Writing a *Successful* Thesis or Dissertation

Fred C. Lunenburg ~ Beverly J. Irby

Writing a *Successful* Thesis or Dissertation

Tips and Strategies for Students in the Social and Behavioral Sciences

CORWIN PRESS
A SAGE Company
Thousand Oaks, CA 91320

For information:

Corwin Press
A SAGE Company
2455 Teller Road
Thousand Oaks, California 91320
www.corwinpress.com

SAGE India Pvt. Ltd.
B 1/I 1 Mohan Cooperative Industrial Area
Mathura Road, New Delhi 110 044
India

SAGE Ltd.
1 Oliver's Yard
55 City Road
London EC1Y 1SP
United Kingdom

SAGE Asia-Pacific Pte. Ltd.
33 Pekin Street #02–01
Far East Square
Singapore 048763

Printed in the United States of America.

Library of Congress Cataloging-in-Publication Data

Lunenburg, Fred C.
 Writing a successful thesis or dissertation : tips and strategies for students in the social and behavioral sciences / Fred C. Lunenburg, Beverly J. Irby.
      p. cm.
Includes bibliographical references and index.
ISBN 978-1-4129-4224-9 (cloth)
ISBN 978-1-4129-4225-6 (pbk.)
   1. Dissertations, Academic--Authorship. 2. Academic writing. 3. Social sciences—Authorship. I. Irby, Beverly J. II. Title.

LB2369.L814 2008
808'.066378—dc22   2007031656

This book is printed on acid-free paper.

07   08   09   10   11   10 9 8 7 6 5 4 3 2 1

Acquisitions Editor:	Elizabeth Brenkus
Managing Editor:	Arnis Burvikovs
Editorial Assistants:	Ena Rosen, Desirée Enayati
Production Editor:	Jenn Reese
Typesetter:	C&M Digitals (P) Ltd.
Proofreader:	Paulette McGee
Indexer:	Nara Wood
Cover Designer:	Monique Hahn

Contents

Preface

PURPOSE OF THIS BOOK

We have written this book to help graduate students write the dissertation from beginning to end successfully. Each of us has taught courses focused on writing the dissertation. We have a combined total of more than 40 years of experience supervising doctoral dissertations. Together we have chaired more than 100 dissertations. In addition, we have been external examiners of doctoral dissertations for several universities in Australia, Canada, New Zealand, the Netherlands, and the United States. Thus, we have written this book to compile the best of our wisdom on how to make the process of writing the dissertation a less mysterious and more rewarding experience. Our approach is applicable also to writing master's theses, which we view as limited-scope dissertations.

From our combined experience, we have found that if the key elements of each dissertation/thesis chapter are clearly identified with corresponding examples of those elements (or sections), it takes the mystery out of writing the dissertation. Thus, we have designed this book to explicitly describe and define the elements (sections) of each dissertation chapter and provide examples of completed dissertations that illustrate typical ways to write the sections of each chapter. We have extracted examples from more than 100 completed dissertations from well-known universities. We present multiple viewpoints that include quantitative, qualitative, and mixed methods approaches. Our writing style throughout is intentionally conversational, as if we were talking directly to the student.

HOW TO USE THIS BOOK

Our goal is to provide advice to those learning how to write the major elements (sections) of a dissertation. Thus, in each chapter of the book, we provide specific information about sections commonly found in dissertations, such as how to write research questions or hypotheses, how to select a sample for the study, how to write descriptions of instruments, how to write results of data analyses, how to interpret the results, and so forth. Our goal is to define and explain the rationale for the common elements (sections) of each chapter of the dissertation. Then we support our advice with numerous examples to illustrate how previous doctoral students have written those sections. The model we use is the traditional five-chapter dissertation. We realize that there are many variations to this model. Students and faculty who are chairing dissertations should feel free to modify the approach to reflect advising style, unique subject area, and institutional requirements.

WHO SHOULD READ THIS BOOK

This book should be of special interest to students in the social and behavioral sciences, including education, psychology, social work, and business. Its contents should be applicable also to those studying nursing and other health sciences with a behavioral base, certain aspects of anthropology, sociology, and criminal justice. Other students will find the book useful as a dissertation guide. As mentioned previously, our approach is applicable also to writing master's theses.

The book can be used as the principal text in courses focused on writing the dissertation or master's thesis. It may be used also as a supplementary text in seminars that introduce students to graduate education or in research methods courses, particularly those in the social and behavioral sciences.

ORGANIZATION OF THE BOOK

This book contains 12 chapters in four major parts and 10 appendixes. In Chapter 1, we discuss how to go about selecting a suitable topic for a doctoral dissertation or master's thesis. We suggest that students begin their search for a suitable topic at the outset of their graduate programs. Good sources of possible topics include: textbooks, professional journals, dissertations, theories, current employment, and existing databases. The characteristics of a good research topic include: whether it is of personal interest, significant, feasible in terms of available data, appropriate to knowledge and skill level, manageable, and attractive for funding.

Chapter 2 includes valuable tips about selecting a chairperson and other committee members. Issues to consider in the selection process include: the reputation of the faculty members, their interest and expertise in the topic, their accessibility, the feedback they provide the student, and the goodness of fit between the student and the dissertation chair and the other committee members. The chapter also deals with ways to identify prospective chairpersons and committee members, including the student's own experience with the faculty member, other students' opinions, and an examination of completed dissertations and faculty Web sites.

Chapter 3 contains quantitative research designs, including descriptive research, correlational research, causal-comparative research, quasi-experimental, and experimental research. In Chapter 5, we discuss qualitative and mixed methods designs, including case study, ethnography, ethology, ethnomethodology, grounded-theory, phenomenology, symbolic interaction, and historical research. The overall purpose of these two chapters is to provide an overview of the two basic approaches to conducting research: quantitative and qualitative. Sandwiched between Chapters 3 and 5 is Chapter 4, which deals with basic statistical procedures.

The overview of basic statistical procedures in Chapter 4 includes descriptive statistics and inferential statistics. Parametric and nonparametric tests are discussed, as are the statistical procedures commonly used in social and behavioral science research. The focus is on the application of the common statistical procedures used in the social and behavioral sciences for given research designs.

Chapter 6 contains the structure and writing of the introduction chapter of the dissertation or master's thesis, including the elements (or sections) that comprise that chapter. These sections include: background of the study, statement of the problem, purpose of the study, significance of the study, definition of terms, theoretical framework, research questions or hypotheses, limitations, delimitations, and assumptions. The section organization of the study, concludes the introduction chapter of the dissertation. We follow specific guidance on what to include in each section of the chapter with examples from completed dissertations.

Chapter 7 is divided into three parts. In the first part of the chapter, we provide an introduction on how to systematically search and review the literature. We discuss six sources: handbooks and encyclopedias, annual reviews, review articles, abstracting and indexing services, government documents, and public search engines. In the second part of the chapter, we discuss eight techniques to help the student write a clear and effective review of the literature chapter. They include: organizing material in a funnel, being specific, making an outline, writing the introduction, using headings, using transitions, writing a summary, and being careful not to plagiarize. The chapter concludes with several additional strategies to help the student critically synthesize the body of literature. We provide examples from dissertations and published articles throughout the chapter.

Chapter 8 includes the structure and writing of the methodology chapter, including the elements (sections) that comprise that chapter. These sections include: selection of participants, instrumentation, data collection, and data analysis. We provide pertinent information related to each of the sections of the methodology chapter, as well as numerous examples of each of these sections from completed dissertations.

Chapter 9 contains information on how to write the results chapter. Each element (or section) of the chapter is described, followed by examples from completed dissertations. We discuss different methods of organizing results for both quantitative and qualitative studies: by research questions or hypotheses, variables, or themes.

Chapter 10 consists of information on how to structure and write the discussion chapter of a dissertation or master's thesis. We discuss each element (or section) that should be included in the discussion chapter, and provide examples of each section of the chapter from completed dissertations.

Chapter 11 contains advice on the steps to be taken to ensure a successful proposal defense and final oral defense of the dissertation. These steps include: preparing a well-written document, knowing the format of the defense, preparing the presentation, practicing the presentation, and anticipating questions. We provide an explanation of how decisions are made by dissertation committees at the defense, and what students should do after a decision has been reached.

Chapter 12 includes suggestions on seeking a wider audience for the completed dissertation. Issues explored include preparing a paper for a professional conference or job interview, finding a publisher for the manuscript, or converting the dissertation into a journal article, monograph, or book.

Appendixes A, B, and C are sample letters used in survey research. Appendix A is the initial letter sent to a prospective participant requesting participation in a study. Appendixes B and C are follow-up letters designed to increase response rate of the study sample.

Appendixes D, E, F, and G contain dissertation proposal outlines for quantitative and qualitative studies. Each dissertation proposal outline uses a different method of analysis. The dissertation proposal outline is the first step in writing the dissertation proposal.

Appendix H contains guidelines used to critique a qualitative research study. Much can be learned from critiquing a qualitative study using the guidelines provided.

Appendix I is a typical agreement between a doctoral student and a dissertation chair, which has been used by the authors of this book. Among other things, it describes guidelines the authors use when agreeing to chair a dissertation. It has been field tested for the past 10 years.

Appendix J is a detailed checklist used by the student for monitoring the quality of a dissertation. The checklist is structured for a traditional five-chapter dissertation and conforms to the elements (or sections) contained within each dissertation chapter.

Acknowledgments

This book has been a cooperative effort between scholars of the field and experienced editors and publishers. We wish to express our appreciation to the reviewers and others whose suggestions led to improvements in this book.

We also wish to thank the people at Corwin Press whose contributions made this a much better book.

We are grateful to our dean, Genevieve Brown, for creating an environment conducive to research and contributing the necessary resources to complete this book. Special thanks are also extended to Alicia Raley and Dacey Ellington, who typed portions of this book.

Fred C. Lunenburg
Beverly J. Irby

Corwin Press gratefully acknowledges the contributions of the following people:

Mary Betsy Brenner, Professor
Gevirtz School of Education
University of California—Santa Barbara
Santa Barbara, CA

Sharon Toomey Clark, Educational Consultant
Clark & Associates
Claremont, CA

Randy L. Joyner, Adjunct Professor
Appalachian State University
Corwin Press Author
Boone, NC

Maria Piantanida, Adjunct Associate Professor
Carlow University and University of Pittsburgh
Pittsburgh, PA

Carol Roberts, Professor
University of La Verne
Corwin Press Author
La Verne, CA

Mark H. Rossman, Professor Emeritus
Capella University
Minneapolis, MN

William A. Rouse, Jr., Assistant Professor
Department of Educational Leadership
East Carolina University
Greenville, NC

About the Authors

Fred C. Lunenburg is the Jimmy N. Merchant Professor of Education and Senior Research Fellow in the Center for Research and Doctoral Studies in Educational Leadership at Sam Houston State University. Prior to moving to the university, he served as a teacher, principal, and superintendent of schools. He has authored or coauthored more than 100 articles and 20 books, including *Educational Administration: Concepts and Practices* (Thomson/Wadsworth, 1991, 1996, 2000, 2004, 2008), *The Principalship: Vision to Action* (Thomson/Wadsworth, 2006), *Shaping the Future* (Rowman & Littlefield, 2003), *The Changing World of School Administration* (with George Perreault) (Rowman & Littlefield, 2002), and *High Expectations: An Action Plan for Implementing Goals 2000* (Corwin Press, 2000).

Beverly J. Irby is Professor and Chair of the Department of Educational Leadership and Counseling at Sam Houston State University. Previously Director of Field Experiences, she has been a school psychologist, educational diagnostician, director of special education, elementary school principal, and superintendent of schools. She has authored or coauthored 12 books and more than 150 articles in education. In addition, she has secured grants totaling more than $25 million and often serves as a consultant to school districts. She is a member of the International Who's Who of Women and has received the Texas Council of Women School Educator's Outstanding Educator Award, the Renaissance Group Research Fellow Award, and the AERA Willystine Goodsell Award.

PART I

Getting Started

1

Selecting a Suitable Topic

The selection of a suitable topic is the first major step in writing a thesis or dissertation. For some students this is an easy task. They have known what they wanted to study from the time they entered graduate school and perhaps even before, but for many others, selecting a thesis or dissertation topic is one of the most difficult parts of their graduate programs. The thought of developing a "completely original" idea for such a large-scale project may seem overwhelming to them.

The notion that a dissertation must be completely original is a misconception, for no research is completely original. All research is based on the work of others to some extent. In fact, the most useful kind of research simply builds on research that has already been done. Some of the most successful theses and dissertations simply extend the knowledge base one step further in an area by examining a new variable within a well-established line of inquiry, collecting data on a different sample, testing a new methodology, or introducing a new statistical technique. Thus, as you begin to focus progressively on a broad search for a topic, you gain a more thorough understanding of what has been done in an area and what needs to be done. Afterwards, originality may cease to be an issue. The Council of Graduate Schools (2002) clarified the point. The term *original* "implies some novel twist, fresh perspective, new hypothesis, or innovative method that makes the dissertation project a distinctive contribution" (p. 10).

Students often ask when the search for a topic should begin. In some universities students do not begin to search for a thesis or dissertation topic until after they have passed the comprehensive examination. We recommend that a serious search for a dissertation topic start as soon as doctoral study begins. By selecting a dissertation topic early in the graduate experience, you can then use assigned course research papers as a means of doing preliminary work on your projected research.

As soon as you select a broad area of study, you need to immerse yourself in the literature in that area, with an eye toward the dissertation (thesis) proposal. Also, you should read and review your university's doctoral handbook, to see if there are guidelines concerning what goes into the proposal and how long it is expected to be.

Most universities have very definite requirements for the dissertation proposal. These requirements can range from a 10- to 20-page description of your proposed study to the completion of the first three chapters of the dissertation. In some universities, the dissertation chair (or advisor) is the only one who has to approve the proposal. Other universities may require a formal oral defense of the proposal before the entire dissertation committee. The purpose of the proposal is to get agreement on the merits of the proposed study before the student begins to collect data and makes formal application to the university's Human Subjects Committee. Even schools or colleges within the same institution may have different requirements. The proposal requirements for master's theses may be less rigorous than they are for doctoral dissertations.

Our institution decided that most dissertation proposals should consist of Chapter One, Two, and Three of the dissertation. Typically Chapter One is titled "Introduction," Chapter Two, "Review of the Literature," and Chapter Three, "Methodology." However, for some qualitative dissertations, the proposal may appear differently. In most cases, after you collect and analyze your data, your Chapters One, Two, and Three will require only minor revisions to be ready for the final dissertation. Even if you must edit some later, you should be writing the proposal and the dissertation simultaneously. For those of you who are doing a qualitative dissertation, you may have to do some major rewriting of the first three chapters as your data emerge.

SOURCES OF TOPICS

As mentioned previously, you should begin your topic selection by identifying two or three broad areas in which many different types of research may be pursued. Examples of what is meant by broad topic areas are: teaching methods, leadership styles, bilingual education, school improvement, and so forth. Sources of ideas for broad topic areas include: (a) textbooks,

(b) professional journals, (c) dissertations, (d) theories, (e) current employment, and (f) existing databases.

Textbooks

Textbooks that you are currently using in your courses or that you have used in previous courses can be a source of ideas for broad topic areas. Often, the authors of textbooks point out areas of controversy or gaps in the research on specific topics. For example, in the first chapter of their textbook *Educational Administration: Concepts and Practices*, Lunenburg and Ornstein (2008) identified some current issues in assessment, which include testing minority students and confidentiality of test data. In a subsequent chapter, they discussed current and emerging issues in the measurement of disabled children. In another chapter, they shared problems with the validation of some leadership theories and the use of majority samples in the development of some of these theories. In each of these chapters, the authors pointed out several broad areas in need of further research.

Professional Journals

Although reading textbooks will give you a broad overview of topic ideas for your thesis or dissertation, you need to steep yourself in the literature in your field and related fields. (If you are an education student, related fields are psychology, sociology, anthropology, economics, and business management.) This will enable you to examine the specifics of how other scholars have conducted research. These specifics can be found in reports of original, empirical research (which include both quantitative and qualitative studies) published in professional journals. Such reports can be accessed electronically. If you are unfamiliar with conducting such searches, consult the research librarian at your university. Some electronic databases provide the full text of research articles; others provide abstracts only. If an abstract interests you, obtain copies of the full article and carefully read it through.

As you read, pay particular attention to the purposes, research questions, or hypotheses that are stated in the articles. Consider the methods used to examine the research questions or test the hypotheses, including participants, instrumentation, data collection, and data analysis the researcher(s) used, and, of course, the findings. Consider reliability and validity issues of the studies you review. You should also pay particular attention to the discussion sections. In their discussions, researchers often describe implications of their research for theory and practice, discuss limitations of their studies, and suggest possibilities for further research. Such an examination of the specifics of empirical research will assist you in developing and refining your own thesis or dissertation proposal.

Reading professional journals related to your field will help you keep abreast of research trends in your discipline and enable you to explore broad topic areas at the same time. Pay particular attention to periodicals that publish review articles, such as the *Review of Educational Research, Harvard Educational Review, Sociological Review, Annual Review of Psychology,* and *Review of Research in Education.* Review articles are helpful to you because they organize a great deal of literature efficiently. A topical review represents the analytical thinking of some scholar who has examined existing literature, interpreted it, and pointed out the theoretical issues it raises. These reviewers are invited to write reviews, because they are considered to be among the best scholars in their fields. A review article also provides you with an extensive reference list that can form the basis for a complete review of the literature once you select a topic for your thesis or dissertation. The review article is also a good model for the dissertation proposal and the abstract of your dissertation. It is relatively short and usually includes the purpose, research questions or hypothesis, methods, results, implications, and limitations.

In some fields, books are published annually that are devoted to the review of significant recent theoretical and practical research developments. Four such annual publications include the *Annual Review of Anthropology, Annual Review of Psychology, Annual Review of Sociology,* and *Yearbook of the National Society for the Study of Education* (NSSE). Each yearly volume of the annual reviews contains highly comprehensive and integrated reviews of numerous research areas in anthropology, psychology, sociology, and education, respectively. Some topics contained in these volumes are reviewed annually, while others are reviewed every five years. The researcher should look over the six or seven most recent volumes to get an idea of topical coverage. Other useful sources of reviews of research include the *Handbook of Research on Teaching, Handbook of Qualitative Research, Encyclopedia of Educational Research, Handbook of Research on Educational Administration,* and *Encyclopedia of Educational Leadership and Administration.* The articles contained in these documents are written by distinguished scholars in specific content areas. The topics are selected for their timeliness at the time of writing and their theoretical or practical value to researchers. Because these volumes are not published annually, some of the contents may not be as current as the aforementioned annual reviews, but may be appropriate for the selection of broad topic areas.

Dissertations

Other completed dissertations can serve as another good source of topic selection. Be sure to secure exemplary projects to serve as models. Try to find: (a) award-winning dissertations in your field or related fields, (b) recent dissertations in the selected field at various universities, (c) good recent dissertations suggested by faculty in your department, and (d) the best dissertations suggested by your dissertation chair.

Examine the titles of these dissertations, as well as titles published in *Dissertation Abstracts International*. If a title interests you, read the abstract of the study. If you are still interested, get a copy of the document and read specifically the review of the literature and the suggestions for further research. Dissertations are now online through most university libraries.

There are certain advantages of searching for a topic from completed dissertations that go far beyond topic selection. For example, a recently completed dissertation includes a comprehensive review of the literature up to the point of completion. Updating the most recent studies will be an easy task. Your study might include a different population, other variable(s), or another methodology. However, other dissertations can help you in identifying acceptable approaches to: (a) writing research questions or hypothesis, (b) choosing an appropriate sample size, (c) examining how data were collected and analyzed, and (d) observing what kinds of conclusions can be drawn from the results, and/or (e) formulating a theory. These specifics of conducting research can be valuable information learned from examining completed doctoral dissertations.

Theories

Theories are developed to explain phenomena in a field or to provide structure or framework to the knowledge base in a field. A new theory may be developed, or an existing theory may be modified or extended. For example, Paul Hersey (1976) did a theory dissertation in which he developed with his dissertation chair, Ken Blanchard, a new leadership theory known as the *situational leadership theory* (see Hersey & Blanchard, 2007 for an explanation of the situational leadership theory). One of our doctoral students, Salvatore Pascarella (1985), did a field test of Hersey and Blanchard's situational leadership theory in a school setting using a sample of elementary school principals (see also, Pascarella & Lunenburg, 1988). Doris Delaney (2005), another one of our doctoral students, completed a dissertation that further field-tested Hersey and Blanchard's situational leadership theory using a sample of prekindergarten principals.

The development and testing of theory is important work and can make an important contribution to the field. Many theories have received only limited empirical testing. In addition, many theories have been tested using only majority populations. For example, many of the management theories developed in industrial settings between 1900 and 1960 used only men as participants.

One of the authors of this book has developed a new gender-inclusive theory of leadership called the *synergistic leadership theory* (SLT) (Irby, Brown, Duffy, & Trautman, 2002). The theory can be applied to any organization. Developed through a qualitative approach, the SLT has been validated quantitatively, qualitatively, and with mixed methods designs nationwide and is currently being validated internationally by our doctoral students, using samples of principals, superintendents, and higher education leaders. These validation studies have included nonmajority populations (Bamberg, 2004; Hernandez, 2004; Holtkamp, 2001; Schlosberg, 2004; Trautman, 2000; Truslow, 2004). All of the aforementioned dissertations have used quantitative, qualitative, or mixed methods designs. Wanda Bamberg and Teresa Schlosberg validated the theory through qualitative methodology. Rose Hernandez and Leslie Holtkamp used a quantitative methodology. Diane Trautman and Kimberly Truslow used a mixed methods design. More details on the methodology used in these dissertations are provided in subsequent chapters.

You should not limit yourself to theories within your own discipline. Many professionals study the same problems educators do, including anthropologists, psychologists, sociologists, business executives, and others. Thus, theories from other disciplines provide new ways of examining topics in your discipline. For example, a social psychological theory such as Bandura's (1997) self-efficacy theory has been tested in applied areas of education and has greatly expanded the existing knowledge base. Woolfolk and Hoy (1990) tested Bandura's self-efficacy theory in relation to prospective teachers' control beliefs. Later, Hoy and Woolfolk (1993) tested self-efficacy theory in relation to the organizational health of schools. Tschannen-Moran and others (1998) modified Bandura's teacher efficacy scale. Building on the work of Bandura, Hoy, Tschannen, and Woolfolk, Lauren Black (2003), one of our doctoral students, developed and validated a new instrument, the principal efficacy scale, which was the subject of her dissertation. Lauren Black used a mixed methods design in her dissertation.

Some dissertations are guided by theory. Others are not. Look for reported research (survey textbooks, research journals, dissertations) that is grounded in a solid theoretical framework. Such works make a substantial contribution to the knowledge base. An excellent way to justify proposed research to your thesis or doctoral committee is to show that your research will either test certain aspects of an important theory or has its foundation in such a theory. Thus, we suggest that you consider whether your research could be guided by a particular theory and how you can create empirical ways of testing the theory or theories.

Many quantitative studies are designed to test a theory that has been developed to explain educational phenomena. Such theory-driven studies use hypotheses as the starting point for designing the research methodology. Qualitative research studies can be designed so that data are collected first, and then a theory is derived from those data (Denzin & Lincoln, 2005; Gall, Gall, & Borg, 2007; Gay, Mills, & Airasian, 2006). Such qualitative studies might be informed by a theoretical or epistemological framework, but formal hypotheses are not typically used to frame the study

(Gall et al., 2007). For example, in grounded theory methodology, hypotheses are the outcome of the study rather than the initiators of it (Glaser, 1978).

Current Employment

Another source of dissertation topics can be derived from your current employment. For example, one of our doctoral students, Vickie Basham (1988), was able to relate her dissertation topic to her employment (see also, Basham & Lunenburg, 1989). Vickie worked for the Kentucky Department of Education as the Director of Assessment. She wanted to determine the relationships between strategic planning, student achievement, and school district financial and demographic factors. At that time, the state of Kentucky had just implemented a statewide strategic planning model. In addition, the state administered annually a standardized achievement test to all students in grades 3, 5, 7, and 10 in three content areas: reading, language arts, and mathematics.

The achievement data, as well as the financial and demographic factors she was studying, were easily accessible to her through the Kentucky Department of Education's database. (However, there was no instrument to measure the use of strategic planning in the state.) The State Superintendent of Schools was very interested in the study and sent a letter to all superintendents in the state requesting them to participate in Vickie's study. The letter from the top administrator in the state opened doors for data collection, resulting in a nearly 80% return rate from the total *population* of superintendents in the state (her study sample); complete access to the state's database; and free assistance from state department measurement experts in the statistical analysis of her data, as well as survey-item construction of the strategic planning instrument. These measurement experts also assisted her with the pilot study needed to validate the strategic planning scale she developed with her dissertation chair. Thus, after a careful review of the literature, Vickie developed an acceptable dissertation topic, conceptualized a problem, and completed a literature review, methodology, and supporting evidence that were firmly grounded in theory.

Existing Database

Drawing on your current employment and having access to an existing database can be a real advantage in selecting a dissertation topic. Keith Clark (2002), one of our doctoral students, was chief financial officer (CFO) for a large, urban school district. Drawing on his work experience in finance, he examined student achievement, financial and demographic factors, and property wealth as related to the educational resources in public school districts. Another one of our doctoral students, Danielle Lutz (2006), was Director of Grants in another large, urban school district.

Drawing on her work experience in grants she examined, using a mixed methods design, the relationship between bilingual federal grant programs and student achievement in public schools. Because the school districts were interested in these students' studies, they received free clerical assistance and access to computer services. Moreover, each student could retrieve a portion of his or her data through the state's existing database.

Sally Craycraft (1999), another one of our doctoral students, became intrigued by the availability of a large database at Hermann International that contained elements from a certified administration of the Herman Brain Dominance: Thinking Styles Assessment Instrument to 366 school superintendents and 599 chief executive officers (CEOs). The sample included individuals from across the United States and included males and females; different ethnic-racial groups; and urban, suburban, and rural organizations, equivalent to the national population. Using this existing database, she examined the relationship between brain dominance and leadership styles of school superintendents and business CEOs by gender, race, and organization size.

Likewise, one of our international doctoral students, Ying-Chiao Tsai (2006), used an existing database of Progress in International Reading Literacy Study (PIRLS) reading achievement for English-language students in the United States and Singapore. She compared reading achievement levels for majority and minority language-students by gender for both countries. The federal government provides national databases related to early childhood, special education, longitudinal household surveys, higher education, the National Assessment of Educational Progress (NAEP), and the like. Most of these are provided through the National Clearinghouse of Educational Statistics (NCES).

Three other of our doctoral students, Melinda Wooderson-Perzan (2000), Darlene Blair (2001), and Heather Thielemann (2004), used an existing database to examine some, but not all, of their study variables. Melinda and Darlene used an existing database for their student achievement and school district financial and demographic factors. For the other variables in their studies (leadership styles and instructional leadership/ management tasks profiles) of superintendents and principals, respectively, they used Bass and Avolio's (1994) Multifactor Leadership Questionnaire (MLQ) and Lunenburg's (1982, 2000) Instructional Leadership/Management Tasks Profile.

Heather collected data on the effectiveness of enrollment management programs in four-year universities and community colleges in Texas using an adaptation of Noel-Levitz enrollment management survey. She compared the data collected in Texas colleges and universities with the Noel Levitz national database of community colleges and four-year universities. After a careful review of the literature, Keith, Danielle, Sally, Ying-Chaio, Melinda, Darlene, and Heather developed an acceptable dissertation and completed their studies.

We have found quite often that research topics (and their accompanying research questions), including the aforementioned studies, need to be reworked by the student and dissertation chair (advisor) before they are approved. In some cases, a research topic may be completely rejected by the dissertation or master's thesis chair (advisor) as inappropriate for a dissertation or master's thesis.

CRITERIA FOR TOPIC SELECTION

In selecting an appropriate topic for a thesis or dissertation, the following criteria should be considered as important: (a) interest, (b) significance, (c) available data, (d) knowledge and skills, (e) manageability, and (f) funding. Let's examine these criteria to see why they are considered important.

Interest

It is the fortunate dissertation student who investigates a topic that is both professionally and personally compelling. Writing a dissertation is hard work. Try to find a topic for which you have substantial curiosity and perhaps even passion to sustain you though the process. Here is an example from one of the authors of this book.

When I began my career as a high school teacher and coach, I was selected to be a member of the school district's teachers' collective bargaining team. While serving as a member of that team, I came in contact with many teachers. In talking with them, it became apparent to me that, in some schools in the district, teacher morale was high and in other schools it was low. I was curious why this was so.

At the same time, I was a master's student in educational administration at the local university. I began reading about organizational climate. In my graduate classes at the university, I heard about a new instrument developed a few years earlier for measuring climate called the Organizational Climate Description Questionnaire (OCDQ) (Halpin & Croft, 1963). Furthermore, the concept of organizational climate and the OCDQ was getting a great deal of attention in the professional literature at that time. There was also some controversy about the eight dimensions of organizational climate and the six climate categories conceptualized through factor analysis by Halpin and Croft, who originally developed the instrument in their study of 71 elementary schools chosen from six different regions of the United States.

The university I attended required a thesis as a requirement for the MA degree in educational administration. I chose as my MA thesis topic: "A Validation of the OCDQ in Elementary Schools" (Lunenburg, 1969). I drew my sample from 35 elementary schools in Newark, New Jersey, a large urban school district. The school was the unit of analysis. I conducted a factor analysis of the OCDQ with my sample of elementary schools and found seven discrete climate categories instead of six, and eight dimensions of climate. However, only three dimensions were particularly strong predictors of open and closed organizational climates for my sample of 35 elementary schools: esprit, thrust, and disengagement. My analysis was based on a description of these schools given by 1,050 teacher respondents and 35 principal respondents. In addition to conducting a factor analysis of the OCDQ, I examined climate in relation to school size, socioeconomic status of the community, and differences in perceptions of principals and teachers.

Over the next few years, my interest in organizational climate led to my doctoral dissertation topic: "Organizational Climate, Dogmatism, and Pupil Control Ideology" (Lunenburg, 1972; see also, Lunenburg & O'Reilly, 1974). I personally administered three instruments (one of which was the OCDQ) during regularly scheduled faculty meetings in 55 elementary schools located in six urban, suburban, and rural school districts in Ontario, Canada. The analysis was based on a description of these variables by nearly 1,200 respondents. I have continued to work with doctoral students in the area of school climate using a variety of climate constructs, other variables, and a variety of research methodologies, including quantitative, qualitative, and mixed methods designs.

Significance

Most university catalogs and dissertation handbooks suggest that the dissertation is a test of your preparation to conduct independent research and make a significant contribution to the field. This is not quite as true for master's theses, however. We view master's theses as limited scope dissertations. Basically, a significant topic has the potential to do at least one of the following: (a) contribute to the development of a new theory, (b) test an existing theory, (c) uncover new facts or principles, (d) challenge existing truths or assumptions, (e) suggest relationships between phenomena, (f) provide new insights into phenomena, (g) suggest new interpretations of known facts, (h) alter other people's perceptions about phenomena, and (i) extend a research methodology or statistical procedure.

Available Data

Earlier in this chapter, we discussed how some of our doctoral students were able to take advantage of existing databases. However, not all students will have the opportunity to use existing databases to collect their data. The ability to collect data needed for your study is a major consideration. Access to data is so important that you might consider identifying your research participants first and then seek to select a topic.

Sternberg (1981) provided an excellent example of a problem with access to data. The key question Sternberg posed is whether a researcher can gain admission to topic-loaded samples or groups. He uses as an example a topic in social psychology to make his point. According to Sternberg, an apparently worthwhile and relevant dissertation topic would be "The National Security Council as a Small Group: A Test of Bales's Interaction Process Matrix." "Bales and his associates, watching, recording, and videotaping Harvard undergraduates for decades through one-way mirrors have constructed a set of 'laws' about how members will behave, which they assert are generalizable to all small 'task-oriented' groups" (p. 48). However, it is not likely that a doctoral student would get a chance to set up shop in a room adjacent to the National Security Council conference room. Therefore, such a topic would have to be eliminated.

Furthermore, you need to be certain the data for your dissertation will be available and accessible when you come to the collection phase of your dissertation. The timing of the data collection is just as important as the topic itself in the calculation of its researchability. If your topic-loaded sample or group will disappear in six months or a year; or if personnel who granted you access change, resulting in new personnel not willing to honor their predecessors' offer of entry, you must drop the topic. These reversals do happen. We recommend that you get your commitments to data access in writing.

Knowledge and Skills

Selecting a topic consistent with your knowledge and skills is also important. First, you will save time, because you will be dealing with a familiar topic. Second, you can talk knowledgeably about your topic. Third, you are more likely to get support from your dissertation chair and committee for a topic about which you have some knowledge. Recall that the doctoral dissertation of one of the authors of this book was a spin off of his master's thesis. Even though master's theses are being phased out of many master's programs, you may have already done research papers and taken courses in a particular subject area. Thus, you may find that you have a considerable amount of work already completed regarding the literature search. Another example of a useful knowledge base, also akin to an experiential base, is observed in a recent dissertation proposal by Yu Fen Lin Li. She is an ordained Presbyterian minister and has a master's degree in theology. Her PhD dissertation in counseling is qualitative and is based on her knowledge of the Bible and feminism, and her experience as a female pastor in a patriarchal culture. Her topic is the development of a feminist therapy for Taiwanese female pastors in the Presbyterian Church.

In addition, selecting a topic that matches your skills is also important. For example, if you undertake a historical study, you must have some familiarity with documentary research techniques. Courses in historiography are helpful. Similarly, qualitative dissertations will demand knowledge of specialized qualitative research techniques, such as interviewing, observing, document analysis, textual analysis, focus groups, visual methods, autoethnography, data management methods, computer-assisted analysis, and applied ethnography (see Denzin & Lincoln, 2005). Choosing a quantitative dissertation may not be a deterrent, for many individuals are available to help with statistical analysis. Many areas will require a combination of skills; all demand literary proficiency.

Manageability

Most doctoral students, and master's students as well, begin with a topic that is too broad. Examples that illustrate what is meant by broad topic areas include the following: teaching methods, leadership styles, school improvement, bilingual education, or counseling theories. Your dissertation chair cannot provide useful advice until you get it clear in your own mind exactly what it is that you want to study. By narrowing your topic, you make the purpose of your research clear to yourself and others. Sufficiently narrowing your topic helps you organize your literature review and produce a specific problem statement with an accompanying theoretical framework. Part of this narrowing process is writing meaningful research questions. A further discussion of writing research questions can be found in Chapter 6.

In addition, we recommend that you try to assess the amount of time you will need to complete the thesis or dissertation early in the selection process. From our experience, although you may have been working on your topic since you began the doctoral program, the average amount of time required for the final completion of dissertations is from one year to 18 months. The time may be longer if you work full time. The average master's student requires from four to nine months to complete the master's thesis. We suggest that you select a dissertation topic that you can complete within a year or so. An example of a topic that does not meet the completion time criterion we suggested is a dissertation topic that proposes to study the development of high school students from freshman to senior years. This is a longitudinal study, which would have to extend over four or more years and, therefore, would not meet the one-year completion time criterion.

Funding

Most thesis and dissertation research is not funded, so you incur all of the expenses associated with the project. These financial constraints greatly limit the scope of the research you can undertake. You may check with your department, college, or university for internal funding opportunities. Many federal agencies and some private foundations offer grants for graduate students to pursue degrees and write dissertations. Grants are usually not available for writing master's theses. Topics that are current and have some unique approach are usually more likely to receive funding. We provide a sampling of grant opportunities related to education and psychology (see Table 1.1). These grants are extremely competitive. Therefore, when considering specific grant applications, you should seek assistance from grant specialists in your university or elsewhere to help you prepare the application.

Table 1.1   Grant Opportunities

Dissertation Fellowship Program
Agency: Spencer Foundation
Deadlines: October 7
Amount: $20,000
Guidelines: http://www.spencer.org/programs/fellows/dissertation.htm

Dissertation Fellowships
Agency: American Association of University Women (AAUW)
Amount: $20,000 (51 awards)
Guidelines: http://www.aauw.org/3000/fdnfelgra/american.html

AERA/OERI *Dissertation Grants Program*
Agency: American Educational Research Association and the U.S. Department
    of Education Office of Educational Research and Improvement
Deadlines: October 15, April 15
Amount: $15,000 for 1-year projects: $25,000 for 2-year projects (four awards
    per year)
Guidelines: http://www.aera.net/anews/announce/af01-002.htm

Dissertation Grants Program
Agency: American Educational Research Association
Deadlines: September 5, January 10, and March 20
Amount: $15,000
Guidelines: http://www.aera.net/programs/

Dissertation Fellowship Program
Agency: Association for Institutional Research (AIR)
Deadlines: January 15
Amount: $15,000
Guidelines: http://www.airweb.org/page.asp/page=40

*Grants for Improving Doctoral Dissertation Research—Human Cognition and
Perception*
Agency: National Science Foundation
Deadline: Continuous
Amount: $8,000 North America; $12,000 other areas
Guidelines: http://www.nsf.gov/cgi-bin/getpub/nsf0111

SUMMARY

In this chapter, we presented guidelines for selecting a suitable topic for a thesis or dissertation. We recommend that you begin looking for a topic as soon as your graduate program commences.

Begin by identifying two or three broad topic areas that interest you. By searching the literature, narrow these broad areas down to one or two specific topics that you might wish to research. Good sources of possible topics include textbooks, professional journals, dissertations, theories, current employment, and existing databases.

The topic you finally select should be interesting to you, significant, feasible in terms of available data, appropriate to your knowledge and skills, manageable, and attractive for funding. In the next chapter, we describe how you select a dissertation/thesis chair and committee.

2

Selecting a Chair and Committee

Selecting your committee is a very important step in the process of preparing your dissertation or master's thesis. The chairperson of the committee usually has broad power and influence throughout the process of completing the dissertation or master's thesis. Therefore, the selection of a chairperson for your project is a very important decision. In collaboration with your chair and committee, you will delimit your topic, develop your proposal, conduct your research, and write your dissertation or master's thesis. Ultimately, your committee will judge the quality of your project. In this chapter, we present some suggestions that might help you in selecting your dissertation or thesis chair and other committee members.

Before choosing a faculty member as your chairperson, consider the chair's role. As mentioned previously, your chair will have broad power and influence over the dissertation or thesis process. While the specifics of this role vary from institution to institution, from department to department, and from chairperson to chairperson, some general functions of the chair are relatively universal. First, the chairperson will approve your dissertation or thesis topic. Second, the chairperson will approve, in consultation with you, the other committee members. Third, the chairperson will approve every line, section, and chapter of the dissertation. Fourth, the chairperson will determine how committee members will be involved in the dissertation or thesis process. Fifth, the chairperson will decide when you are ready to defend your dissertation or master's thesis. And, ultimately, the chairperson will determine whether you will be granted the degree.

Most departments have rules concerning who may and who may not serve as dissertation or thesis chairpersons. Some universities allow only those individuals who are on the graduate faculty to serve as dissertation chairs; that is, faculty who have adequate, recent publication records and who teach graduate classes. These rules are based on the rationale that faculty who do not have active programs of research will lack the necessary skills to guide a doctoral research project. Rules regarding who may chair master's theses may not be as stringent as those concerning doctoral dissertations. Because practice varies on who may and who may not serve as dissertation chairs, we recommend that you learn your institution's rules as soon as possible. Knowing your institution's local ground rules will help you avoid considering a potential chairperson who is not eligible to chair a dissertation or thesis.

CRITERIA TO CONSIDER IN SELECTING A CHAIR

You must consider the following factors in choosing a chair: (a) expertise, (b) accessibility, (c) feedback, (d) success, (e) personality style, and (f) attitudes toward methodology. The importance of each one will be discussed in turn.

Expertise

Ideally, it is in your best interest to find a chair with expertise in your topic area. You may want to read some of your potential chair's publications. In our opinion, following this advice generally will produce a better product. Obviously, the closer your chair's area of expertise is to your topic, the more competent he or she will be to (a) identify difficulties you may encounter as your proceed with your study, (b) direct you toward literature sources pertinent to your topic, and (c) guide your choice of methods for collecting and analyzing data. Furthermore, a chair who has an interest and competence in your topic area is likely to be more invested in your project; that is, think through the project more fully and keep a vigilant eye on your progress than one who is not knowledgeable about your topic area, and, therefore, may lack interest in it as well.

Accessibility

Another important factor to consider in selecting a chair is accessibility. Several things can interfere with a chair being consistently accessible to you during the life of your project. When considering someone as a possible chair, you should think about these things. Nationally known scholars may be too busy with their own research activity to give you the time you need. Other faculty may have active clinical practices or be away from campus frequently due to consulting commitments. Faculty members who have nine-month contracts with the university may not be available during the summer. Faculty who are planning a sabbatical leave may potentially interrupt your progress. Another faculty member may be planning to take a position in another university and, therefore, may not be available during the progress of your project. One of the authors of this book had her chair go on sabbatical leave during the final semester of her dissertation work; therefore, a new chair had to be appointed. Popular chairs may have an excessive number of dissertations or theses to monitor, because they are in high demand.

Then there is the issue of tenure. Whereas nontenured faculty contracts may not be renewed, tenured faculty members are likely to be more stable. You will need to consider the relative accessibility and stability of potential chairs, along with your own time constraints and projections for completion.

Feedback

Typically, the chair provides the first line of quality control for the dissertation or thesis. And usually the chair will approve the proposal and final version of the project before you will be permitted to forward chapters of the dissertation or thesis to other committee members. Therefore, look for a chair with a reputation for reading, critiquing, and returning written drafts promptly.

What is a good turnaround time? A good rule of thumb is to allow two weeks for a response. After that, a tactful inquiry may be appropriate. Obviously, students should recognize that it might take longer during very busy periods (e.g., end of grading periods, holidays, and before graduation deadlines when all students want to finish their projects).

You should balance timeliness of response with the thoroughness with which the potential chairperson reads submitted material. Some chairs provide vague feedback (e.g., rewrite this section), while others may provide detailed comments (e.g., "You need to identify the three main factors and then evaluate them in light of the theories you have discussed."). Waiting longer for a chapter to be returned by a chair may have some positive consequences. First, if you satisfy a chair who provides a thorough critique of your work, you are less likely to encounter serious problems with other committee members. Second, you will be better prepared for your proposal defense and final oral defense of your dissertation or thesis. Third, once you have satisfied your chair's standards, he or she is more likely to support you if one of your other committee members becomes overly or unreasonably critical of your work.

Success

Success at bringing students to graduation is an important factor to consider when selecting a chair. Because you are concerned with completing your degree, count how many successful students your potential chair has;

that is, what percentage of the chair's students finish their degrees. Consider this criterion cautiously, because some faculty members may not have had the opportunity to chair doctoral dissertations or master's theses.

Personality Styles

Personality styles matter to some people. Writing a dissertation or thesis is a collaborative process between you and your chairperson. Obviously, you want a chair with whom you can work reasonably well. You will need to assess the match between what you expect from your chair and your chair's notion of the best way to perform his or her role.

Chairpersons vary greatly in how they work with students on dissertations and theses. Those at one end of the continuum closely monitor each phase of the students' work, in some cases stipulating exactly what is to be done at every step, and then require the student to submit each section of material for critique. Chairs at the other end of the continuum tell students to progress on their own and to finish a complete draft of the project before submitting it for evaluation. Most chairs will probably fall somewhere between these two extremes.

Chairpersons also differ in the way they provide criticism. Some are blunt and even derisive. Others are direct and kindly in critiquing students' work. Still others are so cautious of students' feelings when pointing out weaknesses that they fail to guide their students in correcting deficiencies. In the latter case, someone else on the committee will have to step up and perform that duty; for the role of the chair and committee is to ensure that the candidate has met the university, college, and department standards.

Students also have personal preferences with whom they want to work, in general. For example, some students prefer to work with female faculty members, while others prefer to work with male faculty. Some students prefer to work with older people, while others prefer younger faculty.

Attitudes Toward Methodology

Faculty members often differ concerning their preferences for a particular research method. A research method comprises the strategy followed in collecting and analyzing data. The major distinction in classifying research by method is the distinction between quantitative and qualitative research (Gay, Mills, & Airasian, 2006). Quantitative and qualitative research can be broken down further into several distinct types, each designed to answer a different kind of research question. Quantitative research involves the collection and analysis of numerical data, which are usually rendered in the form of statistics. Advocates of quantitative studies tend to prefer such research types as descriptive (or survey), correlational, causal-comparative, and experimental research. Proponents of such studies claim that their work is done from within a value-free framework (Denzin & Lincoln, 2005).

Qualitative research involves mostly nonnumerical data, such as extensive notes taken at a research site, interview data, videotape and audiotape recordings, and other nonnumerical artifacts. Qualitative researchers stress the socially constructed nature of reality, the intimate relationship between the researcher and the participant, and the situational constraints that shape inquiry. Qualitative researchers emphasize the value-laden nature of inquiry (Denzin & Lincoln, 2005). Proponents of qualitative studies tend to favor such research approaches as case study, ethnography, ethology, ethnomethodology, grounded theory, phenomenology, symbolic interaction, and historical research.

You need to examine the match between your preference and your potential chair's preference for a research method. Many faculty members accept both quantitative and qualitative research methods, including the authors of this text. We believe that the issue is not which method is better, but rather which method (quantitative, qualitative, or mixed methods) will best answer the particular research question or direction of inquiry.

COMPOSITION AND ROLE OF THE COMMITTEE

Dissertation and thesis committees vary in size, composition, and role depending on the institution's rules and the degree awarded. The committee usually consists of the chair and an additional number of faculty members. Typically, the thesis committee has three members, and the dissertation committee has between three and five members.

Sometimes there is a requirement that at least one of the committee members be from a department other than the student's major department. Some universities require that the majority of the committee be members of the graduate faculty. Institutions usually require that the committee chair be a member of the graduate faculty. The committee usually serves through the proposal stage to the satisfactory completion of the dissertation or master's thesis.

Composition

The composition of committee members can be very important to the quality of the completed thesis or dissertation. We recommend that you start at the top. First, select your committee chair. Then, working in collaboration with your chair, you can complete the selection of the other committee members. Your chair will be in the best position to help you. You may offer some suggestions of your own, but you should allow your chair to guide you in the decision. Your chair likely will know what expertise respective committee members can contribute to your project. And your chair may work better with certain colleagues than with others.

Ideally, committee members should supplement your chair's expertise. If your study requires complex statistical procedures and your chair is not a statistician, you may want to add to your committee a faculty member who teaches your department's statistics courses. We call this person a *resident statistician*. At our institution, we include the resident statistician on all committees that involve complex statistical procedures. If your study is qualitative, and your chair is not strong in qualitative research techniques, adding a qualitative researcher to your committee may be useful. Aim for balance on your committee. A well-balanced committee might include a faculty member who is strong in theory, someone who is knowledgeable about the literature in your field, and another person who is a careful editor.

Role

Although specific duties of committee members vary depending on the institution, general roles include the following: (a) the committee provides consultation to the student throughout the process of the research; (b) committee members establish the direction of study by approving the proposal and assisting the chairperson in providing direction for the study; (c) they offer additional assurances to the university, college, and department that the dissertation or thesis standards have been met; (d) they examine the student and approve the final oral defense; and (e) they make judgments about the student's written work, including substance, style, and usage.

In a specific sense, however, the role of committee members can vary greatly by institution or department. In some departments, committee members read the dissertation or thesis proposal and final written document only after the chair has approved these documents. Approval follows extensive work between the student and the chair concerning the research questions/hypotheses, design of the study, and other details of the project. Committee members offer suggestions and criticisms, and participate in the proposal and final oral defense meetings. In other departments, each committee member will actively contribute expertise at each stage of the dissertation (thesis) process. Chapters will be submitted simultaneously to all committee members, after the chair's approval. In most cases, the specific model used will probably fall somewhere between the two extremes.

RESEARCH PROSPECTIVE COMMITTEE MEMBERS

Researching the pool of prospective chairpersons and committee members is essential. There are four main sources of information to explore: (a) your own experience, (b) other students, (c) dissertations, and (d) Web sites.

Your Own Experience

The first source of information to explore is your own experience with the potential chairperson or committee member. You may have taken a class from a particular faculty member. Some questions you might ask yourself include: What kind of relationship did I have with Professor X in class? Do I have confidence that Professor X can guide me through the research process? Am I ready to accept direction and criticism from Professor X? Be open-minded in your exploration. Sometimes faculty members are different in one-to-one relationships than they are in classes.

The relationship between you and your chair and other committee members is collaborative. Ideally, you want to create an equal relationship, but in reality this is rarely the case (Brause, 2004). The student usually conforms to the styles of the professors. Some negotiation of procedures for progressing through the research process may be possible; however, professors usually set the rules. And each professor has idiosyncrasies, to which doctoral (master's) students eventually learn to adapt, or they choose to work with other faculty members. That is to say that faculty members have a history of collaborating in different ways. It is important that you understand the rules for working collaboratively with faculty. It may require you to utilize a different set of interaction skills than you used when taking classes.

Other Students

A second source of information comes from students who have worked with the prospective chair or committee member. Interview several students to get an adequate sample. Listen carefully to students. Ask for opinions. Ask such questions as: Who selected the topic—you or the chair? Did the chair help you improve the proposal? How many substantive changes were made to the proposal once submitted? Was the chair available on a regular basis? How many drafts of each section or chapter did you write? (We think it not unusual for a student to write several drafts of each section or chapter.) What kind of feedback did the faculty member provide—vague, detailed, useful, or not useful? How did the chair respond to issues the committee raised? What issues did the committee raise? Did individual committee members cause any problems during the research process? What were they? Questions such as these ask about specific faculty behavior and not merely subjective opinions.

Dissertations

A third source of information comes from reviewing recent dissertations completed in your department. Data you will gather from reading dissertations will answer questions such as: What method of research (quantitative, qualitative, or mixed methods) do Professor X's students do? Are all dissertations related to a single topic area? Are the dissertations similar in format? What kind of populations and samples were used in the studies? How many pages do the dissertations contain? Who were the committee members? Who were the students? In most universities, the student can download dissertations from their own institution by author, title, or chair. Dissertations can be obtained from University Microfilms International, and through interlibrary loan.

Web Sites

A final source of information comes from department Web sites. Many departments now have Web sites on which faculty research interests are provided. Spending some time researching Web sites may help you locate potential chairpersons and committee members both inside and outside of the department. At this point, you may have a potential list of chairpersons and committee members.

THE DESIRABLE STUDENT

Thus far, we have described desirable qualities of the chair and committee members. What are some desirable qualities of a doctoral or master's student from the standpoint of the chairperson and committee members? In general, they want: (a) a student who will produce a quality dissertation or master's thesis in a reasonable amount of time, (b) a student who accepts guidance and follows through on suggestions and criticisms from the committee, (c) a student who uses the committee's time effectively, (d) a student who has personal integrity, and (e) a student who resists the impulse to give the chair or committee members rough copy or first drafts.

Quality Product

Completed dissertations are archived in *Dissertation Abstracts International*. The names of both the chair and the student, as well as the names of all committee members appear on the signature page of the dissertation. Faculty members with national reputations will be careful about the quality of work with which their name is associated. Chairing or serving on a dissertation committee is something most faculty take seriously. Faculty members will be much more willing to chair or serve on a committee if the student demonstrates that a quality dissertation will result.

Follow-Through

You are likely to write multiple drafts of your dissertation or thesis, with each draft reflecting a more refined understanding of the important issues of your research. As you are writing these drafts, you are learning the genre of scholarly writing acceptable at your institution and as it conforms to the style of writing acceptable in professional journals in your field. Moreover, you need to learn to accept the suggestions and criticisms of your chair and committee members graciously and follow through on them. Nothing is more frustrating for a chair or committee member than to see an error in a final document that was corrected by a chair or committee member previously; that is, the student failed to follow through on committee suggestions. In our combined experience of chairing more than 100 dissertations, we have seen this happen quite frequently.

The Committee's Time

You need to look at the dissertation or thesis process from the chairperson's and committee member's viewpoints. A good chair will provide expertise in your topic area, timely feedback on your drafts, and general support. Assuming you made a good choice, your committee members will be interested in your dissertation (thesis) and will provide competence that supplements your chair's expertise. However, dissertation chairs and committee members also teach classes; do their own research; write journal articles and books; provide service to the department, college, and university; and attend professional conferences. You are one small part of their professional lives. The student who is organized and who exemplifies the stated purpose of a doctorate, one who has the ability to do independent research, will more likely demonstrate that the time demands on committee members will be reasonable.

Personal Integrity

The student with personal integrity will take the writing of the dissertation (thesis) seriously. The focus will be toward producing a high-quality product. The student who lacks personal integrity approaches the task of writing the dissertation (or thesis) as simply "getting the thing done," without investing the time required to produce a good dissertation. A student who accepts guidance and follows through on suggestions and criticism, is organized and uses the committee's time effectively, and produces a quality product has personal integrity.

Polished Drafts

Some students give their chair and committee members rough copy or first drafts. This will give the impression that you are not really serious about your work. Always submit pages on which you have expended serious time and effort. Use the following rule of thumb: Be 100 percent satisfied that your pages, which you are prepared to submit, are the very best work that you can do. Any dissertation or master's thesis may need to go through several drafts. If possible, have someone—preferably an expert in your field—review the chapter after you have written what you consider to be your final draft.

SUMMARY

The composition of your dissertation or thesis committee can be very important to the quality of the finished product. The chairperson of the committee has broad power and influence throughout the process of preparing the dissertation or thesis. Therefore, we recommend that you start at the top. Select the chair of your committee first. Then, working with your chair, select the other members of your committee. Ideally, committee members should supplement your chair's expertise. Collecting reliable information about potential chairpersons is essential. You want a chairperson with whom you can work reasonably well. You will need to assess the match between what you expect from your chair and your chair's notion of the best way to perform his or her role. You will want committee members who can work well together and with your chair.

The next chapter begins Part II, "What You Need to Know." Chapter 3 contains valuable information on quantitative research designs. This chapter is followed by a chapter on basic statistics. Part II is concluded with a chapter on qualitative research designs.

PART II

What You Need to Know

3

Quantitative Research Designs

In this chapter, we share with you an important component of the dissertation process—determining the type of inquiry and research design you will use for your study. This actually will not be a specific chapter in your dissertation, but is all important in developing your proposal and carrying out your research. The inquiry techniques and/or methods presented in this chapter all have their beginnings in basic human observation and curiosity. We are describing science in the broadest sense of the word—a way of reflecting on our world. Just as children experience science via attitudes, processes, and products, we do also as adult researchers.

Your attitude as a researcher is critical. First, you must think of yourself as a researcher and writer, and not just as a graduate or doctoral student. Your attitude will carry you far as a budding scientist. It will encourage you further in your own curiosity of your topic and of others' topics; it will provide you with perseverance for the task of conducting the research; it will pick you up when you fail and help you learn from your mistakes; and it will aid your open-mindedness and assist you in cooperation with others. Furthermore, a positive attitude toward the research will provide you with a desire to seek reliable and valid sources of information; a desire to provide and to tolerate alternative viewpoints; an avoidance of overgeneralizations; a restraint to make a judgment until all evidence is examined or evaluated, or to make claims without having proof or descriptors; and an open mind toward questions related to your own research.

Processes of research will aid you in working through your study in a critical and creative way. In the simplest terms, processes may include observing, classifying, contrasting, communicating, measuring, estimating, predicting, and inferring. You also will use the processes of identifying and controlling variables, operationalizing definitions, hypothesizing, questioning, experimenting, investigating, interpreting data, or forming theories or models.

The product of your research, your dissertation, provides your chosen field with a greater knowledge base; therefore, because knowledge is considered power, you also carry with you during your research much responsibility as you plan your study, choose your method of inquiry, and conduct your research. You have an ethical obligation to do the very best research that can be produced. You ask: even at the dissertation stage? The answer is yes, at the dissertation stage of your research career. Though you may be questioned on your study, you also know that much of science changes over time and that knowledge is challenged as it is produced. Remember this about your research, as Slavin (1992) said, "the best research design is one that will add to knowledge, no matter what the results are" (p. 3). Your research product, whether you find a small or large effect size along with significance, may be interpreted or used differently by different audiences, depending on their circumstances and experiences.

Your dissertation, as a product, may take the form of a hierarchy, such as basic factual or uniconceptual research, principles of research that relate to multiple concepts, or theories, the highest level of research. This hierarchy can be observed in Figure 3.1. The closer the products of the research are to the top point of the pyramid, the more complex the study. In the development of theory, we note that the complexity may involve dual methodologies, both quantitative and qualitative.

A couple of important questions should be considered as you determine your method of inquiry. First, you must ask yourself: what is my intent or purpose of the research? Second: what are my research questions? These initial components will drive the method you select. You may determine that a quantitative analysis will suffice in answering your research question or will respond to your purpose. On the other hand, you may conclude that it is qualitative, the deeper understanding of the topic, that responds to your purpose, or ultimately, you may decide that a mixed methods approach, using both quantitative and qualitative analyses, is the best method of inquiry for your dissertation.

In this chapter, we provide you with an overview of each of the data analysis techniques or inquiry methods you could use if your questions or hypotheses necessitated a quantitative approach. Certainly, this chapter is not all inclusive, and we know that you will want to "dig deeper" on your own once you settle on a specific method of inquiry. For example, you will need to consult statistics and research methods textbooks and review your proposed method with your dissertation advisor. You must be thoroughly familiar with your method of inquiry and the assumptions for the statistical procedures.

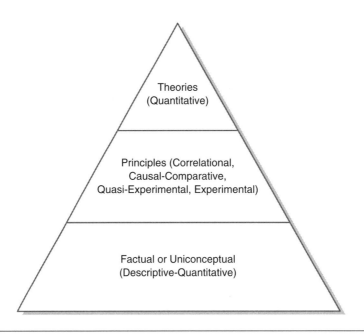

Figure 3.1   Hierarchy of Products of Research

Your research design or method of inquiry for quantitative research will fall into one of four categories of research (a) descriptive research, (b) correlational research, (c) causal-comparative research, and (d) quasi-experimental and experimental research. In addition to providing you with a brief overview of each category, we also provide examples of research purposes or questions that would justify a specific type of quantitative research design or method of inquiry.

DESCRIPTIVE RESEARCH DESIGN

Descriptive research is one of the most basic forms of research. It lies at the bottom of the hierarchy as depicted in Figure 3.1. Even though descriptive research is at the base of the pyramid, it does not mean it is unimportant, unscientific, or unworthy. This type of research involves the description of phenomena in our world. In this type of inquiry, the phenomena described are basic information, actions, behaviors, and changes of phenomena, but always the description is about what the phenomena look like from the perspective of the researcher or the participants in the research; it is not about how the phenomena function. Prior to beginning the research, you will need to have established from theory or from prior research what it is about the phenomenon you will study; from this perspective, descriptive research is theory or research driven.

Descriptive research studies are important to the public and to educators. For example, many reports produced by the federal government are good examples of necessary descriptive research (the U.S. Census Report or the many reports from the National Center for Education Statistics). Such reports provide the impetus for many other research studies.

Descriptive research tends to answer basic informational questions as indicated in the following examples. What leadership behaviors do superintendents who serve rural, suburban, and urban school districts exhibit? What pedagogies can be observed in teachers who teach in bilingual education classrooms? What types of technology are implemented by teachers who have had technology classes at the university level? Which leadership and/or organizational textbooks used in educational or business administration courses include gender-inclusive leadership theory? Such questions in descriptive research will generally ask the question of who, what, when, where, how, or which.

When conclusions are drawn from descriptive research, there is a reporting of the facts, but there should also be researcher-based conclusions connecting the data to theory or prior research.

> . . . illustrating the importance of how a phenomenon is conceptualized in descriptive research, Thurstone, Guilford, and others promoted a different conception of intelligence that emphasized instead the specific nature of human abilities. Thurstone, using a somewhat different mathematical model of factor analysis than had the previous researchers emphasizing general intelligence (Gould, 1981), found, instead of general intelligence, several distinct dimensions of intelligence that he termed "primary mental abilities." Subsequently, Guilford developed and described a complex "structure of intellect" model that first posited 120 separate factors, theoretically derived (Guilford,1967), and later 150 (Guilford, 1977). Notice that the strategy was theory driven: Guilford's complex conceptual model of intelligence, for example, largely based on logically derived theory, provided a basis for designating the specific tasks he then used to measure each specific dimension of intelligence as described in his model. (Anastas, 1999, pp. 128–129)

Guilford used prior research and theory to build his structure of the intellect model that has been used many times in developing curriculum and in research related to gifted children.

Instrumentation

Instrumentation is critical to descriptive research. If you are using archived data, you will likely use an instrument that measures achievement among students or classrooms or schools. Perhaps you are asking the question: What is the achievement among various groups of students based in the state academic achievement test? You define the various groups of students as ethnicities, gender, and special-needs students. You would, of course, need to describe the instrument in detail, along with its norm reports on validity and reliability, particularly as it relates to the various groups of students. Because the research question is based in a standardized achievement test, the results of the study will only be as good as the instrument. Other standardized instruments may include personality inventories, intelligence measures, or attitudinal scales.

In most descriptive research studies, instruments must be developed by the researcher due to the fact that the study is related to a specific phenomenon. You will need to pay special attention to your instrument development and describe all the specifics of (a) how you developed your instrument, (b) where you obtained information to include in your instrument, (c) how you ensured validity and reliability, and (d) if others assisted you in your development. Surveys are some of the most common instruments you will use in descriptive research studies. In fact, sometimes descriptive research is even called *survey research*.

Data

Descriptive research reports data as measures of central tendency, which include mean, median, and mode, and as measures of dispersion, which include deviance from the mean, variation, range, and quartile. It is usually conducted as indicated previously through surveys, or it may be conducted via observation, interviews, portfolios, or cases. Polls, surveys, or questionnaires are typical examples of descriptive research studies. However, antiquities that are archived, film, video, Internet, and e-mail, may also be used for gathering data for descriptive research studies.

Longitudinal Studies

In descriptive studies, there may be more than one variable, but usually descriptive research includes only one variable. This variable may be measured at one point in time, but it also may be measured across time. The latter is considered as a longitudinal descriptive study, or it could be noted as a descriptive trend study. An example of such descriptive studies would be the reports on the National Assessment of Educational Progress (NAEP) or the Longitudinal Early Childhood Studies (for U.S. Department of Education reports see http://www.ed.gov). In longitudinal descriptive studies, data are taken from the same group or sample over varying points in time. In a trend descriptive study, data are gathered from a different group at various points in time, but within a population that changes as well. The NAEP study is an example of this type because students are assessed every year on reading and mathematics in specific grade levels.

In other words, the population for all fourth grade students changes from year to year. Trends are established on a measure over time with changing populations.

Another type of descriptive study is a descriptive cluster study. In the cluster study, data are taken on measures from samples within the same population at various points in time. For example, all children beginning kindergarten in 2006 in a large urban school district or in a state would be considered the population. Those children would be followed throughout their school career; however, each year or at each point when data are taken, a cluster would be sampled within the same population of students who began their school careers in 2006.

Cross-Sectional Studies

A simulated longitudinal descriptive study can be completed by collecting data obtained at a point in time from samples of individuals who represent a cross section of the population. This is typically called a cross-sectional descriptive study. You may survey parents of students at grades K through 5 in a large urban district on their perceptions of teacher attitudes toward their children or on some variable of interest. You may administer a test to a sample of students from grades K through 12 at a point in time to gather data on a particular phenomenon. Mobility of students and attrition are not accounted for in this type of research and are considered limitations.

Several dissertation abstract examples follow that demonstrate effective use of descriptive research design. (See Examples 3.1, 3.2, and 3.3.) Following is an example of a dissertation dealing with a training program for school psychologists completed by Bridgewater (2006). (See Example 3.1.)

Example 3.1

Abstract

Despite the need for early identification and intensive intervention for social emotional concerns in young children, there exists a shortage of personnel trained to provide mental health services with early childhood populations (Klien & Gilkerson, 2000). The purpose of this study was to examine, through descriptive research, the current status of preservice school psychology training in relation to the assessment of social-emotional development in preschool children. Specifically, this study sought to explore the training school psychology programs offer, in preparing preservice school psychologists to provide mental health services for preschool populations, and evaluate the perceptions of trainers and students regarding the coursework, competencies, and instruments necessary for preparing school psychologists to provide social-emotional assessment and mental health services in early childhood settings. Participants in this study included 108 program directors (trainers) of school psychology training programs within the United States, as well as 4 advanced level students from each program, randomly selected from the master's/specialists ($n = 151$) and doctoral level ($n = 74$) of study in each program; a total of 225 students. Two corresponding forms of the *"Preschool Social-Emotional Assessment Training"* questionnaire were developed for this study. Each questionnaire was worded appropriately for the different groups of respondents. The questionnaire items were developed based upon two previous studies conducted by Boyer (1996) and Gettinger, Stoiber, Goetz, and Caspe (1999), and the current literature concerning the preparation of school psychologists and related service personnel in the delivery of early childhood metal health assessment and intervention services. (Bridgewater, 2006, p. ii)

The second abstract example is a dissertation that reports parental regulations on television viewing (Salvato, 2006). (See Example 3.2.)

Example 3.2

Abstract

Childhood obesity is the most prevalent chronic disease among North American children and has reached epidemic proportions. Increased television viewing has been shown to increase the chances of a child becoming obese. The purpose of this descriptive study was to determine the amount of media children are using and the parental practices being used to regulate television viewing among elementary school students. The sampling frame consisted of parents of children attending an elementary school in Connecticut. A questionnaire was adapted to determine the parental regulations being used to monitor children's television viewing. Parents self-reported their child's height and weight so that a correlation could be made between regulations and childhood obesity. The results of this study have increased the data on parental regulations regarding the use of television, and revealed that many parents are not aware of the effects that excessive television use can have on their child's BMI. (Salvato, 2006, p. iii)

The third dissertation example relates to a higher education study on writing centers and the questions that are asked by the tutors. This dissertation was completed by Cook (2006). (See Example 3.3.)

Example 3.3

Abstract

This dissertation examines two research questions: What questions do tutors ask of writers during tutorials, and what apparent effect do such questions have on the tutorial? Writing center theory has largely bulked question types together, causing many to hail questions as harmful while others to view them as essential.

In this study, 20 videotaped tutorials were observed wherein a total of 10 university writing tutors and 20 university student writers collaborated for nearly 427 minutes. During viewing, every question a tutor asked of a writer was logged and each context was analyzed. All sessions were viewed at least three times.

Tutors in this study asked 473 questions, allowing for 16 types of tutor questions to be identified. The types are labeled according to their effect and are further categorized into two categories. The first category is Interpersonal Tutor Questions, and it contains the following types: process, consent, rapport, gauging, filler, distracting, refocusing, and orienting. Effects include the ability to manage tutorials, gain permission, establish rapport, check writer understanding or mood, participate in chat, distract writers, refocus writers, and inform tutors. The second category is Making Meaning Questions, and it contains the following types: clarifying, verifying, transferring, suggesting, prompting, modeling, drawing, and exploring. The effects are the ability to clarify tutor understanding, verify that tutor understanding is correct, transfer expertise, suggest changes, lead writers through discovery, model thought processes, draw out information from writers, and challenge and stimulate writers' ideas and views.

This study is a descriptive study, which examines tutor questions and their effects; it does not examine the mental processes behind questioning. The study's conclusions are: tutors employ 16 tutor question types for various purposes; effective questioning requires the understanding of different question types; without an awareness of question types, tutors may find it difficult to know how to ask *probing* or *challenging* questions; the writing center field's understanding of tutor questions can benefit from question research in other fields, but direct parallels made without consideration of the unique culture of writing centers may lead to tutor confusion. This study provides an important step toward tutor questioning training. (Cook, 2006, pp. iv–v)

CORRELATIONAL RESEARCH DESIGN

Correlational research is based in "relationship" just as its name implies. It is grounded in interactions of one variable to another; for example, as scores on one variable go up the related scores on another variable go down. You might find an inverse correlation between positive praise and acting out behavior—as the amount of praise increases, the amount of acting out behavior decreases. In correlational research, the degree to which the variables are related is important as well as the direction of the relationship. This type of research is not specifically causal-comparative research nor is it ex post facto research. Where correlational research actually relates scores from two or more variables from the same sample, ex post facto research compares scores from two or more groups on the same variable. Generally, correlational research does not signify causality, but some correlational research designs, such as path analysis and cross-lagged panel designs, allow for causal conclusions.

In correlational research, if a relationship is found between two or more variables, then the variables are correlated. This correlation must be interpreted based on the strength and direction via the correlational coefficient that ranges between −1 and +1. The direction of the correlation or the association between the two variables can indicate a positive association (0 to +1). This means that as one variable increases, the other variable also increases, and vice versa. Correlation coefficients between 0 and −1 represent a negative association. In this sense, as one variable increases, the other variable decreases. The magnitude or strength of the correlation or association between the two or more variables is signified as stronger by correlation coefficients closer to 1 (either positive or negative). A correlation coefficient of +1 indicates a perfect positive relationship, while a coefficient of 0 indicates no relationship, and a coefficient of −1 indicates a perfect negative relationship.

The correlational coefficient is represented by the letter r. In education, generally a correlation of 0.30 may be considered significant, and any correlation above 0.70 is almost always significant. A Pearson's product moment correlation, represented by r, is the most widely used statistic of correlation. It is used when variables you want to correlate are normally distributed and are measured on an interval or a ratio scale. As you learned in statistics, the r is not a percentage score, but when you square the r (r^2), then you have an index called the *coefficient of determination* that indicates how much of the variance of X has in common with the variance of Y. For example if r is .50, then the r^2 would be 25%. This means that the two variables have 25% of their variance in common with each other. It can also be interpreted that 25% of the variance in Y can be accounted for by X. The coefficient of determination should be reported as it lends meaning to your findings by giving you the size or degree of the relationship. Cohen (1988) indicated that correlations can yield effect size in the r^2 and determined that a small correlation effect size would be $r^2 = .01$, a medium effect size would be represented by $r^2 = .09$, and a large effect size would be $r^2 = .25$. Effect size is recommended to be reported in the findings as it quantifies the distance from the null hypothesis (in correlational study the null hypothesizes that no relationship exists between the two variables) (Thompson, 2000).

Correlational research is used in a wide array of studies that intend, of course, to determine relationships, but also that aim to assess consistency, as well as predictions. As you may have learned from the chapter on statistics or your course in statistics, when the p-calculated is less than p-critical (in education it is usually established before a study is conducted and set as .05), such a relationship is significant. In correlational research, sample size is an important consideration. As you already know the smaller the sample size, the larger the size of the correlation has to be to be statistically significant; on the other hand, the larger the sample size, the more likely a significant correlation will be found even if it is with small magnitude. Therefore, in research with large sample size, reporting effect size is meaningful and critical.

Following are some types of correlations that may be used in correlation research when data are specific to ratio or interval scales.

Bivariate Correlation

For bivariate correlation, you would be investigating the relationship between two variables. For example, you may be interested in determining the relationship between the amount of time sixth grade students spend reading in structured partnership reading in school and their reading scores at the end of a six-week period. An example of a dissertation that used bivariate correlation was conducted by Siemers (2006). (See Example 3.4.)

Example 3.4

Abstract

Aggression negatively impacts children's psychological and academic well being. The playground environment is more susceptible to aggressive behavior than more structured academic settings like the classroom. In this study, the relation between staff and student reports of student playground aggression was examined. Then, the relation between environmental playground factors (i.e., playground activities, playground supervisor ratios, active supervision, and playground rules) and student reports of aggression was examined. Finally, the relation of playground aggression to student self-reports of playground worries was evaluated. School Climate Theory provided the conceptual framework for evaluating playground characteristics, student aggression, and worry. Participants included 767 third, fourth, and fifth grade students and 57 playground supervisors from 10 Midwest elementary schools. Participants completed reports of aggression (students and staff), playground worries (students only), and playground environmental factors (staff only). Bivariate correlations were used to examine the relation between staff and student reports of aggression. Hierarchical Linear Modeling analyses were conducted to examine the relation among playground factors, aggression, and playground worries. This study used a novel approach to measuring the predictive relation of aggression on children's worries through student self-report measures. Results of this study showed that staff and students' reports of playground aggression were inconsistently correlated. Although overt physical and verbal playground aggression scores were significantly correlated, relational playground aggression and playground conflict were not associated. Additionally, four playground characteristics were linked to playground aggression: cooperative games, supervisor ratios, active monitoring, and playground rules. Finally, when students reported more playground aggression, their reports of playground worry were higher. (Siemers, 2006, pp. ii–iii)

Regression and Prediction

For regression and prediction, you would be assessing if a correlation exists between two variables. You might know the score on one and wish to predict the score on the second variable, and regression is related to how well you can make that prediction. The closer the correlation coefficients are to −1 or +1, the better your predictions become. A strong prediction is evidenced on packs of cigarettes—the more a person smokes, the higher the prediction of the person developing lung cancer or other cancers.

An example of a dissertation related to compensation strategy on non-profit organizations is provided by Hoke (2006). (See Example 3.5.)

Example 3.5

Abstract

This study examined the effects of a total compensation strategy on the culture of a nonprofit. This study also examined employee perceptions of the new total compensation strategy. A paired-samples t test was used to determine whether a statistically significant difference existed between the means of the variables designated as productivity, innovation, and culture before and after the implementation of a new total compensation strategy. A Pearson r was used to determine the degree to which productivity, innovation, and culture variables were associated. A simple linear regression was used to examine how effectively the total compensation strategy variable allowed prediction of the value of the variables designated as productivity, innovation, and culture. The study was initiated in order to increase understanding of those elements that influence organizational productivity, innovation, and cultural change. The setting was a donative nonprofit in St. Louis, Missouri. The data analysis in this study revealed that the independent variable; i.e., the new total compensation strategy, had a statistically significant effect on the culture of the nonprofit organization. The findings presented in this study also illuminated ways in which employees viewed the new total compensation strategy as most helpful; i.e., providing a sense of ownership and motivation, and conversely, as least helpful; i.e., confusion about how the strategy works. An integrated analysis of the quantitative and qualitative data also suggested ways in which the effect of the new total compensation strategy could be increased. For example, the analysis suggested that more support for being creative and doing new things would increase organizational productivity and innovation. As a second example, the analysis suggested that more freedom for employees to exercise discretion in decision making would increase organizational productivity and innovation. Future research that addresses the application of organizational interventions developed in the private sector to the nonprofit sector and considers the impact of personal value systems will further refine the body of evidenced-based interventions. These interventions will assist nonprofit organizations to enhance sustainability, contribute to the effectiveness of organizational functioning, and finally the satisfaction and well-being of those employed by the organization. (Hoke, 2006, pp. i–ii)

Multiple Regression

For multiple regression, you would add more variables and more power in terms of making more accurate predictions. The variable that you would be predicting in multiple regression is called the *criterion, outcome,* or *dependent variable,* while the variables you use to make the prediction are called the *predictor* or *independent variables.* If you are trying to predict English reading scores for English language learners in a structured intervention, you might have as predictor variables the amount of time taught in English, the level of English of the parents, and the amount of time spent in academic oral language engagement with the child. You would have one criterion variable measured by some predetermined reading assessment and you would have three predictor variables. Do not forget to calculate your effect size for multiple regression and other correlational designs. An example of the effect size for multiple regression follows. Cohen's f^2 is the appropriate effect size measure to use in the context of multiple regression or multiple correlations. The f^2 effect size measure for multiple regression is as follows:

$$f^2 = \frac{R^2}{1 - R^2}$$

(R^2 is the squared multiple correlation derived from the regression model).

By convention, f^2 effect sizes of 0.02, 0.15, and 0.35 are considered small, medium, and large, respectively (Cohen, 1988). Other multiple regressions, such as hierarchical multiple regression, will have a slightly different formula for the effect size. You will need to consult a statistics manual.

The following is an example of a dissertation in which multiple regression was used in a correlational research design (Bean, 2007). (See Example 3.6.)

Example 3.6

Abstract

Rates of obesity in children are rising at an alarming rate, particularly among girls and ethnic minorities. Engaging in regular physical activity can help reduce this risk. Little is known about factors associated with physical activity (PA) in preadolescent populations, an age when intervention is ideal. Guided by Social Cognitive Theory, this study used a repeated-measures design to examine PA and its correlates, including PA self-efficacy, outcome expectations, and social influences (from parents and peers), among participants ($N = 57$) in *Girls on the Run,* an innovative

PA intervention for elementary school girls. Participants (M age = 9.4) predominately include girls from ethnic groups at highest risk for obesity, with 74% African American and 18% Hispanic. Multiple regressions indicated that, at baseline, girls with higher self-efficacy were significantly more likely to report greater intentions to be physically active (β = .40, p < .05). Further, although no mean changes in study outcomes were found, an examination of factors associated with the variance in PA behaviors and intentions at posttest can further understanding of PA in this age and ethnic group. Processes of change regressions suggested that, after adjusting for baseline levels, increases in both self-efficacy and social influences were significantly associated with higher physical activity behaviors and intentions at posttest (p < .05). Outcome expectations, or belief in the benefits of physical activity, was not a significant variable in the models (p > .05). Overall, findings suggest the importance of targeting physical activity self-efficacy and fostering high levels of peer and parental support for physical activity to help girls meet recommended guidelines. Implications for future interventions are discussed. (Bean, 2007, p. vii)

Canonical Correlation

Canonical correlation uses multiple correlations and has more than one criterion variable to a prediction equation. It allows you to see which of the variables are most important to relationships between the sets of independent and dependent variables. An example of a dissertation that included canonical correlation as its primary technique was done by McCoy (2005). (See Example 3.7.)

Example 3.7

Abstract

The purpose of this study was to examine hypothesized relationships between participants' characteristics (i.e., academic interest area, prior exposure to persons with disabilities, the positive personal characteristics of humor, hope, and gratitude) and their self-report of cognitive, affective and behavioral responses to persons with disabilities, while controlling for social desirability. Undergraduate student participants at three Mid-Atlantic colleges were recruited from introductory courses in human services to complete survey packets.

The instruments used to gather data for this study consisted of a demographic survey designed by the author, the Marlowe-Crowne Social Desirability Scale (Crowne & Marlowe, 1960), the Humor Styles Questionnaire (Martin, Puhlik-Doris, Larsen, Gray, & Weir, 2003), the Adult Dispositional Hope Scale (Snyder et al., 1991), the Gratitude Questionnaire-6 (McCullough, Emmons, & Tsang, 2002), the Attitudes Toward Disabled Persons Scale—Form O (Yuker, Block, & Campbell, 1960), the Relationships with Disabled Persons Scale (Satcher & Gamble,

2002), the Interaction with Disabled Persons Scale (Gething & Wheeler, 1992), and the Situational Response Questionnaire (Berry & Jones, 1991).

A canonical correlation analysis was used to identify a combination of personal characteristics that are correlated with a combination of reactions to persons with disabilities. The primary multivariate finding of this study was that the combination of some, but not all, of the personal characteristics explored were correlated with the combination of some, but not all, of the measures of reaction toward persons with disabilities. A construct composed of the personal characteristics of affiliative humor and majoring in a human services field and, to a lesser degree, self-defeating humor, hope, and prior exposure to persons with disabilities was correlated with a construct composed of cognitive attitudes toward persons with disabilities, and to a lesser degree, affective responses toward persons with disabilities. Though the findings of this study were significant, the amount of variability in criterion variables that was explained by the predictor variables was relatively small. This suggests that other factors account for the rather large amount of variability unexplained by the predictors included in this study. (McCoy, 2005, p. iii)

Discriminant Analysis

Discriminant analysis is used to compare two or more groups on a set of variables. The criterion variable in this correlational analysis is the group membership. Predictor variables are input and a formula or model results. An example of discriminant analysis employed in a dissertation from Thanasui (2005) follows. (See Example 3.8.)

Example 3.8

Abstract

This study investigated the influence of past witnessed or experienced abuse on heterosexual cohabiting couples' Premarital Personal and Relationship Evaluation for Cohabiting Couples (PREPARE-CC) couple relationship types. The researcher utilized preexisting data from 5,000 cohabiting couples who had previously participated in the PREPARE marriage preparation program and had completed the PREPARE-CC inventory including a demographic section that elicited information about past abuse. Discriminant analysis was conducted in SPSS to answer the question of whether the presence of past witnessed or experienced abuse could successfully predict relationship type among cohabiting couples.

Results of the discriminant analysis yielded no significant ability to classify cohabiting couples by individuals' experience of past abuse, however, isolating females and males with the highest frequencies of past abuse indicated that males abused "very often" had a higher frequency of higher-satisfaction relationship types than the general sample consisting mostly of individuals with little or no history of abuse. Females reporting abuse "very often" did not follow this same pattern. Recommendations were made for future longitudinal studies and for strength-based research on healthy heterosexual cohabiting couples in an effort to understand what contributes to these couples' success. (Thanasui, 2005, p. iii)

Factor Analysis

Factor analysis is another statistical procedure that uses correlations to identify basic patterns of variables. If a large number of variables having intercorrelations are present, then a common factor could be identified for that set of variables. Several factors could be identified among a large set of variables if you are studying leadership and organizations. For example, you might find two factors such as leadership behaviors and organizational structures. The two factors might be helpful in describing the success of superintendents. An example of factor analysis used in a dissertation by Evans (2006) follows. (See Example 3.9.)

Example 3.9

Abstract

The purpose of this study was to examine the validity and reliability of scores from a survey instrument, the Technology Integration Survey (TIS), designed to measure technology integration skills in preservice teachers. All of the items used in the survey were based on the ISTE NETS for Teachers (NETS-T) standards. Participants in the study were undergraduate students enrolled in the preservice teacher education program at a large university in southeastern North Carolina. Validity and reliability studies were conducted on the TIS including: (a) a study of representativeness and alignment of survey items to the NETS-T standards, (b) analysis of the internal structure using exploratory factor analysis, (c) pre/posttest testing after technology intervention, (d) correlations between the TIS and an instrument with known validity and reliability, (e) correlations between TIS and field experiences or online portfolios, and (f) analysis of internal consistency. Four factors were extracted using a principal components analysis. The factors (a) Planning and Designing Learning Environments and Experiences, (b) Teaching and Professional Practice, (c) Social, Ethical, and Human Issues, and (d) Assessment and Evaluation explained 63% of the variance. Reliability coefficients on the four subscales ranged from .83 to .89. Evidence from the study supports the use of the TIS as a viable tool to measure technology integration skills in preservice teachers. (Evans, 2006, p. iii)

Path Analysis

Path analysis may be used to assess which of a number of pathways connects one variable to another. For example, in the relationship of smoking and lung cancer, there might be a small to medium path that runs through healthy activity, but a major path that goes through smoking behavior. In this, you could surmise that even with running, walking, and eating properly, if a person continues to smoke heavily, he or she has a stronger likelihood to develop lung cancer.

A dissertation example that used path analysis was completed by Choi (2005). (See Example 3.10.)

Example 3.10

Abstract

The purpose of this study was to identify the physical activity behavior (leisure-time, household, job-related, and transportation-related) and to examine the relationships between physical activity behavior and the correlates of physical activity including acculturation as well as environmental resource, social support, and cognition (self-efficacy, decisional balance) in 200 adult Korean immigrant women aged 20–64. Although the health benefits of physical activity are well established, the current physical activity level of the U.S. public, particularly for ethnic minority and immigrant women, does not reach the Healthy People 2010 goals. There are few studies of physical activity and its correlates for Asian-American women and none include Koreans. A descriptive cross-sectional survey design was used. Korean ethnic church-based recruitment was the primary means of accessing this population. Physical activity was measured with the long form of the International Physical Activity Questionnaire. Acculturation was measured with proxy measures (language, years of residence in the U.S., age at immigration) and the Vancouver Index of Acculturation. McAuley's Barriers Self-Efficacy measure and Marcus' Decisional Balance measure provided measures of cognition. The mean age of the participants was 41 years, 84.5% were married, and 71% had a college degree or higher. In general, the women were not physically active in their leisure time, but most of them were physically active when other domains of physical activity were examined together. A path analysis showed that years of residence in the U.S., self-efficacy, and decisional balance had direct positive effects, and number of children under five years had a direct negative effect on leisure-time physical activity. Age and American acculturation had indirect positive effects through self-efficacy while depression had an indirect negative effect through decisional balance on leisure-time physical activity. A total of 14 percent of the variance in leisure-time physical activity was explained. The findings showed that acculturation is an important correlate of leisure-time physical activity among Korean immigrant women. In addition, self-efficacy and decisional balance were essential cognitive correlates of leisure-time physical activity and they played mediating roles. Findings provide direction for developing targeted physical activity interventions for Korean immigrant women based on their self-efficacy, decisional balance, and acculturation. (Choi, 2005, n.p.)

Cross-Lagged Panel

Cross-lagged panel (longitudinal) correlational designs measure two sets of variables simultaneously at two points in time. For example, the correlation between early exposure to oral English literacy in prekindergarten and reading achievement in fifth grade is compared with the correlation between later reading achievement in fifth grade and later exposure to oral English literacy in first grade. Some of the data points in this design are treated as temporality delayed or lagged values of the outcome variable. According to Mackinnon, Nohre, Cheong, Stacey, & Pentz (2001):

> Cross-lagged correlation approaches were criticized for several reasons, including problems due to measurement error (Kessler & Greenberg, 1981). Measurement error was later incorporated in the cross-lagged model by the estimation of latent variable models for the observed measures. These methods enjoyed several years of wide and convincing applicability (Bentler & Speckart, 1979, 1981; Kessler & Greenberg, 1981) until their limitations were clearly described (Rogosa, 1980). According to Rogosa and Willett (1985), these models do not explicitly specify individual change, do not easily generalize to more than two waves of data, and the data analysis only includes the covariance matrix and not the means. Stoolmiller and Bank (1995) added that autoregressive models fail when there is high-rank order stability over time and require the questionable assertion that the prior score on a variable causes the subsequent score on that variable. (p. 221)

An example of a cross-lagged panel correlational design was used in a dissertation by Coon-Carty (1998). (See Example 3.11.)

Example 3.11

Abstract

Vygotsky argued that children's development is most likely to occur when, in the course of collaboration, assistance is provided within their zone of proximal development—the distance between what a child can achieve independently and what he or she can do with the assistance of a more competent peer. This dissertation discusses the results from a longitudinal investigation exploring the impact of learning in either a multiage or traditional classroom on students' subject-specific academic self-concepts. Results from a cross-lagged panel correlation analysis, testing the predominant causal flow from subject-specific self-concepts to academic achievement are also described. Participants in the study consisted of 189 first (106) and fourth (93) grade children who were drawn from a public elementary school in Salt Lake City, serving predominantly European-American middle- and lower middle-class students. Eighty-one of the participants were in a multiage classroom with the remaining 108 in a traditional classroom. Multiple self-concept measures and a standardized achievement test were given to the participants toward the beginning and at the conclusion of the academic year. Results indicated no significant differences for math and reading self-concepts between the multiage and traditional participants and the end of the academic year. Learning in a multiage classroom did not increase the participants' math or reading self-concepts over the course of the academic year. Significant differences were found as a function of setting for male participants. Fourth grade males in the multiage classroom reported significantly lower control over performance scores at the end of the academic year compared to the fourth grade males in the traditional classrooms. Results from the cross-lagged correlation design demonstrated a causal flow from reading self-concept to subsequent reading achievement, suggesting that perceptions of reading abilities cause future reading achievement. The study did not show the same significant influence between math self-concept and math achievement. The pattern of associations between math self-concept and math achievement is more suggestive of a reciprocal relationship rather than a causal one. (Coon-Carty, 1998, pp. x–xi)

Other Correlation Coefficients

For data that are represented by rank scores, an ordinate coefficient of correlation, *Spearman's rho (ρ)*, is used. It is interpreted in the same way as the Pearson r and ranges from −1 to +1. A phi coefficient (Φ) is used when both variables are dichotomous scores (1 or 0). This is often used when sex of individuals is a variable. For example, you might want to determine on a particular college campus if drinking is more related to men than to women. The phi coefficient reveals both strength and direction of relationships. Although we have presented only three types of correlation coefficients, there are others that are available to you for use with nominal and ordinal data and that can be used with more than two variables.

Advantages and Disadvantages

There are advantages and disadvantages to correlational designs. First, the advantage is that almost any variable that you wish to study can be investigated. Additionally, it can be used in a predictive manner with one variable or more predicting another. Disadvantages that have been discussed are that correlational research is subject to extraneous variables and that causation cannot be inferred.

CAUSAL-COMPARATIVE RESEARCH DESIGN

Causal-comparative research, or ex post facto (after the fact) research, is the most basic design for determining cause-and-effect relationships between variables. Causal-comparative research is different from experimental research in that you do not manipulate the independent variable since it has already occurred, and as already indicated, you cannot control it. Additionally, causal-comparative research will not meet the experimental research requirement for random assignment of participants from a single population or pool of participants. At least two comparison groups are needed in causal-comparative research to be compared on a dependent variable. One group may be students who have been identified by their teachers as being potentially gifted, and the other group may be those students not identified by their teachers as being potentially gifted. These two groups could be measured on standardized IQ tests to determine if the group differences identified by the teacher perception are accurate as compared by the standardized measures.

When you discuss the groups, you will want to make certain you describe the groups and their characteristics in detail and the independent variable that distinguishes the groups. Why is this important? It is important because the group constitution and definitions can affect the generalizability of your findings. Give ample detail to understand all about each of the groups in terms of their comparability and differences. You may obtain your groups from two independent established populations, such as those students who have had public school prekindergarten and those who did not. You may want to compare these students on English reading achievement at the end of kindergarten or first grade. To obtain your sample you may conduct random sampling (not random assignment from one single population as in experimental research). You will want your groups to be as similar as possible on some variables. For example, in the prekindergarten versus no prekindergarten groups, you may want to go through the random samples and match the samples (to have better control) on age, ethnicity, socioeconomic status, and gender. You want the groups to be as similar as possible so that the difference or lack of differences you see in the end of your research is more likely to be attributed to your independent variable. Because causal-comparative research does not rest on randomization or manipulation or control of variables, you will know up front that is a weakness if you so choose this type of design.

Weakness Controlled

One way to control for that weakness has already been mentioned—match the samples. Another way to control for confounding variables is to compare homogenous groups. In our previous example, we could take all students who had been to prekindergarten and who had not who were all English language learners and who were non-English fluent upon entry to kindergarten. Another way to further control the study would be to take that same group of students and separate them into subgroups that would represent varying degrees of English language fluency. Perhaps you might group the students into non-English fluent and limited-English fluent. This would permit you to determine the influence of English fluency when checking the independent variable's influence on the dependent variable. If you like this approach, you may wish to test control variables by using factorial analysis of variance (known as ANOVA). This approach will allow you to determine the effect of the independent variable, as well as the control variable (separately and combined), on the dependent variable. A factorial analysis provides information about the interaction of the independent variable on the control variable at the different subgroup levels. Students who are limited-English fluent upon entry to kindergarten may indeed show significantly higher beginning English reading (literacy) scores at the end of the kindergarten year.

Another statistical technique that may be used as well is analysis of covariance (ANCOVA). ANCOVA adjusts for initial differences in your groups. For example, if students who have better English skills at the outset of the study and demonstrate in a pretest score significantly higher in English literacy/reading, then the ANCOVA will adjust for that. It adjusts both groups to equal standing. As instruction is then given to both groups using the same curriculum, the final outcome can be better assessed in terms of the actual kindergarten year intervention.

All methods discussed here are univariate analyses. When you have more than one dependent variable you may want to resort to multivariate analysis.

Data analysis techniques used in causal-comparative research designs usually consist of inferential statistical techniques such as t test (comparison between two groups), analysis of variance (comparison among more than two groups), and chi square (when outcome variable is dichotomous). We have a couple of words of caution as you begin your analysis and conduct your statistical tests. First, be careful on your interpretation of causality. Look at your data carefully to make certain in which direction the causal relationship flows. Additionally, remember to conduct a test for effect size for each of the typical statistical tests for this research design. Effect size takes various forms, such as r^2 (see previous sections on correlational research). We present here a basic effect size type for t test for means; however, you will want to consult your committee statistician on this topic for calculating or obtaining these via your statistical package you use for your dissertation. Typically for a t test for testing means, you would use Cohen's d. Here is the formula:

$$d = \frac{\text{mean}_1 - \text{mean}_2}{\sqrt{(\text{SD}_1^2 + \text{SD}_2^2)/2}}$$

You will also want to report confidence intervals as well. The bottom line is that, whether it is chi square or t test, all must be followed by an effect size calculation for your research findings to be rendered worthwhile, as this calculation provides you with the strength of the association to the larger population as it relates to your study.

Following are two examples of causal-comparative research designs used in recent dissertations. (See Examples 3.12 and 3.13.)

Example 3.12

Abstract

The purpose of this study was to determine differences in teacher preparation and retention for two groups of Texas A&M University–Corpus Christi graduates certified in 2002 and 2003. Factors that influenced teacher attrition, such as teaching assignments, working conditions, salary, benefits, scheduling, organizational skills, rapport with administrators, colleagues, parents and students were examined to determine whether graduates who completed a formal mentoring program stay in the teaching profession at higher rates than the graduates who did not participate in the Strategies of Success (SOS) formal mentoring program.

Participants included 95 certified TAMU-CC graduates who met the inclusion criterion of no prior teaching experience.

A causal-comparative research design was used to compare two preexisting groups, non-SOS and SOS TAMU-CC certified graduates applying for certification in 2002 and 2003. Outcome measures examined were retention, reasons for leaving the field of education and satisfaction with the teacher education program at this regional university. The TAMU-CC Teacher Education Survey (Arnold & Ramirez, 2003) was used to collect data for this study. Results of the analyses showed no statistically significant difference between the non-SOS and SOS groups. (Arnold, 2006, pp. iii–iv)

Example 3.13

Abstract

This study analyzed test scores of economically disadvantaged students who attended two elementary schools implementing different types of Title I models from 1999–2001. Test scores from the Texas Assessment of Academic Skills (TAAS), the Iowa Test of Basic Skills (ITBS), and the Stanford Achievement Test (SAT-9) were analyzed. One school implemented the targeted assistance model (less than 50% poverty), which focused resources on students identified as failing or at risk of failing. The other a schoolwide model (95% poverty), which used resources to help all students in a school regardless of whether they ware failing, at risk of failing, or economically disadvantaged.

The quantitative approach was used with a causal-comparative design. A cohort of continuously enrolled students was identified for the TAAS ($n = 155$) and the ITBS/SAT-9 ($n = 135$). Descriptive statistics such as the frequency, mean, and standard deviation, were used to measure differences on the Texas Learning Index (TLI) for the TAAS, and Normal Curve Equivalent (NCE) on the ITBS/SAT-9. Analysis of Covariance (ANCOVA) was used to partially adjust for preexisting differences among the groups and because randomization was not possible. The independent variable was type of Title I model, targeted assistance or schoolwide. The dependent variable was the achievement measure, and the covariate was the initial achievement scores in third grade (pretest).

The ANCOVA reports and descriptive statistics showed that economically disadvantaged students performed better in reading and math on TAAS and ITBS/SAT-9 at the targeted assistance school in 1999 and 2001, with mixed results in 2000. The academic performance of economically disadvantaged students at the targeted model was consistent all three school years. They scored slightly lower than the non-economically disadvantaged students, but higher than their peers at the schoolwide model. The students' third grade pretest score was the most significant predictor of future performance. (Hinojosa, 2005, n.p.)

QUASI-EXPERIMENTAL RESEARCH DESIGN

Even though the best causal research is reflected in true experimental designs, most research in education that requires causal inferences cannot be conducted under true experimentation due to the inability to randomly assign participants to experimental and control groups or the inability to secure a control or comparative group. Additionally, much of true experimentation is expensive in that it often requires training in the intervention and always monitoring for fidelity. In this case, quasi-experimental designs are available to give you adequate control over threats to validity. There are several types of quasi-experimental designs, which we believe would be advantageous to the development of your dissertation research.

Nonequivalent Control Group Design

This design is used most frequently in educational research. This design includes at least an experimental group and a control group with random assignment of participants to groups; however, there is random assignment of intact groups to treatments. Cook and Campbell (1979) outlined 11 nonequivalent control group research designs. Table 3.1 shares several of those 11 possible designs.

Examples of nonequivalent control group research designs from dissertations follow. (See Examples 3.14 and 3.15.)

Table 3.1   Nonequivalent Control Group Research Designs

Research Design	Explanation
One-Group Posttest-Only Design	Because there is no accurate information on pretest data from the group, the results of this type of design cannot be considered completely valid because changes in the dependent variable may be due to treatment, or they may be due to any number of threats to validity, such as history or researcher expectation. A caution is noted to gather and report as much information as possible related to the pretest conditions. However, this design is fairly inexpensive. It allows you to conduct research when there is no comparison group readily available. Often this design is used in evaluation research.
Posttest-Only Design with Nonequivalent Comparison Groups Design	This design consists of the administration of a posttest to two groups—usually a treatment group and a comparison group. Because the two groups may not be the same prior to the beginning of the instruction, it is difficult to draw valid conclusions about treatment effect based solely on posttest information on two nonequivalent groups because effects may be due to treatment or to nonequivalencies between the groups.
One-Group Pretest-Posttest Design	This is a common design (0×0) comparing performances of a single group of participants, but this design has weaknesses. It is subject to such threats to internal validity, such as history, maturation, regression toward the mean, testing, selection, and mortality. It is difficult to determine if the results are from the intervention or from confounding variables between the pretest and posttest.
Two-Group Pretest-Posttest Design Using an Untreated Control Group	In this design, threats to validity are reduced because there is a comparison group; however, the groups are not equivalent. Therefore, there remains the possibility of the threats of selection. Performance trends in both the treatment group and the control group, can be established by using multiple pretests. There should be a change in the trend line for the treatment group but not the control group.

Example 3.14

Abstract

Purpose. The purpose of this study was to describe Advanced Placement (AP) calculus teachers' and administrators' perceptions of AP calculus program characteristics that have increased student enrollment in selected San Bernardino County public comprehensive high schools.

Methodology. Descriptive research methodology and a posttest only, one-group design was used to identify the current characteristics of AP calculus programs in the county of San Bernardino. The study examined the responses of twenty-five AP calculus teachers and twenty-seven site administrators in the county of San Bernardino. Teachers and administrators were surveyed with a questionnaire to obtain information on student preparedness for AP calculus classes, student learning, access, and placement. The study examined the educational/training of AP calculus teachers, as well as the types of instructional, administrative, district, and parental support AP calculus programs received. Free response questions were elicited to determine the teachers' and administrators' perceptions of AP calculus programs.

Findings. Administrators and teachers both perceived that there were gaps to students' preparedness for AP calculus classes. Teachers were more pessimistic that AP calculus classes were supported from their school district. Teachers and administrators perceived that they received a lot of support from their site principal, but teachers were more pessimistic on parental support. The findings confirm that teachers and administrators perceived that students receive AP practice exams for support, after-school sessions, and individual tutoring, but students are not perceived to receive Saturday support sessions or guidance counseling for AP calculus classes.

Conclusions and Recommendations. AP calculus teachers and site administrators must generate strategies to increase student enrollment in AP calculus classes in selected San Bernardino County public comprehensive high schools. The study recommends that AP calculus teachers and site administrators collaborate to develop and implement strategies on student preparedness for AP calculus classes, student learning, access, placement, and the implications of those strategies for the design and integration of curriculum, instruction, assessment, and professional development. The study presents a set of recommended actions that could significantly improve existing programs for approaches to AP calculus courses and serve to promote programs for advanced study in the mathematics discipline. (Rodriguez, 2005, pp. iii–iv)

Example 3.15

Abstract

This study assessed the effects of general and specific supervisory feedback on counselors'-in-training ratings of counseling self-efficacy (CSE). Fifty-four students in counseling-related graduate programs from two universities in the Southeast and one in the Midwest volunteered as participants. Thirty-seven participants were female, 14 were male, and three did not indicate their sex. Forty out of 54 participants indicated they were Caucasian-American, five were African American, one was Hispanic-American, one was Asian-American, and three indicated "other." The median number of months of previous clinical supervision for the participants was one month. This study made use of a two-group pretest-posttest design. The independent variable was performance feedback, with two levels (specific and general). The dependent variables included posttest scores on the Counselor Activity Self-Efficacy Scales (CASES), (Lent, Hill, & Hoffman, 2003). State anxiety was also assessed with the state scale of the State-Trait Anxiety Inventory (STAI-S), (Spielberger, 1982). After completing pretest measures, participants performed a ten-minute mock counseling session with a confederate. After the mock counseling session, the confederate provided either specific feedback or general feedback statements to the participants. Participants then filled out posttest measures. After the measures were collected, participants received an extensive debriefing. The three hypotheses for counseling self-efficacy were: (a) participants receiving specific feedback would obtain higher counseling self-efficacy scores; (b) posttest counseling self-efficacy scores would be significantly higher than pretest scores; and (c) while both groups were expected to score similarly in the pretest measure of counseling self-efficacy, it was predicted that the participants receiving specific feedback would report higher counseling self-efficacy scores in the posttest measures. There was no difference between counseling self-efficacy scores of participants who received general or specific supervisory feedback. Postmeasure counseling self-efficacy scores were significantly higher than the premeasure scores. There was no group × time interaction. There was no difference between anxiety scores of participants who received general or specific supervisory feedback. Postmeasure anxiety scores were significantly higher than the premeasure scores. There was no group × time interaction. Implications and issues to be considered in future research were discussed. (Clark, 2005, pp. vi–vii)

Time Series Design

The time series design is a variation of the one-group pretest–posttest design. Such a design is diagrammed in Figure 3.2. The *one- or single-group time series design* is where one group of participants is tested repeatedly both before and after treatment. The repeated testing establishes stability prior to the treatment, and the repeated testing after the treatment establishes confidence in the effectiveness of the treatment. You would essentially investigate the pattern of test scores pre- and post-treatment. There are threats to validity related to history and instrumentation if the instrument is changed during the research. A *multiple time series design,* adding a control group, can eliminate the threats.

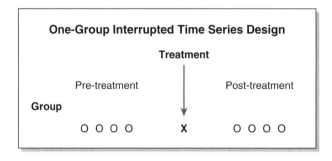

Figure 3.2   One-Group Interrupted Time Series Design

Following are examples from dissertations using time series designs. (See Examples 3.16 and 3.17.)

Example 3.16

Abstract

This study assessed the impact of Pennsylvania's zero-tolerance juvenile drunk driving law. Enacted in Pennsylvania on August 01, 1996, the law lowered the Blood Alcohol Concentration (from .10 mg/ml to .02 mg/ml) necessary to charge a juvenile (under age 21) with the offense of drunk driving. The intent of the law, which was enacted nationally, was to lower motor vehicle fatality accident rates involving juveniles who consumed alcohol and then drove.

Using interrupted time series designs (ITS) two outcome measures (PA juvenile drunk driving arrest rates and PA juvenile alcohol-related motor vehicle fatality accident rates) were used to assess the law's impact. Additional ITS designs, as well as informal, semi-structured interviews with law enforcement supervisors and an archival data review (various newspapers published within Pennsylvania) also were employed to control for validity threats to the research findings.

The data indicated that the law was ineffective in reducing juvenile alcohol-related motor vehicle fatality accident rates. In both Pennsylvania and the control state of Ohio, the data revealed that over the seven year span after the law was initiated juvenile alcohol-related motor vehicle fatality accident rates increased slightly (statistically insignificant), mirroring the effect of juvenile non-alcohol-related motor vehicle fatality accident rates.

The data further revealed that monthly juvenile drunk driving arrest rates in both Pennsylvania and Ohio significantly increased ($p < .000$) after the law was enacted, but the perceived increase in certainty and severity of punishment failed to deter juvenile drivers from drinking and driving. A brief policy analysis is offered as to why deterrence theory failed to reduce incidents of juvenile drunk driving, along with policy recommendations about how to reduce juvenile alcohol-related incidents and accidents by taking an educational approach to juvenile alcohol use instead of a punitive approach. (Lewis, 2006)

Example 3.17

Abstract

The purpose of this study was to examine the relationship between exposure to opportunities inherent in jobs and self-perceived changes in leadership behaviors and characteristics. Qualitative research in the early 1980s pointed out the importance of work-related experiences to development as a manager and leader. Most of the follow-up quantitative research has been on the relationship of on-the-job opportunities and learning or managerial growth. However, there does not appear to be any quantitative research identifying which on-the-job developmental opportunities are related to changes in leadership and characteristics.

This study examined the relationship between exposure to on-the-job challenges and self-reported changes in leadership behavior and characteristics. This quantitative study employed a quasi-experimental, multiple time series design to assess whether exposure to on-the-job developmental opportunities were associated with changes in leader behavior and characteristics. Additionally, the study investigated which on-the-job developmental opportunities were associated with changes in leader behavior and characteristics. On-the-job developmental opportunities were assessed using McCauley, Ohlott, and Ruderman's Job Challenge Profile (JCP). Leadership behavior and characteristics were assessed using Sashkin's The Leadership Profile (TLP).

Results revealed significant, positive relationships between level of job challenge and self-reported changes in leadership behavior and characteristics. Additionally, findings confirmed that job challenges arising from "Managing at High Levels of Responsibility," "Managing Boundaries," and "Creating Change" were associated with significant, positive changes in one or more of the leadership components measured by the TLP for one or more of the cohort groups involved in this longitudinal study. (Thompson, 2003, pp. i–ii)

EXPERIMENTAL RESEARCH DESIGN

Experimental research designs are considered to be the Rolls Royce of quantitative research. Few dissertations in education are completed using a true experimental design; therefore, if you have the opportunity to conduct such a study, it would be advantageous to your academic career.

Experimental design allows you to determine whether a program or treatment intervention *is the cause of* the outcome, and in such a case, you must have strong internal validity. It requires the manipulation of at least one independent variable and an attempt to hold all other variables except for the dependent variable constant. The essence of a truly experimental design is its random selection from population of interest and random assignment to treatment and control groups.

Specifically, Cook and Campbell (1979) mentioned 10 types of experimental design that use or approximate randomization of subjects into treatment and control groups. The control group may receive no treatment, or it may receive a standard or typical practice treatment, such as students receiving enhanced English as second language (ESL) classes versus those receiving typical practice ESL instruction.

Factorial Experiment

The factorial experiment is one in which you would determine the effect of two or more independent treatment variables, both independently and in interaction with each other, on a dependent variable. The main effect is reported as the effect each independent variable has on the dependent variable. The interaction effect is the effect of two or more independent variables on the dependent variable. Some two-factor experiments involve a 2×2 design (four cells)—meaning two variations of one factor and two variations of another manipulated simultaneously. There would be four treatment groups in this design with each group receiving a different combination of the two factors and with participants having been randomly assigned to each group. Statistics typically used for this design are first descriptive statistics, ANOVA, ANCOVA, or multiple regression. There may be three-, four-, or five-factorial experiments as well. There are also single subject experimental designs.

Two major classic experimental designs are:

1. *Between subjects design.* There are different participants for each level of the independent variable(s). A participant is observed in one and only one treatment combination. In this design, you will rely on randomization of subjects among the treatment groups to control for unmeasured variables, though sometimes stratification of subjects is employed to guarantee proportions on certain key variables such as ethnicity or socioeconomic levels.

2. *Within subjects (repeated measures) design.* The same subjects are used for each level of the independent variable. With this design, subjects are observed prior to any treatment, then they receive a treatment, and finally they are observed at posttest. It is possible to extend this design to include a maintenance testing at a designated later time. This type of design may also be called *repeated-measures designs* or *longitudinal experimental designs.* In real-life situations, some measures are time-relevant or dependent; for example, language proficiency, height, leadership skills, and maturity levels. Therefore, a study conducted over a longer period is expected to provide more reliable and valid results. Advanced statistical approaches for this type of research design include structural equation modeling (SEM), and hierarchical linear modeling (HLM). The purpose of using these techniques is to detect the change of outcome on the same unit over time.

SEM analyses subsume confirmatory factor analysis (CFA) and explanatory factory analysis (EFA). The advantage of using SEM finds its consideration of the potential measurement errors that cannot be controlled during the study. It can be employed to identify casual relationship among latent factors that are represented by various observed variables and is particularly useful in trajectory identification upon a factor (known as latent curve modeling) (Bollen & Curran, 2006). You may be interested in evaluating the long-term effect of a running program from fourth grade to eighth grade in terms of students' height growth. With repeated measures (for instance, at the end of each school year over 4 years), you can describe the growth trend of height on individual students, and the sample population as well. You may also compare across multiple samples with different intervention.

HLM is a more recent method of analyzing longitudinal repeated-measure data. It is developed on the concept that the society has complex levels of nesting, such as the family, the school district, and county, or any other community. One may want to explore the effectiveness of a different reading program to see under what circumstances individual participants may benefit from a certain type of program. Because participants are nested within classrooms, and classrooms within school, the influence of such external factors (teachers' instruction and school contexts) may also be studied if there is any.

The application of SEM and HLM usually requires larger sample size ($n > 100$) and normal distribution of observed variables. SEM and HLM are also common in quasi-experimental design.

Note that poor design can never be compensated by sophisticated statistical tools, and scientific research design becomes more valid and generalizable through advanced methods of analyses.

There are other types of experimental designs. For example, one is called **matched-pairs designs**. With this design, the repeated measurement is not of the same subjects but of very similar subjects matched to have like key characteristics. *Equivalent time series designs* are used when treatment cannot be delivered simultaneously to all, also legitimating giving treatment to some participants but, temporarily, not to others, as when all teachers are to receive professional development, but in rotations, such that different types of development can be delivered to different groups of teachers.

Examples of experimental designs used in dissertations follow. (See Examples 3.18, 3.19, and 3.20.)

Example 3.18

Abstract

Working memory is a system that consists of multiple components. The visuospatial sketchpad is the main entrance for visual and spatial information, whereas acoustic and verbal information is processed in the phonological loop. The central executive works as a coordinator of information from these two subsystems. Numerous studies have shown that working memory has a very limited capacity. Based on these characteristics of working memory, theories such as cognitive load theory and the cognitive theory of multimedia learning provide multimedia design principles.

One of these principles is that when verbal information accompanying pictures is presented in audio mode instead of visually, learning can be more effective than if both text and pictures are presented visually. This is called the modality effect. However, some studies have found that the modality effect does not occur in some situations. In most experiments examining the modality effect, the multimedia is presented as system-paced. If learners are able to repeat listening as many times as they need, the superiority of spoken text over visual text seems lessened.

One aim of this study was to examine the modality effect in a learner-controlled condition. This study also used the one-word-at-a-time technique to investigate whether the modality effect would still occur if both reading and listening rates were equal.

There were 182 college students recruited for this study. Participants were randomly assigned to seven groups: a self-paced listening group, a self-paced reading group, a self text-block reading group, a general-paced listening group, a general-paced reading group, a fast-paced listening group, and a fast-paced reading group. The experimental material was a cardiovascular multimedia module. A three-by-two between-subjects design was used to test the main effect. Results showed that modality effect was still present but not between the self-paced listening group and the self text-block reading group. A post-study survey showed participants' different responses to the two modalities and their preferences as well. Results and research limitations are discussed and applications and future directions are also addressed. (Chung, 2006, pp. vi–vii)

Example 3.19

Abstract

This quantitative study derived from an ongoing federal experimental research project targeting Spanish-speaking English language learners (ELLs) receiving services in four program models: control/experimental transitional bilingual education (TBE) and control/experimental structured English immersion (SEI). The purpose of my study was (a) to capture the growth trajectory and rate of oral English acquisition, (b) to investigate the role of oral English development in acquiring English reading skills, and (c) to compare program models in order to identify practices that promote ELLs' English oral and reading competency at the early elementary level. Structural equation modeling was utilized. Participants consisted of 534 Spanish-speaking ELLs who started at kindergarten and continued through first grade in their respective models.

Striking similarities were found among the four instructional models that English oral proficiency improved significantly ($p < .05$) in a linear fashion over two years. However, the magnitude differed in that the experimental TBE demonstrated a steeper growth ($p < .025$) than that of the control group that started at the same level. Even though experimental SEI group started at a much lower level in oral English, they progressed at a rate significantly higher ($p < .05$) than that of the control group.

In relation to English reading comprehension, for experimental SEI groups, the initial level of English oral proficiency is of great concern in reading achievement ($p < .05$). For both TBE groups, effective intervention is desired because the growth of English oral proficiency strongly impacts reading achievement ($p < .05$), and, in addition, initial level strongly predicts reading comprehension.

The intervention was successfully implemented so that students advanced to a substantial amount in academic English oracy. It is also evident that first language (L1) instruction did not impede the learning of a second language. On the contrary, for those students receiving a larger proportion of L1 instruction, alterations in program models are needed to nurture English oracy at a faster rate of growth, which in turn facilitates English literacy acquisition. Findings also indicate that without effective English intervention, students placed in control TBE classrooms remain below all the students in oral English proficiency. (Tong, 2006, pp. iii–iv)

Example 3.20

Abstract

In the past two decades, North American, European, and Pacific countries have experienced record levels of immigration, yet researchers have conducted very few comparative studies to provide policymakers with a clear understanding of the important influences of immigrant achievement. However, research has shown that immigrant student achievement on international tests lags behind that of native students in a substantial number of countries, even when controlling for other background characteristics. The study seeks to provide a more comprehensive understanding of factors related to immigrant success among seventeen immigrant receiving countries by estimating how school context and instructional variables are related to differences in foreign-born student achievement, as well as the relative importance of individual and school variables. This goal is achieved by using data from the Programme for International Student Assessment (PISA) conducted by the Organization for Economic Cooperation and Development (OECD).

This study employs quantitative analytic techniques, including regression and hierarchical linear modeling to examine key policy-related questions: (1) Does immigrant status have a separate effect on student achievement after accounting for socioeconomic status, and how do these two factors appear to relate across countries? (2) Do students in different immigrant status groups get tracked into schools with different contexts and quality and quantity of instruction, and what are the implications for immigrant student achievement? These two research questions serve as the guide for the development of the quantitative results into taxonomy of immigrant student achievement in the seventeen case countries. Finally, I employ additional data from Germany and the United States for a more in depth exploration of immigrant student achievement in these two countries. First, I investigate the role of country of origin and race for immigrant student achievement. I find that there are significant differences in reading and math achievement among different immigrant groups. I also use additional school data to control for tracking between schools (in Germany) and within schools (in the United States). I also find that these controls are important for understanding the relationships between immigrant status, socioeconomic status and student achievement. (Christensen, 2004, p. iv)

THEORY DEVELOPMENT

Developing and testing theory takes research to a level of synthesis, analysis, and evaluation. Because theory is the essence of what drives our actions and because theory describes, explains, and even predicts human phenomena, it is important for theory developers to "get it right," or at least "get it on the right track." Kerlinger (1986) stated of theory, "The ultimate aim of science is the generation and verification of theory" (p. 7). According to Dorin, Demmin, and Gabel (1990), theory (a) provides a general explanation for observations made over time, (b) explains and predicts behavior, (c) can never be established beyond all doubt, (d) may be modified, and (e) seldom have to be thrown out completely if thoroughly tested, but sometimes may be widely accepted for a long time and later disproved.

Theory can be developed and tested quantitatively. Qualitative theory development is discussed in Chapter 5. More often than not, in terms of quantitative analysis, theories are tested quantitatively as opposed to being developed quantitatively. Quantitative analysis generally leads to support of the theory or reconsideration of the theory. As Crown (1998) indicated of policy, and which would be indicative of other concepts in education:

> . . . theory is . . . tested by using data to estimate a statistical model that provides numerical estimates of the relationships between a policy variable (or variables) of interest and a set of explanatory variables. The estimated model may fully support, partially support, or contradict the theory. Of course, from the researcher's standpoint, it is nice to have the estimated model support the theory. This happens when the key variables have the expected signs and are statistically significant. All too frequently, though, key variables to one's theory turn out to be statistically insignificant or to have the "incorrect" sign. When this happens the theory must be reconsidered, the model respecified, or new data collected with which to test the original theory. (p. 2)

A dissertation example from the counseling field by van Eden-Moorefield (2006) is provided that utilized a quantitative design in theory development and testing. (See Example 3.21.)

Example 3.21

Abstract

Given recent calls for theory development and extension relevant to gay relationships, this study examined the relationships of gay men by testing a mid-range model derived from identity theory (Stryker, 1968) and the extant literature. The model asserted that the extent to which one holds a gay status affects his level of identity commitment which, in turn, affects couple verification. Further, couple verification affects couple identity directly and indirectly through distress and relationship satisfaction. Theoretical extensions of the construct of identity commitment included both personal and symbolic dimensions.

Data were collected via an Internet-based survey. The sample consisted of 188 gay men in current relationships of at least 3 months duration and representing 26 states and the District of Columbia; the participation rate was 83%. Overall, the sample was White, well-educated, and middle class.

As a preliminary step, a series of exploratory factor analyses were conducted to assess the factor structure of the measures used. Composite scores were created, and data were fit to the model using path analysis. Results demonstrated that the data did not fit the original model. A modified model was then tested and fit the data. The modified model added direct links from identity commitment to both relationship satisfaction and couple identity. Each path in the modified model was significant except for the path between couple verification and distress, and 54% of the variance in couple identity was explained. Suggestions for theory and future research are discussed. (van Eden-Moorefield, 2006, n.p.)

Another example is provided for you related to the testing of a theory. This example is from Truslow's dissertation (2004). (See Example 3.22.)

Example 3.22

Abstract

Purpose. The purpose of this study was to identify the differences in conflict management modes of male and female public school superintendents and to examine a relationship between superintendents' conflict management modes and the Synergistic Leadership Theory (SLT).

Methods. The target population of this study included all 13,728 public school superintendents in the United States. The stratified random sample included 500 female and 500 male superintendents. Quantitative and qualitative data were collected through the Thomas-Kilmann Inventory (TKI), an open-ended interview protocol, and the Organizational Leadership Effectiveness Inventory to answer the following research questions: (1) Is there a significant difference in gender distribution among conflict management modes of superintendents? (2) Is there a relationship between conflict management modes of female superintendents and the Synergistic Leadership Theory? (3) Is there a relationship between conflict management modes of male superintendents and the Synergistic Leadership Theory? (4) Is there a relationship among gender, conflict management modes, and the four factors of the Synergistic Leadership Theory?

Findings and Conclusions. The data obtained in the current study resulted in the conclusion that male and female superintendents have significantly different conflict management modes as illustrated by gender distribution. A relationship was identified between the four factors of the

Synergistic Leadership Theory and each conflict management mode. There was no difference between gender and the SLT within each conflict management mode. Both male and female superintendents identified the same factors as sources of incongruence within each conflict mode. This suggests that gender is related to each conflict management mode; however, gender is not related to perceived incongruence among factors of the SLT and conflict within each conflict management mode.

Recommendations for Further Research. The following recommendations are suggested for further study and development: (1) Further research should be conducted regarding the length of tenure of superintendents in relation to the alignment of factors of the SLT. (2) Additional research should be pursued in regard to the relationship of the superintendent's conflict management mode to the board president's conflict management mode. (3) Continued research should be conducted to include the introduction of student achievement data and district ratings in relationship to the superintendent's conflict management mode. (Truslow, 2004, pp. 4–5)

SUMMARY

In this chapter, we have reviewed four categories of quantitative research: (a) descriptive research, (b) correlational research, (c) causal-comparative research, and (d) quasi-experimental and experimental research. In addition to providing you with a brief overview of each category, we also provided examples of research purposes or questions that would justify a specific type of quantitative research design or method of inquiry. The next chapter contains specifics on basic statistics.

4

Basic Statistics

Statistics are mathematical procedures for describing, synthesizing, and analyzing numerical data. The statistical procedures you choose will be determined by your research questions or hypotheses and the type of data you will collect. Thus, different research questions or hypotheses and different types of data require different statistical analyses. The statistical procedures you use should be described in detail in your Methodology Chapter under the heading "Data Analysis" and again in your Results Chapter. Data analysis is a very important component of any research study. No matter how well you conduct your study, inappropriate statistical analyses will likely result in inappropriate research conclusions.

Many statistical procedures are available to you. In this chapter, we describe those commonly used in the social and behavioral sciences. The focus is on how to apply these statistics to your dissertation or master's thesis. Contrary to popular opinion, you do not have to be a mathematician to use statistics. All you have to know is when to use an appropriate statistic to accomplish your research purposes, and a computer program will do the rest.

Generally, we recommend using a computer for data analysis, particularly if you have a large amount of data or if multiple analyses are to be performed. The most commonly used software for statistical analysis is the Statistical Package for the Social Sciences (SPSS). Another widely used statistical program is Statistical Analysis System (SAS). Both SPSS and SAS programs can perform all of the statistical procedures described in this chapter.

DESCRIPTIVE STATISTICS

Descriptive statistics are mathematical procedures for organizing and summarizing numerical data. The major types of descriptive statistics are (a) measures of central tendency, (b) measures of variability, (c) measures of relative position, and (d) measures of relationship. These are the types of statistics you will present at the beginning of your Results Chapter under the heading "Descriptive Statistics" in a quantitative dissertation or master's thesis (see Table 9.1, Chapter 9). Descriptive statistics, and even inferential statistics, are sometimes used in some types of qualitative studies as well (see Slater, 2001, referenced in Chapter 9).

Measures of Central Tendency

Measures of central tendency are indices that represent the typical or average score among a distribution of scores. Measures of central tendency can describe a set of numerical data with a single number. The three most frequently used measures of central tendency are the mean, median, and mode. The choice usually depends on two factors: the type of measurement scale used and the purpose of the research. There are four measurement scales: nominal, ordinal, interval, and ratio.

Nominal data classify persons or objects into two or more categories: sex (male or female), type of school (public or private), IQ (high, average, low), political party (Democrat or Republican), personality type (dominant or passive), race/ethnicity (African American, Asian, Hispanic, White). *Ordinal* data not only classify persons or objects but also rank them in terms of degree to which they possess a characteristic of interest. In other words, ordinal data puts participants in order from highest to lowest. For example, 15 doctoral cohort members might be ranked from 1 to 15 with respect to height. Percentile ranks are ordinal data. Most standardized tests, like the GRE, provide a raw score, as well as a percentile rank from 100 to 0. *Interval* data have all of the characteristics of nominal and ordinal data, but in addition, they are based on predetermined equal intervals. Most tests used in social science research, such as achievement tests, aptitude tests, and intelligence tests, represent interval data. *Ratio* data are derived from scales that have an absolute zero and so enable relative comparisons to be made, such as length of school day, class size, age, speed, and dollars.

Mean, Median, and Mode

The *mean* is the arithmetic average of the scores. It is calculated by adding up all of the scores and dividing that total by the number of scores. The mean is the appropriate measure of central tendency when the data represent either an interval or ratio scale. Because most quantitative measurement in the social sciences uses an interval scale, the mean is the most frequently used measure of central tendency.

The *median* is the midpoint of a group of scores. For example, for the scores 10, 20, 30, 40, 50, the median is 30. If the number of scores is even, the median is the point halfway between the two middle scores. For example, for the scores 10, 20, 30, 40, 50, 60, the median is 35. The median is the appropriate measure of central tendency when the data represent an ordinal scale.

The *mode* is the score that occurs most frequently in a distribution of scores. The mode is seldom used because of the problems associated with it. For example, a set of scores may have two or more modes. Such a distribution of scores is referred to as *bimodal*. Another problem with the mode is that equal-sized samples randomly selected from the same target population can have different modes. Nevertheless, the mode is the appropriate measure of central tendency when the data represent a nominal scale.

Measures of Variability

Measures of variability show how spread out the distribution of scores are from the mean of the distribution, or how much, on the average, scores differ from the mean. The three most frequently used measures of variability are (a) standard deviation, (b) quartile deviation, and (c) range.

Standard Deviation

The *standard deviation* is the most frequently used measure of variability. The standard deviation is the appropriate measure of variability when the data represent either an interval or ratio scale. Like the mean, the standard deviation is the most stable measure of variability. It includes every score in the calculation of scores in a distribution of scores. By knowing the mean and standard deviation of a set of scores, you will have a good idea of what your distribution of scores look like. This will become much clearer in the impending discussion of the normal curve.

Quartile Deviation

The quartile deviation is one half of the difference between the upper quartile and the lower quartile in a distribution of scores. Thus, the upper quartile of any distribution of scores is the 75th percentile, that point below which are 75% of the scores. The lower quartile is the 25th percentile, that point below which are 25% of the scores. Calculation of the quartile deviation is done by subtracting the lower quartile from the upper quartile and then dividing the result by 2. If the quartile deviation is small, the scores are close together. If it is large, the scores are more spread out. The quartile deviation is the appropriate measure of variability when the data represent an ordinal scale.

Range

The *range* is the difference between the highest and the lowest score and is the result of subtraction. For example, for the scores 5, 5, 6, 7, 8, 8, the range is 3. If the range is small, the scores are close together. If the range is large, the scores are more spread out. The range is the appropriate measure of variability when the data represent nominal data. The range, like the mode, is not a very stable measure of variability. However, it does give a quick, rough estimate of variability.

The Normal Curve

The normal curve (or bell-shaped curve) is a theoretical distribution in which the height of the curve indicates the percentage of cases under portions of the normal curve. As shown in the example in Figure 4.1, the test scores of the majority of individuals tend to cluster close to the mean. Fewer cases occur as we move farther from the mean. Specifically, about 68% of the sample will have scores within the range of plus or minus one standard deviation from the mean. Approximately 95% of the sample will have scores within the range of plus or minus two standard deviations from the mean. And more than 99% of the sample will have scores within the range of three standard deviations from the mean. Many variables (e.g., height, weight, IQ scores, achievement test scores) yield a curve similar to the one shown in Figure 4.1, providing a large enough random sample is used.

Measures of Relative Position

Measures of relative position indicate how a person has performed in comparison to all other persons in the sample who have been measured on the same variable. This is called *norm referencing*. The two most frequently used measures of relative position are percentile ranks and standard scores.

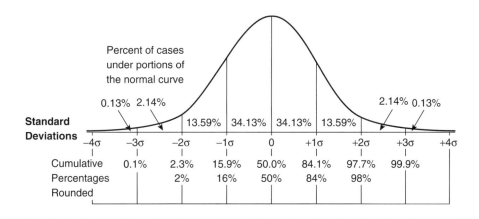

Figure 4.1   Normal Curve

Percentile Ranks

A *percentile rank* indicates the percentage of scores that are at or below a given score. Percentile ranks are appropriate measures of relative position when the data represent an ordinal scale. Percentile ranks are not used much in research studies. They are often used, however, in the public schools to report student's standardized test scores. They are also used in making decisions regarding acceptance to colleges and graduate schools. The SAT and ACT used as one criterion for admission to undergraduate colleges and universities include both a score and the percentile rank associated with that score. This is true for the GRE and MAT used to admit students to graduate school. The percentile rank provides the decision maker with a measure of how well the applicant did in relation to all other test takers.

Standard Scores

A *standard score* indicates how far a given raw score is from the mean, in terms of standard deviation units. A standard score is the appropriate measure of relative position when the data represent an interval or ratio scale. The most commonly used standard scores are z scores and stanines.

z Scores. The *z score* is the most basic standard score, with a mean of 0 and a standard deviation of 1. Thus, a z score of +1 is at the 84th percentile for a normal distribution, −1 is at the 16th percentile, and −2 is at the 2nd percentile. Other standard scores are linear transformations from the z score, with arbitrarily selected means and standard deviations. That is, it is possible to choose any mean and any standard deviation. Most IQ tests, for example, use 100 as the mean and 15 or 16 as the standard deviation. The resultant IQ score is a standard score (the ratio IQ, mental age divided by chronological age times 100, is rarely used today).

Stanines. *Stanines* are standard scores that divide a distribution of scores into nine parts. Stanines, like percentile ranks, are often reported in norms tables for standardized tests. Stanines are often used in the public schools as a basis for ability grouping, and they are used also as a criterion for selecting students for special programs. For example, on the one hand, a remediation program may select students who scored in the first and second stanine on a standardized reading test. On the other hand, a gifted program may select students who scored in the eighth and ninth stanine. Like percentile ranks, the use of stanines is a reporting device that is understandable to most lay people.

Measures of Relationship

The descriptive statistics presented thus far involve the description of a single variable. Measures of relationship indicate the degree to which two variables are related. Correlation is often used for this purpose. The two most frequently used correlational statistics are the product-moment correlation coefficient (r) and rank-difference correlation (rho). For other bivariate correlational techniques (i.e., relationship between two variables), such as the phi coefficient, biserial correlation, correlation ratio (eta), partial correlation, and others, see standard statistics textbooks.

Product–Moment Correlation Coefficient

The product-moment correlation coefficient (r) (sometimes called Pearson r) is the most appropriate measure of relationship when the data represent an interval or ratio scale. In the social sciences, most of the measures represent interval scales. For this reason, the Pearson r is the statistic most often used for determining relationship. For example, if we administer an intelligence test and an achievement test to the same group of students, we will have two sets of scores. Pearson r would be the appropriate correlational statistic to use for determining the relationship between the students' scores on the two measures. The product-moment correlation can also be used to compute a correlation matrix in which subjects' scores on a large number of variables are correlated with each other (e.g., see Basham & Lunenburg, 1989; this study is discussed in greater detail in Chapter 6).

Rank-Difference Correlation (Rho)

Spearman's rho, as it is sometimes called, is used when the data are ranks rather than raw scores. For example, assume the principal and assistant principal have independently ranked the 15 teachers in their school from first, most effective, to 15th, least effective, and you want to assess how much their ranks agree. You would calculate the Spearman's rho by putting the paired ranks into the Pearson r formula or by using a formula developed specifically for rho.

Spearman's rho is interpreted the same as is Pearson r. Like the Pearson product-moment coefficient of correlation, it ranges from -1.00 to $+1.00$. When each individual has the same rank on both variables, the rho correlation will be $+1.00$, and when their ranks on one variable are exactly the opposite of their ranks on the other variable, rho will be -1.00. If there is no relationship at all between the rankings, the rank correlation coefficient will be 0. If you have a computer or calculator program for Pearson r, you can calculate Spearman's rho by putting the ranks into that program.

INFERENTIAL STATISTICS

Inferential statistics deal with inferences about populations based on the results of samples (Gay, Mills, & Airasian, 2006). Most social science research deals with samples drawn from larger populations. Thus, *inferential statistics* are data analysis procedures for determining the likelihood that results obtained from a sample are the same results that would have been obtained for the entire population.

Example 4.1

To illustrate: You have randomly selected a sample of ninth grade students. Based on a pretest in mathematics and other criteria, you have created two closely matched samples of students. Group A will be taught mathematics using a computer, and Group B will be taught mathematics using a traditional method. You want to know if the mean scores for Group A are significantly different from the mean scores of Group B. Results of the posttest in mathematics reveals that Group A has a mean score of 93, and the mean score for Group B is 85.

You have to make a decision as to whether the difference between the two means represents a true, significant difference in the treatment (in this case, method of instruction) or simply sampling error. A true difference is one caused by the treatment (the independent variable) and not by chance (Gall, Gall, & Borg, 2007; Gay et al., 2006). Thus, an observed difference is either caused by the treatment, as stated in the research question (or research hypothesis), or is the result of chance, sampling error.

The Null Hypothesis

The research hypothesis typically states a difference or relationship in the expected direction. A null hypothesis states that no difference or relationship exists. The null hypothesis is preferred when applying statistical tests. You can never prove your hypothesis, only disprove it. Hypothesis testing is a process of disproving or rejecting, and the null hypothesis is best suited for this purpose (see Gall et al., 2007; Gay et al., 2006).

The initial step in hypothesis testing then is to establish a null hypothesis. For instance, the null hypothesis for our example can be stated as follows:

No significant difference exists between the mean mathematics scores of ninth grade students who receive computer mathematics instruction and ninth grade students who receive traditional mathematics instruction.

After formulating the null hypothesis, the researcher carries out a test of statistical significance to determine whether the null hypothesis can be rejected (i.e., whether there is a *true* or *real* difference between the groups). This test enables us to make statements of the type:

If the null hypothesis is correct, we would find this large a difference between sample means only once in a hundred experiments ($p < .01$). Because we have found this large a difference, the null hypothesis quite probably is false. Therefore, we will reject the null hypothesis and conclude that the difference between sample means reflects a *true* difference between population means. (Gall et al., p. 138)

Tests of Statistical Significance

Concepts underlying tests of statistical significance follow:

1. The purpose of using a test of statistical significance is to determine if the difference in two scores (or the characteristics of the sample is different from the population) is significant or the result of chance fluctuation/or sampling error.

2. To determine statistical significance, the data are analyzed via a formula and a score is obtained—a *t* score, chi square score, or *F* score.

3. You then determine the degrees of freedom (number of subjects minus one).

4. Then compare the calculated significance score with the table score in the appropriate probability table using the calculated degrees of freedom. Select the .05 level of confidence. (This would be the minimum level you should accept.)

5. If the calculated significance score is greater than the one in the table (at the .05 level), then this indicates that the difference in student scores is statistically significant at the .05 level of confidence and not the result of chance fluctuation. This means that the difference in student scores is so great that it could only be obtained by chance only 5% of the time. And 95% of the time, the difference between the student scores is the result of the impact of the independent variable on the dependent variable. Hence, the null hypothesis is rejected.

6. If the calculated significance score is less than the one in the probability table (at the .05 level), then this indicates that the difference in student scores is statistically insignificant at the .05 level and is the result of chance fluctuation. This means that the difference in the student scores is so small that the independent variable had no impact on the dependent variable. Therefore, 95% of the time, the difference in student scores is the result of chance fluctuation. And only 5% of the time could the independent variable have impacted the dependent variable. Hence, the null hypothesis is accepted.

Effect Size

One of the reasons that statistically significant *p* values can be misleading is that the value that is calculated is directly related to sample size. Thus, it is possible to have a very large sample, a very small difference or relationship, and still report it as "significant." For example, a correlation of .44 will be statistically significant at $p < .05$ with a sample as small as 20, and a sample of 5,000 will allow a statistically significant .05 finding with a correlation of only .028, which is, practically speaking, no relationship at all.

The American Psychological Association (2001) and several research journals now strongly recommend or require that investigators report appropriate indicators that illustrate the strength or magnitude of a difference or relationship along with measures of statistical significance. These *effect magnitude* measures, as they are called, are either measures of strength of association or effect size. Measures of association are used to estimate proportions of variance held in common, similar to the coefficient of determination. Effect size is more commonly used. It is typically reported in a generalized form as the ratio of the difference between the group means divided by the estimated standard deviation of the population. According to Cohen (1988), the *effect size index* then provides an indication of the practical or meaningful difference. Effect size indexes of about .20 are regarded as small effects, of about .50 as medium or moderate effects, and .80 and above large effects.

Statistical Analysis

Different statistical analyses are appropriate for different types of data. It is essential that you select the appropriate statistical test, because an incorrect test can result in incorrect research conclusions. Basically there are two types of statistical tests: parametric and nonparametric. Your first decision when selecting a statistical test is to determine whether a parametric or nonparametric test is appropriate. The use of a *parametric test* requires that three assumptions be met: the variable measured is normally distributed in the population, the data represent an interval or ordinal scale, and the selection of participants is independent. Most variables examined in social science research are normally distributed. Most measures used in social science research represent an interval scale. And the use of random sampling will fulfill the assumption of independent selection of participants. A *nonparametric test* is an appropriate statistical test to use when the three parametric assumptions are not met and when the data represent an ordinal or nominal scale.

The following parametric statistical tests are described below: (a) *t* test; (b) analysis of variance, including post hoc procedures; (c) factorial analysis of variance; (d) analysis of covariance; and (e) multivariate analysis of variance. In the section following, several important nonparametric tests are discussed.

The *t* Test

In many research situations, a mean from one group is compared with a mean from another group to determine the probability that the corresponding population means are different. The most common statistical procedure for determining the level of significance when two means are compared is the *t* test. The *t* test is a formula that generates a number, and this number is used to determine the probability level (*p* level) of rejecting the null hypothesis.

Two different forms of the equation are used in the *t* test, one for independent samples and one for samples that are paired, or dependent. Independent samples are groups of participants that have no relationship to each other; the two samples have different participants in each group, and the participants are usually either assigned randomly from a common population or drawn from two different populations.

Example 4.2

If you are testing the difference between an experimental group and a control group mean in a posttest-only design, the independent samples *t* test would be the appropriate statistic. Comparing leadership styles of two groups of superintendents would also utilize an independent samples *t* test.

The second form of the *t* test can be referred to by several different names, including paired, *dependent* samples, *correlated*, or matched *t* test. This *t* test is used in situations in which the participants from the two groups are paired or matched in some way.

Example 4.3

A common example of this case is the same group of participants tested twice, as in a pretest–posttest study (e.g., see Pascarella & Lunenburg, 1988). Whether the same or different subjects are in each group, as long as a systematic relationship exists between the groups it is necessary to use the dependent samples *t* test to calculate the probability of rejecting the null hypothesis.

In the Pascarella and Lunenburg (1988) study, elementary school principals from two school districts received leadership training using Hersey and Blanchard's situational leadership framework. Pretests and posttests were administered to the principals and a sample of their teachers before and after training to determine the effects of training on principals' leadership effectiveness and style range. The study provided partial support only for Hersey and Blanchard's situational leadership theory. Using dependent samples *t* tests, principals were perceived as more effective three years after training than before training: t (principals) = 6.46 (15) < .01 and t (teachers) = 3.73 (59) < .01. However, no significant differences were found in principals' effectiveness immediately following training, nor in principals' leadership style range before and after training.

Although the formulas and degrees of freedom are different for each form of *t* test, the interpretation and reporting of the results are the same, the *df* for the dependent *t* test is the number of pairs minus one. Thus, you need not worry about whether the correct formula has been used.

Example 4.4

The *t* test can be used for purposes other than comparing the means of two samples. For example, the *t* test is used when a researcher wants to show that a correlation coefficient is significantly different from 0 (no correlation). The mean of a group can be compared with a number rather than another mean, and it is possible to compare variances rather than means. Because there are so many uses for the *t* test, it is frequently encountered in reading social science research.

Example 4.5

A more concrete explanation of using the *t* test is the following example. Suppose a researcher is interested in finding out whether there is a significant difference between high school boys and girls with respect to mathematics achievement. The research question would be: Is there a difference in mathematics achievement (the dependent variable) of boys compared with girls (the independent variable)? The null hypothesis would be: There is no difference between boys and girls in mathematics achievement. To test this hypothesis, the researcher would randomly select a sample of boys and girls from the population of all high school students. Let us say that the sample mean for boys achievement is 540, and the sample mean for girls is 520. Because we assume the null hypothesis—that the population means are equal—we use the *t* test to show how often the difference of scores in the samples would occur if the population means are equal. If our degrees of freedom (total sample size minus 1) is 60 and the calculated *t* value 1.29, we can see by referring to the *t* test table that the probability of attaining this difference in the sample means, for a two-tailed test, is .20, or 20 times out of 100. We accept the null hypothesis and say that there is no statistically significant difference between the mathematics achievement of high school boys and girls.

One-Way Analysis of Variance

If a study is conducted in which two or more sample means are compared on one independent variable, then to test the null hypothesis the researcher would employ a procedure called one-way analysis of variance (ANOVA). ANOVA is simply an extension of the *t* test. Rather than using multiple *t* tests to compare all possible pairs of means in a study of two or more groups, ANOVA allows you to test the differences between all groups and make more accurate probability statements than when using a series of separate *t* tests. It is called analysis of variance because the statistical formula uses the variances of the groups and not the means to calculate a value that reflects the degree of differences in the means. Instead of a *t* statistic, ANOVA calculates an *F* statistic (or *F* ratio). The *F* is analogous to the *t*. It is a three- or four-digit number that is used in a distribution of *F* table with the degrees of freedom to find the level of significance that you use to reject or not reject the null. There are two degrees of freedom. The first is the number of groups in the study minus one, and the second is the total number of subjects minus the number of groups. These numbers follow the F in reporting the results of ANOVA. For example, in reporting $F(4, 80) = 4.25$, the degrees of freedom mean that five group means are being compared and 85 subjects are in the analysis.

ANOVA addresses the question: Is there a significant difference between the population means? If the F value that is calculated is large enough, then the null hypothesis (meaning there is no difference among the groups) can be rejected with confidence that the researcher is correct in concluding that at least two means are different.

Example 4.6

Let us assume, for example, that a researcher is comparing the quality of school life of three groups of students in urban, suburban, and rural school districts (e.g., see Lunenburg & Schmidt, 1989). The researchers in the cited study selected a random sample from each group, administered a quality of school life (QSL) instrument, and calculated the means and variances of each group. The sample group means for QSL were: urban = 18, rural = 20, and suburban = 25. The null hypothesis that is tested, then, is that the population means of 18, 20, and 25 are equal, or, more correctly, that these are different only by sampling and measurement error. The calculated F in the study was 5.12 and $p < .01$. Lunenburg and Schmidt (1989) concluded that at least two of the means were different, and that this conclusion will be right 99 times out of 100. Many other variables were examined in the study referenced above. Results of the ANOVA indicated that the means were different only, but not where the differences occurred. Post hoc procedures are necessary to determine exactly where the differences in mean scores occurred.

Post Hoc Procedures

When a researcher uses ANOVA to test the null hypothesis that three means are the same, the resulting statistically significant F ratio tells the researcher only that two or more of the means are different. Usually the researcher needs to employ further statistical tests that will indicate those means that are different from each other. These tests are called *post hoc comparisons.*

There are five common multiple comparison tests: Fisher's LSD, Duncan's new multiple range test, the Newman-Keuls multiple range test, Tukey's HSD, and the Scheffé test. Each test is used in the same way, but they differ in the ease with which a significant difference is obtained; for some tests, that is, the means need to be farther apart than for other tests for the difference to be statistically significant. Tests that require a greater difference between the means are said to be conservative, while those that permit less difference are said to be liberal. The listing of the tests above is sequential, with Fisher's test considered most liberal and Scheffé's test most conservative. The two most common tests are Tukey and Scheffé, but different conclusions can be reached in a study depending on the multiple comparison technique employed.

Factorial Analysis of Variance

One-way ANOVA has been introduced as a procedure that is used with one independent variable and two or more levels identified by this variable. It is common, however, to have more than one independent variable in a study. In fact, it is often desirable to have several independent variables because the analysis will provide more information. For example, if a group of researchers investigates the relative effectiveness of three reading curricula, they would probably use a 1×3 ANOVA to test the null hypothesis that no difference in achievement exists between any of the three groups. If the researchers were also interested in whether males or females achieved differently, gender would become a second independent variable. Now there are six groups, because for each reading group males and females are analyzed separately.

Example 4.7

In this hypothetical situation, two independent variables are analyzed simultaneously and one dependent variable (achievement). The statistical procedure that would be used to analyze the results would be a two-way ANOVA (*two-way* because of two independent variables). Because *factor* is another word for independent variable, *factorial* means more than one independent variable. *Factorial ANOVA,* then, is a generic term that means that two or more independent variables are analyzed together. The more specific term, such as *two-way* or *three-way* ANOVA, tells the exact number of independent variables. Researchers can be even more precise in indicating what the analysis is by including the levels of each independent variable. As pointed out earlier, *levels* refers to the subgroups or categories of each independent variable. In the example mentioned above, *reading curriculum* has three levels and *gender* two levels. The levels can be shown by numbers that precede the ANOVA. In our reading example, it is a 2×3 ANOVA.

An *interaction* is the effect of the independent variables together; that is, the impact of one factor on the dependent measure varies with the level of a second factor. Stated differently, it is the joint effect of the independent variables on the dependent variable. An interaction is evident if the differences between levels of one independent variable are inconsistent from one level to another of the other independent variable. In other words, an interaction exists if the effect of one variable differs across different levels of the second variable. Now it is clear how a factorial ANOVA can provide more information than one-way ANOVAs.

Analysis of Covariance

Analysis of covariance (ANCOVA) is a statistical procedure used in cases similar to ones in which a one-way or factorial ANOVA is used. ANCOVA has two major purposes: to adjust initial group differences statistically on one or more variables that are related to the dependent variable but uncontrolled, and to increase the likelihood of finding a significant difference between group means.

Example 4.8

For the first purpose, consider the following example. A researcher uses two classes to investigate whether computer-assisted instruction or noncomputer (traditional) instruction is more effective. On the basis of a pretest, the researcher knows that one class has greater knowledge of the dependent variable (achievement in mathematics) than the other group (for example, the computer group pretest mean is 12 and the noncomputer group pretest mean is 10). If a posttest is given and it is found that the computer group mean is 24 and the noncomputer group mean 20, the researcher might be tempted to conclude that the computer group achieved more than the noncomputer group. This would be likely to happen if the pretest scores were ignored. An alternative approach would be to look at pretest–posttest gain scores and use a *t* test to determine whether the gain scores are significantly different. This approach would result in comparing 12 (24 − 12) to 10 (20 − 10).

While this approach is theoretically better than not using the pretest scores, for reasons beyond the scope of this chapter, there are technical problems with comparing gain scores. The best method of analyzing the data in this circumstance is by using ANCOVA. ANCOVA would statistically adjust the posttest scores by the differences that existed between the groups on the pretest. In this example, the posttest score of the computer group would be lowered by one point, because this group's mean was higher by one point than the mean of both groups on the pretest. Similarly, because the noncomputer group pretest mean is one point lower than the mean of the two pretests, the posttest score of 20 would be raised by one point to 21. Instead of comparing 20 to 24, ANCOVA would thus compare 21 to 23.

The variable that is used in ANCOVA to adjust the scores (in the above example the pretest) is called the *covariate* or *concomitant variable.* Covariates are often pretest scores or results from achievement, attitude, or aptitude tests that would be related to the dependent variable. IQ scores and scores on prior standardized achievement tests, for instance, are commonly used as covariates.

The second purpose of covariance analysis is to increase what is called the *power* of the statistical test to find differences between groups. A full explanation of the concept of power is beyond the scope of this chapter. Briefly, power is the probability of detecting a significant difference. It is used to increase power when the sample size is low or when the researcher has reason to believe that the differences between the groups will be small.

ANCOVA can be used in several situations: with two groups and one independent variable in place of a *t* test; with one independent variable that has more than two groups in place of one-way ANOVA; and with factorial analysis of variance. Studies can also use more than one covariate in a single ANCOVA procedure. The reporting of ANCOVA is very similar to the reporting of ANOVA.

Because ANCOVA is used frequently with intact groups, without random assignment, it should be noted that the interpretation of results should weigh the possibility that other uncontrolled and unmeasured variables are also related to the dependent variable and hence may affect the dependent variable. In other words, while statistical adjustment of the effect of the covariate can be achieved, the researcher cannot conclude that the groups are equal in the sense of random assignment.

Multivariate Analysis of Variance

Multivariate analysis of variance (MANOVA) differs from ANOVA in only one respect: it incorporates two or more dependent variables in the same analysis, thus permitting a more powerful test of differences among means. It is justified only when the researcher has reason to believe correlations exist among dependent variables. Similarly, multivariate analysis of covariance (MANCOVA) extends ANCOVA to include two or more dependent variables in the same analysis. The specific value that is calculated is *Wilk's lamda*, a number analogous to *F* in analysis of variance. Table 4.1 summarizes some multivariate tests that correspond to procedures used with one dependent variable.

Nonparametric Tests

In our discussion of statistical tests up to this point, we have been concerned with procedures that use sample statistics to estimate characteristics of the population. These characteristics of the population are called *parameters,* and the statistical procedures are referred to as *parametric procedures.* In addition, parametric statistics are used when the researcher can assume

Table 4.1   Corresponding Univariate and Multivariate Tests

Univariate Test	Multivariate Test
t test	Hotellings T^2
ANOVA	MANOVA (multivariate analysis of variance)
ANCOVA	MANCOVA

that the population is normally distributed, has homogeneity of variance within different groups, and has data that are interval or ratio in scale.

As long as the assumptions on which parametric statistics are, for the most part, met, the researcher uses a *t* test, ANOVA, ANCOVA, MANOVA, or some other parametric procedure. If these assumptions are not met—that is, if the data are not interval or ratio or are not distributed normally—the researcher should consider using a nonparametric analog to the parametric test. For most parametric procedures, a corresponding nonparametric test can be used. The interpretation of the results is similar with both kinds of tests. What differs is the computational equation and tables for determining the significance level of the results. Both procedures test a hypothesis and report a level of significance for rejecting the null. In contrast to parametric tests, however, nonparametric tests do not test hypotheses about characteristics of a population. Rather, nonparametric procedures test hypotheses about relationships between categorical variables, shapes of distributions, and normality of distribution. While parametric procedures use means, nonparametric techniques are concerned with frequencies, percentages, and proportions. The parametric tests are generally more powerful in detecting significant differences and are used frequently even when all assumptions cannot be met.

Table 4.2 gives the names of nonparametric tests that are analogous to parametric tests we have already discussed. Each one is discussed briefly below.

Chi Square

Chi square is a nonparametric statistical test appropriate when the data are in the form of frequency counts or percentages and proportions that can be converted into frequencies (Gay et al., 2006). These frequency counts can be placed into two or more categories. Thus, chi square is

Table 4.2   Commonly Used Inferential Techniques

	Parametric	*Nonparametric*
Quantitative	*t* test for independent means	Mann-Whitney *U* test
	t test for correlated means	Kruskal-Wallis one-way analysis of variance
	Analysis of variance (ANOVA)	Wilcoxon signed rank test
	Analysis of covariance (ANCOVA)	Friedman two-way analysis of variance
	Multivariate analysis of variance (MANOVA)	
	t test for *r*	
Categorical	*t* test for difference in proportions	Chi square

appropriate when the data are a nominal scale (e.g., male or female, Democrat or Republican). A chi square test compares the proportions actually observed in a study to the proportions expected, to see if they are significantly different. Expected proportions are usually the frequencies that would be expected if the groups were equal, although occasionally they also may be based on past data. The chi square value increases as the difference between observed and expected frequencies increases. To determine whether chi square is significant, you must consult a chi square table.

One-dimensional chi square. The chi square can be used to compare frequencies occurring in different categories or groups.

Example 4.9

For example, you might wish to investigate whether doctoral students prefer to study alone or with others. Tabulation, based on a random sample of 100 doctoral students, might reveal that 45 prefer to study alone, and 55 prefer to study with others. The null hypothesis of no preference would suggest a 50–50 split. In order to determine whether the groups were significantly different, you would compare the observed frequencies (45, 55) with the expected frequencies (50, 50) using a chi square test of significance.

Two-dimensional chi square. The chi square may be used also when frequencies are categorized along more than one dimension, sort of a factorial chi square.

Example 4.10

In the study sequence example above, you might select a stratified sample, comprising 50 males and 50 females. Responses could then be classified by study preference and by gender, a two-way classification that would allow us to see whether study preference is related to gender.

Although 2×2 applications are quite common, contingency tables may be based on any number of categories, for example, 2×3, 3×3, 2×4, and so forth. When a two-way classification is used, calculation of expected frequencies is a little more complex, but is not difficult.

Numerous examples of the aforementioned parametric and nonparametric tests have been provided from sample dissertations in Chapter 3. Many more of the most commonly used parametric and nonparametric statistical tests are presented in Chapter 9.

Other Nonparametric Tests

Of the nonparametric tests of significance, chi square probably is the most frequently used by social science researchers. Other nonparametric tests sometimes are used, particularly when the research data are in the form of rank-order scores or interval scores that grossly violate the parametric test assumptions of normal distribution and homogeneity of variance. They include (a) the Mann-Whitney U test, (b) Kruskal-Wallis one-way analysis of variance, (c) Wilcoxon signed rank test, and (d) Friedman two-way analysis of variance.

Mann-Whitney U Test

The *Mann-Whitney U test* is a nonparametric alternative to the t test used when a researcher wishes to analyze ranked data. The researcher intermingles the scores of the two groups and then ranks them as if they were all from just one group. The test produces a value (U), whose probability of occurrence is then checked by the researcher in the appropriate statistical table. The logic of the test is as follows: If the two groups are essentially similar, then the sum of the pooled rankings for each group should be about the same. If the summed ranks are markedly different, on the other hand, then this difference is likely to be statistically significant.

Kruskal-Wallis One-Way Analysis of Variance

The *Kruskal-Wallis one-way analysis of variance* is used when researchers have more than two independent groups to compare. The procedure is quite similar to the Mann-Whitney U test. The scores of the individuals in the several groups are pooled and then ranked as though they all came from one group. The sums of the ranks added together for each of the separate groups are then compared. This analysis produces a value (H), whose probability of occurrence is checked by the researcher in the appropriate statistical table.

Wilcoxon Signed Rank Test

The *Wilcoxon signed rank test* is used when a researcher wants to analyze two related (as opposed to independent) samples. Related samples are connected in some way. For example, a researcher will try to equalize groups on IQ, gender, age, or some other variable. The groups are matched on these variables. Another example of a related sample is when the same group is both pretested and posttested. Each individual is tested on two different occasions (as with the t test for correlated means).

This test is very easy to use. The researcher simply lines up the pairs of related subjects and then determines how many times the paired subjects in one group scored higher than those in the other group. If the groups do not differ significantly, the totals for the two groups should be about equal. If there is a marked difference in scoring (such as many more in one group scoring higher), the difference may be statistically significant. The probability of this occurrence can be determined by consulting the appropriate statistical table.

Friedman Two-Way Analysis of Variance

If more than two related groups are involved, then the *Friedman two-way analysis of variance test* can be used. For example, if a researcher employs four matched groups, this test would be appropriate.

Multivariate Correlational Statistics

Earlier we discussed two commonly used bivariate correlational statistics: product-moment correlation coefficient (Pearson *r*) and Spearman's rho coefficient of correlation (Spearman's rho). These correlational techniques can be used to analyze the degree of relationship between two variables. Because two variables are involved, these techniques are called *bivariate* correlational statistics. However, many research problems in the social sciences involve interrelationships between three or more variables. There are a number of commonly used multivariate correlational statistics: (a) multiple regression, (b) discriminant analysis, (c) canonical correlation, (d) path analysis, (e) factor analysis, and (f) structural equation modeling (Gall et al., 2007). Many of the dissertation examples discussed in the Chapter 3 used many of these statistical procedures.

Multiple Regression

Multiple regression is a prediction equation that determines the correlation between a combination of two or more predictor variables and a criterion variable. For example, we might use undergraduate GPA, graduate GPA, and GRE scores (verbal, quantitative, and analytical) to predict success in graduate school. Multiple regression is one of the most widely used statistical techniques in the social sciences, because of its versatility and precision. It can be used to analyze data from any of the major quantitative research designs: experimental, causal-comparative, and correlational. It can handle nominal, ordinal, interval, and ratio data. And it provides not only the relationship between variables but also the magnitude of the relationships.

Example 4.11

The use of multiple regression is illustrated in a relationship study conducted by Lunenburg and Columba (1992). The purpose of their study was to identify personality factors and education level that distinguish high performing urban principals from average performing urban principals (*n* = 179). Four independent criteria were used to measure principal performance (dependent variable): supervisor's ratings, paired comparison ratings, peer nomination ratings, and teacher ratings, resulting in an overall performance score. Sixteen personality factors (measured by the 16PF) and education level (master's or doctorate) were the predictors (independent variables). Stepwise multiple regression analysis revealed that factors E (dominant), M (imaginative), Q2 (self-sufficient), A (warm), and doctoral education level were consistent predictors of superior performance of urban principals (see Table 4.3). Because multiple regression is one of the most widely used statistical techniques in the social sciences, we will explain the procedure in some detail using the example as a model.

Table 4.3   Multiple Regression Analysis of Personality Factors and Demographic Variables with Principal Performance

Criterion Variable		X1	X2	X3	X4	X5	Constant	R	R²	F
Prinicpal Performance Rating										
	beta	.48	.28	.12	.09	.13	21.4	.64	.41	4.68*
	R	.49	.60	.62	.62	.64				

X1 = Factor E, X2 = Factor M, X3 = Factor Q2, X4 = Factor A, X5 = Educational Level
* $p < .01$

The first step in multiple regression usually is to compute the correlation between the best single predictor variable and the criterion variable. This procedure yields a multiple correlation coefficient *(R)*, which is shown in Table 4.3. Because Factor E: dominant is the best predictor, it is the first predictor entered into the multiple regression. Unless you specify otherwise, the computer program will start the multiple regression analysis with the most powerful predictor of the criterion variable.

Suppose you have not specified the order in which the predictor variables are to be entered into the multiple regression analysis. In this case, after selecting the best predictor, the computer program will search for the next best predictor of the criterion variable. This second predictor is not chosen on the basis of its product-moment correlation *(r)* with the criterion. Rather, the second predictor is chosen on the basis of how well it improves on the prediction achieved by the first variable.

What qualities should a variable have to be a good second predictor? First, it should correlate as little as possible with the first predictor variable. The second quality of a good second predictor is obvious: It should correlate as highly as possible with the criterion variable. In short, a good second predictor is one that correlates as little as possible with the first predictor and as highly as possible with the criterion.

The third predictor entered in the multiple regression analysis is determined by whether it improves on the prediction made by the first two predictors. The computer program will keep adding predictor variables until none are left. Each new predictor variable will contribute less to *R* than the preceding predictor, however, in which case there are rapidly diminishing returns for adding new predictors.

At this point we can consider further the meaning of R. The multiple correlation coefficient *(R)* is a measure of the magnitude of the relationship between a criterion variable and some combination of predictor variables. The value of R will increase with each variable that enters the multiple regression analysis. Thus, we see in Table 4.3 that the value of R to predict superior performance gradually increases from .49 to .64 as each predictor variable is added. The value of .64 represents the best prediction one can make of superior principal performance from the predictor variables listed in Table 4.3. The value of R can range from 0.00 to 1.00; negative values are not possible. The larger the R, the better the prediction of the criterion variable.

If R is squared, it will yield a statistic known as the *coefficient of determination (R^2)*. The 10th column of Table 4.3 shows the R^2 coefficient corresponding to the R in the ninth column. For example, the R^2 coefficient is .41, which is the square of the corresponding R coefficient (.64). R^2 expresses the amount of variance in the criterion variable that is explained by a predictor variable or combination of predictor variables.

Each b value in the multiple regression equation is a regression weight, which can vary from -1.00 to 1.00. A regression weight (sometimes called a b weight) is a multiplier term added to each predictor variable in a regression equation in order to maximize the predictive value of the variables. The b weights were converted to beta *(B)* weights. *Beta weights* are the regression weights in a multiple regression equation in which all the variables in the equation are in standard score form. Some researchers prefer beta weights because they form an absolute scale. For example, a beta weight of +.40 is of greater magnitude than a beta weight of +.30, irrespective of the predictor variable with which it is associated. In contrast, the magnitude of a b weight is dependent on the scale form of the predictor measure with which it is associated.

There are several variations of multiple regression analysis: stepup (also called *forward*), stepdown (also called *backward*), and stepwise. Each variation uses a different procedure for selecting a subset of predictor variables that yields the best prediction of a criterion variable. In *stepup multiple regression,* the predictor that leads to the largest increase in R is added to the current set until the addition no longer leads to a statistically significant increase. In stepdown multiple regression, all possible predictor variables are entered into the analysis first, and then, step by step, the variable that results in the smallest decrease in R is deleted until a statistically significant decrease occurs. In *stepwise multiple regression,* both the stepup and the stepdown procedures are combined. Lunenburg and Columba (1992) used a stepwise multiple regression procedure.

Multiple regression analysis is sometimes misused by researchers. One common problem is to confuse prediction with explanation. The procedures are relatively straightforward if the purpose is to optimize prediction of a criterion variable. You should be careful, however, if you have a theory that attributes causal significance to the predictor variables. In this situation, you should not confuse the causal significance of a predictor variable with its regression weight or R^2 increment value in a multiple regression equation. If you wish to test a causal theory by using multivariate correlational data, consider path analysis or structural equation modeling rather than multiple regression. Both procedures are discussed later in the chapter.

You should maintain a reasonable balance between sample size and the number of predictor variables used. A rule of thumb is to increase sample size by at least 15 subjects for each variable that will be included in the multiple regression analysis. Using this rule, you would select a sample of at least 45 subjects for a multiple regression analysis involving three predictor variables.

Discriminant Analysis

Discriminant analysis is a statistical procedure related to multiple correlation. It uses a number of predictor variables to classify subjects into two or more distinct groups such as dropouts versus persisters, successful versus unsuccessful students, delinquents versus nondelinquents, and so on. The criterion in discriminant analysis is a person's group membership. The procedure results in an equation, or *discriminant function*, where the scores on the predictors are multiplied by weights to predict the classification of subjects into groups. When there are just two groups, the discriminant function is essentially a multiple correlation equation with the group membership criterion coded 0 or 1. But with three or more groups as the criterion, discriminant analysis goes beyond multiple correlation.

Example 4.12

Discriminant analysis might be used to identify predictors of success in a school of education doctoral program. You could identify the variables that discriminated membership into one of two groups: those who successfully completed doctoral study and those who did not. A number of different predictors might be used: Miller Analogies Test (MAT) scores, Graduate Record Examination (GRE) scores, undergraduate GPA, graduate GPA, time lapse between the master's degree and entrance into the doctoral program, doctoral major, age at entrance, gender, race/ethnicity, and marital status. Complex correlational analysis would produce an equation showing the variables that were significant in predicting the criterion, success or lack of success in a doctoral program.

Canonical Correlation

Canonical correlation is a generalization of multiple regression that adds more than one dependent variable to the prediction equation. Recall that a multiple correlation coefficient shows the correlation between the "best" combination of independent variables and a single dependent variable.

Canonical correlation extends the analysis to more than one dependent variable. In other words, canonical correlation is an analysis with several independent variables and several dependent variables. It takes into account the X and Y scores, the relations between the X variables, between the Y variables, and between the X and Y sets of variables. The result is a *canonical correlation coefficient* that represents the maximum correlation possible between sets of X scores and sets of Y scores. It also indicates the relative contributions of the separate independent and dependent variables to the canonical correlation, so you can see which variables are most important to the relationships between the sets. For more information on canonical correlation, see Thompson's *Canonical Correlation Analysis* (1984).

Path Analysis

Path analysis is a set of statistical procedures designed to test a hypothesized causal model about the relationships among three or more variables. Using theory and existing knowledge, the researcher proposes a causal model and then applies path analysis to determine if the causal model is consistent with the empirical data. Models inconsistent with the data are rejected, whereas those not rejected are viewed as plausible causal patterns to be subjected to further investigation.

Example 4.13

Lunenburg (1984, 1991a, 1991b), Lunenburg and Cadavid (1992), Lunenburg and O'Reilly (1974), and Lunenburg and Mankowsky (2000) tested a path model of the influences affecting teachers' job satisfaction. The model used in the four studies hypothesized that job satisfaction is a function of a teachers' belief systems, locus of control, perceptions of organizational climate, dimensions of school bureaucratization, pupil control orientation and behavior, and several demographic variables including, gender, age, father's education, mother's education, teacher's academic achievement, teaching experience, teacher's commitment to the teaching profession, and race and ethnicity in the later studies (Lunenburg & Cadavid, 1992; Lunenburg & Mankowsky, 2000). There were significant relationships between teachers' job satisfaction and perceptions of teachers' belief system, locus of control, dimensions of school bureaucratization, organizational climate, and pupil-control orientation and behavior. The researchers concluded that the prototypic profile of the dissatisfied teacher is one who has a closed-minded belief system, an external locus of control, perceives a closed organizational climate, a high level of school bureaucratization, and has both a custodial pupil-control orientation and behavior.

The analysis was done separately for samples of African American teachers and White teachers. In general, the path coefficients were similar for African American teachers and White teachers. One exception was found when satisfaction was related to academic achievement. Lower-achieving

White teachers tended to be more satisfied in their jobs than did their higher-achieving counterparts; for African Americans, no such difference was found. Another observed difference occurred when satisfaction was related to gender. African American men tended to be more satisfied with their jobs than African American women, but White women tended to be more satisfied than White men. This finding is consistent with a study by Culver, Wolfe, and Cross (1990). For both groups of White and African American teachers, demographic variables such as age, sex, father's education, mother's education, and years of teaching experience were found to be of little importance to job satisfaction. For further discussion of path analysis, see Loehlin (2004).

Factor Analysis

Another widely used procedure based on correlation is *factor analysis*. This procedure analyzes the intercorrelations among a large set of measures to identify a smaller number of common factors. Factors are hypothetical constructs assumed to underlie different types of psychological measures, such as intelligence, aptitude, achievement, personality, and attitude measures. Factor analysis indicates the extent to which tests or other instruments are measuring the same thing, enabling researchers to deal with a smaller number of constructs. Some factor analysis studies of intelligence tests, for example, have identified underlying verbal, numerical, spatial, memory, and reasoning factors.

The first steps in factor analysis involve selecting variables to be included in the analysis and developing a correlation matrix that shows the correlation of each measure with every other measure. There may be a very large number of correlations in the matrix. The matrix is then subjected to computations with a factor analysis computer program that produces clusters of variables that intercorrelate highly within the cluster but have low correlations with other clusters. These clusters are the factors, and the object is to identify a smaller number of separate underlying factors that can account for the covariation among the larger number of variables.

Example 4.14

Consider the hypothetical correlation matrix in Table 4.4. An "inspection" of the factor analysis shows three clusters. The correlation between vocabulary and analogies is high (.50), but neither correlates highly with the other variables. Arithmetic and numerical reasoning correlate highly with each other, but not with the other variables. A similar pattern can be seen with picture completion and block design. Three factors appear to underlie performance on these six measures—verbal, numerical, and spatial.

Table 4.4   Correlation Matrix of Six Factors Related to Intelligence Tests

	1	2	3	4	5	6
1. Vocabulary	—	.50	.15	.12	.12	.15
2. Analogies	—		.12	.15	.10	.18
3. Arithmetic	—	—		.55	.15	.12
4. Numerical Reasoning	—		—	—	.20	.22
5. Picture Completion	—		—		.	.52
6. Block Design						—

Several variations of factor analysis are available. For example, a factor analysis can be done to yield an *orthogonal solution,* meaning that the resulting factors are uncorrelated with each other. An orthogonal solution is desirable if we seek a pure set of factors, with each measuring a construct that does not overlap with constructs measured by other factors. In certain situations, however, it is desirable to do a factor analysis with an *oblique solution,* meaning that factors can be derived that do correlate with each other.

Example 4.15

Lunenburg and Schmidt (1987) administered a 64-item instrument, which they developed, to 227 public high school educators in Illinois, Iowa, and Wisconsin. A principal components factor analysis using an orthogonal rotation with varimax solution, revealed three interpretable factors. Items that exhibited factor loadings whose absolute value was .40 or greater were used to define a factor. Application of the Scree Test (Cattell, 1966) clearly identified three interpretable factors. The three factors accounted for 45% of the variance. The 35 items that did not conform psychometrically or theoretically to any factor were eliminated. Alpha coefficients (Cronbach, 1951) of .93 for the total scale and for respective factors (.91, .79, and .73) supported their moderately high reliability. Results of the factor analysis are presented in Chapter 8. For readable discussions of factor analysis, see Kim and Mueller (1978) and Thompson (2004).

Structural Equation Modeling

Structural equation modeling is a multivariate technique that can be used to test theories of causal relationships between variables. The method is similar to but more powerful than path analysis, because it provides a more powerful test of causal relationships specified by a theory. LISREL (*Analysis of Linear Structural Relationships*) is the computer program that was developed to run it. For further discussion of structural equation modeling, see Byrne (2006) and Loehlin (2004). A good, recent example of structural equation modeling is provided by Hoy, Tarter, and Hoy (2006). Reference to this study is provided in Chapter 7.

SUMMARY

Statistics are mathematical procedures for analyzing numerical data. The statistical procedures you choose will be determined by your research questions or hypotheses and the type of data you will collect. Thus, different research questions (hypotheses) and different research designs require different statistical analyses. No matter how well you conduct your study, inappropriate statistical analyses likely will result in inappropriate research conclusions. Many statistical procedures are available to you. In this chapter, we described those commonly used in the social and behavioral sciences. In the following chapter, we describe qualitative research designs.

5

Qualitative Research Designs

In this chapter, we continue the discussion of methods of inquiry from Chapter 3; however, in this chapter we guide you through qualitative and mixed methods research designs. Just as quantitative research begins with basic human observation and curiosity, qualitative research does also. The science of qualitative research seeks to have the researcher look deeply into the world of individuals and phenomena.

Your dissertation, as a product of qualitative research, will likely be based on small nonrandom samples, or it may relate to multiple concepts, phenomena, or theories, or it may yield theory. Basic factual information or uniconceptual research in qualitative designs report information on one concept or phenomenon and does not attempt to make broader commentaries on the data. It is confined to one dimension and the small sample. It may be applied to similar groups in similar situations. Qualitative research can become more complex as the researcher uses methods of inquiry that promote cross-analyses or comparisons of data. Theory development, grounded theory, is often the most difficult, but most rewarding outcomes of the methodological techniques.

Just as in quantitative research, also in qualitative research, you must ask yourself: what is my intent or purpose of the research? Second, you must ask: what are my research questions? Again, these initial components will drive the method you select. If you conclude that you need to go obtain a deeper understanding of the topic, you will select qualitative methodology. Ultimately, you may decide that a mixed methods approach, using both quantitative and qualitative analyses, is the best method of inquiry for your dissertation. In this chapter, we provide an overview of each of the data analysis techniques or inquiry methods you could use if your questions or purpose necessitate a qualitative approach. Certainly, this chapter is not all inclusive, and we know that you will want to investigate more fully other options on your own once you settle on a specific method of inquiry. You will need to consult qualitative research methods textbooks and review your proposed methodology with your dissertation advisor. You must be thoroughly familiar with your method of qualitative inquiry.

Your research design or method of inquiry for qualitative will likely fall into one of four major categories of research: (a) phenomenological research, (b) case study research, (c) ethnographic research, and (d) grounded theory research. In addition to providing you with a brief overview of each category, we also provide examples of research purposes or questions that would justify a specific type of qualitative research design or method of inquiry. We also give several other types of research in qualitative inquiry. In a final section of this chapter, we discuss mixed methods research and provide some examples of it.

According to Creswell (2007),

> A qualitative study is defined as an inquiry process of understanding based on distinct methodological traditions of inquiry that explore a social or human problem. The researcher builds a complex, holistic picture, analyzes words, reports detailed views of informants, and conducts the study in a natural setting. (p. 15)

Therefore, qualitative research emphasizes understanding by closely examining people's words, actions, and records, as opposed to a quantitative research approach that investigates such words, actions, and records at a mathematically significant level, thus quantifying the results of observations. Qualitative research examines the patterns of meaning that emerge from data gathered; such patterns are often presented in the participants' own words. Many students believe that qualitative research is easier than quantitative research; however, it takes not only a logical mind, but one that can take and make sense of ambiguity by searching for patterns and connections. Your task in qualitative research is to find patterns within words and observed actions, and to present those patterns for others to inspect while at the same time staying as close to the construction of the world of the participants as they originally experienced it. Again, your job as a researcher is not to make broad generalizations; rather, your job is to contextualize the findings.

PHENOMENOLOGICAL RESEARCH DESIGN

Phenomenological research is one of the most basic forms of research. This type of research involves the description of phenomena in our world. In this type of inquiry, the phenomena described are basic information, actions, behaviors, and changes of phenomena, but always the description is about what the phenomena "look like" from the perspective of the researcher and the participants in the research; it is not about how the phenomena function. Prior to beginning the research, you will need to have established from theory or from prior research what it is about the phenomenon you will study; from this perspective, descriptive research is theory or research driven.

Husserl, the twentieth-century philosopher and the father of phenomenology, was concerned with the study of "experience" from the perspective of the individual, and believed that the researcher could approximate those experiences through intuiting and rigorous examination of the subjects, objects, or people's lived experiences, behaviors, or actions. He believed that researchers could gain subjective experience, essential realities, and insights into a person's or persons' motivations and actions; thus, researchers could minimize presuppositions and traditionally held beliefs. The researchers' interpretations of the phenomena allows it to, as in action research, inform, support, or challenge policy, procedures, and actions in society or organizations.

In a phenomenological research design, the researcher is concerned with clarifying the specific and recognizing phenomena through the eyes of the participants. Deep and rich descriptions of the phenomenon or phenomena are usually gathered through inductive, qualitative methods such as interviews, focus group discussions, and participant observation. Although phenomenological research has been related to other essentially qualitative approaches including ethnography (discussed later in this chapter), hermeneutics (analysis of the written word), and symbolic interactionism (making meaning of individual's interactions), it usually is akin to descriptive research in that it is about describing rather than explaining. Much of this type research has the researcher come to it without any preconceived notions or hypotheses; however, it is extremely unlikely that you, as the researcher, will not have a preconditioned paradigm, purpose, or hypothesis. Therefore, you, as the researcher, never can be removed from your own presuppositions about the phenomena; therefore, you should admit your own perspective under a heading in your dissertation methodology as "Researcher's Perspective" or "My Personal Perspective."

Techniques/Approaches/Methods

Phenomenological research can be based in either single-case designs or purposefully selected samples. A variety of qualitative techniques, approaches, or methods can be used in phenomenological research, including interviews, focus groups, participant or direct observation, and document or personal entry analyses. Of course in any of these approaches, the establishment of trust is important via good rapport and empathetic listening. The techniques are explained in more detail in Table 5.1.

(*Text continues on page 95*)

Table 5.1   Phenomenological Technique, Method, Approach

Phenomenological Technique, Method, Approach Defined	*Explanation*
Interview—The interview, both factual and meaningful, seeks to describe the meanings of central themes in the life world of the subjects. The main task in interviewing is to understand the meaning of what the interviewees say (Kvale, 1996).	The interview can be structured, semistructured, or unstructured. In a structured or semi-structured interview, you will need an interview protocol that has been face validated. The interview is usually recorded and then transcribed with notes taken during the interview added later. Prior to the interview, you must: (a) secure a location with the least distraction, (b) explain the purpose of the interview, (c) address confidentiality and provide a consent form for signature, (d) explain the format of the interview, (e) indicate the length of the interview, (f) give your contact information, (g) allow interviewee to ask any questions about the interview, and (h) determine how you will record the interview data (if the tape recorder is used, verify that it is working periodically throughout the interview and if you take notes, be thoughtful of how and when notes are taken, not to make the interviewee feel uncomfortable—notes may be used for observations during the interview only).
	During the interview, you will need to attend to: (a) careful listening, (b) nonverbal cues, (c) the progress of the conversation, (d) probing when needed, (e) taking notes, and (f) not responding during the interview.
	Questions in the interview should be sequenced as follows: (a) ask factual, basic questions first, simply getting the interviewee involved, then place factual questions throughout the interview, (b) present-based questions should be asked prior to

(Continued)

Table 5.1 (Continued)

Phenomenological Technique, Method, Approach Defined	Explanation
	past-based or future-based questions, and (c) allow the interviewee to add any additional information at the end of the interview. Note: the interview is time-consuming and resource extensive.
Focus Groups—This technique is a form of interview, but with a group. It focuses on data generated via observation and communication between and among participants. Denzin and Lincoln (1994, p. 365) stated that Merton et al., coined the term *focus group* in 1956 to apply to a situation in which the interviewer asks group members very specific questions about a topic after considerable research has already been completed, while Kreuger (1988) defined a focus group as a "carefully planned discussion designed to obtain perceptions in a defined area of interest in a permissive, nonthreatening environment." (p. 18) It is less time consuming and resource intensive than the individual interview.	You, or someone you train, can lead or moderate the group, which usually consists of four to twelve people. The less experienced the interviewer, the more people in the group may be likely to be frustrating or unwieldy; however, the less experienced the interviewer, the fewer people may likely not be encouraged to generate the information needed that a few more in a group could generate. In this technique, you would have an interview protocol established and validated. Additionally, it should be noted that you should not be alarmed if one participant's discussion is influenced by another. This is normal in focus group research. We often call it "piggybacking." The protocol should go from more general questions to more specific and should consist of about 10 questions.
Participant or Direct Observation—The participant observation technique is an observational method in qualitative research that uses the five senses to describe the (a) setting, (b) people, (c) occurrences, and (d) meaning of what was observed. In other words, it examines the intricacies of the interactions and	You will, in participant observation method, intentionally put yourself in the context or location of the phenomena being studied over an extended period. As a participant observer, you will become a part of the group and become fully engaged in experiencing what the participants are experiencing. You may combine

Phenomenological Technique, Method, Approach Defined	*Explanation*
relationships of individuals. It investigates the phenomena of this. This technique is usually done onsite; however, with the virtual world, it may be conducted using photographs, videotaping or streaming, and audiotaping or streaming. In direct observation, you will conduct systematic observation and documentation of phenomena in its usual setting or location.	some unstructured interviews during the time you are also observing. The extent to which you participate and the length of participation is up to you as the researcher. It truly depends on your research purpose. There may be limitations in terms of gender, time, language, age, socioeconomics, or culture that you, as the researcher, will need to consider prior to entering as a participant. You may consider having other researchers make observations at the same time you do. You may wish to observe at other times—vary your times of observation to make your finding more reliable. In direct observation you will be a quiet observer and will not interact with the participants; you will not intervene in situations in an attempt to influence the outcome of the study. As participant observers, you become a part of the group and are fully engaged in experiencing what those in the study group are experiencing. You may, however, conduct focus groups or individual interviews at another time during the study. But, unlike participant observation, the interviews will be considerably more structured and will likely be based on things you have observed so that you can obtain more in-depth understanding about what it is that you observed. In both participant and direct observation, you will want to make notes on: (a) the physical environment, (b) sociological aspects

(Continued)

Table 5.1 (Continued)

Phenomenological Technique, Method, Approach Defined	Explanation
	of community, (c) hierarchical structures, (d) language, (e) communication venues, (f) unspoken communications or norms, (g) activities, and (h) your own thoughts and responses. Take down as much of the direct conversations as possible for reproduction of thoughts of the individuals and group.
Document Analysis—This particular technique in qualitative research is related to the critique or analysis of documents for significance, meaning, and relevance within a particular context and phenomenon. Documents can consist of historical papers, personal entries, clinical records (if available), video, photos, electronic media, collections (stamps, clothes, other materials), books, newsletters, or newspapers (not an all inclusive list).	Using this technique, you will (a) define your purpose(s), (b) collect your documents, and (c) review and analyze your documents. When you review your documents, you will want to label your documents and perhaps use differing colors of Post-it tabs for varying themes you find. You will want to use the constant comparison method as defined by Patton (1990) as "to group answers. . . to common questions [and] analyze different perspectives on central issues." (p. 376)
Discourse Analysis—Discourse analysis is actually not a specific research method, but can inform the phenomenon being studied. It provides a deconstructive reading and interpretation of a problem or text. Discourse analysis can be stated as a set of methods and theories for investigating language in use and language in social contexts (Yates, Taylor, & Wetherell, 2001). It can be used as well in ethnography to understand and examine a person's social world. Approaches to discourse analysis may include discursive psychology; conversation analysis; critical discourse analysis and critical linguistics; and sociolinguistics.	The defining of discourse analysis is part of its explanation. Stubbs (1983) defined it as being (a) concerned with language *use* beyond the boundaries of a sentence/utterance, (b) concerned with the interrelationships between language and society, and (c) concerned with the interactive or dialogic properties of everyday communication. The validity and reliability of discourse analysis may be found in four approaches: (a) deviant case analysis, (b) participant understanding, (c) coherence, and (d) reader's evaluation. (Potter, 1996)

Following are examples of phenomenological studies by Meyertons (2006) and Gitonga (2006). (See Examples 5.1 and 5.2.)

Example 5.1

Abstract

This phenomenological study investigated the experiences of a set of faculty who taught classes in hybrid format at a small liberal arts university in Salem, Oregon. For this study, a "hybrid format" course was defined as a course that includes elements of both traditional face-to-face and technology-enhanced (often Internet) course components. The study consisted of a set of heuristic interviews with faculty members identified through an empirical survey I conducted in Fall 2002 as part of my duties as Director of Instructional Design and Development for the university's technical services department.

Higher education leaders have consistently identified technology integration as an important priority for their faculty. Since in many cases faculty have proven reluctant to do so, it is clear that there has been some dissonance between leadership expectations and faculty experiences. An extensive review of relevant literature indicates that little research has been conducted specifically on the faculty experience with educational technology, although much evidence has been gathered on the student experience and on learning outcomes. The goal of this study was to discover if there were any common elements that faculty experience in working with hybrid formats, and to try to distill these elements into a set of recommendations to higher education leaders for improving faculty experiences with educational technology. The broader goal was to help develop practices that might improve ways faculty use educational technology to enhance teaching and learning. (Meyertons, 2006, pp. 1–2)

Example 5.2

Abstract

The purpose of this study was to explore beginning counselors' experience of their first counseling position in their first year. Four counselors, who shared a similar counselor education background but who also differed by their degree majors, described their experiences. Using phenomenological methodology to collect and analyze data, two rounds of interviews were conducted in order to allow the four participants to individually describe their experiences. A focus group composed of all the participants verified the accuracy of the research findings. The study resulted in a fusion of common themes. Within the theme of hope and expectations, the essence of the beginning counselors' experience revolved around support, clientele, salary, time, and continuity. Other common themes that emerged from the study were: (1) the process of transitioning from students to counselors, (2) exciting as well as challenging experiences as beginning counselors, and their perceptions of their level of preparedness for the first counseling position. In these themes, there were commonalities as well as "uniquenessalities" of the essence of their experience. (Gitonga, 2006, p. x)

CASE STUDY RESEARCH DESIGN

Case studies are specific explorations of individuals, but also such investigations can be on groups, cohorts, cultures, organizations, communities, or programs. If a case study is based in biography, it may be called *life history,* which focuses on major circumstances, situations, events, problems, celebrations, and/or decisions of a person, group, or organization. If a case study is focused on one individual or group, it is called *single-case design.* If the case targets multiple individuals and the same phenomena or it targets various communities related to a similar phenomenon, then this type of design is called *multiple-case study design.* It may even be called a *phenomenological case study,* combining as we indicated the case study and phenomenology.

More than likely, you will be using purposeful sampling in case study design. You must describe your sampling procedure and case selections in detail. Share all the characteristics of the selection criteria and distinctive and uncommon features. Also indicate the duration of the study, as that may have a bearing on the outcome.

Cases may also be classified as one of the following: deviant or extreme case, critical case, convenience case, typical case, or politically important case (Patton, 2002). An *extreme case* study would be if you were to study one or more persons at some extreme. For example, you might study superintendents who have served in urban school districts only as superintendents. A *critical case* would be one that makes a point. It is like this: if it happens in this case, then it will happen in any case, or vice versa. An example of a critical case is related to language. For example, if a letter is sent home in English to predominately Vietnamese-speaking homes and the parents understand the letter, then all parents of other languages and of English would be expected to understand the letter. A *convenience case* is one in which cases are selected based on availability. It is not purposeful or strategic in nature and is the weakest type of case. A *typical case* is one in which you would select to typify the norm when describing a group or program. A *politically important case* would be one in which cases are selected based on political sensitivity. For example, a case study of dual language programs in the state would be politically sensitive and informative in a year in which the legislature was considering funding or not funding dual language programs or other types of bilingual programs.

Your case data may include, but not be limited to: (a) basic demographic information about the individual that is written in narrative format, (b) family history (or if the case is about a program or organization, it would relate the program's or organization's history), (c) document analyses relating to the individuals or programs, (d) interview data, and/or (e) observational records. Once you have sufficient data, you will compile the case data that tells the story of the individual, program, or organization. You likely will have themes, which may be by type of phenomena revealed or from a chronological perspective. When you write, you will need to provide sufficient explanation with deep description, so nothing is left for the reader to surmise. If you have definitions specific to your study, be certain to explain those as well. Just as in a traditional dissertation, it is helpful to have a separate listing of definitions in qualitative dissertations as well in the Introduction Chapter. You must bring your reader right into the case itself. Perhaps if you visited the individual on location, you might take photos to place into your dissertation (see, for example, Christensen's case study dissertation, 2003).

If you have multiple case studies, you will want to analyze each separately, then compare and contrast all of the cases for a final cross-case analysis (e.g., Bamberg's case study dissertation, 2004). Of course, as in all qualitative research, you will need to report themes, categories, subcategories, or subthemes. Any anomalies found must be reported in detail as well. Data reduction, as it spirals from the more general to the specific, may include, as Miles and Huberman (1994) suggested, data matrices, tables, and figures to draw comparisons across cases. When you are writing your interpretation, you must establish the significance of the findings or themes, linking them to your theoretical framework. Implications for practice are also important in conveying the significance of your findings, but generalization to broader populations is typically not appropriate for this type of research. Even in writing your findings, you should be cautious in making what we call, "great leaps," from the data to your implications. Your data represent exactly what they represent and nothing more, so make sure you have given the reader an appropriate amount of information in any claims that you make. Your findings must be credible as well as convincing and, again, based in a theoretical frame and previous literature and studies that are also credible. If you want to build theory itself from your case study, you will need to make certain you have a satisfactory number of case studies that will provide sufficient information to justify the development of a theory.

Examples of case studies conducted for dissertations follow. The first example is of a single case study conducted by Ozawa (2006). (See Example 5.3.)

Example 5.3

Abstract

The purpose of this single case study was to explore authentic communication for Japanese language learning in second-year Japanese classes at a small, private university in the Midwest. Types of authentic Japanese communication and materials in and outside of Japanese class were studied from four learners' and one professor's perspectives.

Data were collected throughout one academic year, the first semester of 2004 through the second semester of 2005. Multiple methods of data collection were used in this study including personal interviews, casual conversations, participant observations of classes and related events, and studying relevant documents, including the textbook, students' study sheets, videos, oral exam transcripts, e-mail copies, reflection sheets, and web log copies.

Qualitative research procedures were used to study second-year Japanese language learners' authentic communication. Data were analyzed by categorizing into codes, then themes and subthemes. Five themes emerged in this study: (1) the e-mail writing process, (2) the e-mail reading process, (3) the learning process, (4) learning through e-mail, and (5) authentic Japanese. Lastly, implications and recommendations based on the data were concluded. (Ozawa, 2006, n.p.)

The second example is a multiple case dissertation by Menconi (2006). (See Example 5.4.)

Example 5.4

Abstract

Looping is an instructional practice that allows the teacher to keep the same students over a two-year period. Multiage grouping is a more complex form of the multiyear configuration where the same teacher instructs students from two or three grade levels until they have completed the highest grade represented in that classroom. Both configurations present a logical approach toward developing long-term relationships which benefit students, teachers, parents, and administrators. Looping and multiage instruction beginnings go back to the one-room schoolhouse long before the Common School Reform Movement which introduced the graded school system of the 1860s. Even though the graded school system is over 150 years old, it still remains entrenched today. Consequently, looping and multiage instruction represent practices that require a paradigm shift from the graded school system.

While there are philosophical differences between looping and multiage instruction, there are also many similarities. Perhaps the most significant similarity is the long-term relationship that is developed between the child, teacher, and parent when the teacher has the same child for two years or two grade levels. This distinction develops many benefits such as curriculum coherence, safety, continuity, and student confidence. Two years with the same child also provides administrators and principals with many benefits. There is a tremendous savings of time because the students do not have to learn new routines and classroom management is easier. And there is a tremendous amount of professional development benefits for the teachers, since the teachers become better acquainted with the child and the curriculum.

Principals have indicated several concerns regarding the implementation of looping and multiage instruction, since it is a change from the standard graded school system. These concerns include the issues of more developmentally appropriate means for educating children, blending the curricula for two grade levels, and identifying staff members willing to undertake this paradigm shift.

The purpose of this study is to identify principal perspectives of the strengths and weaknesses of looping and multiage instruction from principals and lead teachers who have implemented them successfully. A multiple-case study design is used to investigate looping and multiage practices and provide a comparison of sites or cases so a range of generality or conditions is established. These sites include a wealthy, suburban elementary school using multiage practices, an integrated, middle-class, urban elementary school using looping, and a low-income, urban middle school using looping. Different information gathered from multiple sites and principal perspectives establishes a range of aspects or a conceptual framework that can assist principals in understanding these multiyear practices better. It is anticipated that this conceptual framework will be of value to those principals and administrators interested in implementing looping and multiage practices in their own schools or school districts. (Menconi, 2006, p. x)

ETHNOGRAPHIC RESEARCH DESIGN

Ethnographic research requires that you conduct fieldwork to become involved with the individuals or group in a personal manner, using participant observation as a technique for gathering data for telling the group's or individual's story via rich narrative description. You will typically gather the data via interviews during the participant observation, videography, photography, and document analysis. These techniques of data gathering will yield thick and rich descriptions necessary for your ethnographic dissertation in the form of quotations (low inference descriptors), descriptions of the group and the contexts, and parts of documents. You will, as in participant observation, investigate the behaviors of the people, their language, their actions, and their artifacts. You will look for norms, mores, and customs. Prior to going in to conduct such research, you must be clear about your own biases, about colonization, about who the "other" is, about your impact on the group to be studied, and about basic respect. To conduct fieldwork for the ethnography, you will need to gain the trust of the individuals in charge; these are the gatekeepers.

In ethnographic studies, depending on your purpose, you may use *convenience sampling* (as explained previously under case study method). You may use *stratified sampling* that seeks out groups from various levels such as socioeconomic levels. *Snowball sampling* may also be used where referrals from your initial contacts are made to add to the group.

Ethnography does not come without serious consideration. Some critical features to consider prior to the selection of an ethnographic design are: (a) your own understanding of culture and cultural anthropology, the foundation of ethnography; (b) your ability to write in a narrative style so that others may understand the cultural occurrences and norms of the group; (c) your ability to be a part of the group, yet remain apart from the group as the researcher, thus creating a fine line and balance between the researcher and the researched; (d) the ethical implications for studying the group or individuals; and (e) an extensive time commitment for the fieldwork.

Although conversation analysis was mentioned under the approach of discourse analysis within the phenomenological research method previously, we could consider conversation analysis as a separate approach and list it under ethnography and classify it as an ethnographic approach. In this type of analysis, one studies natural conversations in a variety of conventional settings (interviews, courts, schools, telephone conversation, restaurant, family conversations) to determine how the participants interact, construct conversation across time, identify problems, and/or exhibit gestures and eye contact.

We are placing narrative analysis within the larger context of the ethnographic research method, because according to Connelly and Clandinin (1990) narrative analysis is "how humans make meaning of experience by endlessly telling and retelling stories about themselves" (p. 14). Mishler (1986) frames the narrative through four categories: (a) orientation that describes the setting and character, (b) abstract that summarizes the events or incidents of the story, (c) complicating action that offers an evaluative commentary on events, conflicts and themes, and (d) resolution that describes the outcomes of the story or conflict (pp. 236–237).

Examples of ethnographic studies follow. The first ethnographic study comes from a master's thesis by Quon (2006). (See Example 5.5.)

Example 5.5

Abstract

This study examines gendered patterns of participation in teens of classroom floor access and control with elementary school children. Primary participants in the study include approximately 97 students from four intact classrooms and 4 teachers. Eight students were also selected for observation.

Field notes from participant observation, informal interviews, and video/audio taped classroom interactions provided the data for this classroom ethnography. A portion of the data was analyzed in detail for time spent in effort and ratified speaking tone. The remainder of the data was analyzed through constant cross comparison for patterns of student talk participation in whole class interactions.

Findings revealed that success in talk is contingent on teacher organization of talk. Tightly organized floors rendered more equitable distribution of talk between boys and girls. Loosely organized floors rendered more differences in talk distribution in favor of boys. In all four classrooms, however, the girls are just as successful as boys in securing floor spaces, although they had to invest much more effort in hand raises. Data analysis of vocal children revealed that language proficiency can provide a context in which children gain self-confidence. Self-confidence allows the children to learn how to use language proficiency in order to gain status with other children.

The general improvement of women's social status in the workforce and other contexts may help explain why gendered gap in participation is diminishing in the classrooms. (Quon, 2006, pp. 1–2)

The second example is from a doctoral dissertation by Thompson (2006), who employed an ethnographic approach. (See Example 5.6.)

Example 5.6

Abstract

The purpose of this study was to describe and interpret the dimensions of performance creativity within a Montessori culture. Performance creativity is a reconceptualization of how creative activity is recognized and encompasses four elements: self, self-expression, meaning, and cultural significance. The conceptual framework for this study articulates creativity as a dynamic self-construction influenced by the meaning one draws from a cultural learning environment. The reconceptualization of creativity is built upon a frame of neuroscience research, Montessori philosophy, and selected Eastern/Asian, African, and Native American views of creativity.

This qualitative study was conducted in a Montessori primary and elementary school in the western United States, and it employed both the traditional ethnographic techniques of extended observations and artifact analysis. The study also used the performance ethnographic method of the collaborative dialogic interview.

The goal of performance ethnography is to produce a research-based performance narrative which views research participants as collaborators in the composition of the performance script. One of the facets of a performative study is that it initiates a dialogue within a larger community. The goal for this study is that it will invite educators to begin to reexamine how and why children express creativity and how creativity can be envisioned through a multicultural lens.

The findings of this work present emerging connections among neurological, Montessori, and multicultural perspectives of creativity that were observed in a Montessori learning environment. Educational implications related to this study include the potential for the fields of neuroscience and education to be drawn closer together, by using a multicultural avenue through which to describe creativity. The goal of designing curriculum and teacher education that is supported by neurological evidence is one that can be supported by further research in this area. (Thompson, 2006, n.p.)

McFadden (2006) used narrative analysis to conduct her dissertation study. (See Example 5.7.)

Example 5.7

Abstract

Abundant research exists on the relationship that religion or spirituality has played in the lives and recovery of individuals diagnosed with physical ailments, while little research is found regarding the role that religion or spirituality has played in the lives of individuals diagnosed with a chronic or severe mental illness. Therefore, the researcher undertook to explore, investigate, understand, and describe the lived religious or spiritual experiences of these individuals, using a qualitative research inquiry and narrative analysis.

Data were collected during unstructured, informal interviews with seven adult volunteer participants. Data analysis of the interviews provided three major relationship themes common to all participants: with self, others, and God.

All participants acknowledge some form of religious or spiritual upbringing, and all report that their religious or spiritual practices improved once they were diagnosed. The participants identify a holistic approach to their recovery that incorporates their physical, mental, emotional, and spiritual well-being, and they further suggest a need for health care professionals to include a spiritual aspect in their treatment. Finally, all participants report a renewed sense of hope, meaning, and purpose for their lives, which they attribute to their religion and spirituality. (McFadden, 2006, p. iii)

GROUNDED THEORY RESEARCH DESIGN

Grounded theory, first described by Glaser and Strauss (1967), is intended to generate or discover a theory inductively from data gathered about a specific phenomenon. Three elements of grounded theory are concepts, categories, and propositions. Concepts are the basic units of analysis. Corbin and Strauss (1990) stated:

Theories can't be built with actual incidents or activities as observed or reported; that is, from "raw data." The incidents, events, happenings are taken as, or analysed as, potential indicators of phenomena, which are thereby given conceptual labels. If a respondent says to the researcher, "Each day I spread my activities over the morning, resting between shaving and bathing," then the researcher might label this phenomenon as "pacing." As the researcher encounters other incidents, and when after comparison to the first, they appear to resemble the same phenomena, then these, too, can be labelled as "pacing." Only by comparing incidents and naming like phenomena with the same term can the theorist accumulate the basic units for theory. (p. 7)

Catagories is the second element of grounded theory and are defined by Corbin and Strauss (1990) as:

> ... higher in level and more abstract than the concepts they represent. They are generated through the same analytic process of making comparisons to highlight similarities and differences that is used to produce lower level concepts. Categories are the "cornerstones" of developing theory. They provide the means by which the theory can be integrated. We can show how the grouping of concepts forms categories by continuing with the example presented above. In addition to the concept of "pacing," the analyst might generate the concepts of "self-medicating," "resting," and "watching one's diet." While coding, the analyst may note that, although these concepts are different in form, they seem to represent activities directed toward a similar process: keeping an illness under control. They could be grouped under a more abstract heading, the category: "Self Strategies for Controlling Illness." (p. 7)

Propositions, the third category of grounded theory, indicate generalized relationships between a category and its concepts, as well as between discrete categories. As an iterative process, grounded theory is not generated *a priori* and then subsequently tested. Rather, it is,

> ... inductively derived from the study of the phenomenon it represents. That is, discovered, developed, and provisionally verified through systematic data collection and analysis of data pertaining to that phenomenon. Therefore, data collection, analysis, and theory should stand in reciprocal relationship with each other. One does not begin with a theory, then prove it. Rather, one begins with an area of study and what is relevant to that area is allowed to emerge. (Corbin & Strauss, 1990, p. 3)

Four research criteria are important in grounded theory for *validation* of the study and for establishing *reliability* of the findings of the study. Actually, these are recommended for review for all qualitative studies. They are: (a) construct validity, (b) internal validity, (c) external validity, and (d) reliability. *Construct validity* is accomplished by establishing clearly specified operational procedures. *Internal validity* can be reached by establishing causal relationships in which certain conditions are shown to lead to other conditions, as distinguished from false relationships, and it addresses the findings' credibility or "truth value." *External validity* is the extent to which the study's findings can be generalized and to the extent that you, as the researcher, establish the context in which it can be generalized. Generalization is usually to some broader theory or other valid studies (quantitative and qualitative) and not the population. Finally, *reliability* requires demonstrating that the operations of a study—such as data collection procedures—can be repeated with the same results.

Triangulation is another method for ensuring that the study is robust, valid, and reliable. Triangulation may appear as four basic types: (a) data triangulation, involving time, space, and persons, (b) investigator triangulation, which consists of the use of multiple, rather than single researcher/observers, (c) theory triangulation, which consists of using more than one theoretical frame in the interpretation of the phenomenon, and (d) methodological triangulation, which involves using multiple methods. Multiple triangulation may be used when you combine in one dissertation, multiple observers, theoretical perspectives, sources of data, and methodologies.

You may also use reflexivity in the study to establish better credibility and trustworthiness.

> Reflexivity requires an awareness of the researcher's contribution to the construction of meanings throughout the research process, and an acknowledgment of the impossibility of remaining "outside of" one's subject matter while conducting research. Reflexivity then urges us to explore the ways in which a researcher's involvement with a particular study influences, acts upon and informs such research. (Nightingale & Cromby, 1999, p. 228)

Willig (2001) indicated:

> There are two types of reflexivity: personal reflexivity and epistemological reflexivity. "Personal reflexivity" involves reflecting upon the ways in which our own values, experiences, interests, beliefs, political commitments, wider aims in life, and social identities have shaped the research. It also involves thinking about how the research may have affected and possibly changed us, as people and as researchers. "Epistemological reflexivity" requires us to engage with questions such as: How has the research question defined and limited what can be "found?" How has the design of the study and the method of analysis "constructed" the data and the findings? How could the research question have been investigated differently? To what extent would this have given rise to a different understanding of the phenomenon under investigation? Thus, epistemological reflexivity encourages us to reflect upon the assumptions (about the world, about knowledge) that we have made in the course of the research, and it helps us to think about the implications of such assumptions for the research and its findings. (p. 10)

Two examples of grounded theory methodology used in dissertation research follow. The first example is from Jodry (2001), and the second example is from Ericksen (2006). (See Examples 5.8 and 5.9.)

Example 5.8

Abstract

Purpose. The overarching purpose of this study was to develop a grounded theory that can guide action in advancing the academic achievement for Hispanic students. Specifically, the study focused on the discovery of relationships and factors within the contexts of the home, school, and community that positively influenced the academic achievement of six academically able Hispanic students in an urban area, non-border, high school advanced diploma program.

Methods. Following an extensive review of pertinent literature, I developed a conceptual framework of factors of support, motivation, and education within the contexts of the home, school, and community found to have an impact on Hispanic student achievement. The research questions focused on identifying the factors that were present in relationships within the home, school, and community that positively influenced the achievement of academically able Hispanic students in an urban, nonborder, high school advanced diploma program. Using ethnographic case study methodology, findings were applied to the development of a theory and an accompanying model titled, The Hispanic Academic Advancement Theory.

Results. From a research-based conceptual framework and data gathered in an ethnographic study, a grounded theory that can guide action in advancing the academic achievement of Hispanic students was developed. The Hispanic Academic Advancement Theory includes three factors, 18 subfactors, and 12 relationships. The three factors are: (a) supportive factors, (b) motivational factors, and (c) educational factors. The 18 subfactors are (a) positive communication, (b) positive adult relationships, (c) a climate of caring, (d) collaboration, (e) value for academic goals, (f) students viewed as assets, (g) advocacy orientation, (h) positive adult role models, (i) service learning, (j) safe environment, (k) high expectations, (l) programs, (m) development of self-advocacy, (n) respect for language and heritage, (o) culturally and linguistically responsive pedagogy, (p) shared culture and language, (q) parents as assets, and (r) culturally and linguistically responsive leadership. The 12 relationships are: (a) mother, (b) father, (c) older siblings, (d) grandparent, (e) aunts/uncles, (f) elementary bilingual educator, (g) secondary special area teacher, (h) secondary counselor, (i) principal, (j) peers in the advanced program, (k) college/university relationships, and (l) church relationships. (Jodry, 2001, pp. iv–v)

Example 5.9

Abstract

This dissertation utilized primarily qualitative methods of data collection and analysis to examine how 11 early elementary special education teachers in 10 schools in a large school district in the Mid-Atlantic region of the United States approached the task of developing and providing literacy instruction to students with significant disabilities who received most of their education in a self-contained setting. An environmental observation, semistructured interviews, and classroom observations were used to (1) describe the teachers' existing practices related to early emergent reading, writing, and communication, (2) explore the extent to which teachers followed recommended best practices, and (3) to develop a beginning theory of how early elementary special education teachers approach early literacy learning given the many challenges of their students.

Six critical features were identified from the literature related to literacy instruction for students with significant disabilities. Those features were: (a) a responsive and supportive literacy rich environment, (b) integration of computers, assistive technology (AT) and alternative and augmentative communication (AAC) strategies, (c) direct instruction, (d) social engagement and meaning-making, (e) individualization based on local understanding, and (f) high expectations. Most of the teachers were actively engaged in teaching literacy skills to their students. In general they provided a responsive and supportive literacy environment and direct instruction. Computers were widely used as were AT and AAC; however, AT and AAC strategies were not systematically integrated across activities. Teachers had high hopes for their students but did not expect many of them would achieve conventional literacy. Emphases on meaning-making and social engagement were not observed, nor did teachers share these perspectives during interviews.

Using grounded theory methodology, a theory was constructed of five related concepts: (a) instructional outlook, (b) institutional expectation, (c) instructional set, (d) instructional fit, and (e) vigilance-adaptation. This theory was used to explain how teachers approach literacy instruction. It was also found useful for predicting poor instructional fit, which was defined as the match among the teacher, her students, and the instructional demands and supports in an instructional setting. (Ericksen, 2006, p. x)

MIXED METHODS RESEARCH DESIGN

Mixed methods research can refer to those studies that have engaged both quantitative and qualitative research questions and/or that have used both probability and purposeful sampling. It is a field of research that is still emerging.

According to Johnson and Onwuegbuzie (2004), mixed methods research is "the class of research where the researcher mixes or combines quantitative and qualitative research techniques, methods, approaches, concepts, or language into a single study" (p. 17). They further indicated:

Mixed methods research offers great promise for practicing researchers who would like to see methodologists describe and develop techniques that are closer to what researchers actually use in practice. Mixed methods research as the third research paradigm can also help bridge the schism between quantitative and qualitative research

(Onwuegbuzie & Leech, 2004a). Methodological work on the mixed methods research paradigm can be seen in several recent books (Brewer & Hunter, 1989; Creswell, 2007; Greene, Caracelli, & Graham, 1989; Johnson & Christensen, 2004; Newman & Benz, 1998; Reichardt & Rallis, 1994; Tashakkori & Teddlie, 1998, 2003). (p. 15)

Johnson and Onwuegbuzie further iterated eight distinct steps in mixed methods design: (a) determine the research question, (b) determine whether a mixed design is appropriate, (c) select the mixed methods or mixed-model research design, (d) collect the data, (e) analyze the data, (f) interpret the data, (g) legitimate the data, and (h) draw conclusions (if warranted) and write the final report.

Examples of mixed methods research in dissertation studies follow. The first example is from Christopher (2006) and the second is from Wilbur (2005). (See Examples 5.10 and 5.11.)

Example 5.10

Abstract

Secondary English language learners (ELLs) spend most of their school day in classes with regular education teachers who have little or no training in methods for teaching English for Speakers of Other Languages (ESOL). This mixed methods (qualitative and quantitative) study investigated teacher use of accommodations and strategies for ELLs and assessed how the format of the resources made available to them affected their teaching. The participants were mainstream secondary teachers at the district-designated ESOL high school in an urban Midwestern city. The participating teachers were randomly divided into 2 groups and presented with a lesson plan addendum designed to help them increase their use of accommodations and strategies for ELLs. The first group received a CD version of the addendum which included Internet-linked resources explaining the strategies and accommodations. Participants in the second group received a paper version of the lesson plan addendum, and printed versions of the Internet-linked resources were available in the school media center. The researcher observed the teachers' classes before and after receiving the lesson plan addendum. She recorded the strategies and accommodations demonstrated in their teaching, (before and after), in order to determine if the teachers in both groups changed their strategy use. Additionally, she compared the results from each group to ascertain if there was a difference in the frequency of strategy use between the two groups. Finally, the teachers were interviewed after the quantitative data were collected to determine if their self-perceptions about using strategies for ELLS aligned with the researcher's observation of their teaching.

The results of this study showed that providing mainstream teachers with a lesson plan addendum focusing on English language learners does, in fact, lead to an increase in strategies and accommodations used.

The results on the preferred way to provide the lesson plan addendum are inconclusive, although there is evidence that the resources linked via the Internet are more likely to be accessed than those that are made available in the media center at the school. Finally, based on interviews with the participants, the researcher concluded that they had a good understanding of how they changed their teaching as a result of using the lesson plan addendum. (Christopher, 2006, p. ii–iv)

Example 5.11

Abstract

This dissertation focused on the application of a known organizational development strategy to facilitate the conversion of a vast administrative software system at an institution of higher education. Castle and Sir (2001) reported on how to use what they called the five I's of instructing, informing, involving, intervening, and incenting to bring employees directly involved in the change through the adaptive work they needed to do during the process. In applying this 5 I strategy, I used as a platform the theoretical framework of Bennis, Benne, and Chin (1965), using people technologies during change in thing technologies to assist workers in adapting to the change. Using the participatory action research methodology of planning, acting, observing, and evaluating results, this study employed a mixed method approach to data collection, using both qualitative and quantitative methods, as defined by Johnson and Onwuegbuzie (2004). The purpose of the study was to discover the fears, needs and concerns of the staff involved in the conversion through the collection of field notes, journal entries, interviews, and surveys. I then applied the appropriate five I strategy to the change process to mitigate feelings of fear and loss during an imposed organizational change process. The impact of the action research project was the result of intentional interventions to mitigate feelings of fear and loss during an imposed organizational change process. This study also sought to engage the researcher in the practice of reflective leadership. A mixed methods approach to the data collection for this part of the study included taking field notes, journaling, and the administration of the Leadership Practices Inventory (LPI) of Kouzes and Posner (2003). The study showed a first-order change at Orchard University as a result of the intentional insertion of organizational development strategies into the learning process. The study also showed how reflective leadership practice changed a leader's self-perception and set the stage for individual leadership growth. (Wilbur, 2005, n.p.)

Your choice of methodology, whether it is qualitative or mixed methods, will certainly depend on your purpose and research questions. A mixed methods study offers a way to lend credibility to your study and triangulate your data while providing rigor to your study. Be sure to discuss this option with your dissertation chair or advisor.

SUMMARY

In this chapter, we provided an overview of several data analysis techniques or inquiry methods you could use if your questions or purpose necessitate a qualitative approach. We offered you four major categories of qualitative research: (a) phenomenological research, (b) case study research, (c) ethnographic research, and (d) grounded theory research. In addition to providing you with a brief overview of each category, we provided examples of research purposes or questions that justified a specific type of qualitative research design or method of inquiry. We also offered several other types of research in qualitative inquiry and briefly discussed mixed methods research, and provided some examples of it. In the next section, we share the typical approach to writing the dissertation chapters.

PART III

The Dissertation Chapters

6

Writing the Introduction Chapter

One of the things a doctoral or master's student wants to know is "What does a dissertation or master's thesis look like?" While there are variations among universities, among departments, and even among dissertation committees, faculty members and doctoral (master's) students are recognizing the need for some skeletal structure around which to assemble the researchers' ideas, the data, and their conclusions.

Chapter One, the introduction of your dissertation or master's thesis, provides an orientation to your study. In the first chapter, you begin with a background of study, describe the problem, state the purpose of the study, and tell why the study is important. This is followed by a definition of key terms used in your study. A synopsis of the theoretical framework undergirding your study constitutes a major component of the introductory chapter. This is followed immediately by the research questions or research hypotheses.

Some qualitative studies are designed so that data are collected first, and then a theory is derived from those data (Glaser, 1978). Moreover, some qualitative research studies might be informed by a theoretical or epistemological framework, but formal hypotheses are not typically used to frame the study. An exception is a type of qualitative research that is framed within grounded theory methodology. In this type of qualitative research, hypotheses are the outcome of the study rather than initiators of it (Gall, Gall, & Borg, 2007).

Next, limitations, delimitations, and assumptions of the study are addressed. Chapter One concludes with a section called "Organization of the Study," which provides an overview of the contents of each chapter of your dissertation or master's thesis.

In this chapter, we discuss the components that are usually found in Chapter One of a dissertation or master's thesis; however, as mentioned previously, not all dissertations will follow this protocol. Not all students will include each of the elements we recommend. Nevertheless, the contents typically found in Chapter One of a dissertation or master's thesis are shown in Table 6.1.

Table 6.1   Contents for Chapter One of a Dissertation

CHAPTER I

INTRODUCTION

> Background of the Study
> Statement of the Problem
> Purpose of the Study
> Significance of the Study
> Definition of Terms
> Theoretical Framework
> Research Questions (or Hypotheses)
> Limitations
> Delimitations
> Assumptions
> Organization of the Study

The contents of the chapter will be presented in the same order as depicted in Table 6.1. We provide a more detailed description of each of these elements (sections), as well as examples from completed dissertations.

BACKGROUND OF THE STUDY

Use this section of your dissertation or master's thesis to acquaint the reader with your study. You can do a number of things to make this section useful. First, identify the context within which your study will be conducted and give any background information needed to clarify the context. Second, tell the reader why the study is important and timely. Third, build a case for the statement of the problem to follow. Finally, highlight the key theoretical constructs you will describe in greater depth later in this chapter, and in more detail in Chapter Two, "Review of the Literature."

An example background of the study from Ying-Chiao Tsai's (2006) dissertation follows. (See Example 6.1.)

Background of the Study

Educational researchers have long been intrigued by the effects schooling can have on overcoming the impact of student and family characteristics. For the past 20 years, research has shown a positive correlation between effective schools and high student achievement (Hallinger & Heck, 1997). From the history of effective schools and school effects research, the general findings showed that the quality of schooling shares a noticeable portion of the educational outcomes and cannot be ignored. Cuttance (2001) indicated that national and international research revealed approximately 10% to 18% of the variance in student academic achievement was due to between-school differences, while 50% was due to between-classroom differences. Therefore, both school factors and teachers' classrooms practices assume a substantial role in students' success. This study intended to verify the schooling effects into an international context. Two language groups of student populations were examined: English-language majority students and English-language minority students in the United States and Singapore. The Progress in International Reading Literacy Study (PIRLS), conducted by the International Association for the Evaluation of Educational Achievement (IEA) in 2001, was the data source for this study. (Tsai, 2006, p. 1)

Example 6.1 contains only the first paragraph of Tsai's dissertation. Her "Background of the Study" section continued for an additional six pages in which she incorporated two additional subheadings "Challenges in the United States" and "Rationale for Studying PIRLS Data and Singapore." After reading the background of the study, a reader should be able to determine fairly accurately what the research problem is. The background of the study leads logically to the statement of the problem, the next section in Chapter One of a dissertation or master's thesis.

STATEMENT OF THE PROBLEM

The statement of the problem is a definition of what you investigated in your study. It is actually a formal and succinct version of the process you went through in selecting and delimiting your topic (see Chapter 1). Accordingly, it clarifies, outlines, limits, and brings into existence an expression of the problem you investigated. It answers the question of *what* is being done in the study.

In conducting your study, the statement of the problem performs two major functions: (a) to give direction to the study, and (b) to unify all of the efforts undertaken during the conduct of the study (Castetter & Heisler, 1984). The directional function of the statement of the problem may be compared to a school district policy. A school district policy statement clarifies intent. It is a promise to follow a specific course of action. It follows that the statement of the problem acts as a control mechanism. It identifies the dimensions of the problem, defines the research design, determines literature sources and data collection, influences data analysis techniques needed to explain the data, focuses the findings on the purpose of the study, and serves as a basis for discussing conclusions and recommendations in subsequent chapters of the dissertation or master's thesis.

The unifying task of the statement of the problem means that the steps taken to solve the problem are determined by the intent specified in the statement of the problem. The presentation and analysis of data, and the findings, conclusions, and implications found in subsequent chapters of your dissertation or thesis are all focused on the statement of the problem.

Researchers spend time doing research because there is a problem that needs an answer. Such problems arise because of a lack of clear or complete information in a discipline. More specifically, the problem usually evolves out of four circumstances (Martin, 1980):

1. Little or no research on a particular topic exists.

2. There is some research, but it has not been applied to enough samples or in enough situations to be considered a reliable phenomenon.

3. Research abounds, but the findings are contradictory.

4. Two theories explain the same phenomena but recommend or predict different outcomes.

An example statement of the problem from Lauren Black's (2003) dissertation follows. (See Example 6.2.)

Example 6.2

Statement of the Problem

   Considering the demands of the principalship, what influence does the principal's belief in his/her own abilities and skills impact his/her success as a principal? Extensive research has been conducted on self-efficacy (Bandura, 1977; Bandura, 1997; Cervone, 2000; Choi, Fuqua, & Griffin, 2001; Hoy, 1998; Pajares, 1996) and teacher efficacy (Benz, Bradley, Alderman, & Flowers, 1992; Coladarci, 1992; Dembo & Gibson, 1985; Gibson & Dembo, 1984b; Guskey & Passaro, 1994; Herbert, Lee,& Willamson, 1998; Hoy & Woolfolk, 1993; Parkay, Greenwood, Olejnik, & Proller, 1988; Petrie, Hartranft, & Lutz, 1995; Tschannen-Moran, Hoy, & Hoy, 1998). While these studies have described and developed the construct of teacher efficacy, there is little empirical research on principal efficacy (Hoy, 1998). Exploring principal efficacy may provide a source of valuable information for educational leaders. Unless principals "believe they can make a difference through their actions, there is little incentive to act" (Hoy, 1998,

p. 4). A core task of administrators is decision making, which requires the synthesis of multiple cognitive processes to incorporate knowledge into creative solutions. Principals pull from personal knowledge and experience to make decisions on a daily basis.

Bandura (1997) suggested that a strong sense of self-efficacy is necessary to access skills and knowledge while at the same time remaining focused on the task in a complex environment. Hoy (1998) proposed that self-efficacy is equally important for administrators in the processes of communication, leading, and motivating others. Additionally, Hoy (1998) added, "The concept of administrator efficacy, unlike the concept of teacher efficacy, has been neglected in the educational arena" (p. 157). This study sought to identify the components of principal efficacy and develop an instrument to measure principal efficacy. (Black, 2003, pp. 1–2)

Note how skillfully and succinctly Black provided her readers with the intent of her study. Notice how she supported her intent with appropriate literature related to it. Her statement of the problem provided direction to all phases of the study resulting in the development of an instrument to measure principal efficacy.

PURPOSE OF THE STUDY

A section titled "Purpose of the Study" follows the statement of the problem. The purpose of any study is to help solve the stated problem. This section of your dissertation or master's thesis is designed to give the readers a brief overview of how you plan to solve the problem defined previously. This is a section that committee members may go back to several times to make certain they understand exactly what your purpose is in conducting the study. Developing this section often helps you become much clearer about the purpose of your study as well.

An example purpose of the study from Darlene Blair's (2001) dissertation follows. (See Example 6.3.)

Example 6.3

Purpose of the Study

The purpose of this study was to explore the relationship of principals' leadership styles and their school ratings of Exemplary, Recognized, Acceptable, or Low-Performing, assigned by the Texas Education Agency. A second purpose was to explore the relationship between principals' leadership styles and the time they spend on instructional leadership and management tasks. Thirdly, this study determined how time spent by principals on instructional leadership and management tasks is related to their school ratings. Finally, data collected for the study provided evidence as to whether or not principals devote different amounts of time to instructional leadership and management tasks. (Blair, 2001, pp. 4–5)

Note how Blair, in one brief paragraph, stipulated the four main purposes of her study. She described her purpose succinctly. As mentioned previously, this is a section of the dissertation that readers will go back to several times to make sure they understand exactly what the researcher's purpose is in conducting the study.

SIGNIFICANCE OF THE STUDY

The significance of the study is your argument that the study makes a significant contribution to the field. Do not assume that just because there is little research on your topic that the subject is worthy of investigation. You must convince your committee members that your topic has not been examined in the way you examined it. Perhaps you may be using variables that have never been examined before; or the instrument that you are developing and validating is better for your purpose than others that are on the market to measure the same variable; or that your study is the next logical step in a continuous line of inquiry that will eventually solve an important problem in your discipline.

In preparing the significance section in your dissertation or master's thesis, contemplate the following questions: (a) Why is my study important or valuable? (b) Will it revise, extend, or create new knowledge? (c) Does it have theoretical and/or practical application? You must build a case for the study's contribution to the field. Arguments for the research might include such things as the recommendations of prior research, conflicting findings in other studies, new and improved methodologies, or political, social, or psychological trends. Your committee members will be in a better position to understand your study and its relationship to the field by learning the significance of finding answers to the problem.

An example significance of the study from Scott Barrett's (2000) dissertation follows. (See Example 6.4.)

Example 6.4

Significance of the Study

The significance of this study is paramount as it contributes valuable insight and theory into the successful implementation of technology as a decision-making tool, especially in light of the amount of resources being dedicated to the implementation of information systems. Visscher and Spuck (1991) observed "there is great need for systematic research, not only because of its scientific value but also because of its ability to improve the practice of school administrative computing and consequently school effectiveness" (p. 166). The results of this study may be utilized to develop improved training models, environments, and implementation strategies to promote the effective use of student management information systems. Igbaria et al., (1997) stated that "while system usage may not ensure improvement user task performance, it remains a critical variable for organizations to derive any benefit from new technology" (p. 88).

It is increasingly important for school principals to be able to utilize information technology for immediate insight and decision making in support of the accountability factors associated with job performance and campus accountability. By identifying utilization variables, a conceptual starting point can be established for the successful implementation of training. Providing appropriate training in the proper contextual environment can enhance the use of a management information system to support informed decision making.

Gustafson (1985) summarized the importance of this research on the campus-wide impact of computerized information systems.

> Teachers will have access to the same information to which only administrators were privy, thus eliminating the need for a school hierarchy. Site administrators will have the information available which would make curriculum specialists, superintendents, school boards, and even those in higher positions on the county and state levels, obsolete. The computer, if fully implemented, will force new organizations and policy-making structures upon the school. (p. 153)

> It is evident that the potential impact of a MIS cannot be overlooked. The results of this study may contribute valuable insight and theory into the successful implementation of technology as an accountability tool, especially in light of the amount of resources being dedicated to the implementation of information systems. (Barrett, 2000, pp. 15–16)

Note how Barrett provided a convincing argument for the significance of his study of the value of implementing a MIS system in the public schools. He supported his argument with appropriate literature. For example, quotes from Visscher and Spuck, "there is great need for systematic research," and Igbaria et al., "it remains a critical variable for organizations to derive any benefit from new technology," are powerful statements used to support his position.

DEFINITION OF TERMS

You should define all key terms central to your study and used throughout your dissertation or master's thesis. The key terms selected to be defined should be chosen based on the following scientific principle: Distinctions are made between a *constitutive definition* and an *operational definition.* A constitutive definition involves using other words to define a term. An operational definition ascribes meaning to a term according to specific operations used to measure it (Kerlinger, 1986). Typically researchers define all variables contained in a research question or hypothesis. You should define attributes of a population, also called *control variables.* And you should define theories and models on which your research is based. Constitutive definitions should be specific (e.g., behavior, knowledge, imitation). Operational definitions (e.g., intelligence, attribution, reinforcement) should be specific enough so that another researcher can replicate your study.

Your definition of terms can be obtained from a dictionary or a professional reference source, such as a handbook or encyclopedia in a specific discipline. Scholars you reference in your dissertation (or thesis) will likely have defined the term in their studies. Also, you can review the various definitions that have surfaced in your review of the literature. List your terms in alphabetical order, with appropriate citations.

An example of definition of terms from Diane Trautman's (2000) dissertation follows. (See Example 6.5.)

Example 6.5

Definition of Terms

To avoid confusion, this study provided definitions and delineations to distinguish between an approach, model, and theory. Additionally, a distinction was made between a leadership, management, and organizational theory. And, finally feminist theory was defined to differentiate a feminine style of leadership and feminist theory. Many people tend to confuse and mix these terms in their studies; therefore, it was necessary to separate them and show them as individual terms.

Approach

An approach is a "theoretical orientation" or "theoretical perspective," not an actual theory (Bogdan & Biklen, 1998). It is similar to a paradigm or a loose collection of logically related assumptions, concepts, or propositions that orient thinking and research (Bogdan & Biklen. 1998). It is a way of examining the world, the assumptions people have about what is important, and what makes the world work.

Model

A model is a construct or diagram that explains the underpinnings of a theory base; however, the model itself is not the theory and therefore will not be tested or validated (Bogdan & Biklen, 1998). Daresh and Playko (1995) describe a model as interrelationships of variables or factors in a theoretical statement depicted graphically. These graphic depictions or theoretical models constitute part of the basic theory-building cycle (Daresh & Playko, 1995). A model is a description used to show complex relationships in easy-to-understand terms (Stoner, Freeman, & Gilbert, 1995).

Theory

"Theory is an attempt to describe phenomena and interrelationships found in the real world in terms that reflect the true nature of the world"

(Daresh & Playko, 1995, p. 72). One approach to theory development is to start by formulating a theory and then submitting it to a test by collecting empirical data. This process includes three steps: (1) formulation of a hypothesis, (2) deduction of observable consequences of the hypothesis, and (3) testing of the hypothesis by making observations and collecting research data (Gall, Borg, & Gall, 1996). Theory often serves as the basis for further empirical research, in which "theory-testing and theory-verification" is a stated goal and leads to the generation of new research (Daresh & Playko, 1995, p. 73).

Macro Organizational Behavior

This type of organizational behavior is described as structures and processes within major subsystems, organizations, and their environments, and the linkages between them (Miles, 1980). It focuses on the broader definition of organizational behavior (Robbins, 1990).

Micro Organizational Behavior

Micro organizational behavior looks at structures and processes (cognitive, emotional, and physical) within individuals, small groups, and their leaders, and the linkages between them (Miles, 1980). The focus here is on relatively isolated or immediate social settings (Robbins, 1990).

Organizational Theory

Organizational theory can be defined as the discipline that studies the structure and design of organizations, referring to the descriptive and prescriptive aspects of the discipline (Robbins, 1990). This type of theory describes how organizations are actually structured and offers suggestions on how they can improve their effectiveness (Robbins, 1990). It can also be thought of as a group of related concepts, principles, and hypotheses that is used to explain the characteristics of organization and how they behave (Hodge & Anthony, 1991). Organizational theory takes a macro perspective, because it is concerned with the overall organization's ability to adapt and achieve its goals (Robbins, 1990).

Organizational Behavior

Organizational behavior presents a micro view by emphasizing individuals and small groups; it focuses on behavior in organizations and a narrow set of employee behaviors such as employee productivity, absenteeism, turnover, and job satisfaction (Robbins, 1990). Individual behavior topics in organizational behavior include perception, values, learning, motivation, and personality (Robbins, 1990). Others define organizational behavior by four processes: individual processes, group and interpersonal processes, organizational processes, and organizational issues (Hellriegel, Slocum, & Woodman, 1998).

Feminist Organizational Theory

Feminist organizational theory examines and critiques current organizational bureaucracy and hierarchy and contests the ideal of impersonal, role based, and instrumental social relations characteristic of bureaucracy (Morgen, 1994). This theory asserts that organizations of any kind should pay attention to the personal needs of members, not just the instrumental needs of the organization (Morgen, 1994). This type of organizational theory would take a micro view because of its concern with the individual needs and interpersonal processes (Miles, 1980).

Management Theory

Management theory is an explanation of how managers behave and management behavior consists of the things a manager does in carrying out his or her responsibilities (Hodge & Anthony, 1991). The basic activities of a manager are planning, organizing, leading and controlling (Stoner et al., 1995). These activities can be grouped into two basic functions: decision making and influence (Hodge & Anthony, 1991). All organizations require managerial functions; therefore, management theory is the study of how managers consciously and continually shape organizations (Stoner et al.).

Leadership Theory

Leadership theory is the study of leader behavior and its effects on the organization (Lunenburg & Ornstein, 2000). Where managers are concerned with shaping the structures and processes of the organization to produce desired results, leaders have a commitment or vision and inspire others to follow it (Lunenburg & Ornstein, 2000). Stanford et al. (1995) contend that there are three classifications of leadership theories: personal behavior theories, trait theories, and contingency theories. Personal behavior theories focus on what the leader does to carry out the managerial job; trait theories describe certain inherent characteristics that will make individuals effective leaders; and contingency theories hypothesize that the situation is the main determinant of what constitutes an effective leader (Stanford et al.).

Feminist Theory

According to Rosemarie Tong (1989) in her book *Feminist Thought*, there are several types of feminist theory including liberal, Marxist, radical, psychoanalytic, socialist, existentialist, and postmodern. This study would be concerned with liberal feminist theory, which states that because society believes that females are by nature less intellectually and or/physically capable than males, it excludes them from the academy, the forum, and the marketplace (Tong, 1989). As a result of this exclusion, the true potential of women goes unfulfilled (Tong, 1989).

Feminine Leadership Theory

A feminine-inclusive leadership theory can be defined as a leadership theory that takes into consideration the female perspective and experience yet can be applied to both males and females. It includes a leadership and management style that reflects the current leadership paradigm of site-based decision making, collaborative arrangements, empowerment of employees, and strong interpersonal skills that promote a shared vision (Brown & Irby, 1994).

Androcentric

> Androcentric is used to show a male-biased or man-centered view of the world (Shakeshaft, 1989). To label a theory or concept androcentric is an attempt to establish parameters for the consumer to internalize and apply the results as well as heighten the awareness of producer and consumer as to the limitations of a one-sided system of knowledge. (Trautman, 2000, pp. 15–19)

Trautman's dissertation was an initial test of a new gender-inclusive leadership theory, namely the synergistic leadership theory (Irby, Brown, & Trautman, 1999; see also, Irby, Brown, Duffy, & Trautman, 2002). Therefore, it was necessary for her to provide rather extensive definitions of important concepts related to theories in general, leadership theory, and feminine theory. Most dissertations and master's theses will not require such extensive definitions as presented here. Note that Trautman (2000) used appropriate citations to define her terms. This is standard practice when using technical terms.

THEORETICAL FRAMEWORK

A theory is an organized body of interrelated concepts, assumptions, and generalizations that systematically explains regularities in behavior. Thus, a sociological theory may attempt to explain the relationship between home conditions and child-abuse behavior of a parent. A psychological theory may identify factors affecting antisocial behavior. An educational theory may propose how teachers' collective efficacy in a school may affect students' academic achievement in that school. Theory can provide a framework to generate hypotheses or research questions. In turn, they guide significant parts of the research design, including the data collection, data analysis, and presentation and interpretation of the findings.

Your task is to find a theoretical framework within which to pursue your study. One way to select an appropriate theoretical framework for your study is to review the related literature. As you review the literature, ask yourself: Is there a theory, or a variation of some theory to which my study has reference? You may find theories, which you will test empirically, revise, extend, or create. Make a note of these. You may not find a specific theory in the literature; rather, the comprehensive review of the literature may need to serve as the theoretical framework.

If you are seeking direct answers to certain questions, it may not be necessary to state hypotheses and design your study to test them. If you believe, however, that relationships may exist between variables, based on theory, or if it appears that one variable may be the cause of another, a hypothesis may be the best way to state what you are attempting to find. We encourage you to consult with your dissertation or master's thesis chair whether a given research problem might be better approached through formulating hypotheses or by posing research questions.

Many quantitative studies are designed to test a theory that has been developed to explain regularities in behavior. Such theory-driven studies will use hypotheses as the starting point for designing the research methodology. Qualitative research studies might be informed by a theoretical or epistemological framework, but formal hypotheses are not typically used to frame the study (Gall et al., 2007). An exception is a type of qualitative research that is framed within grounded theory methodology. In this qualitative research tradition, studies can be designed so that data are collected first, and then a theory is derived from those data. The resulting theory is called grounded theory, because it is grounded in a set of real-world data (Denzin & Lincoln, 2005; Glaser, 1978).

MODELS

When you are concerned with a larger picture than the relationship between two variables in a quantitative study, and you begin to look at interrelationships among a set of variables, you are involved in the construction of models. Thus, in an effort to synthesize separate pieces of a larger picture, you construct a representation of how each variable influences and/or is influenced by other variables. Usually this results in the construction of a model with arrows indicating direction of influence. Your task in a quantitative dissertation (or thesis) is to provide evidence of relationships, direction, and size. Most such dissertation models are quite simple; confirming complex relationships requires large-scale studies unlikely to be undertaken by doctoral or master's students (Krathwohl & Smith, 2005).

An example of theoretical framework from Vickie Basham's (1988) dissertation follows. (See Example 6.6.)

Example 6.6

Theoretical Framework

With the emphasis on accountability in education today, school administrators are faced with the challenge of developing and implementing educational systems that are effective and efficient. Local, state, and federal mandates are requiring increased justification and documentation of program results. Communities are questioning school district programs, policies, and procedures. Parents and other constituencies are demanding grater participation in school programs. Educational administrators must respond by devising more effective methods of administrative management. Strategic planning is considered to be important to effective administrative management (Ivancevich et al., 1980, p. 52; Huntsman, 1986, pp. 11–12).

For planning to be effective, it needs to eventually affect students in some way. In describing the first step in providing instructional leadership, Wallace (1985) asserted that "one must begin with an analysis of standardized tests results" (p. 7). No planning process in education is complete unless a direct attempt is made, through goal setting, to improve student academic learning (Lewis, 1983, p. 68). William Bennett (1988), former Secretary of Education, proclaimed the importance of student achievement when he said, "And the entire project of American education—at every level—remains insufficiently accountable for the result that matters most: student learning" (p. 2).

While business has devoted a great deal of attention to strategic planning (Camilus, 1986; Gardner et al., 1986; Pfeiffer, 1986; Bryce, 1987; Below et al., 1987; Morrissey et al., 1988), it is only recently that any emphasis has been placed on the study of strategic planning in school settings. And the investigation of the relationship between strategic planning and student achievement has been neglected. The research reported here seeks, on a modest scale, to begin to remedy that situation. More specifically, this study examined relationships among three broad sets of variables: (1) strategic planning in school districts; (2) school district achievement in reading, language arts, and mathematics; and (3) ten school district financial and demographic factors including (a) current expenses, (b) pupil-teacher ratio, (c) cost of instruction, (d) dropout rate, (e) percent Local Education Agency (LEA) supplement for instructional salaries, (f) percent economically deprived, (g) local financial index, (h) attendance rate, (i) assessed property value per child, and (j) percent revenue from local sources.

No other study shows a direct tie-in between strategic planning in school districts and school district performance on standardized achievement tests (or results management), which constitutes what might be referred to as an Interrelated Planning Process. A strategic planning model was devised to guide the research. (See [Figure 6.1].) The strategic planning model incorporates the three broad sets of variables, which were examined in this study. As shown in the model, strategic planning begins with a mission statement consisting of beliefs and goals of the school district's personnel, which provide guidelines for conducting a critical analysis of the internal and external environments, preparing planning assumptions, selecting action goals, developing objectives and evaluation procedures, designing an action plan, and monitoring and reporting results.

As shown in [Figure 6.1], I have placed student achievement and the other ten selected demographic and financial school district factors in the context of a macroenvironment. Within that context these variables represent an important consideration of the strategic planning process and actions initiated to effect school district plans by analyzing, synthesizing, and evaluating this environment. (Basham, 1988, pp. 11–13)

Basham's dissertation is an example of the use of a model to synthesize the interrelationships among a large set of variables. You do not necessarily have to use a model when describing your theoretical framework.

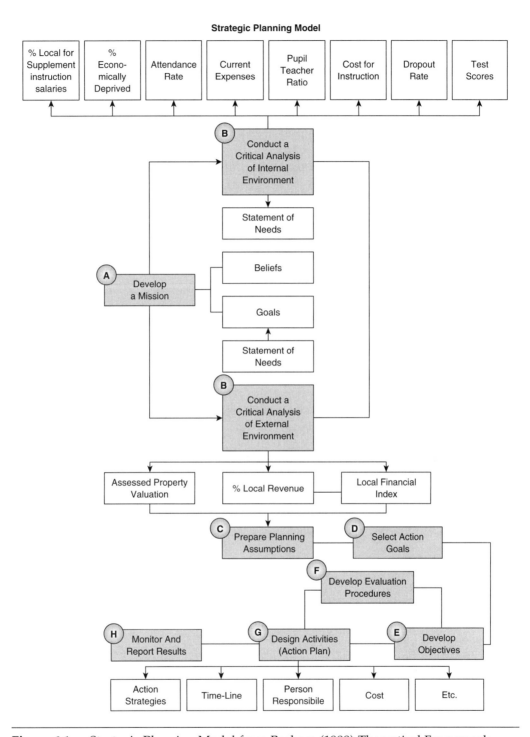

Figure 6.1   Strategic Planning Model from Basham (1988) Theoretical Framework

However, a model is useful if your study involves a number of interrelated variables.

RESEARCH QUESTIONS (OR HYPOTHESES)

Research questions and hypotheses are critical components of the dissertation or master's thesis. Teamed with a tightly drawn theoretical framework, the research questions or hypotheses become a "directional beam for the study." In essence, the research questions or hypotheses should flow directly from the preceding theoretical framework and identify questions that have not been addressed previously or remain unanswered in the literature. Your committee members should be able to understand how your theoretical framework has led to the research questions (and, subsequently, the research hypotheses, if you choose to use them).

Your committee members should be able to learn a great deal about your study simply by reading the research questions or hypotheses. For example, committee members should be able to identify independent and dependent variables; whether the focus of the study is descriptive, relationship, or difference oriented; what types of analysis will be used to examine each research question or hypothesis; the sample size that will be needed to adequately test the research questions or hypotheses; what literature should be reviewed; and forecast elements of the results and discussion chapters.

As mentioned previously, qualitative studies might be informed by a theoretical or epistemological framework, but formal hypotheses are not typically used to frame the study (Gall et al., 2007). Moreover, in some qualitative traditions, studies can be designed so that data are collected first, and a theory is derived from those data (Denzin & Lincoln, 2005; Glaser, 1978). We now turn to the types of research questions used in both the quantitative and qualitative traditions.

Types of Research Questions

Technically, a research question, in the quantitative tradition, explores the relationships between and among variables (Heppner & Heppner, 2004; Heppner, Kivlighan, & Wampold, 1999). For example, a research question could be: Is there a relationship between teachers' collective efficacy in a school and students' academic achievement in that school? Drew (1980) identified three general categories of research questions: descriptive, relationship, and difference.

Descriptive Questions

Descriptive questions ask what some phenomena are like. With descriptive questions, researchers collect information from interviews, questionnaires, observation, or document analysis. Such questions can be either quantitative or qualitative in nature. Rarely do descriptive questions involve experimental research. An example of a descriptive question might be: What are the coping processes ethnic, racial minority students use in response to the stressors of acculturation when attending a predominantly White college or university? Such a question could be examined using either a quantitative or qualitative methodology. For more on this topic, see Creighton's (2006) dissertation.

Relationship Questions

Relationship questions examine the degree to which two or more variables are related to each other. The essential feature is some kind of correlation between two variables. Although this was not the major focus of Creighton's dissertation, an example of a relationship question with her topic would be: Is there a relationship between stressors of acculturation and psychological distress of ethnic, racial minority students attending a predominantly White college or university?

Difference Questions

Difference questions examine whether differences exist between or within individual groups or participants. The essential feature in difference questions is some type of comparison. Such questions can be either quantitative or qualitative in nature. Again, this was not the major focus of Creighton's dissertation, but it was a component within her study. An example of a difference question with her topic would be: Are there differences in stressors of acculturation for ethnic, racial minority students attending a predominantly White college or university as compared to those attending a culturally diverse, urban college or university? This question could be examined using either a quantitative or qualitative methodology.

At this point, you must describe whether you will be asking a description question, a relationship question, or a difference question. Write down the question. Do not worry about form right now. Identify each type of research question you write. It is possible for you to have all three types of research questions addressed in the same dissertation or master's thesis.

Writing research questions for a dissertation (or thesis) is not a linear process; instead it is an iterative process. As you become more knowledgeable about your topic, you will be able to write clear, concise, and meaningful research questions. It usually takes several rewrites to develop research questions that are optimally clear and concise. In addition, different types of research questions require different types of research designs, and different types of data collection and data analysis procedures.

Specifying Research Hypotheses

Research questions ask about relationships among variables. Hypotheses are more precise. They speculate about the nature of these relationships. Research hypotheses predict an expected relationship between variables. The following examples illustrate the point.

Research Questions:

1. Is there a relationship between teachers' collective efficacy in a school and students' academic achievement in the school?

2. Is there a relationship between external pressure from the community on their schools and students' academic achievement in the schools?

Research Hypotheses:

1. The greater the teachers' collective efficacy in a school, the higher the level of students' academic achievement in the school.

2. The greater the external pressure from the community on their schools, the higher the level of students' academic achievement in the schools.

A few observations can be made about the aforementioned examples of research questions and research hypotheses. First, each research question and research hypothesis clearly and concisely describe a relationship between variables. Second, each research question and hypothesis is testable; that is, it can be measured empirically. Third, carefully drafted hypotheses are more precise statements than research questions. Moreover, research hypotheses can be grouped into the same three categories as research questions: descriptive, relationship and difference hypotheses.

Some dissertations and theses are exploratory in nature. Exploratory studies are based on little, if any, theory or previous research. For exploratory studies, it is not always possible to formulate hypotheses, because theoretical support for the hypotheses cannot be provided. You should state hypotheses only for those problem statements for which you can provide a rationale from your theoretical framework. Furthermore, qualitative research studies might be informed by a theory, but formal hypotheses are not typically used to frame the study. However, in qualitative research framed within grounded theory methodology, hypotheses may be the outcome of the study rather than used to frame the study at the outset (Gall et al., 2007).

Write hypotheses in the present tense and as positive assertions. Avoid using the words *significant* or *significance* in a research question or hypothesis. The terms *significant* and *significance* usually refer to tests of statistical significance. Most empirical studies include these tests; therefore, reference to them in hypotheses is not necessary. Your committee members will assume that the issue of statistical significance will be handled in the results chapter of a quantitative dissertation or master's thesis.

Qualitative studies usually do not contain hypotheses derived from theory or previous research. Nevertheless, if your study is qualitative, you need to state a research question at the outset of your study, even if the question is quite general. Qualitative researchers typically "follow the data." That means that during the course of their interviews they may shift directions based on initial respondents' replies, change the nature of the questions for subsequent respondents, and as a result, they might modify their initial research question. In quantitative research, however, the specific research design, including hypotheses or research questions, is very seldom modified during the course of the study.

Some dissertations contain both research questions and research hypotheses. In this case, researchers use research questions as more general investigatory themes, which are then followed by specific research hypotheses that make predictions in a testable form. Two dissertation examples from our students in which both research questions and research hypotheses (or null hypotheses) were used follow.

The first example is from Vicki Stanfield's (2000) dissertation. (See Example 6.7.)

Example 6.7

Research Questions

The following research questions were addressed to determine which, if any, of the 19 scales of the College Student Inventory distinguish enrollment status and academic success in students attending community colleges:

1. What differences exist between students attending community colleges who persist, (also called persisters), and nonpersisters (those who drop out)?

2. What differences exist between academically successful students and academically unsuccessful students attending community colleges? (Stanfield, 2000, p. 5)

Hypotheses

In order to determine whether the College Student Inventory distinguishes enrollment status and academic success in community college students, the following two null hypotheses were tested.

Null Hypothesis 1. There is no difference between students who persist (persisters) and those who do not persist (dropouts) on all 19 scales of the College Student Inventory.

Null Hypothesis 2. There is no difference between academically successful students and academically unsuccessful students on all 19 scales of the College Student Inventory. (Stanfield, 2000, p. 62)

Another example of the use of both research questions and research hypotheses (or null hypotheses) comes from Sally Craycraft's (1999) dissertation. (See Example 6.8.)

Research Questions

The major question guiding this study was to discover what patterns of brain dominance are exhibited by school superintendents and business chief executive officers. The three specific research questions addressed were:

Question 1. What are the brain dominance preferences of school superintendents and chief executive officers?

Question 2. Which brain dominance patterns are most prevalent among school superintendents and chief executive officers?

Question 3. What differences exist between dominance profiles in terms of (a) affiliation (business or education), (b) gender, (c) years of experience, and (d) age? (Craycraft, 1999, pp. 10–11)

In answer to these questions, it was important to determine where "pronounced" (statistically significant) differences exist between the various groups (school superintendents and chief executive officers and between males and females) followed by post hoc tests and descriptive analyses to assess the basis of dissimilarities/differences. The hypotheses to be tested that provided key insight where "pronounced" differences exist between the brain profiles of the various groups were:

Null Hypothesis 1. There is no difference in brain dominance preferences exhibited between school superintendents and chief executive officers.

Null Hypothesis 2. There is no difference in brain quadrant scores between school superintendents and chief executive officers.

Null Hypothesis 3. There is no difference in brain quadrant scores between males and females in both groups of leaders.

Null Hypothesis 4. There is no difference in brain quadrant scores due to experience level.

Null Hypothesis 5. Age is not an influence in determining brain quadrant scores. (Craycraft, 1999, p. 66)

Both students used research questions in Chapter One and null hypotheses in Chapter Four of their dissertations when they presented and analyzed their data. You may wish to review the use of research questions, directional hypotheses, and null hypotheses, and their use, discussed earlier in this chapter.

Additional Examples of Research Questions

Because the development of research questions is so important when writing a dissertation or master's thesis, examples of research questions extracted from four other dissertations follow. They have used only research questions. The first two examples were based on quantitative studies, and the following two examples were drawn from qualitative studies. From our experience in chairing doctoral dissertations, we have found that most doctoral students have a very difficult time writing clear, concise, and meaningful research questions. The examples that follow may help. (See Examples 6.9, 6.10, 6.11, and 6.12.)

Example 6.9

Quantitative Dissertations:

Research Questions

Following are the seven research questions, which guided this study of content reading area subjects of science and social studies in 17 third grade Spanish/English transitional bilingual classrooms in an urban district in Southeast Texas:

1. Which language of instruction do teachers predominantly use?

2. To what extent is the language of instruction used by teachers associated with language content?

3. To what extent is the language of instruction associated with language mode?

4. To what extent does each level of language content occur with each activity structure?

5. To what extent do associations exist among the following variables: language mode, language content, activity structure, students' language of instruction, and teacher's language of instruction?

6. Is there an association between classroom observations and teachers' perceptions of their language of instruction?

7. What are the associations between the four dimensions of the Transitional Bilingual Protocol (TBP) theory and bilingual student achievement on the high-stakes assessment, Texas Assessment of Academic Skills (TAAS)? (Meyer, 2000, p. 8)

Example 6.10

Research Questions

Quantitative and qualitative data were collected through the Thomas-Kilmann Conflict Mode Instrument (Thomas & Kilmann, 1974), an open-ended protocol, and in conjunction with the Organizational Leadership Effectiveness Inventory (OLEI) (Irby et al., 2002) to answer the following research questions:

1. Is there a difference in gender distribution among conflict management modes of superintendents?

2. Is there a relationship between conflict management modes of female superintendents and the Synergistic Leadership Theory?

3. Is there a relationship between conflict management modes of male superintendents and the Synergistic Leadership Theory?

4. Is there a relationship among gender, conflict management modes, and the four factors of the Synergistic Leadership Theory. (Truslow, 2004, p. 5)

Example 6.11

Qualitative Dissertations:

Research Questions

Four research questions guided my dissertation:

1. What are the leadership behaviors of the superintendent?

2. Is the organizational structure of each district aligned with the superintendent's leadership behaviors?

3. How do the leadership behaviors of the superintendent impact the relations between the district and external forces?

4. Are the attitudes, values, and beliefs of the superintendent aligned to the attitudes, values, and beliefs of the school board member and the administrative team member? (Bamberg, 2004, p. 12)

Example 6.12

Research Questions

The following research questions guided my study:

1. What are doctoral students', recent graduates', and program directors' perceptions of positive and negative aspects of the cohort structure used in educational leadership programs in six universities?

2. What recommendations do doctoral cohort students, recent graduates, and program directors make to improve their respective doctoral programs?

3. What recommendations do doctoral cohort students, recent graduates, and program directors make to those people entertaining a doctoral endeavor?

4. What are the perceptions of doctoral cohort students, recent graduates, and program directors concerning the dissertation stage of the doctorate within a cohort structure? (Miller, 2003, p. 3)

Note that we have provided examples of research questions from quantitative, qualitative, and mixed methods dissertations. These can serve as models for your own work.

LIMITATIONS

Limitations of a study are not under the control of the researcher. Limitations are factors that may have an effect on the interpretation of the findings or on the generalizability of the results. Limitations may arise from the methodology, data, or method of analysis. For example, the findings of a case study cannot be generalized to an entire population. Data derived from a study of drug use in an attendance area of a large, urban school district may not be representative of all school age children in the United States or in other school districts in the same state, or even in other schools within the same school district. A finding that school size correlates negatively with student behavior problems may not justify the inference that small schools cause student behavior problems. You need to state the limitations of your study to avoid misinterpretation of the findings as illustrated in the aforementioned examples.

An example of limitations from Clark's (2002) dissertation follows. (See Example 6.13.)

Example 6.13

Limitations

The study has the following limitations:

1. The financial information obtained in PEIMS comes directly from 1,042 school districts in Texas. This information could vary because of variations in the local interpretation of expenditures.

2. The sample of school districts was drawn from a single state; therefore, results may not be generalizeable to all states.

3. Many variables outside the control of the researcher could impact the student achievement and financial information. These variables may include: uncontrollable variations in the prices that school districts pay for various resources, ancillary services provided by the district, the quality of the school facilities, the quality of the instructional programs, parental involvement in the district, graduation rates, course-completion rates, honors program enrollments, and the diversity of course offerings.

4. There are statistical and design problems inherent with correlation studies. (Clark, 2002, pp. 18–19)

DELIMITATIONS

Delimitations are self-imposed boundaries set by the researcher on the purpose and scope of the study. Studies in the social and behavioral sciences typically have many variables that could be affected by circumstances of time, location, populations, or environment (including both physical and social conditions). For example, let's examine the dissertation title of one of our doctoral students: "Principal Leadership, Trust, and Teacher Efficacy" (Azodi, 2006). The title is clear and concise, and it describes the three major variables examined in the study. We have no quarrel with the title. Using it to illustrate elements of a study's delimitations, there is no indication therein of the characteristics of the population or sample. Is it restricted to school principals in the United States, Texas, or Harris County? Does the sample include elementary school principals, middle school principals, high school principals, or all three levels? Does the sample include urban, suburban, and rural schools or merely big city schools? Does the sample include ethnic, racial minorities and gender diversity consistent with the population? Is the time period over a shorter or longer duration—one month? Six months? One year? Five years? The point is that boundaries and qualifications are inherent in every study, which must be noted in this section of the dissertation or master's thesis.

An example of delimitations from Craig Coleman's (2003) dissertation follows. (See Example 6.14.)

Example 6.14

Delimitations

The delimitations utilized by the researcher in this study were determined by a desire to better gain an understanding of the complete relationship that exists between the superintendent and the school board, and how that relationship affects student achievement. In order to gain the perspectives of superintendents and school boards, the researcher only sought participants in the study who were superintendents and school board members of public schools. This use of public schools in this study did not allow the researcher to gain the views of those individuals involved in private and charter schools located in the state.

A second delimitation used by the researcher was the use of only school board presidents as participants. Due to the nature of the board presidents' role, the president serves as the spokesperson for the Board of Trustees.

The nature and closeness of the relationship that is required between the superintendent and school board president in fulfilling the responsibilities of the district, led the researcher to analyze only those superintendents and school board presidents that had a relationship of working as a leadership team for a period of three or more years. The researcher believed, based upon the work of Senge (1990) and Nygren (1992), that the process of creating a successful organizational system required an extended period of time, and, in order to gain a true picture of the leadership team, determined to only use those teams that had been in their current positions together for a period of three or more continuous years. (Coleman, 2003, pp. 13–14)

ASSUMPTIONS

Assumptions are postulates, premises, and propositions that are accepted as operational for purposes of the research. Assumptions include the nature, analysis, and interpretation of the data. For example, "This sample is typical of the total population" (nature); "this instrument will measure what it purports to measure when applied to these data" (analysis); "this criterion is valid when applied to these findings" (interpretation). Assumptions influence the entire research endeavor. Specifically, delineation of assumptions provides a basis for formulating research questions or stating hypotheses and for interpreting data resulting from the study; and assumptions provide meaning to the conclusions and lend support to the recommendations.

An example of assumptions from Scott Barrett's (2000) dissertation follows. (See Example 6.15.)

Example 6.15

Assumptions

This study included the following assumptions: (a) the selected principals responded to the survey accurately and indicated their perceptions in the use of a management information system (MIS); (b) the selected principals understood the vocabulary and concepts associated with a management information system and decision making; (c) the data collected measured the knowledge, skills, and perceptions of the principal's involvement in the utilization of a MIS to support decision making; and (d) the interpretation of the data accurately reflected the perceptions of the respondents. (Barrett, 2000, p. 20)

Note how Barrett succinctly described the assumptions of his study, attending to one or more of the critical elements of assumptions (nature, analysis, interpretation) delineated above.

ORGANIZATION OF THE STUDY

Each chapter of a dissertation or master's thesis contains three main sections: the *introduction*, where you tell your readers what you are going to tell them; the *body*, where you tell them; and the *summary*, where you tell them what you told them. However, because Chapter One is titled "Introduction," it does not begin with the heading "Introduction" like the chapters of a dissertation or master's thesis that follow; nor does it end with the heading "Summary." Instead it begins with the heading "Background of the Study" and ends with the heading "Organization of the Study." This section of a dissertation or master's thesis describes the content found in subsequent chapters of the entire dissertation or master's thesis.

An example of organization of the study from Donna Azodi's (2006) dissertation follows. (See Example 6.16.)

Example 6.16

Organization of the Study

This research study is presented in five chapters. Chapter I includes the background of the study, statement of the problem, purpose of the study, significance of the study, definition of terms, theoretical framework, research questions, limitations, delimitations, and the assumptions of the study.

Chapter II presents a review of the literature, which includes efficacy theory, teacher efficacy, principal leadership, trust, and principal trust. Chapter III describes the methodology used for this research study. It includes the selection of participants, instrumentation, data collection, and data analysis procedures.

Chapter IV presents the study's findings including demographic information, testing the research questions, confirmatory factor analysis, and results of the data analyses for the three research questions. Chapter V provides a summary of the entire study, discussion of the findings, implications of the findings for theory and practice, recommendations for further research, and conclusions. (Azodi, 2006, p. 17)

SUMMARY

In this chapter, we discussed the contents that should appear in Chapter One of a dissertation or master's thesis. Chapter One contains an orientation to your study. In Chapter One, you describe the background of the study, statement of the problem, purpose of the study, significance of the study, definition of terms, theoretical framework, research questions or hypotheses, limitations, delimitations, and assumptions, and you conclude the chapter with an organization of the study. We provided dissertation examples from some of our doctoral students to illustrate each section of the dissertation or master's thesis we described. The next chapter contains advice on reviewing the literature and writing the literature review chapter.

7

Writing the Literature Review Chapter

The review of the literature will provide the basic rationale for your research from which will emerge the statement of the problem, research questions or hypotheses, and design of your study. Therefore, we recommend that you begin work on Chapter Two, "Review of the Literature," prior to writing Chapter One, for you will need to know the theory and previous research relevant to your problem.

The review of the literature can illuminate every aspect of a research problem by (a) providing a historical background for it, (b) describing its current status, (c) supporting the purpose of the study, (d) identifying gaps in the literature, (e) becoming aware of variables relevant to the problem, (f) understanding the seminal studies widely cited, (g) identifying the leading scholars relevant to the problem, (h) proposing useful theoretical constructs for the study, (i) understanding the application of appropriate methodological procedures, and (j) observing comparative studies that assist in analyzing your data and interpreting the results. Thus, a properly executed review of the literature becomes a potent unifying element through its interrelationships with other sections of the dissertation or master's thesis.

In the first part of this chapter, we provide an introduction on how to systematically search and review the literature for a dissertation or master's thesis. In the second part of the chapter, we provide you with techniques to help you write a clear and effective Review of the Literature Chapter. We conclude the chapter with several additional strategies to help you critically, synthesize empirical research reports, which will constitute the body of your literature review. We provide examples from dissertations and from published articles that you can use as models in writing your Review of the Literature Chapter.

SEARCHING THE LITERATURE

To conduct a thorough review of the literature, you need to examine a broad range of sources that are directly related to your problem. These sources include: (a) handbooks and encyclopedias, (b) annual reviews, (c) review articles, (d) abstracting and indexing services, (e) government documents, and (f) major public search engines. None of these sources alone will provide a thorough review of the literature. However, by using all of them together, you will ensure a reasonably comprehensive review of the literature. It is possible to search a wide variety of these sources online, providing your university library subscribes to the various electronic databases. In addition to the aforementioned six sources, many of which contain empirical studies, utilize journals in your field as well. A discussion of the use of professional journals in your literature search is provided in Chapter 1 under the heading "Sources of Topics," subheading "Professional Journals."

Handbooks and Encyclopedias

Handbooks and encyclopedias provide an excellent place to begin your literature search. Handbooks and encyclopedias summarize major research contributions in specific areas. Specialized topics, contained in these sources, are written by experts in the field. Chapters contained within these sources provide extensive references related to important research in a specialized area. You can follow the references later. Examples of handbooks and encyclopedias in education and related fields are the *Handbook of Research on Teaching, Handbook of Research on Educational Administration, Handbook of Industrial and Organizational Psychology, Handbook of Social Psychology, Handbook of Qualitative Research, Encyclopedia of Educational Research*, and *Encyclopedia of Educational Leadership and Administration*. The contents of handbooks and encyclopedias are usually not provided online, but instead are housed in your library's reference section.

Annual Reviews

Annual reviews are published yearly and provide comprehensive reviews of the literature on specific topics. These topical reviews are written by specialists in the field. Annual reviews can be excellent resources if your topic has been reviewed recently. Not only do these annual reviews provide comprehensive reviews on a specific topic, but also they provide prototypes for how to write a critical review of the literature. Examples, of annual reviews in education and related fields are the *Review of Educational Research, Harvard Educational Review, Annual Review of Anthropology, Annual Review of Psychology, Annual Review of Sociology,* and the annual yearbooks of the *National Society for the Study of Education.*

Review Articles

Another excellent source for a literature search are review articles. Some journals in education and related fields periodically devote entire issues of the journal to specific topics. These are comprehensive reviews of research on a specific topic. They include *Educational Leadership, Educational and Urban Society, National Association of Secondary School Principals Bulletin, Phi Delta Kappan, Psychological Bulletin,* and *The Counseling Psychologist.* Some universities, such as the University of Minnesota, Pennsylvania State University, and others, offer a monograph series devoted to a specific topic. For example, one of the authors of this book used University of Minnesota *Research Monograph*s Nos. *1, 2,* and *3* devoted to organizational climate and *Pennsylvania State University Studies No. 24* on pupil control ideology as background information for his dissertation: *Organizational Climate, Dogmatism, and Pupil Control Ideology* (Lunenburg, 1972).

Abstracting and Indexing Services

Abstracting and indexing services can assist you with your literature search. For example, the Educational Resources Information Center (ERIC) is a major clearinghouse for literature related to education. PsycINFO (*Psychological Abstracts*) and Sociofile (Sociological Abstracts*)* respectively contain abbreviated abstracts from psychological and sociological journals, and indexes these abstracts by topic and author. Dissertation Abstracts International is a similar reference source for dissertations. Psych Books indexes chapters in books.

Another very useful abstracting and indexing service is Social Scisearch (*Social Science Citation Index*). It covers the social and behavioral sciences literature and permits you to search who has cited a particular article since its publication. For example, if you were examining the relationship between teachers' collective efficacy and students' academic achievement, you would probably find that Bandura's social learning theory is cited by numerous authors of research articles. You will want to locate the pivotal article written by Bandura that was published several years ago. By using Social Scisearch, you can identify other literature in which Bandura's article has since been cited.

Also published by the Institute for Scientific Information (ISI), Inc., are two other citation indexes. The *Science Citation Index* covers the current literature in more than 100 fields of science and technology. The *Arts and Humanities Citation Index* thoroughly covers the current literature in the arts and humanities field. Using all three of these citations indexes, you can cover most of the journal literature you will probably care to search. Moreover, to keep you abreast of the very latest developments in the field, *Current Contents: Social and Behavioral Sciences* indexes the most recent tables of contents from the major journals in the social and behavioral sciences.

You may also find *Business Periodicals Index* useful for searching industrial and organizational topics. Other useful abstracting and indexing services include CINAHL (nursing, allied health, biomedical, and consumer health), LLBA (linguistics and language behavior abstracts), Medline (nursing, public health, medicine), MLA (literature, language, linguistics, and folklore), NCJRS (corrections, drugs and crime, juvenile justice, law enforcement, statistics, and victims), PAIS International (social sciences, emphasis on contemporary society, economics, political issues, and on public policy), *Social Sciences Abstracts* (sociology, psychology, anthropology, geography, economics, political science, and law), and *Social Work Abstracts* (social work and related fields).

Table 7.1 shows the range of database resources available in the social and behavioral sciences in most research university libraries. This list is not exhaustive; in fact, many large research libraries will have many more research services than are listed in this table.

As you examine your sources, make a list of authors who have been important contributors to the literature in your area. Using a variety of search engines, search by author's name. Most library databases allow you to conduct both topical and author searchers. OVID is one of the broader search engines that allow you to search by topics and authors. Searching documents by key authors may identify additional publications that were omitted from your previous searches.

Government Documents

Government documents are another useful source of information. Government documents provide a massive amount of information that is published regularly. Various government agencies also have created Web sites (see, e.g., http://www.firstgov.gov) on which they post newly funded projects. Two excellent search tools for government documents are the *Monthly Catalog of Government Documents* and the *Index to U.S. Government Periodicals.* Some university libraries may have an online electronic database, such as *Government Documents Index.*

FedStats is a valuable source of statistical information on the Web. At http://www.fedstats.gov, you can access statistics from more than 100 federal agencies. The FedStats search engine automatically searches all agencies for relevant links to federal statistics—you no longer have to search each government agency separately.

State and local governments (including public and private universities) frequently post recent statistics on the Web. Thus, you can obtain more current statistical information from nonfederal government sources.

Table 7.1   Selected Library Databases

Anthropological Abstracts

Arts and Humanities Citation Index

Business Periodicals Index

CINAHL

Current Contents: Social and Behavioral Sciences

Dissertation Abstracts International

ERIC

LLBA

Medline

MLA

NCJRS

PAIS International

PsycBOOKS

Psychological Abstracts

Science Citation Index

Social Science Citation Index

Social Sciences Abstracts

Social Work Abstracts

Sociological Abstracts

This is because the federal government collects data periodically, with years intervening in some cases (e.g., the national census). Local agencies must report timely information to their superordinates, such as mayors and city councils.

Major Public Search Engines

Major search engines used by the public at large can also provide helpful information for use in literature reviews for dissertations and master's theses. You can use search engines (browsers) such as Microsoft Explorer, Netscape, Opera, or Safari to search for information on a variety of topics using keywords, wherever the search engine has indexed the Web. AltaVista, Ask.com, Google, and Yahoo! are popular search engines. Furthermore, meta search engines such as Alltheweb.com, Dogpile, Metacrawler, and Vivisimo simultaneously submit your search to multiple search engines. Other useful sources for additional reading on literature searches are Heppner and Heppner (2004); Krathwohl and Smith (2005); and Reed and Baxter (2003).

When sorting through a long list of Web sites retrieved by a search engine, note the extensions in your Web searches. The extension *edu* in a URL means "education," *gov* means "government," *org* means "organization," *net* means "network," and *com* means "commercial." You should begin your search with those URLs with extensions of *edu* and *gov*, because these will likely produce more relevant research information pertaining to your topic. The other extensions may be useful as well.

In sum, computerized searches using search engines can be very helpful in conducting a literature search. Many search engines have an accompanying thesaurus, such as the *Thesaurus of ERIC Descriptors* for educational topics or the *Psychological Abstracts Thesaurus of Psychological Index Terms* for psychological topics. Keywords must be used to enter online electronic databases such as those listed in Table 7.1.

Finding the right keywords is the key to a productive computer search. This is not easy. It may take considerable trial and error to determine the most appropriate keywords to use. Here are a few tips: Begin by underlining the keywords in the working title of your dissertation or master's thesis. For example, the dissertation title of one of our doctoral students is *Principal Leadership, Trust, and Teacher Efficacy* (Azodi, 2006). Logical keywords for her literature search would be *principal leadership, trust,* and *teacher efficacy.* (Brief titles help considerably when doing computerized literature searches. We find that most dissertation titles are much too long.) Another method of locating keywords is to find abstracts of journal articles pertinent to your topic. Words that surface frequently are typically good keywords to use in a literature search. Still another method to uncover keywords to use in a literature search is to write down the independent and dependent variables used in your study. These probably will be the same or similar to the words used in your title, and they more than likely will be words used in the research questions or hypotheses of a quantitative study. Finally, many journals now list keywords by which the study will be indexed. Nevertheless, a major problem with computerized searches is to believe that you have done a thorough literature search using this method alone. Using all of the six aforementioned methods together will likely result in a reasonably thorough literature search.

WRITING THE LITERATURE REVIEW

At this point, you have searched and reviewed the literature pertaining to your research problem. Now you are ready to begin writing the chapter. Chapter Two, "Review of the Literature," has three distinct parts: the introduction, in which you tell your readers what you are going to tell them; the body, in which you tell them; and the summary, in which you tell them what you told them. Table 7.2 provides an example of the contents of the Review of the Literature Chapter of a dissertation or master's thesis. In any given study, the headings and subheadings contained in the body of the chapter will usually be determined by the variables investigated in the study. Qualitative studies may be organized around themes or participants interviewed.

Table 7.2   Contents for Chapter Two of a Dissertation

CHAPTER II

REVIEW OF THE LITERATURE
   Introduction
   Headings and Subheadings (These will be determined by the type of study being conducted)
   Summary

The Review of the Literature Chapter is often a lengthy chapter in a dissertation or master's thesis. Therefore, is it important to provide a structure that will help you organize and integrate the material you present. The following techniques can be used to organize your Review of the Literature Chapter: (a) organize your material in a funnel, (b) be selective, (c) make an outline, (d) write the introduction, (e) use headings, (f) use transitions, (g) write a summary, and (h) be careful not to plagiarize.

Organize Your Material in a Funnel

A funnel, a structural writing tool, has a wide portion at the top and a narrow portion at the bottom (Heppner & Heppner, 2004; Martin, 1980). The funnel provides a good analogy for the shape of the review of the literature. The idea is that the literature review is organized so that more general information is discussed first, and the information most closely related to the research reported in your thesis or dissertation is discussed last. Your literature review may have four or five sections, each with a heading. Each section (heading) may have one or more subsections (subheadings). That is, divide your review into headings and organize the sections so that the most general material is discussed first, followed by more specific material related to your study. The subsections of the review should be organized in a funnel structure as well.

Specifically, articles of historical interest or the articles utilizing different types of participants or methods than those utilized in your study are presented first. The more recent articles utilizing participants and methods similar to those you are using in your study are then presented.

Each article should not receive the same degree of coverage. An obvious sign of a poorly conducted literature review is one in which all the articles/research reports are given the same coverage and something is said about the participants, method, results, and discussion of each piece of research. Here is a technique you might use in organizing your review. Divide your material into three parts: (a) material that will be described in detail, because it is highly related to your study, (b) material that will be briefly discussed, and (c) material that is tangential to your study, which may or may not be included in your literature review depending on the amount of information available in the literature directly related to your topic.

A common problem of beginning writers is that of providing too much information on a topic and not enough on the specific area that their thesis or dissertation will cover (Heppner & Heppner, 2004). Another common problem of beginning writers is that they frequently switch from the general to the specific and back again to the general. As you are writing your review, think funnel. Look at the shape of your literature review chapter. Do you see the shape of a funnel? Do you begin with more general material and then move toward more specific information until you are providing the research questions or hypotheses of your thesis or dissertation? Do the same for sub-sections of your literature review, again starting from the general and moving to the specifics. The funnel structure is depicted in Figure 7.1.

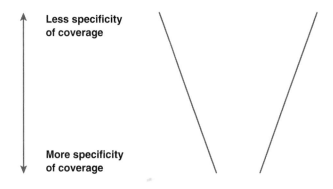

Figure 7.1   The Funnel Structure

Consult models of appropriate writing style and organization. Study the well-integrated reviews of literature found in the *Annual Review of Anthropology, Annual Review of Psychology, Annual Review of Sociology, Review of Educational Research,* the annual yearbooks of the *National Society for the Study of Education,* and other such reviews. These reviews should be used as models of writing style and organization of your literature review and not as material for your own review of the literature. More information on the use of primary sources is provided later in this chapter.

Be Selective

A good literature review needs to be selective. It is permissible to draw upon the research of others and incorporate them into your own thesis or dissertation. This is consistent with the cumulative process that characterizes the development of science (Kuhn, 1962). However, a skillful researcher draws on primary source material rather than relying on review articles and secondary sources. Do not rely on others' descriptions of studies, often referred to as *secondary sources* (Cone & Foster, 2007). If you cannot locate the original article, follow American Psychological Association (APA) guidelines to indicate the citation as a secondary source (e.g., Irby, 2003, cited in Lunenburg, 2008).

A common problem of novice writers is that they sprinkle references liberally around their literature reviews with insufficient thought as to how they fit into the theory or the theme of their study. Make a habit of consistently asking yourself: Why am I including this study or reference? In other words, what is this reference adding to the development of my theory; how does it follow the thread of my dissertation, and how does it relate to my research questions? Examine the reasons why each reference will illuminate or complement your thesis or dissertation. One or more of the following must apply (Swetnam, 2004, p. 77):

- It deals with theory that undergirds your study.
- It makes a definitive statement about an aspect of your study.
- It deals with your subject matter or overlaps it.
- It assists in the maintenance of a coherent argument.
- It puts your study into an external context.
- It defines the current state of research in your area.
- It shows your acknowledgement of the work of others.

As your literature review develops, references should become more specific to the topic, use more journals that are current, move from the general to the specific, and finish with a direct lead-in to your research questions or hypotheses.

You need to adopt a critical perspective in reading and referencing the work of others. Sentences beginning with "Smith found . . ." should be kept to a minimum, because it shifts the focus of the review from your own argument to the work of others. A preferred strategy is to develop a theme and then cite the work of relevant authors to support your argument or to provide examples of your point. In addition, the overuse of quotations tends to limit your own authority. Restrict the use of quotations to proven luminaries on a given topic or that are stated in a unique way that is difficult to recapture (Rudestam & Newton, 2007).

The literature review is not a compilation of facts or narrative, but a coherent argument that leads to a description of your study. There should be no mystery about the direction you are going. A good question to repeatedly ask yourself while writing the review of the literature is: Where am I going with this? State at the outset of the literature review the goal of the review and the structure of your argument. Similarly, each sentence in the dissertation must be there for a purpose. It should never serve as a filler (Rudestam & Newton, 2007). By the end of the literature review, the reader should be aware of the current state of the literature and what you will be doing to extend the state of that knowledge. Your summation of pertinent literature is a significant contribution to the knowledge base.

Make an Outline

Make an outline of the major headings you plan to use in your review of the literature. Developing and following an outline while writing will accomplish two things: (a) It will produce focused, logical prose, and (b) it will help you avoid becoming overwhelmed by the sheer volume of material to be covered in a lengthy review of the literature. Example 7.1 shows an outline of Linda Creighton's (2006) Review of the Literature Chapter. Note that Creighton has divided her literature review chapter into 44 headings and subheadings. This gives her chapter coherence. Coherence is how well a chapter holds together as a unified document. Headings and subheadings help to unify a document's structure and keep the reader focused, as do transitions. (See Example 7.1.)

Example 7.1

Outline

   I. Introduction

  II. Retaining African American Students
     A. Pre-Entry Attributes
     B. Goals and Commitments
     C. Institutional Experiences
     D. Personal and Normative Integration

 III. Issues Impacting Hispanic College Student Retention
     A. Personal Factors
        1. High grade point average
        2. Academic self-concept
        3. The family
        4. Finances
     B. Environmental Factors
        1. Racial climates
        2. Presence of an ethnic community
        3. Working and living off campus
     C. Involvement Factors
        1. Faculty-student interaction
        2. Mentorship
        3. Participation in student organizations
     D. Sociocultural Factors
        1. Immigrant status
        2. Ethnic identity development
        3. Languages/ESL issues
        4. Community orientation
        5. The role of religion

IV. College Persistence and Asian-Pacific American Students
   A. Individual Factors
      1. Academic underpreparedness
      2. First generation status
      3. Language/ESL issues
      4. Low-income backgrounds
      5. Other family demands
      6. Cultural adjustment
   B. Institutional Factors
      1. Marginalization on campus
      2. Racial discrimination on campus

V. Retention of Native American Students
   A. Cultural Discontinuity
   B. Resistance Theory and Transcultural Hypothesis
      1. Alienation from the institution
      2. Disillusionment
      3. Emotional rejection
      4. Physical rejection

(Creighton, 2006, pp. 21–45)

Make an outline before you begin writing the chapter. It will help you structure a lengthy review of the literature.

Write the Introduction

The Review of the Literature Chapter begins with a brief introduction, usually between one and three pages. The introduction should introduce the research problem, including the key variables examined in the study, and describe the scope and organization of the review. Conclude the introduction with a paragraph that describes the sequence of the literature you will cover, often referred to as an *advance organizer,* using the exact headings that appear in the chapter. This format is illustrated in Example 7.2 taken from Donna Azodi's (2006) dissertation. We have provided the first paragraph of each section of Azodi's Review of the Literature Chapter to illustrate the flow and function of the advance organizer concept. This advance organizer should flow from section to section of the chapter, beginning with a topic sentence to start each paragraph in a section, and ending each section with a transition that leads the reader to the next section in the chapter. (See Example 7.2.)

Example 7.2

Introduction

This chapter presents the rationale for conducting research on relationships between principals' and teachers' perceptions of principals' leadership behaviors; principal trust in teachers, students, and parents; and the teachers' sense of efficacy. Educational researchers have studied the constructs of teacher efficacy and leadership for several decades. Both principal and teacher efficacy have been reviewed within the framework of school improvement and student achievement in those studies. My study sought to build upon this body of research through the combined lenses of teachers and principals. I studied similarities and differences in the perspectives of these key contributors in the educational organization.

The recognition of trust as a critical element in the school environment has become a more recent focus of educational researchers. In the context of societal pressures that create stress, even strife, within the educational community, the importance of trust within schools has assumed increased significance. Thus, this study sought to examine the relationship of principal trust and leadership behaviors supportive of teacher efficacy.

The following review of the literature represents the literature pertinent to my research study, namely, teacher efficacy, principal leadership, and principal trust in teachers, students, and parents. Specifically, Chapter II is organized into five sections: (a) efficacy theory, (b) teacher efficacy, (c) principal leadership, (d) trust, and (e) principal trust. (Azodi, 2006, p. 18)

The following five sections contain the first paragraphs of the five sections of Azodi's review of the literature to show the implementation of the advance organizer concept and the use of transitions.

Efficacy Theory

Bandura's (1997) social learning theory provided the foundation from which the concept of teacher efficacy used in this study was developed. Bandura posited a central processor of efficacy information in which "people process, weigh, and integrate diverse sources of information concerning their capability, and they regulate their choice of behavior and effort expenditure accordingly" (p. 212). He defined two concepts of efficacy: efficacy expectations and outcome expectations. "An outcome expectancy is defined as a person's estimate that a given behavior will lead to certain outcomes. An efficacy expectation is the conviction that one can successfully execute the behavior required to produce the outcomes" (p. 193). (Azodi, 2006, p. 19)

Teacher Efficacy

In what has become a seminal study on teacher efficacy, researchers for the Rand Corporation analyzed factors that contributed to success in raising reading scores in selected Los Angeles minority schools. One of the results of that study was the conclusion that a teacher's sense of efficacy had an effect on student achievement. The students, as well as their commitment and morale, helped to determine how much children learn (Amor, Conry-Oseguera, Cox, King, McDonnell, Pascal, Pauly, & Zellman, 1976). This finding has been supported throughout the years of research on teacher efficacy (Ashton & Webb, 1986; Brownell & Pajares, 1996; Corbett, Wilson, & Williams, 2005; Henson, 2001; Smylie, Conley, & Marks, 2002; Spillane & Louis, 2002; Tschannen-Moran, & Hoy, 2001; Tschannen-Moran & Hoy 2002; Tschannen-Moran,Hoy, & Hoy, 1998). (Azodi, 2006, p. 21)

Principal Leadership

In his study of exceptional leadership within industrial organizations, Burns (1978) discussed effective leadership using the terms "transformational and transactional." In transactional leadership, leaders deal with followers by exchanging one thing for another, for example, work for increase in salary or promotion. A transformational leader seeks to understand motives of followers and strives to meet higher needs. Transformational leadership also has the potential to convert followers into leaders. Burns (1978) expressed the belief that relationships were an important component of power in the context of leadership. (Azodi, 2006, p. 27)

Trust

Most of the time people act in ways that are expected not because they are obliged to do so, but rather because on some unconscious level they intuitively know that they are part of a network of trust (Solomon & Flores, 2001). However, we notice trust most by its absence. Baier (1986) indicated that "we inhabit a climate of trust as we inhabit an atmosphere and notice it as we notice air, only when it becomes scarce or polluted" (p. 234). Our day-to-day interactions that make up our lives and support our personal growth and happiness are possible only insofar as we trust. Our trust is based upon perceived protection inherent in such devices as reference, brand names, reputations and in this age of electronic commerce, the security encryption codes in computer transactions (Solmon & Flores, 2001). Moreover, as our lives have grown more complex with the increasingly rapid changes in our society and economy based, in part, on greater immediacy of dissemination of information, we are beginning to pay closer attention to trust (Tschannen-Moran & Hoy, 2000). (Azodi, 2006, pp. 36–37)

Principal Trust

"Schools play a special role in society, and as such, understanding trust relationships in school is vital" (Tschannen-Moran & Hoy, 2000, p. 551). Bryk and Schneider (2003) further explain that trust among school leaders, teachers, and parents not only refines the day-to-day work of schools but is also a critical resource for improvement. For this reason, principals need to understand how trust is developed and how it is lost if they are to gain the trust of stakeholders needed for building successful schools. Moreover, as the school's leader, the principal holds greater institutional power and thus must assume the responsibility for building and maintaining trusting relationships within the school. Through their behavior, principals either support or weaken trust within their schools, thus setting the tone of trust for their campus. Trust more and more has been identified as a critical element of leadership, in so doing establishing a need for greater understanding of the relationship between trust and leadership (Tschannen-Moran & Hoy, 2000; Tschannen-Moran, 2003, 2004). (Azodi, 2006, pp. 43–44)

Note how Azodi used the *advance organizer* concept in the last paragraph of her introduction to outline for readers the headings that constitute the body of her literature review. Also note how the headings she outlined in her advance organizer paragraph are worded exactly as stated in the advance organizer paragraph. This technique helps the reader stay focused on each topic of the literature review and provides coherence to the chapter. This is an especially useful technique when the literature review is very long.

Use Headings

Divide your literature review into useful major sections (headings) and subsections (subheadings). Judicious use of headings and subheadings serves two functions: (a) It helps readers understand the organization of your review, and (b) it helps readers follow your transitions from one topic or subtopic to another.

Note that Creighton (see Example 7.1) divided her Review of the Literature Chapter into five major sections (headings). She further divided her literature review into 12 subsections. She further divided these 12 subsections into 27 additional subsections. Azodi (see Example 7.2) divided her Review of the Literature Chapter into five major sections (headings). Although difficult to quantify in the abstract, a general guideline is that there should be at least one heading or subheading for every six paragraphs of manuscript. This provides coherence and keeps the reader focused on the topic, particularly transitions from one topic to another.

Use Transitions

Use transitions between paragraphs to provide connections between ideas. Use transitions within paragraphs to provide a change from one sentence to another or from one section of the paragraph to another.

Example 7.3 shows transitions (italicized) both between and within paragraphs from Johnson and Fauske's (2000) qualitative study. (See Example 7.3.)

Example 7.3

That organizations such as schools interact with their environments is the focus of little debate. *Indeed*, organizations influence and are influenced by the environments in which they exist (Hall, 1991; Jacobs, 1974;

Katz & Kahn, 1978; Meyer & Scott, 1992; Scott, 1995, 1998). *On one hand*, the presence or absence of critical environmental resources and information constrains or facilitates organizational processes and the realization of organizational goals (Aldrich, 1979; Pfeffer & Salancik, 1978, 1995). *On the other hand*, the environment is something that organization participants act on in a variety of ways and with varying degrees of sophistication to achieve organizational goals (Lawrence & Lorsch, 1967; Weick, 1978, 1995). *In either case*, the environment is consequential for organizations.

Effective organizations are those that act on their environments in strategic ways. *More specifically*, effective organizations are those that create *bridges and buffers* between themselves and the environment (Aldrich, 1979; Thompson, 1967). Organizational leaders often develop *bridging or buffering structures* to mitigate environmental effects on the organization (Scott, 1998; Thompson, 1967). The nature of those *bridging and buffering structures* found in the public school organization have been described in some detail (Corwin & Wagenaar, 1976; Goldring, 1995; Ogawa, 1996; Rowan, Raudenbush, & Cheong, 1993). These studies underscore the importance of the *environment* for school and leadership effectiveness.

The *environment* of the school organization is something that vies for the attention of school administrators. As such, it is subject to strategic and tactical *manipulation* (Selznick, 1957). Although there are limits to this *manipulation*, the fact that *manipulation* is possible highlights an important component of the managerial imperative, namely, the management of the *external environment* of the school.

Of specific interest *here* are questions regarding *what* principals attend to and act on (or react to) in their *external environments* and *how* they explain that interactive behavior. Principals are not equally effective in attending to or managing the environment of the school organization. *To be sure*, there are those who prove adept at mapping, managing, and adapting to a variety of *environmental* constraints and demands. *Likewise*, there are those who prove equally inept. Many known and unknown factors account for these differences—intelligence, years of experience, socialization, the richness of ones' past experiences, and other contextual factors (Greenfield, 1995; Parkay, Currie, & Rhodes, 1992; Weick, 1978).

Purpose and Rationale

Using these ideas as a guiding context, the purpose of this study is to examine and explore *(a)* how a group of principals enact or structure the internal and external environment of their school and *(b)* the cognitive processes guiding these attention and selection processes. The article will address *two* questions: What actions lead to principals' development of strategic *environmental* initiatives and what are the underlying cognitive processes for principals selectively attending to certain aspects of the *environment* while ignoring others (Cyert & March, 1963)? (Johnson & Fauske, 2000, pp. 159–160)

Note how effectively Johnson and Fauske have used both internal and external transitions in the five paragraphs presented above. For example, words and phrases such as *indeed, on the one hand, on the other hand, in either case, more specifically, to be sure, likewise,* as well as seriations, such as *(a), (b),* provide internal transitions. Beginning the fifth paragraph with *Using these ideas as a guiding context* connects (transitions) their fifth paragraph with the preceding four. Also note how they repeat several keywords critical to an understanding of their content: *bridges and buffers, bridging and buffering, environment,* and *manipulation.* This example can serve as a model for your own use of transitions in your review of the literature.

Write a Summary

We began this chapter by stating that each chapter in a dissertation or master's thesis has three distinct parts: the introduction, in which you tell your readers what you are going to tell them (often referred to as an *advance organizer*); the body, in which you tell them; and the summary, in which you tell them what you told them. Your Review of the Literature Chapter should end with a brief summary of the literature you reviewed. Thus, the summary provides an overview of the historical, theoretical, and empirical literature that supports your investigation. It makes the rationale of your study and its research questions or hypotheses apparent to the reader. You should draw on this summary when you are writing your statement of the problem section in Chapter One and describing the theoretical framework for your research questions and/or hypotheses, or setting the context of your study in a qualitative thesis or dissertation. It is for this reason that we recommend that you begin work on your review of the literature prior to writing Chapter One, for you will need to know what has been done and how it relates to your research problem.

Scott Barrett (2000) provided a good example of a summary of the Review of the Literature Chapter in his dissertation. (See Example 7.4.)

Example 7.4

Summary

According to Lucas (as cited by Telem, 1995), research on the implementation of information technology has evolved through four generations. The first generation was characterized by the building of models, such as the Theory of Reasoned Action (Fishbein & Ajzen, 1975), the Technology Acceptance Model (Davis, 1989), and the Theory of Planned Behavior (Ajzen, 1985). The characteristics of second-generation research focused on testing and extending the original models, such as the Extended Technology Acceptance Model (Morris, 1996), the Decomposed Theory of Planned Behavior Model (Taylor & Todd, 1995), and the Psychological Acceptance Model (Malhota, 1998).

Third generation characteristics of information technology research focused on factors associated with implementation, such as Visscher's (1991a) framework and the Perceptions Model for Effective Usage

(Barrett, 1999). The fourth generation of research examines the development of a project, dealing with issues of relationships between designers, users, and the impact of an MIS on an organization, such as the Task Technology Fit Model (Dishaw & Strong, 1999), the Integrated Model of Microcomputer Usage (Igbaria et al., 1997), and the Integrated TAM/TTF Model (Dishaw & Strong, 1999).

According to Johnson and David (1990), "MIS is not a well-defined terminology in the discipline of student affairs. The review of higher educational journals led on numerous occasions not to MIS or other computer-based information systems, but to the uses and benefits of the computer and microcomputer" (p. 28). Based upon the review of relevant literature, the preponderance of research focuses on evaluating and/or predicting the acceptance and utilization of technology applications outside of the educational administration arena. Telem (1990) warned of the potential dangers of relying on information system models developed outside the field of education.

It is evident that valid and reliable instruments to assess the success of information systems that measure, predict, and explain use are increasingly important in determining what causes people to accept or reject information technology. By gaining a better understanding of how the constructs of perceived ease of use, perceived usefulness, external variables, and postadoption experiences impact system usage, a more theoretical understanding of technology acceptance can be determined. Understanding these constructs can promote the successful implementation of an MIS in the proper contextual environment to support a willingness to adopt and utilize these systems. (Barrett, 2000, pp. 64–65)

Barrett's summary provides an overview of different positions researchers have taken on the empirical puzzle selected by the author, and explains how the author's dissertation contributes to its understanding. His summary allows an outside reader to become acquainted with a complex and comprehensive review of the literature and how it supports the author's current investigation.

Be Careful Not to Plagiarize

When writing a thesis or dissertation, it is often necessary to include extracts from journal articles, books, or research reports. These extracts are used to support your arguments and to help set the context for your research. It is important for you to give credit to the author(s) of the work you have extracted. Plagiarism is "to steal and pass off (the ideas or words of another) as one's own" (*Merriam-Webster's Ninth New Collegiate Dictionary*, 1986, p. 898). Taking someone's exact words without using quotation marks is obviously plagiarism. Closely paraphrasing another person's sentences without giving credit to the person is plagiarism. Presenting another person's ideas as though they were your own is plagiarism. The plagiarism may not be intentional, but it is the responsibility of the student to cite others when appropriate. This is not only an ethical matter but a legal issue as well.

SYNTHESIZING THE LITERATURE

We've said that a review of the literature is more than a string of annotations. Annotations are brief summaries of the contents of articles. For example, "Smith found...," "Jones argued...," "Harris stated...." Stringing together several annotations in the body of the literature review may describe what research is available in an area of study, but it fails to organize the material. A good review of the literature is a critical synthesis. That is, you describe and analyze the literature to show how previous studies are related to each other and to your study. You can do this by using one or more of the following strategies: (a) provide a historical context to help the reader understand a phenomenon, (b) point out gaps in the literature, (c) show how a study differs from a group of previous studies, (d) identify themes in a group of studies, (e) report practical significance, (f) reconcile conflicting theories concerning an important variable, (g) use tables to summarize research on a single variable, (h) clarify inconsistent findings, and (i) signal a continuing line of inquiry. We discuss each of these nine strategies in the following sections.

Historical Context

One way of analyzing a body of literature is to provide a historical context that may be helpful to your readers in understanding a new construct. The following article by Hoy, Tarter, and Hoy (2006) is a good example. (See Example 7.5.)

Example 7.5

Coleman startled educators with his finding that the characteristics of a school mattered little in explaining student achievement (Coleman et al., 1966). He argued that schools had only a negligible effect on student performance and that most of the variation in student learning was a product of differences in family background. Edmonds (1979) was one of the first to dispute Coleman's conclusions. His familiar list of effective school characteristics—strong principal leadership, high expectations for student achievement, an emphasis on basic skills, an orderly environment, and frequent and systematic evaluation of students— seemed to refute Colman. Good schools were the product of good administrators. As simple as the connection seems, empirical demonstrations of direct administrative influences on student achievement have been elusive.

It is one thing to identify high-performing schools in neighborhoods of low socioeconomic status (SES) and attribute their performance to leadership characteristics or climate or an orderly environment, any of which may be present at those schools. It is quite another matter to demonstrate a priori that school leadership or other school properties will be directly and systematically related to student success in a controlled study involving a large sample. Although, administrators do not perceive this to be the case, the weight of the evidence suggests that little or no direct relationship exists between principal leadership and student achievement (Hallinger & Heck, 1996). In fact, it is difficult to find school properties that are consistently related to student achievement when controlling for the socioeconomic level of the school (for a notable exception in private high schools, see Byrk, Lee, & Holland, 1993). Nevertheless, educational leaders and policymakers alike have been reluctant to conclude that schools have little or no effect on student achievement. Instead, the quest has turned to identifying school characteristics that make a difference in achievement, in spite of student SES.

Coleman was not wrong; socioeconomic factors are powerful shapers of student performance. In fact, in large-scale studies such as those of Coleman et al. (1966) and Jencks (1972), SES overwhelms the association between school properties and achievement; the influence of school factors vanishes after social factors have been controlled. But Coleman was not entirely right; there are a few school characteristics that consistently predict student achievement, even after controlling for socioeconomic factors. Three organizational properties seem to make a difference in student achievement: the academic emphasis of the school, the collective efficacy of the faculty, and the faculty's trust in parents and students. We suspect that there are other such school properties, but they have not been readily revealed despite continuing research.

Academic emphasis, collective efficacy, and faculty trust are tightly woven together and seem to reinforce each other as they positively constrain student performance. We first examine the research on each of these three school prosperities, and then we explore the theory and research that link the three together as a single powerful force explaining school performance. We call this force academic optimism, which has been demonstrated to be a general latent construct. (Hoy et al., 2006, pp. 425–426)

Note how Hoy et al., provided a historical context for understanding a new construct, academic optimism, and used it to explain student achievement. Such an introduction will help the reader to understand a new construct such as academic optimism. You can use this as a model for your own study if you are introducing a new construct.

Gaps in the Literature

Another way to analyze a body of literature is to point out gaps in the literature. The qualitative study by Brunner (2000) is a good example. (See Example 7.6.)

Example 7.6

With a foundation laid by Patricia Schmuck, Flora Ida Ortiz, Charol Shakeshaft, and others, a previously neglected area of study—women in educational administration—began to take shape, and questions about the dearth of women in administration were asked. Even with this new foundation, however, research focused on women superintendents was and is as scarce and scattered as the women themselves. To be sure, after approximately 75 years of extant scholarship on the superintendency that relied primarily on White, male participants, it is only during the past 20 years that one finds research directed specifically to women superintendents (Tallerico, 1999, p. 290).

Certainly, when women find themselves in the position of superintendent of schools, it is immediately apparent to them that of their colleagues the greatest number are men. In fact, during this 1999–2000 school year, approximately 13% of superintendents are women (Glass, Bjork, & Brunner, 2000). Furthermore, it is shocking to see that when a line graph is constructed using the percentages of women in the superintendency from each year over the past century, the graphed line is, for all practical purposes, flat (Blount, 1998). And with the additional information that more than half of the students in educational administration classes are women, one is left with obvious questions: Why are there so few women in the superintendency? What part does gender inequality play in this phenomenon? Is gender inequality an experience of women in the role? (Brunner, 2000, pp. 76–77)

Note how Brunner used her study of women superintendents' experiences of inequality to point out gaps in the literature and why they exist. You can use this format as a model in pointing out gaps in the literature related to your study.

Different Approach

Another way to analyze studies is to show how a study differs from a group of previous studies. The mixed methods study by Davis (1998) is a good example. (See Example 7.7.)

Example 7.7

Many educators maintain that the principalship is the most demanding of all public school administrative roles. Dwindling resources, burgeoning paperwork, crumbling facilities, increasing public criticisms and expectations, growing numbers of students with special needs, and increasing demands by teachers and parents to participate in decision making pose serious challenges to principals at virtually all levels and in nearly every area of the country. At best, principals strive to provide vision and unity of purpose within challenging, dynamic, and highly political settings.

At worst, they are faced with the unrelenting task of maintaining structure and order within increasingly hostile, unpredictable, and conflict-laden environments. Even the most skilled and experienced principals run the risk of failing in their jobs as a result of actions, events, outcomes over which they may not always have direct control (Deal & Peterson, 1994; Gorton & Snowden, 1993; Martin-Lucchesi, 1990; Sergiovanni, 1995).

The precarious nature of the principalship reinforces the need for continued research on factors related to leadership behavior, especially behavior that may jeopardize a principal's job security. Most studies about school principals focus on the characteristics and outcomes of effective leadership. Few studies have fully examined factors relating to ineffective school leadership. Such knowledge in concert with information about effective leadership, can help principals assess and refine their own leadership behavior and more effectively navigate the increasingly complex and challenging contexts of public school administration. (Davis, 1998, pp. 58–59)

Note that Davis pointed out that most studies about school principals focus on the characteristics and outcomes of effective leadership. He suggested that few studies examined factors relating to ineffective leadership and that benefits are to be gained from such an approach. You can use the "different approach" technique in reviewing the literature in your dissertation or master's thesis.

Trends and Themes

In your review of the literature, you may find a group of studies that employ a similar theme. The following article by Lunenburg (2003b) is a good example. Lunenburg identified a theme in our continuing quest for school improvement. (See Example 7.8.)

Example 7.8

Accountability for school improvement is a central theme of state policies. The No Child Left Behind Act of 2001 (Public Law 107–110) sets demanding accountability standards for schools, school districts, and states, including new state testing requirements designed to improve education. For example, the law requires that states develop both content standards in reading and mathematics and tests that are linked to the standards for grades 3 through 8, with science standards and assessments to follow. States must identify adequate yearly progress (AYP) objectives and disaggregate test results for all students and subgroups of students based on socioeconomic status, race/ethnicity, English language proficiency, and disability. Moreover, the law mandates that 100 percent of students must score at the proficient level on state tests by 2014. Furthermore, the No Child Left Behind Act requires states to participate every other year in the National Assessment of Educational Progress (NAEP) in reading and mathematics.

Will schools, school districts, and states be able to respond to the demand? In an ideal system, school improvement efforts focus educational policy, administration, and practices directly on teaching and learning. This will require districtwide leadership focused directly on learning. School leaders can accomplish this by (a) clarifying purpose, (b) encouraging collective learning, (c) aligning with state standards, (d) providing support, and (e) making data-driven decisions (Lunenburg, 2002). Taken together, these five dimensions provide a compelling framework for accomplishing sustained districtwide success for all children. (Lunenburg, 2003b, pp. 36–37)

Note how Lunenburg identified a theme in our continuing quest for school improvement. Using trends and themes is another strategy you can use to synthesize the review of the literature in your dissertation.

Reporting Practical Significance

As you provide the reader with a review of literature and as you look for significance and potential problems related to your topic, investigating practical significance of the reported studies is very important. You should consider reporting the type of study, the number of participants, and significance with effect size if applicable.

Drees (2006) provided an example of reporting practical significance in his review of the literature. (See Example 7.9.)

Example 7.9

Balogun (1988) reaffirmed his conclusions from 1986. PPGPA ($r = 0.55$, $p < 0.01$) and mean AHPAT score ($r = 0.50$, $p < 0.01$) showed a significant relationship to academic achievement. Unlike the earlier study, Balogun found no significant relationship between the essay score and academic achievement. The single best predictor for clinical achievement was found to be the interview score ($r = 0.59$, $p < 0.01$). (Drees, 2006, p. 23)

Drees also reported a section of the review of literature in this manner:

Platt, Torocy, and McGlumphy (2001) investigated whether the Scholastic Aptitude Test (SAT) scores and high school grade point average (HSGPA) had any ability to predict college grade point average (CGPA) in six allied health programs at a private, northeast university. Descriptive data, HSGPA, CGPA, SAT mathematics (SATM), SAT verbal (SATV), and SAT total were compiled for 373 students of six programs: athletic training, health management, systems, occupational therapy, perfusion technology, physician assistant, and physical therapy. Using stepwise regression analyses, HSGPA and SATV scores were significantly predictive, $F (2, 370) = 31.32$, $p = .00$, of CGPA when looking at all 373 allied health students. (Drees, 2006, p. 16)

Note how Drees included specific information within his review of literature as he reported specific studies. This also indicates that Drees used primary sources of data.

Reconciling Conflicting Theories

One way of analyzing a body of literature is to reconcile conflicting theories concerning an important variable. The study by Hoy and Sweetland (2000) is a good example. (See example 7.10.)

Example 7.10

Virtually all modern organizations are bureaucracies; that is, they have the classical bureaucratic properties (hierarchy of authority, division of labor, impersonality, objective standards, technical competence, rules, and regulations) described by Weber (1947) in his seminal analysis of organizations. In practice, the word *bureaucracy* takes on many connotations, most of them negative. But Weber claims that "Experience tends to universally show that the purely bureaucratic type of administrative organization . . . is, from a purely technical point of view, capable of attaining the highest degree of efficiency" (1947, p. 337). Yet, contemporary criticisms of bureaucracy are rampant. For example, Scott (1998) describes four bureaucratic pathologies—alienation, overconformity, unresponsiveness, and relentlessness—each of which is pervasive and has negative consequences for participants. Feminists attack bureaucracy and argue that it is fundamentally a male invention that rewards masculine virtues and values such as competition, power, and hierarchy (Ferguson, 1984; Martin & Knopoff, 1999). And school executives criticize state bureaucracies for impeding local control of schools and preventing them from delivering educational programs that meet community needs. What most of these critics have in common is the human frustration and aggravation with hierarchy, technical procedures, and unfair and restrictive rules (Hirschhorn, 1997).

While it is true that bureaucracies frustrate participants, that is only half the story, because research also suggests they can improve worker satisfaction (Michaels, Cron, Dubinsky, & Joachmisthaler, 1998), increase innovation (Craig, 1995; Damanpour, 1991), reduce role conflict (Senatra, 1980), and lessen feelings of alienation (Jackson & Schuler, 1985). Indeed, organizational research depicts two conflicting views of the human consequences of bureaucracy. The negative side suggests that bureaucracy alienates, fosters dissatisfaction, stifles creativity, and demotivates employees; the positive view maintains that bureaucracy provides new guidance, clarifies responsibility, reduces role stress, and helps individuals feel and be more effective (Adler & Borys, 1996; Hoy & Miskel, 2001). The purpose of this research is twofold; first, to reconcile theoretically these two views, and second, to develop and test empirically a new construct—enabling bureaucracy. (Hoy & Sweetland, 2000, pp. 525–526)

Note how Hoy and Sweetland reconciled conflicting theories concerning bureaucracy. This is another technique that can be used to synthesize a body of literature for a dissertation or master's thesis.

Using Tables

Another way of synthesizing a large body of research on a single variable is to use a summary table (see Example 7.11). Table 7.3 provides a summary of the major Organizational Climate Description Questionnaire (OCDQ) studies completed between 1963 and 1987. This strategy should not be used unless at least 10 studies examine the effects of a single variable.

Example 7.11

Table 7.3   Summary Data from Major OCDQ Studies

Study	Findings
Anderson (1964)	Principals of open schools are more confident, sociable, and resourceful than principals in closed schools.
Andrews (1965)	Climate type is not related to teacher characteristics, satisfaction, principal effectiveness, and student achievement, but is related to some climate dimensions.
Appleberry (1969)	Schools with open climates are more humanistic in pupil control ideology than schools with closed climates.
Brown (1965)	Validation of the OCDQ resulted in seven discrete climate categories rather than six found by Halpin & Croft (1963).
Feldvebel (1964)	Climate types are not related to SES or school achievement, but climate dimensions are related to principal behavior.
Flagg (1965)	Climate type is not related to student achievement but is related to school size, teacher turnover, and principal characteristics.
Guy (1970)	Climate type is not related to student achievement but to some dimensions of climate.
Hale (1965)	Language achievement (not mathematics and reading) is related to some climate dimensions.
Hartley & Hoy (1972)	There is a relationship between climate openness and the absence of student alienation.

Hoy & Clover (1986)	A revised version of the OCDQ—the OCDQ-RE—was developed for use in elementary schools.
Kanner (1974)	Teachers are more satisfied and loyal to principals in open schools.
Kottkamp, Mulhern, & Hoy (1987)	A revised version of the OCDQ—the OCDQ-RS—was developed for use in secondary schools.
Lunenburg (1969)	Validation of the OCDQ revealed seven discrete climate types instead of six found by Halpin & Croft (1963). Several climate dimensions and open climates were related to school size but not SES. Principal and teacher perceptions of climate are incongruous.
Lunenburg (1972)	Openness of climate (esprit plus thrust minus disengagement) was related to humanistic pupil control ideology but not to open-mindedness.
Maxwell (1967)	Achievement is positively related to principal "consideration" and negatively related to teacher "disengagement." Teacher and principal perceptions of climate are incongruous.
Miller (1969)	Climate type is related to school achievement, with teacher dimensions more important than principal dimensions.
Nicholas, Virgo, & Wattenberg (1965)	SES, school size, and behavior problems are related to climate type.
Null (1967)	Teachers' attitudes toward children are related to climate dimensions.
Nwankwo (1979)	Climate type is related to school discipline.
Plaxton (1965)	Principal personality types are not related to overall climate types but are related to four of the eight climate dimensions: production emphasis, aloofness, thrust, and hindrance.
Randles (1964)	Open climate is related to favorable attitudes of teachers on MTAI.
Rice (1968)	Overall climate type is not related to student achievement. Some dimensions of climate are related to student achievement.
Sargeant (1967)	Difference in climate type are related to teacher satisfaction, school effectiveness, and role, but not school department, size, and community composition.
Watkins (1968)	Climate type is related to school size, accountability, and role.
Wiggins (1972)	Climate type is not related to principal behavior but remains stable with principal turnover.

Using a table like the one above is a very effective way to help the reader visualize a large body of research related to a singe variable. The studies reported in Table 7.3 may seem dated to some readers, but the study of organizational climate throughout the 1960s and later had a tremendous impact on the literature. Note that the same measuring instrument was used to assess organizational climate, the OCDQ, in the studies reported in Table 7.3. The information is provided as a model for your own review of the literature using other variables to synthesize a large body of research on a single topic.

Inconsistent Findings

Another way of analyzing a body of literature is to clarify inconsistent findings. The study by Grejda and Hannafin (1992) is a good example. (See Example 7.12.)

Example 7.12

Interest in the potential of a word processor to improve writing has grown substantially during the past decade. Various authorities have lauded the capability to increase writer productivity (Zaharias, 1983), to reduce tedious-ness of recopying written work (Bean, 1983; Daiute, 1983; Moran, 1983), to increase the frequency of revising (Bridwell, Sirc, & Brooke, 1985; Daiute, 1986), and to improve both attitudes toward writing (Rodriguez, 1985) and the writing process (McKenzie, 1984; Olds, 1982). Some researchers have argued that word processors alter both individuals' writing styles and the methods used to teach writing (Bertram, Michaels, & Watson-Geges, 1985).

Yet research findings on the effects of word processing have proved inconsistent (Fitzgerald, 1987). Some researchers have reported positive effects on writing (Dauite, 1985), whereas others have reported mixed effects (Wheeler, 1985). Although word processing seems to increase the frequency of revision, the revisions are often surface level and do little to improve the overall quality of composition (Collier, 1983; Hawisher, 1987). In some cases, word processing has actually hampered different aspects of writing (Grejda & Hannafin, in press; Perl, 1979).

However, comparatively little has been demonstrated conclusively. Attempts to study word processing have been confounded by both typing requirements and limited word-processing proficiency. Inadequate definition has also plagued word-processing research. Many studies have isolated only mechanical attributes of revision, such as punctuation, requiring only proofreading rather than sophisticated revision skills (Collier, 1983; Dalton & Hannafin, 1987). Other research has focused only on global writing measures, with little attribution possible for observing changes in writing quality (Boone, 1985; Woodruff, Bereiter, & Scardamalia, 1981–82). Both mechanical and holistic aspects of writing are important, but they are rarely considered concurrently (cf. Humes, 1983).

Although comparatively few studies have focused on young writers, the results have been encouraging. Dauite (1986) reported that junior high schools students using word processors were more likely to expand their compositions, as well as to identify and correct existing errors, than were paper-and-pencil students. Likewise, word-processing students were more likely than paper-and-pencil students were to revise their language-experience stories (Barber, 1984; Bradley, 1982). Boone (1985) reported that the compositions of fourth, fifth, and sixth graders become increasingly sophisticated through revisions focusing on both mechanics and higher-level organizations. In contrast, despite improving students' attitudes, word processing has failed to improve overall compositions based upon holistic ratings of writing quality (Woodruff, Bereiter, & Scardamalia, 1981–82).

The purpose of this study was to examine the effects of word processing on the holistic writing quality and revision patterns of sixth graders. We predicted that word processing would improve both the accuracy of revisions as well as the overall holistic quality of student writing. (Grejda & Hannafin, 1992, p. 114)

Note how Grejda and Hannafin pointed out inconsistent findings in a study of the effects of word processing on the accuracy and quality of students' writing. This technique can serve as still another model for synthesizing the review of literature in a dissertation or master's thesis.

Continuing Line of Inquiry

In analyzing a body of literature, you may find an article that started a new line of research that has continued into the present, using additional measurement instruments. The review prepared by Miskel and Ogawa (1988) in their chapter for the *Handbook of Research on Educational Administration* is a good example. Miskel and Ogawa reviewed the literature on the organizational climate of schools from 1963 to around 1982. Lunenburg and Ornstein (2008) continued the review up to 1997. (See Example 7.13.)

Example 7.13

The literature on the organizational climate of schools is largely rooted in four conceptualizations (Hoy & Miskel, 1982): Halpin and Croft's (1963) concept of open and closed climates; Likert's (1961) concept of managerial systems that range from exploitive-authoritative to participative; Steinhoff's (1965) and Stern's (1970) needs-press model; and Willower, Eidell, and Hoy's (1967) concept of pupil-control orientation. Each has led to the development of measurement instruments and subsequent research on schools. These conceptualizations of climate share two important features: They are extensions of theories or perspectives concerning what Tagiuri (1968) has called the social-system dimension of climate, and they operationalize climate as the average of organizational members' perceptions. (Miskel & Ogawa, 1988, pp. 290–291)

Two revised versions of the OCDQ were developed in the 1980s, one for elementary schools—the OCDQ-RE—(Hoy & Clover, 1986) and one for secondary schools—the OCDQ—RS (Kottkamp, Mulhern, & Hoy, 1987). Another instrument to assess the climate of the school is the Organizational Health Inventory (OHI) developed by Hoy and Tarter (1997). Whereas the OCDQ examines the openness/closedness of teacher-teacher and principal-teacher interactions, the OHI describes the health of the interpersonal relations in schools among students, teachers, administrators, and community members.

Hoy and Tarter conceptualize organizational health at three levels: institutional, administrative, and teacher. The institutional level connects the schools with its environment. The administrative level controls the internal managerial function of the organization and learning process. A healthy school is one that keeps the institutional, administrative, and teacher levels in harmony, meets functional needs and successfully copes with disruptive external forces, and directs its energies toward school goals. (Lunenburg & Ornstein, 2008, p. 83)

Note how Miskel and Ogawa and Lunenburg and Ornstein synthesized a continuing line of inquiry on school climate. You may wish to use this strategy in reviewing your literature for a dissertation or master's thesis.

SUMMARY

In this chapter, we provided you with an introduction on how to systematically search the literature. We discussed six sources for such a search: handbooks and encyclopedias, annual reviews, review articles, abstracting and indexing services, government documents, and public search engines. In addition, eight techniques to help you write a clear and effective Review of the Literature Chapter were provided. They include: organizing your material in a funnel, being selective, making an outline, writing the introduction, using headings, using transitions, writing a summary, and being careful not to plagiarize. We concluded the chapter by discussing nine additional strategies to help you critically synthesize the body of literature. Examples from dissertations and from published articles may serve as models for your own work. In the next chapter, we provide advice for writing the Methodology Chapter of your dissertation or master's thesis.

8

Writing the Methodology Chapter

In a typical dissertation or master's thesis, the Introduction and Review of the Literature Chapters are followed by a description of the research methodology. The chapter is usually titled "Methodology." Thus, in Chapter Three you describe the specific steps you have taken to address the research questions or hypotheses that you presented in Chapter One, and that you connected to the prior research you reviewed in Chapter Two. You need to describe the methodology in enough detail so that other researchers may replicate your study.

The Methodology Chapter is typically divided into the following sections: (a) selection of participants, (b) instrumentation, (c) data collection, and (d) data analysis. Although qualitative studies (case study, ethnography, ethology, ethnomethodology, grounded theory, phenomenology, symbolic interaction, and historical research) tend to be less formal in nature and procedure than quantitative studies (descriptive, correlational, causal-comparative, and experimental), much of what is suggested here can apply to all dissertations and master's theses. The typical contents for Chapter Three are provided in Table 8.1.

As discussed previously, each chapter has three distinct parts: the introduction, where you tell your readers what you are going to tell them; the body, where you tell them; and the summary, where you tell them what you told them. You will note from Table 8.1 that Chapter Three begins with an introduction and ends with a summary. The headings in the middle constitute the body of the chapter. A more detailed description of each of these sections follows.

Table 8.1   Contents for Chapter Three

CHAPTER III

METHODOLOGY
    Introduction
    Selection of Participants
    Instrumentation
    Data Collection
    Data Analysis
    Summary

INTRODUCTION

In the introduction, you provide an overview of the chapter. The overview, containing one or two paragraphs, provides the reader with the structure of the chapter, an *advance organizer*. This advance organizer prepares the reader for what is to follow. In some dissertations, the student restates the research questions or hypotheses that were presented in Chapter One. In others, the student simply makes reference to the research questions or hypotheses presented earlier.

An example from Melinda Wooderson-Perzan's (2000) dissertation follows. (See Example 8.1.)

Example 8.1

Introduction

The primary goal of this study was to test the research questions that relate to transformational leadership, student achievement, and selected school district financial and demographic factors as stated in Chapter I. Separate instruments to measure these variables were utilized to this end. The methodology employed to test the research questions is presented in this chapter. The chapter is organized into four sections: (a) selection of participants, (b) instrumentation, (c) data collection, and (d) data analysis. (Wooderson-Perzan, 2000, p. 58)

Note how Wooderson-Perzan, in her brief introduction to her chapter, provided her readers with an advance organizer of the contents of the chapter. Note also that she included all elements typically found in a Methodology Chapter. Additionally, you may add your research design in the introductory section of Chapter Three, or the heading "Design of the Study" may stand alone after the heading "Introduction."

SELECTION OF PARTICIPANTS

In studies involving humans, the term *participants* is generally preferred to the term *subjects* to communicate the active and consensual relationship the participant had in the study. The purpose of the "Selection of Participants" section is to describe (a) who participated in the study, including their characteristics (e.g., age, gender, race/ethnicity), (b) how the participants were selected, and (c) how many participated in the study. We discuss each element in turn.

Who Participated in the Study?

The reason for selecting a sample is to gain information concerning your target population. For example, if you were interested in the effect of conflict resolution training on the number of student discipline referrals for fifth-grade inner-city students, it would not be possible to include all fifth grade students in the United States in your study. It would be necessary for you to select a sample of the population. Because inferences concerning a population are made based on the behavior of a sample, it is important that the sample be representative, sufficiently large, and free of sampling error and bias. However, in qualitative studies, samples tend to be smaller, nonrandom, and purposive. Sampling in qualitative research is discussed later in the chapter.

The first step, then, in sampling in quantitative studies is to define your target population. The target population is the group of interest to the researcher, the group to which you would like the results of the study to be generalizable. Generalizability is the extent to which the results of one study can be applied to other populations. Examples of populations are all principals in the United States, all elementary school gifted and talented children in Texas, and all first grade students in Harris County who have attended preschool. These examples illustrate two important things about populations. First, populations may be any size and cover any geographic area. Second, the entire group the researcher would like to generalize is rarely available.

For example, suppose you decide to do a study of high school principals' attitudes about teaching mathematics using traditional instruction versus online instruction. Suppose that you wish to generalize your results to all high school principals in the United States. You quickly realize the difficulty of getting information from every high school principal in the United States, so you decide to obtain a representative sample of high school principals in the United States. But even this would be a difficult, time consuming, and expensive task. So instead, you decide to study only principals in a single state. By selecting from a more narrowly defined population, you would save time and money but you would be losing generalizability. Your results would be generalizable to all high school principals in that state only, but not to all high school principals in the United States. The key is to define your population in sufficient detail so that other researchers may determine how applicable your findings are to their study.

Regardless of what sampling approach is used, it is important to describe the characteristics of the sample. This description should include the number of participants in the sample and a description of the demographics of the sample (e.g., gender, race, age, experience, education). The nature of the demographic data varies with the sample; that is, the demographic information used to describe a sample of principals would be different from that used to describe a sample of teachers, students, or parents.

The number of characteristics you might use to describe the participants is almost limitless; therefore, you must be selective in deciding on which sample characteristics to report. Following is an example of a description of participants from Linda Creighton's (2006) dissertation to further illustrate issues pertaining to selecting and describing participants. A table such as the one in Example 8.2 makes it easy for readers to scan information that describes the participants. (See Example 8.2.)

Example 8.2

Selection of Participants

The sample was comprised of 63 universities within the University Council for Educational Administration (UECA) membership. The UCEA is a consortium of 72 major public and private doctoral-degree granting research universities in the United States and Canada. It includes doctoral granting universities with the Carnegie Classifications: Very High Research Activity (RU/VH), High Research Activity (RU/H), and Master's Colleges and Universities Larger Programs (Master's L).

Very High Research Activity (RU/VH)

These institutions offer a wide range of baccalaureate programs and are committed to graduate education through the doctorate. They award 50 or more doctoral degrees per year across at least 15 disciplines (The Chronicle of Higher Education, 2005).

High Research Activity (RU/H)

These institutions offer a wide range of baccalaureate programs and are committed to graduate education through the doctorate. They award at least 10 doctoral degrees per year across three or more disciplines, or at least 20 doctoral degrees per year overall (Chronicle of Higher Education, 2005).

Master's Colleges and Universities Larger Programs (Master's L)

These institutions offer a wider range of baccalaureate programs and are committed to graduate education through the master's degree. They award 40 or more master's degrees annually (Chronicle of Higher Education, 2005).

The colleges and universities studied were selected from the four regions of the United States into which the *U.S. News & World Reports* places schools for ranking purposes: North, South, Midwest, and West. Within these regions were UCEA colleges and universities classified as: (a) two universities located in small towns having an average total full-time undergraduate enrollment of 16,799 students; (b) 33 universities from mid-size cities having an average full-time undergraduate enrollment of 27,350 students; (c) three universities located in large towns having an average full-time undergraduate enrollment of 16,249; (d) 19 universities with an average full-time undergraduate enrollment of 32,096 located in or near large cities; and (e) six universities with an average full-time undergraduate enrollment of 14,453 located in or on the fringe of large cities. The Carnegie Classification for the universities is: (a) RU/VH, 50; (b) RU/H, 8; and (c) Master's L, 5. [Table 8.2] displays the participants included in the study based on region, location, student enrollment, and Carnegie Classification.

Table 8.2   Participants Based on Region, Location, Enrollment, and Carnegie Classification

Region	*Participants*	*Location*	*Participants*	*Enrollment*	*Carnegie Classification**	*Participants*
North	5	Small Town	2	16,799	(RU/VH)	50
South	12	Large Town	3	16,249	(RU/H)	8
Midwest	26	Midsize Town	33	27,350	Master's L	5
West	20	Large City	19	32,096		
		Fringe of Large City	6	14,453		

* This denotes the new Carnegie Classifications which took effect in 2005.

(Creighton, 2006, pp. 48–50)

Note how comprehensively Creighton describes her sample of UCEA universities. She follows the textual description with a table, which makes it easy for readers to scan information quickly describing the participants.

Sampling Procedures

In writing Chapter Three, your purpose is not to discuss all the major sampling procedures but instead to describe what method you used to obtain your sample. However, knowledge of the major sampling procedures is a prerequisite to developing an appropriate description of your sample. One desirable characteristic of a sample is *representativeness.* Representativeness enables results from the sample to be generalized to the population. The major sampling procedures that provide representativeness are (a) simple random sampling, (b) stratified random sampling, (c) cluster sampling, and (d) systematic sampling. Each procedure is discussed below.

Simple Random Sampling

Simple random sampling is the process of selecting a sample in such a way that all individuals in the defined population have an equal chance of being selected for the sample. Simple random sampling involves defining the population, identifying each member of the population, and selecting individuals for the sample on a chance basis using a table of random numbers. Simple random sampling is the single best way to obtain a representative sample.

An example of simple random sampling from Diane Trautman's (2000) mixed methods dissertation follows. (See Example 8.3.)

Example 8.3

Selection of Participants

The target population of this study were all superintendents, assistant superintendents, secondary principals (grades 6–12), and elementary principals (grades K–5), male and female, in the United States. This population included only those school leaders in public schools. The Market Data Retrieval Company (2000), a company of the Dun and Bradstreet Corporation located in Chicago, Illinois, was used to determine the target population. The following is a breakdown of the target population for each group: 11,542 male and 2,060 female superintendents; 4,269 male and 2,267 female assistant superintendents; 24,591 male and 29,305 female elementary principals; and 21,230 male and 7,929 female principals. This would make a total target population of 103,193 members.

According to Krejcie and Morgan (1970), when the population is 100,000, a sample size of 384 is recommended. The quantitative sample taken from the population of 103,193 was 800 educational leaders randomly selected by computer through the Market Data Retrieval Company (2000). This group provided the quantitative data for the study obtained from the Organizational and Leadership Effectiveness Inventory. The Market Data Retrieval Company randomly selected by computer from each of the above groups 100 females and 100 males giving a total sample of 800 or .007% of the total population. (Trautman, 2000, p. 84)

Technically, the example above from Trautman's dissertation is not a simple random sample but a stratified random sample. The target population of superintendents, assistant superintendents, secondary principals, and elementary principals in her study were divided into equal numbers of males and females. Thus, she stratified her sample on the basis of gender, which results in a sample that is representative in terms of this characteristic. Stratified random sampling usually provides a more representative sample than strictly simple random sampling does and, therefore, is usually the sampling procedure chosen.

Stratified Random Sampling

Stratified random sampling is the process of selecting a sample in such a way that identified subgroups in the population are represented in the sample in the same proportion that they exist in the population. It can also be used to select equalized samples from a number of subgroups if subgroup comparisons are desired. For example, equal-sized samples would be most useful if you wanted to compare the performance of different subgroups. Suppose, for example, that you were interested in comparing the achievement of students of different ability levels (high, average, and low) being taught by two different methods of mathematics instruction, traditional and computer. The steps in stratified sampling are similar to those in random sampling except that the selection is from subgroups in the population rather than the population as a whole.

An excerpt from Darlene Blair's (2001) dissertation follows. (See Example 8.4.)

Example 8.4

Selection of Participants

There are 1,041 school districts in the state of Texas represented by 7,395 schools. The population of this study consisted of the principals of the 6,367 public schools located in those districts that were rated by the Accountability Rating System of the Texas Education Agency for the year 2000. A sample size of 364 was required for the given population as suggested by Krejcie and Morgan (1970). A stratified random purposive sample ($N = 400$) was selected that represented a proportional sample of the principals of Exemplary, Recognized, Acceptable, and Low-Performing elementary and secondary schools. Based on Texas Education Agency (TEA) data for the 1999–2000 school year, of those randomly chosen, 20 percent represented schools that were rated Exemplary, 30 percent represented schools that were rated Recognized, 43 percent represented schools that were rated Acceptable, and 5 percent represented schools that were rated Low-Performing (TEA, 2000). The sampling and contact information for the potential principal participants was obtained from the Texas Education Public School Directory. (Blair, 2001, pp. 39–40)

Note that Blair stratified her sample based on school ratings of "Exemplary," "Recognized," "Acceptable," and "Low Performing." The goals of her research were to (a) determine relationships between principals' leadership styles and student achievement as evidenced by school ratings, and (b) examine relationships between the amount of time principals spend on instructional leadership and management tasks and school ratings. Therefore, her sample of principals needed to be stratified by school ratings to determine the relationships tested.

Cluster Sampling

Cluster sampling is the process of selecting groups, not individuals. For example, instead of randomly selecting from all ninth graders in a large school district, you could randomly select all ninth grade classrooms and use all the students in each classroom. Examples of clusters include classrooms, schools, school districts, city blocks, and hospitals. The steps in cluster sampling are not very different from those involved in random sampling. The major difference is that random selection of groups (clusters) is involved, not individuals.

Just as it is highly unlikely that one randomly selected student could ever be representative of an entire population, it is also unlikely that one randomly selected school could be representative of all schools in the population. To overcome this problem, be sure to select a sufficiently large sample of clusters.

Following is an example of cluster sampling from Linda Schmidt's (1987) dissertation. (See Example 8.5.)

Example 8.5

Sample

The sample for the study consisted of 239 elementary and secondary teachers and their students from two elementary and four secondary schools in five school districts in a midwestern state. Although the school sample was not random, it was diverse and distributed among urban, suburban, and rural areas and spanned the entire range of socioeconomic status. Extremely small elementary schools were not included in the sample; in fact, only schools with 10 or more faculty members where considered candidates for the sample. Schools that participated ranged in size from 468 to over 3,000 students, with a mean of 1,098 students. Two of the secondary schools were located in a large metropolitan city. Another high school and one elementary school were in its suburbs. The two remaining schools, one elementary and one secondary school, were located in another area of the same state and could be described as rural-small town. Furthermore, the sample represented a group of educators diverse in age, race, gender, experience, and educational level. The student sample was also diverse in grade level, racial composition, gender, and socioeconomic status.

After the schools were selected, trained researchers personally collected data from faculty and students in each school. PCI data were obtained from virtually the entire upper grade level elementary faculty and the entire secondary faculty in each school. However, only teachers who taught major subjects that met five periods per week were asked to participate. Each of the 293 teachers, 49 elementary and 190 secondary teachers, completed PCI Forms and personal data sheets. Similarly, PCB and QSL data were collected from one class taught by each of these teachers by a researcher during regularly scheduled classes. In elementary schools fifth through eighth grade classes were selected by the throw of a die for each grade level. In high schools 9th through 12th grade students were chosen by the throw of a die for each grade level. Except for a few, all of the students selected in this manner completed the forms, which were reverse ordered in approximately half of the classes. A total of 5,172 students furnished usable PCB Forms and 5,199 students completed usable QSL Scales for an average of 26 students per classroom. In all, more than 5,000 faculty and students in 239 classes returned usable questionnaires. (Schmidt, 1987, p. 38)

Cluster sampling was used to obtain the participants for Schmidt's dissertation. Rather than drawing individual names at random and then trying to contact individual teachers and students who would be scattered throughout the schools, she found it more effective to draw a random sample of school districts, schools, and eventually classrooms within those schools (i.e., clusters) and request the classroom teachers to help gather the data for her (i.e., ask them to help her distribute the student questionnaires). This method of sample selection resulted in the completion of questionnaires from 239 teachers (100% return rate) and more than 5,100 students (approximately 96% useable returns). Thus, all teachers completed the instruments. Except for those students who were absent on the day the questionnaires were administered, virtually all students completed the instruments administered in the respective elementary and secondary classrooms.

Systematic Sampling

Systematic sampling is sampling in which individuals are selected from a list by taking every nth name. What N actually equals depends on the size of the list and the desired sample size. For example, if $N = 4$, selection involves taking every 4th name, if $N = 10$, every 10th name, and so forth.

Following is an example from Scott Barrett's (2000) dissertation. (See Example 8.6.)

Example 8.6

Systematic sampling. The total population of Texas public school principals that utilize Pentamation at the time of this study was 662. This number was determined by identifying the Texas public school districts that utilize Pentamation, then acquiring a directory of principals from those school districts from the Texas Education Agency Ask TED (Texas Educational Directory), which provides current directory and mailing information for Texas schools. To avoid any possibility of periodicity, the list of principals was sorted by the name of the city where the school was located. To ensure a sufficient sample size, as determined by the Olejnik chart of Minimal Total Sample Size (as cited in Gall et al., 1996), every fourth name was selected from the list for participation in the study, resulting in a pool of 165 candidates. (Barrett, 2000, pp. 81–82)

The representativeness of your participants is crucial to the external validity of the study. Representativeness of a sample is jeopardized by persons who refuse to participate in a study and using volunteers. Nonresponse can be a problem in studies using mailed and online questionnaires. The seriousness of the problem depends on the amount of nonresponse. You can minimize nonresponse by following the initial questionnaires with follow up requests after two and three weeks respectively (see Appendixes A, B, and C for sample letters). Differences between volunteers and nonvoluntures with respect to the variables examined in the study will affect the representativeness of the sample. Therefore, you need to report not only differences between volunteers and nonvolunteers but also the percentage of nonresponse.

Selecting a Nonrandom Sample

Although random sampling techniques provide the best opportunity to obtain unbiased samples, it is not always possible for researchers to use random sampling. Nonrandom sampling approaches include (a) convenience sampling, (b) purposive sampling, and (c) quota sampling.

Convenience Sampling

Convenience sampling involves including in the sample whoever happens to be available at the time. Examples include the use of volunteers and the use of existing groups just because they are there. If you will be using a convenience sample, generalizations from it to a population will have to be made cautiously. It is best to address this issue directly when describing your sample.

If you must use a convenience sample, consider the possibility of using one that has diversity like Cindy Loeffler (2005) did in her dissertation. Her sample was drawn from several universities. Drawing your sample from several universities (groups) will make your study stronger than if you rely on participation from one institution (or group).

An excerpt from Loeffler's dissertation follows. (See Example 8.7.)

Example 8.7

The second population was represented through a convenience sample of graduate students at both the masters and doctoral level currently enrolled in participating professors' ($n = 72$) education leadership classes during fall 2004. The national student sample for this study can only be estimated ($n = {} < 500$) since the information from each professor indicated an approximation of the student enrollment in online education leadership classes at the time of this study. Professors reported that their classes ranged from hybrid or blended to Web-enhanced to online computer-mediated asynchronous. The number of students surveyed and their geographical distribution over 15 states enable the generalization of this study's results to online graduate classes in education leadership courses and programs in public and private universities and colleges in the continental United States, thereby strengthening the external validity of this study. (Loeffler, 2005, p. 38)

Note how Loeffler strengthened her convenience sample by drawing it from several universities in 15 different states. Obviously, the broader the sample, the more representative it tends to be.

Quota Sampling

Quota sampling is most often used in survey research when it is not possible to list all members of the population of interest. When quota sampling is involved, data collectors are given exact characteristics and quotas of persons to be interviewed (e.g., 30 unmarried teenage pregnant girls between the ages of 13 and 17).

Purposive Sampling

Purposive sampling involves selecting a sample based on the researcher's experience or knowledge of the group to be sampled. For example, if a researcher planned to study exceptional high schools, she would choose a group of schools to study based on her knowledge of exceptional schools. Clear criteria provide a basis for describing and defending purposive samples. For example, the selection of exceptional schools might be based on criteria such as high proportion of students going to four-year colleges, large numbers of AP students, high passing rates on state-mandated tests, extensive computer facilities, and high proportions of teachers with graduate degrees. Much of the research in qualitative research is purposive. Purposive sampling is used in quantitative research as well.

Following is an example from Vicki Stanfield's (2000) quantitative dissertation. (See Example 8.8.)

Example 8.8

Selection of Participants

In special situations the use of a purposive sample is chosen as the form of data collection (Neuman, 1997). In the current study, the purposive sample provided the means to investigate a specialized population of students attending community colleges in the United States. The exploration of the purposive sample allowed for the examination of enrollment data and students' responses to the College Student Inventory from community colleges only, which had not taken place prior to this study. The researcher sought and received approval from USA Group Noel-Levitz, Inc. to utilize the necessary components of their comprehensive database for the purposes outlined in this study. An agreement to preserve both confidentiality and anonymity of institutions and individuals was signed by the researcher and returned to Noel-Levitz prior to receiving the raw data files (see Appendix). Each institution supplied information regarding each CSI respondent's cumulative GPA, terms of enrollment, current enrollment status, and reason for leaving college. A questionnaire containing institutional demographic information was included in the database.

For the purpose of this study, a total of 1,368 students at eight community colleges were selected from the Noel-Levitz database. The institutions were locating in the northern, eastern, and western regions of the United States. Each of these institutions administered the College Student Inventory to incoming freshman students in the first semester of college between the years 1996 to 1999. Student information included in the College Student Inventory included the following attributes: native language, ethnicity, marital status, and mother's and father's highest level of education. (Stanfield, 2000, pp. 42–43)

Sampling in Qualitative Research

Sampling in qualitative research is almost always purposive. Within the domain of purposive sampling are a number of specific approaches useful in qualitative research including:

1. *Intensity sampling:* selecting participants who permit study of different levels of the research topic (e.g., good and bad students, experienced and inexperienced teachers, or teachers in self-contained classrooms and teachers in departmentalized teams).

2. *Homogeneous sampling:* selecting participants who are very similar in experience or philosophy; this produces a narrow, homogeneous sample and makes data collection and analysis simpler.

3. *Criterion sampling:* selecting participants who meet some criterion (e.g., students who have been retained for two successive years, teachers who left the field to raise children and then returned to teaching, female administrators with more than 15 years of experience).

4. *Snowball sampling:* selecting a few people who can identify other people who can identify still other people who might be good participants for a study; this approach is most useful when a study is carried on in a setting in which possible participants are scattered or not found in clusters.

5. *Random purposive sampling* (with small sample)*:* selecting by random means participants who were purposively selected and who are too numerous to include all in the sample; for example, if 25 potential participants were purposively identified by the researcher, but only 10 participants could be studied, a random sample of 10 from the 25 potential participants would be chosen; this approach adds credibility to the sample but is still based on an initial sample that was purposively selected.

Qualitative research uses sampling techniques that produce samples that are predominantly small and nonrandom. This is in keeping with qualitative research's emphasis on in-depth description of participants' perspectives and context.

As mentioned previously, the purpose of qualitative research is to obtain an in-depth understanding of purposively selected participants from their perspective. Thus, if you conduct qualitative research, you should purposively select participants who meet criteria that will provide a sample that is likely to yield the type of information you need to achieve your purpose. For example, suppose the purpose of your study is to apply a theory to the leadership experiences of superintendents leading successful school districts. The theory you have selected is the Synergistic Leadership Theory (SLT) (Irby, Brown, Duffy, & Trautman, 2002). The SLT is a gender-inclusive theory containing four factors that impact successful leadership: (a) attitudes, values, and beliefs, (b) leadership behaviors, (c) organizational structure, and (d) external factors. Your research goal is to test the SLT theory with superintendents leading successful school districts. Specifically, you want to examine the alignment of the four factors of the theory with the leadership experiences of a national sample of school superintendents.

Obviously one criterion you will use is that the superintendent-participants will need to be successful superintendents. Other criteria you might consider include: (a) Will you restrict the sample to superintendent self reports, or will you include other role incumbents in your sample, superordinates and subordinates to the superintendent (i.e., school board members and associate/assistant superintendents, respectively) to obtain their assessments of the superintendent? (b) Will you include superintendents and others from urban, suburban, and rural districts, or will you limit the sample to those in one type of district? (c) Will you include male and female superintendents in your sample? After thinking about such questions, you should prepare a statement of the criteria for the selection of participants to include in Chapter Three of your dissertation.

The following is an excerpt from Wanda Bamberg's (2004) qualitative dissertation containing such a statement. (See Example 8.9.)

Example 8.9

Selection of Participants

The purposive (Gall, Borg, & Gall, 1996) sample for this study included 15 participants. Five female superintendents who participated in the original Learning First Alliance (LFA) study conducted in 2001–2002 comprised one third of the sample and were the primary focus for the study. They were the leaders for the school districts chosen for the LFA study.

Five districts where identified from among 60 districts nationally, a study conducted by LFA in 2001–2002 based on the following criteria: (a) the district's ability to exhibit at least three years of improvement in student achievement in mathematics and/or reading across multiple grades and across all races and ethnicities; and (b) the district's representation of a cross section of characteristics, including size, region, urbanicity, and union affiliation (Togneri, 2003). After LFA researchers identified five school districts, they discovered that all five districts had female superintendents.

The sample for my study included the five superintendents identified by LFA and also included central office administrative team members and school board members from each district for a total of 15 participants. The administrative team members from the districts included top-level administrators in positions with experience working directly with the superintendent to make the district successful. In each case, the administrative team member would be considered the second in command or the second in command responsible for instruction or strategic planning. Board members for the study included experienced members who had worked with the superintendent for several years and were judged by the district contacts or superintendents to be knowledgeable of the district work and success over three to five years. Some board members and administrative team members were also participants in the LFA study. (Bamberg, 2004, pp. 45–46)

Note that sample size in qualitative research is typically smaller than in quantitative studies. This is because you will be striving for in-depth information in qualitative research. It is more important for you to spend sufficient time with a small number of participants than to work superficially with a large number.

How Many Participated in the Study?

One question students often ask when planning their dissertation or master's thesis is: How many participants do I need? The response from committee chairs is likely to be: It depends. Researchers use four major ways of making the decision: (a) heuristics, (b) literature review, (c) formulas, and (d) power analysis.

Heuristics

A heuristic is a rule of thumb that can help the decision maker find a solution to a complex problem (Lunenburg, 2006). We offer very rough guidelines for sample sizes that might be used in studies of different types: (a) For qualitative research, use from 1 to 20 participants (on the lower end if you are using groups); (b) for survey research, drawn from very large populations such as superintendents, assistant superintendents, secondary principals, elementary principals in the United States, use 800 or more participants (see Example 8.3); (c) for correlation research, use 100 to 200 participants; (d) for causal-comparative research, use more than 30 participants; (e) for experimental research, use 30 or more participants; (f) for factorial statistical designs, at least 15 participants is required per cell; and (g) for multiple regression statistical designs, use at least 10 participants for each variable.

Literature Review

Another way to determine sample size is to review the literature. Look at studies that are similar to yours. Pay attention to past studies that employed the same method of research as yours and that used similar variables to the study you are planning. Be cautious, however, when using such norms, because many published studies have used too few participants to have sufficient statistical power, even those published in the most prestigious journals.

Formulas

A third method of determining appropriate sample size is to use a formula. Krejcie and Morgan (1970) generated a model of appropriate sample size (S) required for given population sizes (N). Their model is based on a formula originally developed by the U.S. Office of Education (see Table 8.3).

As shown in Table 8.3, the following general guidelines are helpful in determining sample size (Gay, Miles, & Airisian, 2006).

1. The larger the population size, the smaller the percentage of the population required to get a representative sample.

2. For smaller populations, say, $N = 100$ or fewer, there is little point in sampling; survey the entire population.

3. If the population size is around 500 (give or take 100), 50% should be sampled.

4. If the population size is around 1,500, 20% should be sampled.

5. Beyond a certain point (about $N = 5,000$), the population size is almost irrelevant and a sample size of 400 will be adequate. (p. 110)

Of course, these numbers or percentages are suggested minimums. If it is possible to obtain more participants, you should do so.

Table 8.3   Sample Sizes (S) Required for Given Population Sizes (N)

N	S	N	S	N	S	N	S	N	S
10	10	100	80	280	162	800	260	2800	338
15	14	110	86	290	165	850	265	3000	341
20	19	120	92	300	169	900	269	3500	346
25	24	130	97	320	175	950	274	4000	351
30	28	140	103	340	181	1000	278	4500	354
35	32	150	108	360	186	1100	285	5000	357
40	36	160	113	380	191	1200	291	6000	361
45	40	170	118	400	196	1300	297	7000	364
50	44	180	123	420	201	1400	302	8000	367
55	48	190	127	440	205	1500	306	9000	368
60	52	200	132	460	210	1600	310	20000	370
65	56	210	136	480	214	1700	313	15000	375
70	59	220	140	500	217	1800	317	20000	377
75	63	230	144	550	226	1900	320	30000	379
80	66	240	148	600	234	2000	322	40000	380
85	70	250	152	650	242	2200	327	50000	381
90	73	260	155	700	248	2400	331	75000	382
95	76	270	159	750	254	2600	335	100000	384

SOURCE: From R. V. Krejcie and D. W. Morgan, "Determining Sample Size for Research Activities," *Education and Psychological Measurement, 30*, p. 608, copyright © 1970 Sage Publications, Inc., Reprinted by permission of Sage Publications, Inc.

Power Analysis

A fourth and more precise method of determining an appropriate sample size for your research is to calculate a power analysis. The purpose of a power analysis is to determine how many participants you will need to detect how much of a difference your independent variable makes in relation to the dependent variable. Thus, power analysis allows you to estimate how many participants you will need to detect small effects, medium effects, and large effects.

Cohen (1988) and Olejnik (1984) explain how to calculate power analyses. Cohen (1992) and Olejnik (1984) provide brief, very readable discussions of power analysis as well as tables you can use to estimate the number of participants you will need to detect small, medium, or large effect sizes at the $p < .01, .05,$ and $.10$ levels. The tables cover t tests, analysis of variance, correlations, chi square, and multiple regression analysis.

INSTRUMENTATION

Up to this point in Chapter Three, you introduced your chapter under the heading "Introduction." This was followed by a description of the population and sample under the heading "Selection of Participants." Your next heading in Chapter Three is "Instrumentation," under which you will describe the psychometric adequacy of the instruments you have used in your study. Each description should include the following key points: (a) name of the instrument, (b) acronym, (c) author(s), (d) key reference(s), (e) purpose of the instrument (i.e., what it measures), (f) number of items, (g) subtests or subscales and their definitions, (h) response format (e.g., Likert, multiple choice, yes/no, open-ended), (i) scoring of the instrument, (j) reliability, and (k) validity (Heppner & Heppner, 2004).

All of the aforementioned key points provide important information about the instrument(s), but reliability and validity are critical. The measurement instrument that you use must be both valid and reliable. On the one hand, validity is the most important characteristic of an instrument. On the other hand, reliability is necessary for validity; an instrument that does not provide reliable measures cannot provide valid ones.

Validity

Validity is the degree to which an instrument measures what it purports to measure. There are three main types of validity: (a) content validity, (b) criterion-related validity, and (c) construct validity.

Content Validity

Content validity is the degree to which an instrument measures an intended content area. Content validity is of particular importance for achievement tests. A test score cannot accurately reflect a student's achievement if it does not measure what the student was taught and was expected to learn. For example, most standardized achievement tests have good content validity. Content validity is determined by expert judgment.

Criterion-Related Validity

Criterion-related validity has two forms, concurrent and predictive. Concurrent validity is the degree to which scores on one test correlate to scores on another test when both tests are administered at about the same time. Predictive validity is the degree to which a test can predict how well individuals will do in a future situation. Predictive validity is important for tests that are used to select individuals. Examples are the use of the SAT or ACT as a criterion for admission to colleges and universities, and the Graduate Record Examination (GRE) or Miller Analogies Test (MAT) scores to select students for admission to graduate school.

Construct Validity

Construct validity is the most important form of validity, because it deals with what the instrument is really measuring. As mentioned earlier, all variables derive from constructs, such as intelligence, achievement, personality, and so forth.

Content and criterion-related validity are used in studies to determine an instrument's construct validity. No single validation study can establish the construct validity of an instrument. Instead, a serious of studies would be required to establish construct validity. Construct validity provides justification of the instrument being used in a research study and the appropriateness of the intended instrument interpretations.

Reliability

Reliability is the degree to which an instrument consistently measures whatever it is measuring. There are five different types of reliability, each of which deals with a different kind of instrument consistency: (a) test-retest reliability, (b) equivalent-forms reliability, (c) internal consistency reliability, (d) alpha reliability, (e) split-half reliability, and (f) interrater reliability.

Test–Retest Reliability

Test-retest reliability is the degree to which scores on the same instrument are consistent over time. The procedure for determining test-retest reliability is as follows: Administer the instrument to an appropriate group. After about two weeks has passed, administer the same instrument to the same group. Correlate the two sets of scores. Evaluate the results. If the resulting coefficient is high, the instrument has good test-retest reliability.

Equivalent-Forms Reliability

Equivalent forms of an instrument are two instruments that are identical in every way except for the actual items included. Examples are equivalent forms of a norm-referenced standardized achievement test. Also, in some research studies, two forms of an instrument are administered to the same group, one as a pretest and the other as a posttest. The procedure for determining equivalent-forms reliability is as follows: Administer one form of the test to an appropriate group. At the same session, or shortly thereafter, administer the second form of the instrument to the same group. Correlate the two sets of scores. Evaluate the results. If the resulting coefficient of equivalence is high, the instrument has good equivalent-forms reliability.

Internal Consistency Reliability

Internal consistency is a commonly used form of reliability that deals with one instrument at a time. There are three different approaches to obtaining internal consistency reliability: split-half, Kuder-Richardson, and Cronbach's alpha.

Kuder-Richardson and Cronbach's Alpha Reliabilities

Kuder-Richardson (KR) and Cronbach's alpha estimate internal consistency reliability by determining how all items on an instrument relate to all other instrument items and to the total instrument. An internal consistency coefficient of .80 is acceptable for an instrument containing 40 items. If an instrument contains subscales, internal consistency coefficients should be obtained for each subscale. Instruments containing fewer items and subscales will typically have smaller reliability coefficients.

Split-Half Reliability

Split-half reliability involves breaking a single instrument into two halves. The procedure for determining split-half reliability is as follows: Administer the total test to a group. Divide the test into comparable halves, most commonly by dividing the instrument into odd and even numbered subtests. Compute each subject's score on the two halves; each subject will have a score for the odd items and a score for even numbers. Correlate the two sets of scores. Apply the Spearman-Brown correction formula. Evaluate the results. If the coefficient is high, the instrument has good split-half reliability.

Interrater Reliability

Reliability must be investigated also when scoring potentially subjective instruments. Essay tests, performance tests, projective tests, and observations—almost any instrument that requires more than a one-word response—raise concerns about the reliability of scoring. In such situations, researchers are concerned with interjudge (interscorer, interobserver, interrater) reliability. Estimates of interjudge reliability are typically obtained by correlation techniques but can also be expressed as a percentage of agreement.

A note of caution: When you discuss your instrument and the related reliability and validity, remember that reliability is related to the scores or the data derived from your instrument; therefore, it is the scores that are either reliable or unreliable. You would not say, "The instrument is reliable." Reliability is a function of the scores and is related specifically to your sample or the norming sample for a standardized instrument. You should also be cautious in stating that the test or instrument is valid. The items of the instrument have, for example, content, criterion, or construct validity and should be discussed under those conditions. You may also wish to discuss the items related to face validity.

Examples of instrument descriptions from two dissertations follow. The first example of instrumentation is from Victoria Cadavid's (1986) dissertation. The second example is from Linda Schmidt's (1987) dissertation. (See Examples 8.10 and 8.11.)

Example 8.10

Instrumentation

Maslach Burnout Inventory

The Maslach Burnout Inventory (Maslach & Jackson 1981), which was entitled Human Services to disguise the purpose of the study, was used to measure dimensions of teacher burnout. It consists of 22 items forming three subscales: Emotional Exhaustion, Personal Accomplishment, and Depersonalization and is rated on both frequency of feeling and intensity of the feeling on each subscale producing six dimensions. The frequency scale ranges from 1 (a few times a year or less) to 6 (every day). A value of zero is given if the respondent never experiences the described attitude or feeling; a separate box labeled "never" is used in this event. The intensity scale ranges from 1 (very mild, barely noticeable) to 7 (major, very strong).

The Emotional Exhaustion subscale, consisting of nine items, describes feelings of being emotionally overextended and exhausted by one's work. The five items on the Depersonalization subscale describe unfeeling and impersonal responses to coworkers or recipients of services. The Personal Accomplishment subscale consists of eight items describing feelings of competence and success towards one's achievements. The higher mean scores of Emotional Exhaustion and Depersonalization subscales correspond to greater degrees of experienced burnout, whereas lower scores on Personal Accomplishment correspond to greater degrees of burnout. One final score for burnout is not computed; instead, six separate scores are derived for burnout.

Internal consistency of the MBI was estimated by Cronbach's alpha (Cronbach, 1951) for two samples ($n = 1316$ for frequency) and ($n = 1789$ for intensity). The reliability coefficients for the subscales were as follows: .90 for Emotional Exhaustion Frequency, .87 for Emotional Exhaustion Intensity, .79 for Depersonalization Frequency, .76 for Depersonalization Intensity, .71 for Personal Accomplishment Frequency, and .73 for Personal Accomplishment Intensity (Maslach & Jackson, 1981). Data on test-retest reliability ($n = 53$) ranged from .53 to .89 for the six dimensions of the MBI and were significant beyond the .001 level (Maslach & Jackson, 1981). Convergent validity was established by Maslach and Jackson (1981). Individual MBI scores were correlated with behavioral ratings made independently by persons who knew the individual well, such as a spouse or co-worker. Second, MBI scores were correlated with the presence of certain job characteristics that were expected to contribute to experienced burnout. Third, MBI scores were correlated with measures of various outcomes that had been hypothesized to be related to burnout. All three sets of correlations provided substantial evidence for the validity of the MBI. (Cadavid, 1986, pp. 54–55)

Locus of Control

The Internal-External Locus of Control Scale (Rotter, 1966), called the Social Reaction Survey for purposes of this study, was used to measure the extent to which faculty had an internal or external locus of control. It consists of 29 forced-choice items of which 23 are keyed and six are fillers. Respondents choose one statement out of each pair of 29 statements. It is scored in the direction of externality such that a higher score indicates external orientation. A total score of 12 or less out of 23 assesses an individual as internally controlled and a score of 13 or more assesses one as externally controlled. Test-retest reliability coefficients of .43 to .84 have been reported by Hersch and Scheibe (1967). Internal consistency of the scale ranged from .65 to .79 (Rotter, 1966). (Cadavid, 1986, pp. 53–54)

Pupil Control Ideology

The Pupil Control Ideology Form (PCI) measures the pupil control ideology of educators on a humanistic-custodial continuum. It consists of 20 Likert-type items. Responses are scored from 5 (strongly agree) to 1 (strongly disagree); the higher the overall score, the more custodial the ideology of the respondent.

Prior studies by Willower, et al. (1973) using the PCI Form determined split-half reliability coefficients in two samples of .95 ($N = 170$) and .91 ($N = 55$) with the application of the Spearman-Brown formula. Validity of the instrument was supported by principals' judgments of some of their own teachers. Further evidence of validity was established by a comparison of PCI scores of personnel from schools known by reputation to be humanistic, with scores of personnel from other schools that were not humanistic at the same grade levels (Cadavid, 1986, pp. 57–58)

Example 8.11

Instruments

Quality of School Life

The Quality of School Life Scale (QSL) is a standardized 27-item forced-choice, multidimensional measure of three basic aspects of the quality of school life. The initial validation study (Epstien & McPartland, 1976) indicated the existence of three factors: satisfaction with school (SAT), commitment to classwork (COM) and reactions to teachers (TCH). The *satisfaction with school* subscale examines student's general reactions to school. Because school is a major part of youngsters' lives, students who are positive in their evaluation of life in school may be more likely to experience feelings of general well-being. They also may be more likely to behave in socially acceptable ways and help other students in the school setting. The *commitment to classwork* subscale deals with the level of student interest in classwork. Tasks and assignments are what makes school different from non-school settings. In short, the work is what makes school a school. Students who find class assignments and projects interesting and important may learn facts and concepts more completely and may develop more positive attitudes toward learning. The *reactions to teachers* subscale examines student evaluations of instructional and personal interactions with teachers. Student-teacher relationships may be the key to student acceptance of educational goals, student understanding of school procedures, differences in students' independent or dependent behavior and attitudes toward authority in and out of school.

The first factor (SAT) consists of 5 items and the other two factors (COM) and (TCH) include 11 items each. Items use positive and negative statements and several response patterns to minimize response set. Examples of items include the following: "I like school very much" (SAT); "Work in class is just busy work and a waste of time" (COM); and "I feel I can go to my teacher with the things that are on my mind" (TCH). Responses to the questionnaire are scored so as to yield measures on each of the three qualities of school life factors, and the sum of the factor scores represents a global measure of the quality of school life. Substantial evidence as to the validity of the QSL Scale has been reported. The overall Kuder-Richardson reliability for the QSL is .87 and .89 for secondary and elementary students ($N = 4,266$), respectively. For the subtests, reliability coefficients range from .79 to .81 for the SAT subscale, .72 to .80 for the COM subscale and .64 to .73 for the TCH subscale (Epstein & McPartland, 1978). (Schmidt, 1987, pp. 48–49)

First, note how efficiently most of the 11 key points related to psychometric adequacy, discussed earlier, are addressed in the instrument descriptions from the dissertations of Cadavid and Schmidt. Second, note how the writers have provided key references pertaining to the psychometric properties of the instruments rather than attempting to summarize hundreds of investigations. Third, we recommend that you include a copy of each instrument in the appendix of your dissertation or master's thesis, if possible. If the instrument(s) are copyrighted, you will need to get permission in writing not only to *use* the instrument but also to *publish* it in your dissertation. Both permissions must be clearly stated in the letter for inclusion in your dissertation.

There should be a close match between your research questions and hypotheses and the measuring instruments you use. When there is no published instrument that closely matches your research purposes, there are three alternatives: modify slightly an existing instrument; combine existing instruments; or develop a new instrument. The first two alternatives may make the norms invalid and may affect both the validity and reliability of the instrument. Developing and assessing a new instrument is a valid dissertation topic in itself (e.g., see Lauren Black's 2003 dissertation, referenced earlier in this book).

If you develop a new instrument to be used in your study, you will not have information on the psychometric adequacy of the instrument. In this case, you will need to conduct a pilot study and report the results of that study. Your report should include the number and demographic characteristics of the participants, the criterion used to develop the initial item pool and final items, and information concerning the reliability and validity of the instrument.

The following example from Vickie Basham's (1988) dissertation shows how this might be accomplished. (See Example 8.12.)

Example 8.12

Instrumentation

Strategic Planning

Having defined the concept of strategic planning, the next step was to develop a measure of that concept. Since a validated instrument had not yet been developed, the need arose to devise an operational measure of strategic planning.

One of the early decisions that had to be made in an attempt to measure strategic planning centered on the method of measurement to be used. It was decided that a descriptive questionnaire was the most feasible and appropriate for this initial attempt to map the domain of strategic planning. This decision was prompted by the success previous investigators have experienced using the descriptive questionnaire technique (Stogdill & Coons, 1957; Halpin, 1956; Halpin & Croft, 1963; Gross & Herriott, 1965; Punch, 1967; Willower et al., 1967). While there are criticisms of this technique, especially those that have called into question respondents' perceptions as a measure of "true" behavior (Charters, 1964; Erickson, 1965, 1967), it was deemed appropriate for this study. It was decided to adopt the symbolic interactionist viewpoint taken by a number of previous developers and users of description questionnaires; i.e., that the technique is justified " . . . more because of than in spite of the susceptibility of these descriptive statements to projective distortion . . ." (Brown, 1967, pp. 62–73). The metaphysical problem is provided by assuming that how an individual really behaves is less important than the way he is perceived to behave, since it is perceptions of strategic planning behavior that determines the perceivers' own actions. Best (1981) states that "descriptive design . . . describes and interprets what is. It is concerned with conditions or relationships that exist, opinions that are evident, or trends that are developing" (p. 93).

As an operational measure of strategic planning, an instrument called the Strategic Planning in Kentucky Schools (SPKS) Scale was developed. The final form of this instrument consists of twenty items with several response categories in a Likert-type format.

Construction of the instrument was begun by writing 63 statements, which described specific strategic planning concepts. These statements were based on a review of the literature, the authors' experience in administering public school districts, and items developed by members in a research methods class.

The items were then screened for ambiguity, wording, and content overlap. To insure content validity, the resultant pool of items was subjected to the scrutiny and evaluation of four experts: a professor of educational administration at the University of Louisville, a superintendent of schools, an independent planning consultant, and an administrator in the Department of Planning and Development in the Kentucky Department of Education. As a result of this initial work with the instrument, a 37- item form emerged for further modification.

In order to gather more systematic data on the instrument, the 37-item version of the SPKS Scale was then administered in 89 (urban, suburban, and rural areas) school districts outside of Kentucky. A total of 66 usable returns were collected from the superintendents of the selected districts. As a result of this field test of the instrument, several statements were modified and a number of statements were omitted, leaving twenty items in the final form of the instrument. An alpha coefficient (Cronbach, 1951) of .59 supported the moderate reliability of the scale. From these data, it was determined that the SPKS Scale was a relatively valid and reliable measure of strategic planning. (Basham, 1988, pp. 58–59)

Note the thoroughness with which Basham described the development of the SPKS Scale. Also note that the scale went through intensive scrutiny by four experts in the field (construct validity) and pilot testing by a relatively large sample of 66 superintendents selected from 89 school districts outside of the state in which the study was conducted.

Another example of the development of a new instrument, from Lunenburg and Schmidt (1987), follows. A description of the procedures used in developing the instrument together with a copy of the instrument is provided. This study was funded by a grant. (See Example 8.13.)

Example 8.13

Method

Test Construction

Construction of the instrument was begun by generating items from a review of the literature and from suggestions from practicing school administrators. In addition, members of the first author's graduate classes in research methods contributed statements as an exercise in item construction. The items, which were statements describing specific pupil disruptive behavior, were placed in questionnaire format using an eight-point Likert scale ranging on a continuum from "no action" to "expulsion." The items were then screened for ambiguity, wording, and content overlap. To insure content validity, the resultant poll of items was subjected to the scrutiny and evaluation of four experts: a high school principal, an assistant principal, a professor of education administration, and a statistics professor. The critics were individually instructed to determine which items represented school realties. If a majority of the judges agreed (*interrater reliability*), an item was retained. This process generated 64 items.

Subjects

Subjects were 227 full-time educators from three states: Illinois ($N = 106$), Iowa ($N = 83$), and Wisconsin ($N = 38$). Included were regular education teachers (51%), special education teachers (21%), school administrators (16%), and school counselors (12%). The subjects had an average of 15.2 years of experience and an average age of 43.4. Of the 227 subjects, 141 were male and 86 were female. All subjects were employed in high schools.

Data Analysis

A principal components factor analysis, using an orthogonal rotation with varimax solution, provided the best solution. In order to maximize simple structure and theoretical clarity, items that exhibited factor load-ings whose absolute value was .40 or greater were used to define a factor. Application of the Scree Test (Cattell, 1966) clearly identified three inter-pretable factors. The three factors accounted for 45% of the variance. The 35 items, which did not conform psychometrically or theoretically to any factor were eliminated. Alpha coefficients (Cronbach, 1951) of .93 for the total scale and for the respective factors (.91, .79, and .73) supported their moderately high reliability.

Results

The final form of the PDB together with their factor loadings are pre-sented in [Table 8.4].

Factor 1 had salient loadings on eleven items dealing with general indifference to school rules. Included were items about unexcused absences from school or class, tardiness to school or class, smoking in unauthorized areas of the school building, and minor acts of insubordi-nation and classroom distractions.

Factor 2 contained ten items, which appeared to be more serious vio-lations of school rules and, in some cases, violations of state law. It was comprised of items concerned with fighting, theft, profanity, vandalism, battery, and the possession, use, and sale of drugs.

The eight items loading on Factor 3 dealt primarily with minor dis-ruptions of school and classroom activity. Included were items concerning disobedience of posted school rules, inappropriate dress, cheating on examinations, and classroom interruptions.

Conclusion

The purpose of this present study was to develop an operational mea-sure of pupil disruptive behavior. The instrument empirically identifies incidents of disruptive behavior in schools and their dimensions. While more narrowly defined, the incidents of disruptive behavior in the pre-sent study seem closely related to those suggested in the literature and by practicing school administrators. The study suggests that the PDB is a short, direct, reliable measure useful at the high school level for research and evaluation. (Lunenburg & Schmidt, 1987, pp. 1082–1084)

Table 8.4   Factor Structure for the PDB Scale Items

Item	Factor
Factor 1	
58. A boy skips school and goes skiing.	.746
19. A girl is observed smoking in the girls' lavatory.	.706
12. A boy is late for school and submits a forged note as an excuse.	.672
61. A girl skips a class and spends her time roaming the school corridors.	.669
16. A girl refuses to participate in physical education activity.	.661
11. A boy is seen smoking in the school cafeteria.	.635

(Continued)

Table 8.4 (Continued)

Item	Factor

Factor 1

09.	A girl is late for school and uses the excuse that her car wouldn't start.	.604
39.	A boy is summoned to the assistant principal's office and arrives one hour later without an explanation.	.599
07.	After being reprimanded by her teacher, a girl makes an obscene gesture using the middle finger of her right hand.	.584
27.	A girl tears a page out of a reference book in the library.	.561
54.	A girl is observed setting a fire in a waste basket in the girl's lavatory.	.555

Factor 2

44.	A boy is observed stealing money from another boy's locker.	.762
15.	Two girls are observed fighting in the school cafeteria.	.690
60.	A girl is seen smoking marijuana in the school parking lot shortly before school.	.641
32.	A boy is discovered carving his initials in a desk during class.	.627
30.	A boy is observed selling drugs to another student.	.603
57.	A boy is seen puncturing the tire of a teacher's car.	.595
51.	After being reprimanded by his teacher, a boy shouts, "kiss my ass," to the teacher.	.564
33.	During an authorized search of a boy's locker, drugs are discovered in the student's locker.	.516
46.	A boy is observed throwing a rock through a window of the school building shortly after school.	.508
52.	After being reprimanded by his teacher, a boy strikes the teacher in the face with his fist.	.469

Factor 3

35.	A boy comes to school with an earring in his ear.	.645
41.	A boy is observed playing basketball in the gymnasium in his street clothes after being warned that such behavior is in violation of gymnasium rules.	.620
13.	A girl walks across the grass on the school campus in an area marked "keep off."	.547
08.	A girl is discovered copying answers from her own prepared "crib notes" during an examination.	.522
18.	A boy interrupts a classroom activity by shouting at a friend in the corridor.	.505
42.	A boy is observed riding his bicycle in the school corridor shortly after school.	.502
23.	A girl interrupts a class by laughing and talking while the teacher is lecturing.	.440
55.	A boy disrupts a class by throwing an eraser at another student.	.401

Response Categories:

No Action	Mild Reprimand	Severe Reprimand	Detentions 1 to 3 Hours	Detentions 4 to 8 Hours	Suspension 1 to 3 Days	Suspension 4 to 10 Days	Expulsion

You will note that the instrument Basham developed for use in her dissertation was a unifactor instrument. A factor analysis of the instrument was conducted as part of her dissertation. The second instrument, developed by Lunenburg and Schmidt, was a multifactor instrument consisting of three distinct subscales. Note how content validity and reliability (internal consistency) of the instrument and its subscales, using Cronbach's alpha, were reported. All newly developed instruments as well as all existing instruments used in a dissertation must be subjected to a factor analysis using your research sample. Whether master's theses need to follow the same procedure will depend on your committee's requirements.

We have described the psychometric adequacy of instruments followed by examples of instrument descriptions from several dissertations. We have discussed also the development of new instruments followed by examples of them. Where do you look for such measures?

Locating Instruments

Instruments are available to you, if you know where to look for them. The following published documents provide valuable information about instruments.

1. *Mental Measurements Yearbooks (MMYs)* represent the most comprehensive source of test information available to educational researchers.

2. *Tests in Print (TIP)* is a comprehensive bibliography of all tests that have appeared in preceding MMYs. It includes more listings than MMYs and is a good source for locating addresses and journal articles relevant to a particular instrument. However, it is rather dated and will not have listings for instruments available after 1974.

3. *Pro-Ed Publications* provide information on over 3,000 instruments intended for assessment in psychology, education, and business.

4. *Educational Testing Service (ETS) Test Collection* is an excellent source of test information, especially for recently developed tests. It includes a library of 20,000 tests and other instruments from the early 1900s to the present. The ETS Test Collection can be accessed via the Internet at: http://www.ets.org.

5. Professional journals regularly publish information of interest to researchers. Journals of interest to researchers include: *Journal of Applied Measurement, Journal of Consulting Psychology, Journal of Educational Measurement, Journal of Educational Psychology, Journal of Personnel Psychology, Educational and Psychological Measurement*, and *Psychological Abstracts*.

6. Test publishers provide additional information on instruments. For example, publishers' test manuals typically include: detailed validity and reliability data, a description of the population for whom the instrument is intended, a detailed description of norming procedures, conditions of administration, detailed scoring instructions, and scoring interpretation.

7. *Dictionary of Behavioral Assessment Techniques* provides descriptions of 286 devices and is a very good source of introductory information about an assessment measure. Reviews and references are provided to locate instruments used by researchers in the social and behavioral sciences.

8. Search features are available online in the ERIC/AE Test Locator at http://ericae.net/testcol.htm. (This is the same Web address as that of the ETS Test Collection Database.) These are the Test Review Locator and *Buros/ERIC Test Publisher Directory.* The Test Review Locator allows you to search for citations about a particular testing instrument in MMY and Pro-Ed directories. *The Buros/ERIC Test Publisher Directory* permits you to search for the names and addresses of more than 900 major commercial test publishers.

Qualitative Instrumentation

Paper-and-pencil measurement devices are not the only data collection instrumentation. Interviews, observations, and archival data all constitute valid sources of data collection for dissertations and master's theses. Such types of instrumentation are frequently used by qualitative researchers.

Interviews

Qualitative researchers often use open-ended interviews (i.e., questions are asked but respondents are not provided choices to use as answers, such as Likert scales, multiple choice, yes/no). Typically, these are semistructured questions. That is, some questions are developed in advance. Follow-up questions are developed as the interview progresses based on participant responses.

The following excerpt from Wanda Bamberg's (2004) qualitative dissertation shows how this might be accomplished. (See Example 8.14.)

Example 8.14

Instrumentation

The first instruments in my study were semi-structured, open-ended interviews, with 15 respondents from the five school districts. Merriam

(1998) defined semi-structured interviews as interviews that evolve from inquiry composed of a mix of both structured and unstructured questions. The unstructured questions were open-ended to allow the respondents (participants) more freedom and creativity to respond to the questions (Sowell & Casey, 1982).

I used semi-structured, open-ended interviews with the five superintendents and semi-structured, open-ended interviews with board members and central office administrative team members. The semi-structured interview approach provided reasonably standard data across participants but also allowed me the flexibility to probe answers more deeply and gather more information than is found in a structured interview (Gall et al., 1996). To relate my study to previous work with SLT, questions from the revised Organizational and Leadership Effectiveness Inventory (OLEI) were reviewed to create the interview questions. Three sets of interview questions were developed: one set for the superintendents, one set for the board members, and one set for central office administrative team members (see Appendixes A, B, and C for interview questions). All the interview questions were directly correlated to the research questions and based upon the four factors of the Synergistic Leadership Theory. Questions were designed to allow participants an opportunity to reflect upon the five superintendents' leadership styles and how they relate to the SLT. (Bamberg, 2004, pp. 51–52)

Note how effectively Bamberg described her qualitative instrumentation. Note also that there can be many variations to this example. Your objective is to write a description that is as specific as possible while providing you with the flexibility consistent with qualitative research.

Observations

Another measurement technique frequently used by qualitative researchers is observation. Observation can take two forms: participant observer and nonparticipant observer. A participant observer is one who participants as a member of a group while making observations. A nonparticipant observer is one who makes observations but is not participating. If you plan to use observations, consider asking yourself the following questions to help you write this section of your dissertation or master's thesis: (a) What will I be observing; (b) who will I be observing; (c) when and where will my observations take place; (d) how will I record the observations; (e) how long will I observe; and (f) will I solicit feedback from my participants?

Archival Data

A third technique often used by qualitative researchers is analysis of records or documents. Qualitative researchers examine various types of documents, including archival documents (e.g., student records, standardized test scores, retention rates, minutes of meetings, newspaper clippings); journals; maps; videotapes; audiotapes; and artifacts.

In your section on instrumentation, you should address the issue of demographics (e.g., gender, race/ethnicity, age, years of experience, education level). Demographic data will provide your readers with a picture of your participants. Demographic information should be included in both quantitative and qualitative dissertations and master's theses. We mention it here again because you need to decide how to attach a "demographic data sheet" to your measuring instruments. If you fail to gather demographic data at the time the instrument(s) are administered, it is unlikely that you can obtain this important information later.

DATA COLLECTION

In the "Data Collection" section of your dissertation or master's thesis, describe precisely the physical things you did to obtain data from your participants. Indicate what steps were taken before, during, and after data collection. Before collecting data, it may be necessary for you to develop materials, obtain informed consent from participants, acquire or develop questionnaires or other instruments, screen participants from a list, mail a precontact letter, train experimenters or assistants, conduct a pilot study, and comply with your university's Human Subjects Committee. During data collection, describe what participants will be asked to do, what interventions were used, the order instruments were administered, precise instructions given to each participant, time elapsed between activities, and how data were collected. When data collection procedures are complex and require multiple phases over multiple time periods, a flow chart presenting the procedures visually may be very helpful to the reader. After data collection, describe how participants will be debriefed. In sum, this section should be written in enough detail so that the procedures could be replicated by another investigator.

Following are examples from "Data Collection" sections from students' dissertations. The first example from Diane Trautman's (2000) dissertation provides a model of a data collection section from a mixed methods (quantitative/qualitative) study. (See Example 8.15.)

Example 8.15

Data Collection

This study employed a qualitative and quantitative methodology of data collection and analysis. These two methodologies will be explained separately.

Quantitative

Data Collection. The first step in the quantitative data collection process included mailing to the 800 participants in the sample a copy of the Organizational and Leadership Effectiveness Inventory for validation of the Synergistic Leadership Theory. Address labels received from the Market Data Retrieval Company (2000) were numbered 1 to 800, and then the inventories were coded accordingly in the same way in order for each participant to be identified by the researcher. A master list of all 800 participants was retained by the researcher and were recorded as responses were returned. This list was kept so that follow-up and reminder letters could be mailed to participants and also to select the purposeful sample for telephone interviews. Once participants were selected, the numbers and lists were destroyed.

The first mail-out included a cover letter explaining the study, a copy of the Organizational and Leadership Effectiveness Inventory, and a postage paid return envelope. Respondents were given two weeks to return the inventory, and only 73 out of 800 were returned by that deadline giving a 9.12% return rate. A bright yellow post card including a new deadline of two more weeks was sent out reminding respondents to return the inventory. The second mail-out resulted in a return rate of 16.25% with a total of 130 surveys returned. In the third and final mail-out, a cover letter explaining the importance of the study and a new deadline of two additional weeks, a new copy of the inventory, and a postage paid return envelope was mailed out resulting in a final return rate of 30% with 243 of 800 surveys returned.

Qualitative

The qualitative method of data collection incorporated telephone interviews and open-ended responses from the further comments area of the OLEI to validate the theory. The following steps were taken in the telephone interviews:

1. Twelve names were chosen from eight separate lists comprised of male and female superintendents, assistant superintendents, secondary principals, and elementary principals. The level of management represented was as follows: 2 superintendents (1 male selected from 71 names, 1 female selected from 75 names); 2 assistant superintendents (1 male selected from 65 names, 1 female selected from 70 names); 6 secondary principals (4 males selected from 55 names, 2 females selected from 62 names); and 2 elementary principals (1 male selected from 74 names, and 1 female selected from 76 names).

2. These participants were telephoned and asked if they would participate in a telephone interview about the new theory. The model and description of the Synergistic Leadership Theory were faxed to participants along with interview consent forms, and a request for a convenient time for the telephone interview.

3. During the telephone interviews, respondents were asked to give their perceptions of the Synergistic Leadership Theory and examples of the theory in action. The participant was encouraged to give examples of situations, people, and organizations that fit their specific perception of the theory, making the interview more of an informal conversational interview. The strength of the informal conversational approach to interviewing is that

is allows the interviewer to be highly responsive to individual differences and changes (Patton, 1987). One of the benefits of this type of interview is that questions can be individualized to establish in-depth communication with the person being interviewed (Patton, 1987). Interviews were taped and transcribed and lasted approximately ten to fifteen minutes.

4. Finally, the 243 inventories were sorted through to find those that were returned with open-ended responses in the further comments area of the OLEI. The 22 inventories that were returned with further comments were sorted demographically as well and included the following: 3 female and 4 male superintendents; 3 female and 1 male assistant superintendents; 3 female and 1 male secondary principals; and 6 female and 1 male elementary principals. (Trautman, 2000, pp. 89–93)

Note how Trautman described many of the details that should be included in a "Data Collection" section using a mixed methods research design.

The following is a data collection section from Joan Slater's (2001) qualitative study in which she used multiple sources of data collection divided into three separate phases. (See Example 8.16.)

Example 8.16

Data Collection

The study was conducted using multiple sources of documentation: questionnaires, focus groups, and student essays. This is concordant with Yin's (1994) recommendation to use multiple sources of evidence that connect the questions asked to the data collected and conclusions drawn. This study employed a qualitative method of data collection that helped the researcher to analyze the motivation of at-risk ninth grade students enrolled in online courses and to generalize findings to the target population.

Before data collection began, written consent from the school district administration office and from the Committee for the Protection of Human Subjects at Sam Houston State University was granted to conduct the study (see Appendix D). Three separate phases of data collection were included as part of this study.

Phase I

The first phase of data collection included the administration of an open-ended questionnaire of 10 questions to 24 ninth grade student participants who had been identified as being at-risk and who had been enrolled in both core and elective courses online. All questionnaires were administered to students at their respective campuses. Students were given an unlimited amount of time to answer the questions. Lines provided on the questionnaire helped students to avoid answering questions with a few words or phrases. Students filled out all the lines that were provided on the questionnaire. Through this phase of data collection, emerging themes were identified, and additional ideas and attitudes were highlighted so that they could be incorporated into Phase II. I administered the questionnaire at one of the high schools, and the lead teachers for the initiative at each of the other two high schools administered the questionnaires at each of their respective schools.

Phase II

The second phase of the data collection employed four focus groups, each comprised of six students who had been receiving online instruction for nine months in both core courses and electives. Students participating in the focus groups responded to questions that were based on data collected during Phase I. A scheduled and designated area was set up for the researcher to conduct focus groups at all three campuses. Each focus group lasted approximately 30 minutes, and each focus group interview was tape-recorded and transcribed with the permission of the participants and their parents. The focus group was conducted to gain information regarding the student's perceptions of the impact of online instruction on their motivation. At each focus group, the researcher was accompanied by another central office administrator who was unknown by the student participants. This phase of data collection validated data collect in Phase I, and it resulted in the emergence of additional information.

Bogdan and Biklen (1998) noted that group interviews could be useful in bringing the researcher into the world of the subjects. In this situation, a number of people are brought together and encouraged to talk about the subject of interest. Group interviews are particularly useful if adolescents' perspectives on a particular issue are being studied. Young people tend to be stimulated to talk more expansively when others of their age join them.

Phase III

The third phase of data collection included two focus groups, comprised of six students each who had participated in both Phase I and Phase II of data collection. Questions asked in these interviews were based on questions previously asked since participants were asked to validate responses provided previously. These selected interviews for member checking also referenced the responses provided by the student essays that were administered during the first week of online instruction. This approach employed the strategy of member checking, the process of having research participants judge the accuracy and completeness of statements made in the researcher's report (Gall, Borg, & Gall, p. 763). Students were shown a written summary of Phase I and Phase II results. Also, during this phase, participants were also encouraged to add any pertinent information that had not been included in the data.

During all phases of data collection, the students' identities and confidentiality were ensured. Names and student identification numbers were not included in any summary information. (Slater, 2001, pp. 63–65)

Note how thoroughly Slater describes the details of each of the phases of data collection she used in her qualitative study.

The following is a data collection section from Scott Barrett's (2000) quantitative dissertation in which he used two different data collection methods: mailed survey and online survey. (See Example 8.17.)

Example 8.17

Data Collection

Data were collected by the administration of the MIS utilization survey to school principals in two ways. The first method consisted of mailing the survey to selected principals. From the systematic sample list of principals, every second principal was selected to receive a mailed survey. A total of 82 survey packets were mailed, which included the survey form (survey on the front with a stamped, return address on the back) and a consent form. The second method consisted of distributing the survey utilizing electronic mail and a web-based technology to the remaining principals on the list. This strategy incorporated sending the consent form to the principals through electronic mail. Within the message was the universal resource locator (URL) address of the on-line survey form (http://www .conroe.isd.tenet.edu/doctoral/misus.htm). The principal provided consent by visiting the specified URL and completing the on-line survey. Once the on-line survey was completed and submitted for processing, the results were automatically entered into an on-line FilmMaker database running on a Macintosh G3 server utilizing StarNine's WebSTAR Internet web server software. The resulting data from the mailed survey and from the on-line survey were entered into a computer program that allowed for aggregation and disaggregation of the data according to the criteria identified by the study. (Barrett, 2000, pp. 82–83)

Although Barrett's description of the data collection procedure is not as detailed as the previous models, he does walk the reader through the process just as the participant experienced it.

The following is a data collection section from a correlational study. The data collected was used to predict graduation rates at UCEA public universities using correlation and multiple regression analysis (Creighton, 2006). (See Example 8.18.)

Example 8.18

Data Collection

The data used were the student and institutional factors that could predict graduate rates at University Council for Educational Administration

(UCEA) public universities. Data were collected on: (a) students' SAT scores; (b) percentage of students graduating in the top 10% of their high school class; (c) percentage of students paying out-of-state tuition; (d) percentage of students of underrepresented populations (i.e., African American, Hispanic, Asian, and Native American); and (e) percentage of students age 25 and older. Data were also collected regarding: (f) percentage of full time faculty; (g) the average salary of full time faculty; (h) class size (i.e., percentage of classes with less than 20 students; percentage of classes with 50 or more students); and (i) total student expenditures (i.e., tuition and fees, instruction, research, student services). The variation, if any, in the educational outcomes for the 63 universities in the sample group is explained by the variation of the student and institutional factors as a result of a multiple regression analysis. (Creighton, 2006, pp. 53–54)

Note how succinctly Creighton described the 11 student and institutional factors that were used to predict graduation rates at all 63 UCEA public universities in her sample.

The following data collection section is from a mixed methods study focused on the development of a new instrument for measuring principals' efficacy (Black, 2003). (See Example 8.19.)

Example 8.19

Data Collection

As an initial information gathering part of the study, an expert panel on educational leadership and efficacy reviewed the preliminary model of principal efficacy and provided feedback on strengths, weaknesses, omissions, and recommended changes. Experts of educational leadership came from the list members of the National Council of Professors of Educational Administration (NCPEA). Authors and researchers who have contributed to the body of research on self-efficacy and teacher efficacy were contacted for participation in gathering information on factors that contribute to principal efficacy and review of the preliminary principal efficacy model (see Appendixes A and B). All individuals were contacted via electronic mail to elicit participation. Follow up electronic mail messages were sent to targeted participants in this phase of the study (see Appendix C). All participants were provided an explanation of the researcher's purpose of the study and the intended outcome of the research process. Each participant was guaranteed anonymity and assured his/her feedback would be kept confidential. Participants were also provided the assurance that the option to remove themselves from the research process at any time was afforded.

A preliminary Principal Efficacy Scale was devised from the body of research on self-efficacy and teacher efficacy and on the role of the principal. Additional information incorporated into the Principal Efficacy Scale was gleaned from analysis of current instruments that measure self-efficacy and input from the initial information-gathering phase described above.

Upon completion of development, the Principal Efficacy Scale was presented to the stratified random sample derived in the selection process described previously (see Appendix D). The researcher chose participants randomly from every state's department of education website that lists school districts and principals from district schools. Addresses that were returned as undeliverable by the Web server were replaced by another principal from the same region of the state as the original individual selected in the random sampling procedure. Contact was made via electronic mail with a Web link to the Principal Efficacy Scale that was designed on an Internet survey website (see Appendix D). General demographic questions were posed to obtain information on gender, years of experience as a principal, state, school geographic descriptor (urban, suburban, rural), and level of school (elementary, middle/junior high, high, alternative, other). Participants were provided the opportunity to enter their own electronic mail address to indicate an interest in reviewing the results of the study. A follow up request was made via electronic mail two weeks after the initial request for participation (see Appendix E) to encourage potential participants to respond. (Black, 2003, pp. 53–54)

Note how Black described the development of a new instrument, the Principal Efficacy Scale, and how she referred readers to five separate Appendixes for further information concerning instrument development.

DATA ANALYSIS

The next section in the Methodology Chapter is titled "Data Analysis." In this section, you describe the statistical tests that you used to address your research questions on hypotheses. You should carefully consider each of your research questions or hypotheses and determine the respective statistical analysis that would be appropriate to test each one. Following this procedure will help you when you actually analyze your data. Furthermore, a complete description of your analysis will benefit other researchers who wish to replicate your analysis.

Presentation of statistical analysis should include: the name and description of each technique, the dependent and independent variables, the level of significance, and the research questions or hypotheses addressed by the analysis. If the type of statistical analysis is commonly employed by researchers in the field, it is not necessary to include a lengthy description of the analysis technique. However, a reference, formula, and a more detailed description should be provided for established types of analyses that are not commonly employed, as well as techniques that are unnamed or little known in the field.

Describe any subsequent analyses, commonly known as *post hoc analyses*, you need to perform should you find statistical significance using analysis of variance and chi square. There are six common multiple comparison tests: Fisher LSD, Scheffé test, Turkey HSD, Newman and Kewls multiple range test, Duncan new multiple range test, and Dunn Bonferroni *t* statistics. Furthermore, the American Psychological Association (2001) and several research journals now require that investigators report appropriate indicators that illustrate the strength or magnitude of a difference or relationship along with measures of statistical significance. This requirement applies to dissertations and master's theses as well. These effect magnitude measures, as they are called, are either measures of strength of association or *effect size*. Consult Field (2000) or Sprinthall (2000) for a complete treatment of post hoc tests, and Cohen (1988, 1992) and Olejnik (1984) for examples for calculating and reporting effect size.

The appropriate use of a given statistical technique should depend ultimately on the ability of the procedure to address your research questions or hypotheses, not on the complexity of the statistical analysis. You should be aware of the statistical techniques used in your field and where to find information about them. We believe that most graduate students are capable of mastering the statistical aspects of their dissertations or master's theses. We devote an entire chapter in this book to statistical techniques used in the social and behavioral sciences (see Chapter 4, "Basic Statistics").

Careful, systematic attention to analysis of qualitative data is required of the serious qualitative researcher. If you are doing a qualitative dissertation, you should describe in detail which methods of analysis you will employ and the major steps you will follow. We devote an entire chapter to qualitative methods (see Chapter 5, "Qualitative Research Designs"). In addition, we have provided several examples of qualitative methods in this chapter.

An example of data analysis from Diane Trautman's (2000) dissertation follows. It is a mixed methods study. (See Example 8.20.)

Example 8.20

Data Analysis

The study employed a qualitative and quantitative methodology of data collection and data analysis. These two methodologies will be explained separately.

Quantitative

Quantitative analysis of the data included numerical ratings obtained from items 10–79 on the Organizational and Leadership Effectiveness Inventory. Responses ranging from 1 to 4 were input into SPSS 9.0 for each of the 243 respondents along with their demographic data.

Data were analyzed by using the SPSS 9.0 program to run statistical tests. Tests of statistical analysis were performed to determine theory validation. The frequency and percentage of responses to items 10–79 on the inventory were displayed using descriptive statistics and tables. A table showing the demographic breakdown of the sample was obtained from the SPSS program. An item analysis indicated the mean response of males and females for each of the 70 items on the Organizational and Leadership

Effectiveness Inventory. Then, a *t* test for independent means was per-formed on each item, 10–79, for males and females to determine any dif-ferences between male and female response on each item. A *t* value of −1.96 or less indicated statistical significance at $p = .05$. A two-sample *t* test for independent means was calculated to compare male and female responses on all 70 items for statistical differences as well.

Finally, mean responses were determined for females from each of the four levels of management, and then a one-way analysis of variance was conducted to determine any statistical differences between female admin-istrators at different levels of management. The level of significance was set at $p = .05$ for the ANOVA.

Qualitative

The qualitative analysis of data was comprised of analysis for similarities and differences, coding and categorizing, and constant comparison. Twenty-two of the 243 inventories returned included open-ended responses under the further comments section of the OLEI and were analyzed for similarities and differences. The 12 telephone interviews were taped and transcribed word for word. Using the constant comparative method, interviews were compared to each other as they were collected to determine similarities and differences. Categories were formed, coded, and triangulated for both the open-ended response data and the telephone interview data by using a color code representing different themes that emerged from the data. Themes were determined for each research question and those themes were compared to each other for further analysis. Additionally, themes from the data were com-pared to existing literature on leadership theory, characteristics of feminine leadership style, and the Synergistic Leadership Theory.

The constant comparative method is a research design for multi-data sources similar to analytic induction in that the formal analysis begins early in the study and is nearly completed by the end of data col-lection (Bogdan & Biklen, 1998). This method of data collection was implemented after each phase of the data collection, constantly analyz-ing and comparing each new interview received to the Synergistic Leadership Theory.

Procedural Fidelity

Quantitative. An extensive review of the literature is a characteristic of procedural fidelity for quantitative studies. The review should be intensive and significantly affect the particular study (Gay & Airasian, 2000). This study did conduct an extensive review of current leadership theories with an androcentric bias which did affect the study in that it illustrated a need for a new theory inclusive of the feminine perceptive.

Additionally, the sample was randomly selected which also adds to the generalizability of the study. According to Gall, Borg, and Gall (1998), random selection shows an intent to select a large representative sample in order to generalize results to a population. This study conducted a random selection of a large, nationwide sample, which included equal numbers of males and females.

Measurement and analysis of quantitative data is standardized and numerical and gives greater objectivity to results (Gay & Airasian, 2000). In this study, numerical data was obtained from the Organizational and Leadership Effectiveness Inventory and was analyzed by a computer analysis program for greater objectivity. Additionally, quantitative analysis usually involves statistics, which can be used to make inferences from the findings (Fitzgibbon & Morris, 1987). Statistical tests of significance were conducted in this study such as t tests and an ANOVA to provide a value-free and objective result.

Qualitative. Triangulation (Lincoln & Guba, 1985) is a process used in qualitative studies to address questions of validity. The researcher must consciously utilize designs, which seek counter patterns as well as convergence if data are to be credible (Lather, 1991). Denzin (1978) identifies three basic types of triangulation: data triangulation, investigator triangulation, and theory triangulation (Denzin, 1978).

Data triangulation is the use of a variety of data sources or subjects in a study. This study employed data triangulation by interviewing male and female public school executives in secondary and elementary levels as well as positions in central office administration to obtain their perspectives on leadership styles. Generalizability is promoted when replication is done with other subjects matched as closely as possible who share the same problems (Gay & Airasian, 2000).

Investigator triangulation is defined as the use of several different evaluators, and the study accomplished this by letting the subjects become part of the investigation team in helping to validate the theory since the theory is built on their perspectives. Additionally, an expert group of university professors validated the Organizational and Leadership Inventory and telephone interview questions for face validity. Also, the researcher used a three-person team composed of scholar practitioners in several stages of data collection and interpretation. The team was composed of 3 male principals, one Hispanic and two Anglo, who reviewed and discussed the findings of this study with the researcher and were given opportunity for feedback. The feedback provided by the team reflected their experiences were the same as the findings and on no points did they differ from the researcher's findings.

Theory triangulation is the use of multiple perspectives/theories to interpret a single set of data, and the comparison of feminine leadership theory to 12 other leadership theories does exactly that. "Tying emergent theory to existing literature enhances the internal validity, generalizability, and theoretical level of the theory building . . ." (Eisenhardt, 1989, p. 545). (Trautman, 2000, pp. 89–96)

Note how thoroughly Trautman described her quantitative and qualitative data analyses. She included the name and description of each technique for both the quantitative and qualitative aspects of her study.

Note also that she discussed procedural fidelity for both the quantitative and qualitative aspects of her study.

SUMMARY

The last section of Chapter Three is titled "Summary." The summary should be substantive in nature; that is, it should repeat the contents of the headings that appeared in the body of the chapter ("Selection of Participants," "Instrumentation," "Data Collection," and "Data Analysis") but in a condensed form. The summary should conclude with a transition sentence such as, "The following chapter contains a presentation and analysis of data."

An example from Rose Hernandez's (2004) dissertation follows. (See Example 8.21.)

Example 8.21

Summary

This chapter restated the purpose of this research and presented the research questions. The participants were chosen through a stratified random sample of public school superintendents and their respective school boards in the United States. The selection of the 2,000 participant sample from the target population was discussed. In addition, the validity and reliability of the instrument was presented, including the tests of reliability of the revised instrument. Data reliability tests (see Table II) performed on the pilot study of the revised OLEI indicated the instrument was reliable. The data collection procedures and response rates were also discussed in this chapter. Finally, the methods of data analysis for each of the research questions were presented, followed by a discussion of statistical power analysis. Results of the data analysis are presented in the following chapter. (Hernandez, 2004, p. 122)

Note how efficiently yet comprehensively Hernandez summarized Chapter Three of her dissertation, and how she provided the reader with a transition to the next chapter.

CONCLUSION

Chapter Three, "Methodology," of the dissertation or thesis contains a detailed description of your research plan. In it, you describe the selection of participants, instrumentation, data collection, and data analysis. We provided details concerning these four sections contained in the Methodology Chapter. The Methodology Chapter is extremely important, particularly at the proposal stage, because it defines how your study will be conducted. This is the section of your proposal where you will receive the most questions. In essence, it is the "blueprint" of your study. We provided several excerpts from both quantitative and qualitative dissertations, which you may find helpful in writing your Methodology Chapter.

After you have completed writing the first three chapters of your dissertation and have received approval from your dissertation chair, some universities require you to engage in a dissertation proposal defense. There is great variability among universities and departments concerning exactly how the dissertation proposal approval process works. In some institutions the proposal may consist of a description of your research plan consisting of 10 to 20 pages. In others the approval of your research plan may consist of the first three chapters of your dissertation. In some schools, the dissertation chair is the only person who must approve your proposal. In other schools you may be required to participate in a formal oral defense of your dissertation proposal before your entire dissertation committee (see Chapter 11 for a description of both the proposal defense and the final oral defense of the dissertation). The following chapter deals with the presentation and analysis of your data.

9

Writing the Results Chapter

C hapter Four of a dissertation or master's thesis is usually titled "Presentation and Analysis of Data." It contains a clear and comprehensive presentation of the results of your data analysis. Plan the presentation of your tables and figures before you begin writing the chapter.

In planning the outline of Chapter Four, concentrate on purely objective analysis, without interjecting inferences and value judgments. Resisting the temptation to generalize at the same time data are being analyzed makes the writing of your dissertation or master's thesis a more manageable task, particularly for one who is inexperienced. Judgments, inferences, and questions will surface as you analyze your data. You should record these ideas for use in the subsequent chapter, which will be devoted to interpretation, comparison with other research findings, and recommendations. References to the literature and a restatement of the theoretical framework or methods are unnecessary and will detract from the purpose of the Results Chapter.

We are aware that there are alternative formats for writing qualitative dissertations. Some qualitative researchers recommend combining results and discussion chapters. Some dissertation chairs may encourage students to present the results and discussion as one interconnected chapter. We acknowledge that such an approach may even improve the readability of a qualitative dissertation or master's thesis. And some qualitative dissertations may exceed five chapters. Nevertheless, we recommend the general organizing principles for Chapter Four on the assumption that both quantitative and qualitative dissertations will contain separate results and discussion chapters, albeit the writing in Chapter Four may be quite different according to the methodology of choice (quantitative or qualitative).

Though the model we use is the traditional five-chapter dissertation, students and faculty chairing dissertations should feel free to modify the approach to reflect advising style, unique subject area, and institutional requirements. For example, Joan Slater (2001) and Teresa Schlosberg (2004) combined the results and discussion of their qualitative dissertations into one chapter, resulting in a four-chapter dissertation. (See Examples 9.1 and 9.2.)

Example 9.1

CHAPTERS

I   INTRODUCTION
II   REVIEW OF THE LITERATURE
III METHODOLOGY
IV   RESULTS AND IMPLICATIONS

(Slater, 2001, pp. viii–x)

Example 9.2

CHAPTERS

I   INTRODUCTION
II   REVIEW OF THE LITERATURE
III METHODOLOGY
IV   RESULTS AND IMPLICATIONS

(Schlosberg, 2004, pp. vii–viii)

On the other hand, Judy Christensen's (2003) qualitative dissertation contains nine chapters. She followed our five-chapter model for the first three chapters, then she organized her case study results into four chapters using themes. This was followed by a cross-case analysis chapter. She concluded the dissertation with a summary chapter. (See Example 9.3.)

Example 9.3

CHAPTERS

I	INTRODUCTION
II	REVIEW OF THE LITERATURE
III	METHODOLOGY
IV	CASE A: MAGNETIC ATTRACTION
V	CASE B: PREMEDITATED PROGRESS
VI	CASE C: BUSINESS PARTNERSHIP
VII	CASE D: DELIBERATE DESIGN
VIII	CROSS-CASE ANALYSIS OF FINDINGS
IX	SUMMARY, CONCLUSIONS, AND RECOMMENDATIONS

(Christensen, 2003, pp. vii–x)

Wanda Bamberg's (2004) qualitative dissertation contains nine chapters as well. Like Christensen, she followed our five-chapter model for the first three chapters. She organized her case study results into five additional chapters focusing on each of the major participants of her study and concluded with a summary chapter. (See Example 9.4.)

Example 9.4

CHAPTERS

I	INTRODUCTION
II	REVIEW OF THE LITERATURE
III	METHODOLOGY
IV	CASE STUDY SUPERINTENDENT A
V	CASE STUDY SUPERINTENDENT B
VI	CASE STUDY SUPERINTENDENT C
VII	CASE STUDY SUPERINTENDENT D
VIII	CASE STUDY SUPERINTENDENT E
IX	SUMMARY AND CONCLUSIONS

(Bamberg, 2004, pp. viii–xii)

As shown in the previous four examples, qualitative dissertations may use alternative formats to the traditional five-chapter dissertation model we propose. Most quantitative dissertations and many qualitative dissertations follow the traditional five-chapter model we have been discussing in this book.

For the sake of brevity, we will refer to Chapter Four as the Results Chapter. As mentioned previously, each chapter, including Chapter Four, has three distinct parts: the introduction, where you tell your readers what you are going to tell them; the body, where you tell them; and the summary, where you tell them what you told them. Table 9.1 contains the typical headings found in the results chapter of a dissertation or master's thesis.

Table 9.1   Contents of Chapter Four

CHAPTER IV
PRESENTATION AND ANALYSIS OF DATA

   Introduction

   Descriptive Statistics

   Testing the Research Questions (or Hypotheses) (quantitative study)

      Research Question (or Hypotheses) 1
      Research Question (or Hypotheses) 2
      Research Question (or Hypotheses) 3
      Etc.
      (For a qualitative dissertation, themes, participants, or other organizing format may be used.)

   Additional Analyses

   Summary

A more detailed description of each of these sections follows.

INTRODUCTION

As in previous chapters, you begin the Results Chapter with an introduction, containing one or two paragraphs. In it, you provide an overview of the chapter, an *advance organizer.* The advance organizer lays out the structure of the chapter; it prepares the reader for what is to follow.

   The following is an example from Ying-Chiao Tsai's (2006) dissertation. (See Example 9.5.)

Example 9.5

Introduction

   This study intended to investigate the effects of student, teacher, and school factors on PIRLS reading achievement for both English-language majority and minority students, and it intended to investigate school and teacher factors that moderated the student effects including the language achievement gaps and students' reading attitudes in the United States and Singapore. The purpose of this study was achieved by examining the explanatory power of the combined models with student, teacher, and school factors on the students' reading achievement in the United States and Singapore. This chapter presents the results of the data analysis for the four stated research questions.

The descriptive statistics including univariate and bivariate statistics were first reported followed by the results of unconditional models and the HLM model overview for the change of students' mean reading achievement and language achievement gaps across the five HLM models. The presentation of the findings is arranged by the four research questions. The HLM student background models (Model 2) and the final student models were used to answer research question one: "To what extent do student factors have a direct impact on students' reading achievement for both English-language majority and minority students in the United States and Singapore?"

The HLM school models (Model 4) provided the findings for research questions two and three: "To what extent do school and teacher background variables influence students' reading achievement for both English-language majority and minority students in the United States and Singapore?" and "To what extent do school and teacher classroom instructional factors have a direct impact on students' reading achievement for both English-language majority and minority students in the United States and Singapore?" The HLM full school models were used to answer research question four: "To what extent do school and teacher classroom instructional factors have differential effects on both English-language majority and minority students' reading achievement and on students' reading attitudes in the United States and Singapore?"

Univariate and Bivariate Statistics

(Tsai, 2006, pp. 75–76)

Note how Tsai identified each section of her Results Chapter. Through this advance organizer, she provided her readers with what was to follow. We included her next major heading following her introduction to show the sequence of headings following the introduction.

The next heading that typically appears in the Results Chapter is titled "Descriptive Statistics." Here you summarize the univariate statistics of your study. The most frequently used statistics for this purpose are the mean (M), standard deviation (SD), median, mode, frequency, and percentages (see Chapter 4, "Basic Statistics," for a description of these basic descriptive statistics). When your data set contains many variables, presenting descriptive summary table(s) with an explanation of the descriptive nature of the variables is helpful to the reader.

DESCRIPTIVE STATISTICS

Descriptive statistics are often reported in the Results Chapter to begin the presentation and analysis of data. Following is an example from Keith Clark's (2002) dissertation. (See Example 9.6.) We display *one* table only for each of the three variables (student achievement variables, demographic variables, and expenditure variables) Clark examined in his dissertation.

Example 9.6

Descriptive Statistics

Student Achievement Variables

The TEA Snapshot for the years 1999 and 2000 was used to gather student achievement information. These data on student achievement are utilized to study the achievement of the students in each district included in this study. Student achievement is defined in this study as the percentage of a district's total student population who passes the TAAS test in reading, writing, and mathematics across all grade levels tested. Tables 1 and 2 report the mean percentage and standard deviation for student achievement by subject in all school districts included in this study.

Table 1

Table 9.2   Percent of Students Passing TAAS by School Year

| | *School Year* | | | | | |
| | *1998–1999* | | | *1999–2000* | | |
TAAS Subject	*n*	*M*	*SD*	*n*	*M*	*SD*
% Passed All Test	1,035	81.06	9.08	1,041	82.47	9.09
% Passed Reading	1,035	88.57	9.08	1,041	82.47	9.09
% Passed Writing	1,028	89.32	7.10	1,033	89.82	7.16
% Passed Mathematics	1,035	88.35	6.85	1,041	89.69	6.78

(Clark, 2002, p. 71)

Demographic Variables

Demographic information is another relevant data source related to the type of students who attend each of the school districts. These data include the demographic variables relating to the ethnicity of the student population of a district. Tables 4 and 5 demonstrate the percentage of total African American, Hispanic, White, or Other students in each district in this study. This information comes from data collected for the two years of information included in this study by the Texas Education Agency regarding ethnicity.

Table 4

Table 9.3   Ethnicity of the Student Population of Texas School Districts by School Year

| | *1998–1999* | | | *1999–2000* | | |
	n	*M*	*SD*	*n*	*M*	*SD*
% African American	1,035	7.95	11.82	1,041	8.07	12.16
% Hispanic	1,035	27.38	26.55	1,041	28.15	26.80
% White	1,035	63.82	26.46	1,041	62.91	26.84
% Others	1,035	1.03	1.97	1,041	1.03	1.88

(Clark, 2002, p. 72)

Expenditure Variables

District function level expenditures data was taken from the Public Education Information Management System (Texas Education Agency, 2000). Each of these expenditures is characterized by their functional group. Each are summarized into a per pupil expenditure. This amount is calculated by dividing the total functional expenditure by the total number of students in each given district. Tables 9 and 11 depict the mean per pupil expenditures and standard deviation for each of the eight functional categories for all districts in this study for the academic years of 1998–1999 and 1999–2000.

Table 11

Table 9.4   Total School District's Functional Level Expenditures 1998–1999 through 1999–2000

		1998–1999 and 1999–2000 School Years		
Function	*N*	*Mean (in $)*	*SD (in $)*	*% Total*
Instruction	2,076	4,071	1,101	60.23%
School Leadership	2,076	431	188	6.38%
Student Support	2,076	698	262	10.33%
General Administration	2,076	467	385	6.91%
Non-Student Services	2,076	849	406	12.56%
Ancillary Services	2,076	6	16	0.09%
Debt Services	2,076	64	152	0.94%
Facilities Acquisition	2,076	173	447	2.55%

(Clark, 2002, p. 76)

Testing the Research Questions

Descriptive and inferential statistics were used to investigate the four research questions of this study. To investigate the first research question, Analysis of Variance (ANOVA) was used to compare the amount of variance between group AEIS school district ratings of exemplary, recognized, acceptable, and low performing and the eight functional expenditure categories of (a) instruction and instructional related services, (b) school leadership, (c) student support services, (d) general administration, (e) non-student services, (f) ancillary services, (g) debt services, and (h) facilities acquisition resources per pupil. The other three research questions were studied using regression analysis. The first of three regressions tested the correlation between student scores on the TAAS test and each district's functional expenditures. The last two research questions also compare the eight functional groups to financial and demographic factors. The level of significance .05 was used for each statistical analysis used in this study. This is consistent with commonly used statistical practices (Gall, Borg & Gall, 1996). (Clark, 2002, pp. 70–77)

Note that Clark described student achievement variables, demographic variables, and expenditure variables using 11 tables (3 tables reported here). We included the first paragraph of the next heading of Clark's dissertation, "Testing the Research Questions," which typically follows the heading "Descriptive Statistics" in quantitative dissertations. Note how Clark provided an overview of his plan of analysis for each research question in this section.

TESTING THE RESEARCH QUESTIONS (OR HYPOTHESES)

We recommend that you use research questions (or hypotheses) to organize the presentation of quantitative results. Address one research question (or hypothesis) at a time. Thus, each research question (or hypothesis) would compose one subsection of the Results Chapter under the major section (heading) "Testing the Research Questions (or Hypotheses)." This main heading serves as the topic paragraph(s) for the analyses, by each research question (or hypothesis), to follow. Use narrative, accompanied by appropriate tables and figures.

Following is an outline of the way you might structure the presentation of your results for a quantitative dissertation or master's thesis. Use the following six steps to report the results of each research question (or hypothesis).

1. Restate the first research question (or hypothesis) exactly as it appeared in Chapter One of your dissertation or master's thesis.

2. Reference the table or figure in the text that contains the statistics related to the research question (or hypothesis).

3. Discuss the highlights of the data contained in the table or figure.

4. State the outcome of the analysis for research question or hypothesis one, together with the statistical procedure used.

5. State the disposition of the research question (or hypothesis).

6. State the next research question or hypothesis, and follow the previous five steps until you have reported the results of each research question or hypothesis.

An example from Kimberly Truslow's (2004) dissertation follows. (See Example 9.7.)

Example 9.7

Research Question One

Question 1: Is there a significant difference in gender distribution among conflict management modes of superintendents? The first research question examined the results of the TKI. On each of the 30 questions, participants were asked to respond to a forced choice item to indicate how they would handle a conflict scenario. Each of the 30 questions represented one of the conflict management modes and were assigned nominal values of 1 to 5. All 30 questions were analyzed to answer research question one using cross-tabulation and nonparametric statistics. Chi square analysis and Cramer's V were used to identity if statistically significant relationships existed between the number of males and females in each of the five conflict management modes. The magnitude of association for this research question was reported using Cramer's V.

Cramer's V measures the strength of the relationship between variables and reflects how closely variables are related (Gall, Borg, & Gall, 1996.) Cramer's V, symbolized by V, is based on measures of association from 0 to 1. Rutgers (2003) established that when the measure of V is between (a) 0 to .10, a weak relationship exists between variables; (b) .11 to .29, a moderate relationship exists between variables; and (c) .30 to 1, a strong relationship exists between variables.

Table 5 illustrates the cross-tabulation results of the number of males and females in each conflict management mode. The number of males in each conflict management mode was recorded as follows: 44 for competing, 28 for collaborating, 56 for compromising, 28 for avoiding, and 7 for accommodating. The number of females in each conflict management mode was divided as follows: 8 competing, 25 collaborating, 95 compromising, 22 avoiding, and 6 accommodating.

Table 5

Table 9.5   Fequencies of Gender Reponses for TKI Modes

Gender	TKI Modes					
	Competing	Collaborating	Compromising	Avoiding	Accommodating	Total
Male	44	28	56	28	7	163
Female	8	25	95	22	6	156
Total	**52**	**53**	**151**	**50**	**13**	**319**

A significant relationship χ^2 (4, N = 319) = 35.826, p = .001, was found to exist between gender and conflict management modes of superintendents. No cells in the cross-tabulation analysis had expected counts less than five. The minimum expected count in each cell was 6.36. The magnitude of the association of the relationship as described by Cramer's V is V = .335 indicating a large effect size of gender as being a factor in conflict management modes (Rutgers, 2003). Table 6 illustrates the results of the chi square test and Cramer's V degree of relationship.

Table 6

Table 9.6   Analysis of Chi Square Test with Cramer's V

	Value	*df*
Person Chi Square	35.826	4
Cramer's V (Nominal)	.335*	
N of Valid Cases	319	

* $p < .001$

One-sample t tests were also performed on the TKI data to analyze the gender distribution of males and females in each of the conflict management modes. Two of the conflict management modes, competing and compromising, had significant differences in gender distribution. There was a significant difference between the number of males and females in the competing conflict management mode, t (51) = −6.852, $p = .000$. The difference between the gender distribution of superintendents with a compromising conflict management mode was also significant, t (150) = 3.274, $p = .001$. Table 7 illustrates the results of the one-sample t tests for each conflict management mode.

Table 7

Table 9.7   One-Sample t Test for Conflict Management Modes

Conflict Management Mode	*N*	*t*	*df*	*Sig.*	*Mean Diff.*
Competing	52	−6.852	51	.000	−.3462
Collaborating	53	−0.409	52	.684	−.0228
Compromising	151	3.274	150	.001	.1291
Avoiding	50	−0.267	49	.402	−.0038
Accommodating	13	−0.267	12	.794	−.0038

Research Question Two

Question 2: Is there a relationship between conflict management modes of female superintendents and the Synergistic Leadership Theory? To answer research question two, a qualitative approach was employed. A telephone interview of five female superintendents who scored the highest on each of the five conflict management modes was conducted. Each superintendent was contacted to obtain permission to be interviewed by telephone, an audiotape of the interview was made and major themes were identified. Participants also provided written permission to participate in the interview. Each interview was transcribed and returned to the superintendent for member checking. Corrections were made to each transcript where noted by the participant. Major themes were identified in regards to the four factors of the SLT. Each factor was coded a different color on the transcript as follows: organizational structure was coded pink; leadership behaviors were coded purple; beliefs, attitudes, and values were coded green; and external forces were coded yellow. These phrases that were indicative of each of the factors were loaded in the matrix that grouped them for discussion purposes. For ease of reading, the narratives that follow are organized by participant responses in each of the four factors. (Truslow, 2004, pp. 62–65)

Note how efficiently Truslow followed all six steps we recommend for reporting quantitative results. We included the first paragraph of her second research question to show continuity. You will note from Truslow's second research question that she has done a mixed methods dissertation. The method of analysis for research question two was qualitative.

Assumptions of Statistical Tests

Sometimes it may be necessary for a student to discuss the assumptions of the statistical tests used, particularly when the data may not be normally distributed. The placement of this discussion should precede each research question (or hypothesis) to which the statistical procedure applies.

An example from Linda Creighton's (2006) dissertation follows. (See Example 9.8.)

Example 9.8

The first stage in any data analysis is to explore the data collected to get ideas of any patterns. In addition, it is important to see whether the data meet the criteria necessary for the statistical procedures used (Field, 2000). Since many of the statistical tests used are parametric, it is important to check the assumptions required of parametric tests. Using a parametric test when the data are not parametric increases greatly the risk of inaccurate decisions. Parametric tests are based on the normal distribution and have four basic assumptions that must be met for the test to be accurate: (a) normally distributed data, (b) homogeneity of variance, (c) interval data, and (d) independence (Field, 2000).

Normally Distributed Data

In addition to using histograms to determine normality, my study extends the inspections of normality to include measures of kurtosis and skewness. All variables revealed normal distributions with the exception of two: (a) Hispanic graduation rates and (b) African American graduation rates. Both of these data sets were positively skewed, revealing lower than normal graduation rates. The Spearman's rho correlation test, which is appropriate for non-parametric data, was used with these two distributions, and the Pearson correlation test was used with the normal distributions.

Homogeneity of Variance

Variances should not change systematically throughout the data. A thorough analysis of the data revealed similar stable variances across all of the variables.

Interval Data

Data must be at the interval scale to be analyzed with parametric tests. Pearson correlation was used with all parametric data, and variables not meeting parametric assumptions were analyzed with Spearman's rho correlations. All variables with significant relationships were subjected to multiple regression analysis.

Independence

This assumption was met in all data. Simply, to meet independence, no individuals can be counted in more than one variable or influence the effect on another participant. Each university and its students in this study were independent of other students and universities. (Creighton, 2006, p. 67)

Note how Creighton explored her data to see whether it met the criteria necessary for the statistical procedure she planned to use. She examined the four basic assumptions required to use parametric statistics: normally distributed data, homogeneity of variance, interval data, and independence.

Clarity and Consistency

The Results Chapter requires maximum clarity. One way to achieve clarity is to minimize variety in sentence structure when presenting your results. A good rule to follow is "Be monotonously repetitive" (Cone & Foster, 2007, p. 222). Decide on a particular sentence structure that most clearly presents the results of a particular statistical procedure, and use that structure for all similar results. For example, suppose you wanted to examine the influence of teachers' collective efficacy and community pressure for academic achievement (two independent variables) on students' academic achievement in reading, writing, and mathematics (three dependent variables). You will use a 2 (high/low teacher efficacy) × 2 (high/low community pressure) × 1 ANOVA that involves three dependent variables (student achievement in reading, writing, and mathematics). Conduct three separate ANOVAs, one for each dependent variable. To achieve clarity and consistency, you would present the results for each dependent variable (reading, writing, and math achievement) in exactly the same way. Thus, begin with your first independent variable (teacher efficacy), and present results for it first, followed by your results for your second independent variable (community pressure for achievement), followed by the interaction, if any. Use this order as you present the data for each dependent variable. Furthermore, if you discuss high teacher efficacy first for the first dependent variable, discuss it first for all dependent variables.

Another way to achieve clarity is to place the statistics related to a result at the end of the sentence. For example, "Females were more humanistic in pupil control ideology than males (M females = 48.1; M males = 53.4), $F(1,924) = 6.84 < .01$." Compare this statement with the following: "The mean for the females on the PCI Form was 48.1, which the ANOVA $F(1,924) = 6.84$, $p < .01$, revealed to be significantly lower than the males' mean of 53.4." Note how the first example is much easier to read than the second example. Moreover, in the first example, reference is made to the dependent variable (pupil control ideology) when comparing females and males, and not the instrument used to measure it. In the second example, the researcher would have to explain what "lower" means.

Tables

Most dissertations contain one or more tables. If you have a large amount of data, which are also complex, tables can make it easier for you to present the data. Tables usually help organize both descriptive data and the results of statistical analyses.

Tables typically contain five major parts: (a) number, (b) title, (c) headings, (d) body, and (e) notes (Rudestam & Newton, 2007).

Number. Every table must be numbered with Arabic numbers in the order in which they first appear in the text (American Psychological Association, 2001). Begin with Table 1, and continue throughout the dissertation or master's thesis.

Title. Every table must have a title. Generally, a good title provides the name of the major variable(s) and type of analysis.

Headings. Every table must have a heading. Headings include the variables and statistics presented in the table. Common abbreviations are permissible: M (mean), SD (standard deviation), df (degrees of freedom), f (frequency), % (percent), N (number in sample). Avoid using mnemonics for variables and acronyms for describing instruments. Include a note indicating their meaning at the bottom of the table.

Body. The body of the table contains the data. Consider readability; that is, allow sufficient space between entries, align columns of numbers on decimal points, and do not present data beyond two decimal points. Enter a dash (—) when cells of a table are empty. Tables presented vertically are less cumbersome than tables presented horizontally. If you must use the horizontal format, be certain the table appears along the binding side of the page.

Notes. Two kinds of notes may appear at the bottom of a table: general notes and probability notes. General notes include the meaning of symbols or abbreviations. Probability notes indicate the outcome of significance tests. Asterisks indicate the probability levels as follows: * $p < .05$. ** $p < .01$. *** $p < .001$.

The generally accepted rules concerning how to present the results of statistical tests have been documented in the fifth edition of the *Publication Manual of the American Psychological Association* (2001). The general rule when presenting inferential statistics in the text is to present the symbol of the statistic followed by the degrees of freedom, such as, $F(1, 924)$, then the value of the statistic (e.g., 6.84), and finally the probability level (e.g., $p < .01$); thus, from the previous example: $F(1, 924) = 6.84$, $p < .01$. When a chi square is used, the degrees of freedom and sample size are reported in parentheses: $\chi^2 (4, N = 319) = 35.83$, $p < .001$. When correlation is used, the statistical statement indicates both the strength of the relationship and its significance: $r (62) = .484$, $p < .01$. The 62 in parentheses following the r is the degrees of freedom associated with the statistical test and is one less than the sample size (i.e., $N - 1$). The APA manual provides more details.

Following are examples of tables taken from the dissertations of Clark (2002), Truslow (2004), and Creighton (2006) to illustrate ANOVA, χ^2, and r, respectively. (See Examples 9.9, 9.10, and 9.11.)

Example 9.9

Table 9.8 Means and ANOVA Summary Table per Pupil Expenditures for Instruction

District Rating	N	M	S.D. (in $)
Exemplary	290	4,540	1,664
Recognized	822	4,083	975
Academically Acceptable	952	3,920	936
Low Performing	12	4,071	1,204
Total	2,076	4,071	1,101

Source	df	SS	MS	F	η^2
Rating	3	85,800,422	28,600,141	24.4011*	.04
Error	2,072	2,428,554,379	1,172,082		
Total	2,072	2,514,354,801			

Note. η^2 = effect size.

*$p < .001$.

(Clark, 2002, p. 79)

Example 9.10

Table 9.9 Analysis of Chi Square Test with Cramer's V

	Value	df
Person Chi Square	35.826	4
Cramer's V (Nominal)	.335*	
N of Valid Cases	319	

* $p < .001$

(Truslow, 2004, p. 64)

Example 9.11

Table 9.10   Pearson Correlations between Top 10 % and Graduation Rates

	% in Top 10%	4-Year Rate	5-Year Rate	6-Year Rate
% in Top 10 %	1.00			
4-Year Rate	.484**	1.00		
5-Year Rate	.455**	.840	1.00	
6-Year Rate	.534**	.886	.952	1.00

** Correlation is significant at the .01 level (2-tailed)

(Creighton, 2006, p. 67)

Statistical significance does not deal with the power of a relationship between variables (called *effect size*). Include measures of effect size in all tables when presenting the results of statistical tests. It is not enough to discuss effect size in the narrative preceding the insertion of the table.

Reference each table by number in the text before inserting the table in the manuscript. Tables should be placed in your dissertation as close to where they have been described as possible. Alternate tables with textual description rather than placing tables consecutively one after another, unless the tables are clearly connected. Thus, considerable planning should precede the construction of tables. Think carefully about the number of tables to include in your document and their content. Also, think about how to organize your tables throughout the chapter. Therefore, construct all tables you intend to include in your Results Chapter before writing the text for the chapter. This will help you with the placement of tables and the avoidance of white space at the bottom of the page in your dissertation or master's thesis.

Figures

Many dissertations contain figures. Figures include graphs, charts, photographs, drawings, and anything that is not text or a table. Some examples of when a figure would be helpful include the following:

1. Trends in longitudinal data

2. Scatter plots in correlational analysis

3. Testing a moderating effect in a hierarchical multiple regression

4. Cluster analysis

5. Path analysis

6. Structural equation modeling

Many of the qualities of good tables apply equally to figures.

Presenting the Results of Qualitative Research

If you have conducted a qualitative study, the organization of your Results Chapter may differ from that used for a quantitative study (Long, Convey, & Chwalek, 1985). We recommended using research questions (or hypotheses) to organize the presentation of results for a quantitative study. As with all research (quantitative or qualitative), the first priority is to adopt a well-organized strategy that makes sense of your data and presents them clearly and comprehensively (Rudestam & Newton, 2007).

Qualitative researchers typically gather large amounts of data in the form of words and ideas rather than numbers and statistics. The methods of gathering such data in qualitative research include in-depth interviews, focus groups, participant and nonparticipant observation, and document analysis. Instead of using research questions (or hypotheses) to organize the presentation of results in your qualitative study, consider using major themes as headings in your Results Chapter. For example, in a qualitative study of 12 women superintendents' experiences of inequality, Brunner (2000) identified five topics of talk that emerged from the narrative data: power, silence, style, responsibility, and people. These themes became the headings in her analysis. Each of these topics was examined for settled and unsettled taxonomies. (See Example 9.12.)

Example 9.12

Within the taxonomy of unsettled talk, there were five topics: (1) power-understood as control or dominance, (2) overt silencing, (3) negative consequences for being direct, (4) barriers that blocked their ability to perform the verbal responsibilities of role, and (5) the need to use others as mouthpieces. Clearly, inequality because of gender bias was a consistent part of these women's experiences. When the women broke the normative cultural rules governing gender-appropriate behavior, they faced negative consequences.

Within the taxonomy of settled talk, the women shared experiences that fell within the traditional normative behavior of women in culture. The five topics of talk within the settled taxonomy were: (1) power as shared, (2) positive silence-listening, (3) positive consequences for having a soft approach—being a "lady," (4) finding ways to be verbally responsible in spite of barriers, and (5) working for equality of voice for everyone. (Brunner, 2000, p. 106)

The stated purposes of Brunner's qualitative research study were (a) to examine the women superintendents' perceptions of their experiences of inequality within the contextual constraints of their positions, and (b) how they overcame these experiences. Rather than using research questions to organize the presentation of results, Brunner used themes (or topics) to organize her analysis of results.

Previously we provided a six-step strategy for reporting the results of quantitative analyses. Qualitative researchers also need to devise a well-organized strategy for wading through volumes of qualitative data. We suggest the following eight-step strategy:

1. Read and reread all of the data you have collected to get a feel for the whole (Creswell, 2007).

2. Summarize the data in the form of memos and reflective notes.

3. Give participants copies of your summaries or transcripts (called *member checks* or *reciprocity*).

4. Reduce your data by developing codes for further sorting.

5. Sort your data into some kind of coherent pattern or themes.

6. Once you have determined your overall themes, give each theme a color code and attach a matching color tape flag to the page(s). Include the narrative (quotations) and speaker for that theme, and create a file.

7. Continue the process for each theme.

8. For each major theme, find subthemes and affix smaller color-coded, Post-it notes to the larger tape flags.

Earlier in this chapter we mentioned four qualitative dissertations that deviated from the traditional five-chapter dissertation model we have been discussing in this book: Slater (2001), Schlosberg (2004), Christensen (2003), and Bamberg (2004). The first two dissertations were four chapters each, and the latter two were nine chapters each. Christensen's dissertation was organized according to themes and Bamberg's dissertation was organized according to participants. Both dissertations used the case study method. (See Examples 9.3 and 9.4.) Providing excerpts from these chapters would not do justice to the rich narrative contained therein. Therefore, we recommend that you read Christensen's entire nine-chapter, 274-page qualitative dissertation and Bamberg's entire nine-chapter, 462-page qualitative dissertation.

All four qualitative researchers—Slater, Schlosberg, Christensen, and Bamberg—analyzed their data by following the eight-step strategy we recommended for organizing the results of qualitative data.

ADDITIONAL ANALYSES

This section of your dissertation or master's thesis is reserved for data not covered by the research questions (or hypotheses) in a quantitative study. The heading for this section in your Results Chapter is typically "Additional Analyses" (see Table 9.1). For example, in a study of the effects of teacher self-efficacy, locus of control, and pupil-control orientation on teacher burnout, you may have an interest in examining the relationships among the three independent variables (self-efficacy, locus of control, and pupil-control orientation) even though these relationships were not the subject of the research questions (or hypotheses). Such analyses would be placed in the section titled "Additional Analyses."

We mentioned previously that all instruments used to collect data for a quantitative dissertation should be factor analyzed with your own study sample. Assume that you found that, as a result of your factor analysis, several items of the instrument(s) you used in your study produced low reliability and validity, or the items of a multidimensional instrument did not load as in previous research, and therefore you choose to eliminate those items from the questionnaire(s). You decide to retest the research questions (or hypotheses) using the modified paper-and-pencil instrument. You cannot place the results of these analyses in the section titled "Testing the Research Questions (or Hypotheses)," but you place these additional analyses in the section titled "Additional Analyses."

Furthermore, suppose you decide to perform statistical analyses of demographic variables (e.g., gender, race/ethnicity, grade level taught) with each of the independent variables (i.e., self-efficacy, locus of control, and pupil-control orientation), but these variables were not the subject of the research questions (or hypotheses). As a result of these analyses, you found some interesting things. You found differences between elementary and secondary school levels on one or more of the independent variables (self-efficacy, locus of control, pupil-control orientation). The placement of the results of these additional analyses belong in the "Additional Analyses" section of the Results Chapter.

SUMMARY

The last major heading in the Results Chapter is "Summary" (see Table 9.1). Concluding the Results Chapter with a summary has two advantages. First, results can be generalized at a higher level in the summary than that found in the preceding text analysis. Now results extracted from tables and figures in quantitative dissertations and from rich narrative in qualitative dissertations can be synthesized and summarized in ways that were not possible earlier because of the organization of the chapter. Results that support or contradict each other can be identified and related to each other. Segmentation due to chapter organization (by research questions/hypothesis, themes, or participants) can be overcome in the summary.

The second advantage is that the results have been generalized to the degree necessary for making comparisons with the findings of other studies. The summaries of Chapter Two, "Review of the Literature," and Chapter Three, "Methodology," provide the supports needed for development of the Discussion Chapter to follow. Without such a basis from which to proceed, the next chapter invariably will be a repetition of the information found in the tables, figures, and narrative preceding it. From our experience, such repetition occurs with some frequency. It makes the task of writing the Discussion Chapter quite difficult. Furthermore, it serves to emphasize the importance of chapter summaries. The last sentence of the summary should introduce the following chapter.

The following comes from Diane Trautman's (2000) mixed methods dissertation. (See Example 9.13.)

Example 9.13

Summary

In this chapter, an introduction was given regarding the analysis and statistical tests that were to be discussed and in which order they would be addressed. This was followed by a demographic analysis of the sample, an item analysis with individual t tests of items 10–79 from the Organizational and Leadership Effectiveness Inventory, results of a t test for overall difference between groups, and results of an ANOVA between four levels of management.

Results from the first quantitative research question revealed that although there were slight statistical differences between males and females on how they perceived the leadership behavior factor of the Synergistic Leadership Theory, male and females perceived the leadership behaviors included in the leadership behavior factor of the theory to be statistically reflective or non-reflective of their leadership styles thus yielding construct validity to the factor. Similarly, female leaders at different levels of management acknowledged the validity of the leadership behavior factor of the Synergistic Leadership Theory. Further, the factor was validated by a strong level of internal consistency of scores on the OLEI which measured the factor at $\propto = .928$. The quantitative findings contradicted current literature that only females exhibit feminine leadership behaviors or that only males exhibit masculine behaviors.

The next chapter will present and analyze the qualitative data obtained from the open-ended response section of the Organizational and Leadership Effectiveness Inventory and the telephone interviews. (Trautman, 2000, pp. 120–121)

CONCLUSION

In this chapter, we discussed the common sections and headings that typically appear in a Results Chapter. We also included typical examples found in some qualitative dissertations. We provided a step-by-step guide to writing the Results Chapter, together with examples from dissertations on how to present each section of the chapter (both quantitative and qualitative), including the use of tables and figures. In the next chapter, we provide advice on how to write Chapter Five, "Summary, Discussion, and Conclusions."

10

Writing the Discussion Chapter

Chapter Five of your dissertation or master's thesis typically contains the following elements: (a) a summary of the study, (b) discussion of the findings, (c) implications for practice, (d) recommendations for further research, and (e) conclusions. These five elements comprise the sections (or headings) that are contained in Chapter Five (see Table 10.1).

Table 10.1   Contents of Chapter Five

CHAPTER V

SUMMARY, DISCUSSION, AND CONCLUSIONS
    Introduction
    Summary of the Study
    Discussion of the Findings
    Implications for Practice
    Recommendations for Further Research
    Conclusions

The concluding chapter of a dissertation or master's thesis can have any number of titles: "Summary," "Discussion," "Implications," "Recommendations," and/or "Conclusions." We prefer the title shown in Table 10.1. For the sake of brevity, we will refer to Chapter Five as the Discussion Chapter. A more detailed description of each of the above sections follows.

INTRODUCTION

As in previous chapters, you begin the Discussion Chapter with an introduction, which contains one or two paragraphs. In it, you provide an overview of the chapter, an *advance organizer*. The advance organizer lays out the structure of the chapter; it prepares the reader for what is to follow.

The following is an example of an introduction from Donna Azodi's (2006) dissertation. (See Example 10.1.)

Example 10.1

Introduction

In the preceding chapter, the presentation and analysis of data have been reported. Chapter V consists of a summary of the study, discussion of the findings, implications for practice, recommendations for further research, and conclusions. The purpose of the latter sections is to expand upon the concepts that were studied in an effort to provide a further understanding of their possible influence on leadership practice, and to present suggestions for further research targeting the understanding of trust and principal leadership behaviors and their impact on teachers' sense of efficacy. Finally, a synthesizing statement is offered to capture the substance and scope of what has been appempted in this research. (Azodi, 2006, p. 347)

Note how Azodi, in the brief introduction to her chapter, provides her readers with an advance organizer of the contents of the chapter. Note also that she includes all elements typically found in a Results Chapter.

SUMMARY OF THE STUDY

The next heading that typically appears in the Discussion Chapter is titled "Summary of the Study." In this section, briefly restate the problem and purpose of your study, the theoretical framework, research questions or hypotheses, methodology, and findings. The findings are the most important part of the dissertation and should receive the heaviest emphasis. The summary of the study should be brief, containing two or three pages.

We provide the summary from Diane Trautman's (2000) mixed methods dissertation as an example. (See Example 10.2.)

Example 10.2

Summary of the Study

This chapter begins with a summary of the purpose and structure of the study and is followed by the major findings related to the Synergistic

Leadership Theory. Conclusions from the findings of this study are discussed in relation to the definition, function, and characteristics of a good theory. Finally, implications for practice and recommendations for further research are presented and discussed.

The purpose of this study was to validate a feminine-inclusive leadership theory, the Synergistic Leadership Theory, by analyzing the perceptions of male and female educational administrators across the United States through quantitative and qualitative research.

The Organizational and Leadership Effectiveness Inventory (OLEI), a self-report inventory related to the four factors of the Synergistic Leadership Theory developed in a previous study by Irby et al. (1999), was revised for this study with face validity established by a group of university professors and educators. Participants were asked to score items 10–79 of the leadership behavior factor of the OLEI because this data could most effectively measure agreement or disagreement with the leadership behavior factor of the theory. Reliability was established for the leadership behavior factor studies at $\propto = .98$. By scoring their own leadership behaviors and effectiveness, respondents indicated their perceptions of the leadership behavior factor of the Synergistic Leadership Theory. Scores from the OLEI were used as quantitative data and were used to determine theory validity.

Respondents also wrote comments to an open-ended question of the OLEI, which were included in the qualitative analysis. Additionally, telephone interviews were conducted with administrators to determine their perceptions of how the four factors of the Synergistic Leadership Theory interacted and whether they perceived the theory as valid. Respondents often related real-life experiences to illustrate how the four factors of the model interacted.

The study included 243 participants (65 superintendents, 67 assistant superintendents, 52 secondary principals, and 57 elementary principals) randomly selected from a computer database compiled by the Market Data Retrieval Company (2000) for the quantitative sample. A demographic breakdown was provided for gender, ethnicity, management level, and years of experience. Additionally, a qualitative sample of 34 was composed of 12 educational leaders chosen from those who did not reply to the OLEI and 22 participants who added comments on the OLEI. This study included four research questions:

Quantitative

1. To what extent do differences exist between male and female educational leaders regarding the leadership behavior factor of the Synergistic Leadership Theory?

2. To what extent do differences exist among female educational leaders at different management levels regarding the leadership behavior factor of the Synergistic Leadership Theory?

Qualitative

1. In what ways do male and female leaders perceive the four factors of the Synergistic Leadership Theory to be interactive?

2. How do female leaders at different levels of management perceive the interaction of the four factors of the Synergistic Leadership Theory?

Questions one and two were answered quantitatively from the data obtained from participant scores on the leadership behavior factor of the OLEI. Question one was answered using the results from a *t* test for independent means comparing means of male and females' scores for each item and for group differences. To answer question two, an ANOVA was performed comparing means of females in the four different management levels. The quantitative results addressed only one of the four factors of the Synergistic Leadership Theory, the leadership behavior factor.

To answer the two questions to the qualitative phase of the study, data were obtained from telephone interviews as well as responses to the open-ended questions of the OLEI. Data were categorized, coded, and triangulated to determine levels of management. Where quantitative research questions addressed only one factor of the Synergistic Leadership Theory, the qualitative questions addressed possible interactions of all four factors of the Synergistic Leadership Theory. (Trautman, 2000, pp. 146–148)

Note how skillfully Trautman summarized her study up to the findings. Instead of summarizing findings in this section, she summarized her findings in the next section of her dissertation, titled "Discussion of the Findings," incorporating a discussion of each finding.

The five elements may be positioned in a variety of ways, as long as each element is addressed in Chapter Five, or the concluding chapter, if the dissertation contains more or fewer than five chapters as some qualitative dissertations do.

DISCUSSION OF THE FINDINGS

In Chapter One, "Introduction," you presented the theoretical framework undergirding your study. In Chapter Two, "Review of the Literature," you presented other empirical studies that were related to your study. In a theory-driven study, you present your interpretation of your results by linking them with the theoretical framework and the existing literature. As you discuss your results, you evaluate what your results mean, how they fit with your theoretical framework and the literature you reviewed earlier, and what you can conclude about the research questions or hypotheses you posed at the outset. Of course, you will need to cite some of the relevant studies that you discussed previously in Chapter Two.

In many qualitative traditions, studies might be informed by a theoretical or epistemological framework; but the researcher does not typically set out to test a theory by collecting empirical data. Instead studies may be designed so that data are collected first, and then a theory is derived from those data. In other words, the theory is grounded in the particular data that the researcher has collected. The usefulness of the theory can be tested in subsequent research (Denzin & Lincoln, 2005; Gall, Gall, & Borg, 2007; Glaser, 1978). This is the case with testing the usefulness of the Synergistic Leadership Theory (Irby, Brown, Duffy, & Trautman, 2002), which was developed using a qualitative methodology and tested in subsequent research by Bamberg (2004), Hernandez (2004), Holtkamp (2001), Schlosberg (2004), Trautman (2000), and Truslow (2004), and which is currently being tested in other countries.

Regardless of the methodology you use, you will need to base your interpretations on the data (i.e., "Stay close to the data"). Thus, when making statements about what the data mean, you must be able to reference the specific data to support your statements. To write an effective discussion section, you will need a thorough knowledge of your data, your theoretical framework, or epistemological framework, and the existing literature.

The discussion section in Chapter Five, or the concluding chapter, may be organized in many ways. Research questions (or hypotheses), variables, or themes can be used to organize this section. Present them in the same order they were presented in the Results Chapter. Following are guidelines that may help you structure the discussion section in Chapter Five or your concluding chapter.

GUIDELINES TO STRUCTURE YOUR DISCUSSION SECTION

First, briefly restate each research question (or hypothesis), variable, or theme. Present the results that relate to it. Do not reiterate technical details of the analysis, such as F and p values. Analyses have already been presented in the Results Chapter. Here you discuss, analyze, and explain the results of each research question (or hypothesis), variable, or theme. Examine the extent to which the data answered your research questions, supported/failed to support your hypotheses, showed functional relationships between variables, or made sense of the themes. Also identify any confounding or mediating variables that may have affected the results, and discuss their implications for your study.

Second, indicate how the results of your study support, contradict, or extend the knowledge base in your discipline. It requires you to return to the literature you reviewed in Chapter Two to integrate results of your study with other empirical studies that have examined the same phenomena. If your results support previous findings, highlight points of similarity. But if your results contradict what other researchers have found, discuss why your results differ from previous research. If your study was guided by a theoretical framework or epistemological framework, discuss your results in relation to that framework. However, if your study was not based on theory, discuss how your study related to theory in your discipline. Recall that in some qualitative traditions, theory may be derived directly from the immediate data that the researcher has collected rather than from prior research and theory (Gall et al., 2007).

Third, in some cases, your results may not have turned out as expected. You must explain why this happened. Consider several explanations. Causes of unexpected results usually fall into three major categories: (a) sampling, (b) instrumentation, and (c) research design.

Sampling

One problem that may limit your results is sampling, including inadequate sample size, low consent rates, high percentage of nonresponse from participants, participants dropping out of the study, use of volunteers, and improper sampling procedures. Lack of representativeness of a sample can bias the results of a quantitative study. You should examine these issues to determine if sampling has affected your results.

Instrumentation

Another problem that could affect the results of your study is instrumentation. Perhaps the instruments you used did not adequately operationalize the variables you measured. Other instrument issues include lack of validity and reliability of your instruments, unreliable ratings or observations, missing data, and possible biases. Review the appropriateness of each instrument concerning these issues.

Research Design

Still another problem that may limit your results is your research design. The design of your study involves issues of internal validity, including confounding variables, and many others. Space does not permit a full discussion here. You can review specific issues concerning internal validity associated with particular research designs by consulting Campbell and Stanley (1963) and Cook and Campbell (1979). They provide detailed descriptions of internal validity issues for experimental and quasi-experimental designs. Bogdan and Biklen (2007), Creswell (2007), and Denzin and Lincoln (2005) provide information on issues of research design for qualitative studies.

An example of a discussion section taken from Linda Creighton's (2006) dissertation follows. Creighton proposed nine research questions and regression models for student and institutional factors in her dissertation, which focused on predicting graduation rates at University Council for Educational Administration (UCEA) public universities. Due to space limitations, we present three of her research questions and a discussion of her regression models in the following example. (See Example 10.3.)

Example 10.3

Discussion of the Findings

Previous researchers (Astin, 2005; Goenner & Snaith, 2003; Pascarella & Terenzini, 2005) studied extensively what phenomena affect and ultimately predict a student's decision to remain in school or not. The goal of my study was to predict what factors were statistically significant at 63 UCEA public universities. This section discusses the implications of the findings for each of the nine research questions and two prediction models.

Research Question One

Is there a relationship between graduation rates at University Council for Educational Administration public universities and student SAT scores?
The findings resulting from research question one indicate a positive and significant relationship between graduation rates for the universities in this sample at the four-, five-, and six-year graduation level and student SAT scores. This finding speaks to the selectivity of the colleges and universities regarding their admission criteria and the curriculum in which the students are enrolled. Universities that are highly selective in their admission policies (e.g., accepting only those students achieving higher than average scores on the SAT test) may raise graduation rates. An institution requiring an average SAT score greater than 1100 should expect a higher graduation rate than a less selective required SAT score that is in the range of less than 990.

Students who meet the admission requirements of highly selective universities already come possessing the attributes for academic success; thus, it is imperative that colleges and universities offer academic programs and support services to ensure the continued success of these students. The graduation rate performance of students is an indicator that the university's programs and policies are perhaps meeting the needs of students better than those colleges and universities evidencing lower graduation rates.

Research Question Two

Is there a relationship between graduation rates at University Council for Educational Administration public universities and students graduating in the top 10% of their high school class?
As in research question one, the findings for research question two revealed a significantly positive relationship between graduation rates at the sample universities and students graduating in the top 10% of their high school class. This finding is consistent with previous research (Astin, 1991, 1993, 1997, 2005; Pascarella & Terenzini, 2005; Tinto, 1999) which indicated that one of the most accurate predictors of graduation rates was the percentage of students enrolled in the university who had graduated in the top 10% of their high school class. The implication here is that students, by virtue of their high academic ranking in high school, are equipped to handle the separation from family and high school friends, make a successful

transition from high school to college, and become successfully integrated into the society of the college. A note of caution is warranted in interpreting this finding: it may be that not all high schools maintain the same standard of rigor in their academic curriculum. In addition, some students may have achieved this status because of inflated grading procedures and may not in reality have the ability to assimilate into the society of the college that this ranking would imply; however, the results of the statistical test used to analyze this factor indicates a positive relationship between students' high school class rank and graduation rates.

Research Question Three

Is there a relationship between graduation rates at University Council for Educational Administration public universities and the percentage of students from underrepresented populations (i.e., African American, Hispanic, Asian, and Native American)?

As evidenced by the review of literature, the underrepresented populations identified in this study do not graduate from college at the same rate as the majority population (U. S. Department of Education, National Center for Education Statistics, 2004). However, there were approximately 11 UCEA institutions identified in the current study that experienced graduation rates for these underrepresented populations ranging between 70% and 93%. The literature (Agboo, 2001; Flowers, 2004; Hernandez, 2000; Hurtado, 2000; Nora, 2001) named numerous factors including: (a) environmental factors (i.e., racial climate, presence of an ethnic community, and working and living off campus); (b) involvement factors (i.e., faculty-student interaction, mentorship, participation in student organizations); and (c) social-cultural factors (immigrant status, ethnic identity development, community orientation). A further implication for the low graduation rates of these underrepresented populations is that many of the students may not speak English as their primary language and struggle with language issues, resulting in the need for remediation courses. As earlier research indicated (Kerr, 2001), many minority students experience academic difficulties because of their language barrier. The college environment may be alienating for these students and places them at risk of dropping out. The implication here is that the 11 UCEA institutions having higher than average (i.e., 70%–90%) graduation rates for underrepresented populations may have programs in place to further their academic success. Perhaps they show a high regard for diversity and foster a college climate of genuine concern regarding the possible effects that anticipatory stress could have on the interaction of minority students. In addition, it is possible that the faculty and student affairs professionals are acutely aware of the varied effects that ethnic group membership have on the social encounters of these students and exert collaborative effort to actively address issues related to the social experiences of racial-ethnic group members.

The findings of my study also have implications for the counseling of minority students. The counseling programs at the 11 UCEA institutions cited as having high graduation rates for these students may have programs in place that help foster students' self-efficacy. These schools may have professional counselors or graduate student advisers available to assess and evaluate students' academic and personal needs. Taking physical, economic, social, and cultural environments into consideration, counseling staff members work to involve students in academic and extracurricular activities that integrate them into the campus community and promote personal well being and success. These programs help and encourage students to maintain respective cultural values and simultaneously employ strategies to negotiate negative messages possibly perpetuated by the dominant society (Lesure-Lester & King, 2004). (Creighton, 2006, pp. 97–101)

Student Factor Regression Results

The regression model for student factors revealed a student's SAT score and high school rank as the strongest predictors of graduation rates. Though universities commonly take these variables into account, they are mostly doing so for selection and admission purposes. Administrators and policymakers must shift their focus to consider both of these variables for the purpose of increasing graduation rates. Selection and admission are important, but the major objective for universities is to graduate students. For example, many of the UCEA institutions have high SAT scores and high-school rank requirements for admission, but continue to have graduation rates in the 30–40% range. This is problematic. The point is: universities can predict that a 100-point increase in SAT requirements will affect graduation rates by approximately 10%. For example, if the graduation rate of a university is 40% while average SAT scores are 1100, the prediction can be made that by increasing its SAT average to 1200, its graduation rate would increase from 40% to approximately 50%. In addition, increasing the percentage of students admitted who are in the top 10% of their graduating high-school class by 10% will likely result in a four percent rise in graduation rate. Combining these two factors can affect rates by nearly 15%, having powerful and significant implications for accomplishing the real goals of education—degree completion.

The percentage of students enrolled over the age of 25 also had an effect on graduation rate, albeit a negative one. This issue is very complex with obvious confounding variables already identified in research studies (Berger, 2001; Caison, 2004; Carey, 2004). The implication here is that universities should not be quick to limit the enrollment of this age group. Evidence exists (Kuh, 2005; Mangold, Bean, Adams, Schwab, & Lynch, 2002; Pascarella & Terenzini, 2005; Schnell & Doetkott, 2002) that indicates student support systems and activities focus mostly on university freshmen (e.g., First Year Experience programs). Rarely are there support programs and activities geared toward the student over the age of 25. Programs must be designed and implemented that include support for this group of non-traditional students. For example, if we find that family emergencies interrupt a student's program of study, there must be an alternative plan available to the student. Even in doctoral programs, students can take a semester off to attend to family emergencies, then return to their program the following semester. This kind of option must be made available to undergraduate students in the over-25 age group.

Institutional Factor Regression Results

The regression model for institutional factors revealed the percentage of full-time faculty, percentage of classes with less than 20 students, and educational expenditures as the strongest predictors of graduation rates. In addressing these three factors several difficulties arise. First, in a time of economic constrictions, adding faculty, increasing expenditures, and reducing class size will not likely occur. Second, finding qualified faculty and additional classroom space continue to be problematic. But the implications here can be encouraging. Rather than addressing these issues *directly*, perhaps universities can approach them more creatively and *indirectly*. For example, many universities are implementing two- and three-tier faculty load status. Faculty can elect to focus more on teaching with a reduction in expectations for research—resulting in faculty teaching additional sections of courses. If this practice is rewarded and encouraged, it seems that the result would be a reduction in class size, due to increased sections of courses.

The correlation between student expenditures and graduation rates is not surprising. Currently, there is much emphasis on such things as increasing expenditures for programs that assist students from underrepresented populations, programs that provide more one-on-one advising, and programs that help at-risk students. The implication, though, is that universities must also focus on *indirect* effects of expenditures. As an example, if more funding is funneled to improving the technological infrastructure, the result may actually be more academic support for students, which in turn could have a positive effect on graduation rates. If library holdings are increased to support the addition of undergraduate programs and degrees, it seems that the result might be increased graduation rates in the long run. (Creighton, 2006, pp. 107–109)

As recommended, Creighton discussed each research question in the same order she presented them in Chapter One, "Introduction" and Chapter Four, "Presentation and Analysis of Data." She carried forth a discussion of her two regression models from Chapter Four. Note that Creighton refrained from repeating the technical details of her statistical analyses, which had already been presented in Chapter Four. Here she discussed and explained the results of each research question and regression model.

As mentioned at the beginning of this chapter, the concluding chapter of a dissertation or master's thesis can have any number of titles, including: "Summary, "Discussion," "Implications, "Recommendations," and/ or "Conclusions." And we have also mentioned elsewhere in this book that qualitative dissertations often deviate from the traditional five-chapter dissertation or thesis model we have been discussing throughout this book. Such is the case with Wanda Bamberg's (2004) qualitative dissertation. Bamberg's dissertation is nine chapters. After following our model for the first three chapters, she devoted five chapters to a discussion of her results: Chapters IV, V, VI, VII, and VIII, one chapter each devoted to the rich narrative she developed from interviewing five female superintendents, five school board members, and five administrative team members from the districts that participated in the 2001–2002 study conducted by Learning First Alliance. The Learning First Alliance identi-fied the five female superintendents as being the "most effective" superin-tendents in the nation. This constituted Bamberg's sample, including board members and administrative team members in these superinten-dents' school districts. All were female superintendents.

Bamberg's concluding chapter of her 2004 dissertation, Chapter IX, is titled "Summary and Conclusions." In Example 10.3 we provide the intro-duction to her concluding chapter, followed by the remainder of the sections (headings) contained in her chapter. (See Example 10.3.)

Example 10.3

CHAPTER IX

SUMMARY AND CONCLUSIONS

Introduction

Five female superintendents have been presented in five case studies in Chapters IV through VIII. My study examined the professional leader-ship experiences of the superintendents as they related to the Synergistic Leadership Theory (SLT) (Irby et al., 2002). In each case study, the data were presented from the interviews, responses on the Organizational Leadership and Effectiveness Inventory (OLEI) (Irby et al., 2000; Hernandez, 2004; Holtkamp, 2001; Trautman, 2000; Truslow, 2004), the LFA case studies, organizational charts, and newspaper and journal arti-cles to address the four research questions in the study. Each case study ended with a summary of the relationship between the leadership experi-ences of the superintendent and the alignment of the four factors of the SLT: attitudes, values, and beliefs; leadership behaviors; organizational structure; and external forces.

The chapter presents a summary of the cases of five superintendents as their leadership experiences related to the alignment of the four factors in their respective school districts. The chapter also offers conclusions about the superintendents and a description of theory into practice through the application of the SLT in implications for practice. Recommendations for further study are also included. (Bamberg, 2004, p. 410)

Below are the remaining headings in Bamberg's concluding chapter of her dissertation.

Summary of the Five Superintendents

Factor 1: Attitudes, Values, and Beliefs
Factor 2: Leadership Behaviors
Factor 3: Organizational Structure
Factor 4: External Forces
SLT Leadership Experiences: Alignment Summary

Implications for Practice

Recommendations for Further Research

Conclusions

Note that Bamberg included all but one of the elements, "Discussion of the Findings," we recommend for inclusion in the concluding chapter of a dissertation or master's thesis. Nevertheless, Bamberg provided an excellent discussion of her findings, which she skillfully integrated into Chapters IV, V, VI, VII, and VIII while discussing her results of the interviews she conducted. This is another technique many qualitative researchers use, the integration of results with discussion of those results. Of course, the ultimate decision as to what sections (headings) constitute a given chapter rests with the dissertation or thesis chair. We recommend that you read Wanda Bamberg's (2004) entire nine-chapter, 462-page dissertation in order to capture the rich narrative contained therein.

IMPLICATIONS FOR PRACTICE

The section on implications for practice in the Results Chapter is your opportunity to suggest how the results of your study may be applied to practice. Of course, some studies have more implications for practice than others. Typically, studies that involve education populations are likely to have a great many practical applications. Inferring those implications for practitioners can be challenging, but educators must be able to make those connections. For example, dissertations or master's theses in education might include a section on implications for teachers, counselors, department heads, and administrators. You also can provide implications of your study for other researchers. Implications for research and practice should be drawn as your study evolves rather than waiting until it is completed. Of course, you can do both.

For example, Keith Clark (2002) discussed implications of his study of the relationship between the allocation of educational resources and student achievement. (See Example 10.4.)

| Example 10.4 |

Implications for Practice

The era of school accountability in the United States started several years ago (Murphy, 1990). Many community members as well as lawmakers have called for greater accountability for schools. State and federal legislatures have answered the call and are investing large amounts of financial resources into schools. These agencies are closely examining how this investment in education is being utilized by the country's school districts. Many reports have shown that this increase in funds has not significantly improved student achievement (Barry & Hederman, 2000; Coate & VanderHoff, 1999).

The findings of this study have far-reaching implications for many persons interested in the United States educational system. This study identified several links between school district expenditure patterns and student achievement. Persons interested in school finance, policy, and research will find the evidence of links between expenditures of educational resources and student achievement very useful.

For educational administrators, this study offers insight into what resource allocation strategies are more likely to positively influence student achievement. It will also give the administrator a good idea of which strategies may negatively influence student achievement. In particular, this study suggests expenditures for instructional purposes can help boost student outcomes. Research questions one and two demonstrate these phenomena. In both research questions using different methodologies, instructional expenditures were identified as significant predictors of student achievement.

This study will also be useful to persons interested in school finance research and policy development. Many researchers have indicated that the money spent on schools does not matter when looking at student achievement. These studies, in most cases, looked at school district spending in the aggregate. This study looked at the actual functional expenditure areas in which school districts expend their resources. The information contained in this study indicates that the money spent on education does make a difference in student outcomes. What really matters is how and to what activities or programs the resources are directed.

Another important finding that relates to policymakers is the discovery that resource allocation strategies can positively or negatively effect student achievement. Many state school allocation systems are designed to equalize funding to school districts. These equalization-funding systems are designed to give every school district substantially equal funding in order to give every student the same level of education. This study implies that equalization strategies may not work to enable students to achieve at higher levels. The data suggests that even though school districts may receive the same funding, the way they expend their financial resources may not result in equal educational environments for students. This information should have a direct effect on the way state education agencies allocate resources. For example, the data suggest that the allocation of more money for instruction will increase student achievement. State agencies that want to increase student achievement could require specific percentages of state funds be used for instructional related activities. (Clark, 2002, pp. 128–130)

Note that Clark discussed implications of his research for school administrators, policymakers, and those persons interested in school finance research. Note also that Clark has observed our maxim mentioned earlier in this chapter: "Stay close to the data." His discussion of implications for research and practice are tied to his findings.

RECOMMENDATIONS FOR FURTHER RESEARCH

Recommendations for further research are frequently generated during the course of the study. Such recommendations can be valuable to other researchers, particularly other graduate students, who are seeking ideas for research topics. For example, when our doctoral students are searching for appropriate topics for their dissertations, we advise them to examine the final chapter of completed dissertations or discussion sections of professional journals to get ideas from other researchers about areas that warrant further research.

In addition to providing ideas for researchable topics, the recommendations section contains suggestions for ways that your study can be improved or extended. As you ponder how you might improve or extend your study, ask yourself the following questions: What additional independent variables need further study? What important dependent variables should be studied? What methodological improvements are needed? What questions remain unanswered? These questions and others prompt recommendations for further research. Data gaps, such as these, may have weakened your study and may have caused qualifications in the support of some of your predictions. Thus, their resolution is important to the goal of extending the knowledge base in your area of study. Similarly, qualitative researchers can ask similar questions related to research designs in the qualitative tradition.

Be certain that your recommendations are based on your results and not on opinion. Recommendations should not be generalized beyond the scope of your study. Adhere to the maxim we suggested earlier: "Stay close to the data." Furthermore, be careful not to make recommendations without considering their possible consequences, or taking into account their practicality. Finally, be careful that your recommendations are not stated so they sound like conclusions.

For example, Clark (2002) discussed recommendations for further research in which he followed our suggestions. (See Example 10.5.)

Example 10.5

Recommendations for Further Research

The goal of this study was to investigate the effect resource allocation strategies had on student achievement. Data was collected to test four research questions relating to this goal. The information was studied and many significant findings resulted from the examination of the data. The findings, although significant, have some limitations. One limitation is that the findings explain only a small proportion of the activities that are affecting any individual student's academic achievement. Another limitation is the design of the study. The study focused on aggregate functional expenditures. By only using functional level expenditures, the researcher could not explain in any detail what actual expenditures caused the significant effects discovered by this study. Based on the inadequacies of the study design, as well as the lack of statistical evidence in explaining a large part of the variance in test scores, suggestions are made for further research. The first two research questions examined the relationship between a school district's student achievement and their allocation of financial resources by functional expenditures. It was found that higher budget allocations for instructional purposes were significantly related to higher student achievement. It was also found that some budgetary expenditures have a negative effect on student achievement. The problem is that the statistical methods used to analyze the data could not provide complete answers to the complex relationships between budget allocations and student achievement. Further research along these lines should use a variety of data collection methods. Quantitative analysis can identify relationships between school district expenditure patterns and student achievement in reading, writing, and mathematics, as well as school district ratings. Qualitative studies can be used to map specific examples of relationships among the variables. A study in this format could go beyond simply discovering what expenditure functions have an effect on instruction. It would allow researchers who have discovered a relationship to delve far deeper into the factors causing the relationship. This could include case studies or interviews with school personnel who are intimately involved in the allocation of financial resources.

Future research into this subject should also include more detailed expenditure information. This study broke information down into expenditure functions. Functional level expenditure data is much more detailed than earlier studies looking only at total district expenditures. The problem is that the information is not detailed enough. Future studies should break financial expenditure data down to the object level. Object level expenditure information is a disaggregate of functional expenditures. It provides detailed spending information at a more detailed level than expenditures at the aggregate functional level. At this level of detail, the researcher would be able to tell what instructional level expenditure was having the greatest effect on student achievement. For example, if this study had utilized functional level expenditure information, the results would be able to show more than the fact that instructional level expenditure increased student achievement. It would also be able to show if higher teacher compensation or greater expenditures for instructional supplies were significant factors in this increase.

Another avenue of research could be to institute a case study of several successful districts to discover their unique allocation practices. The information from the case studies could be combined to ascertain if there are common practices successful school districts are using. These practices could include financial as well as nonfinancial information. This type of research could also be used to study successful student instructional programs or strategies. The researchers could study successful programs that create structures allowing the researchers to report the amount of student academic gain for each unit of monetary resources.

This study has shown that it is not enough to simply assume that increasing the dollars spent on education will improve the existing system. It has shown that the allocation of resources within a school district does have a limited impact on student achievement. The one factor that was shown to have a strong positive impact on student achievement was expenditures for instruction. This was shown to be the single strongest indicator of a district's success in improving student achievement. This is not to say that simply throwing money at school districts will not ensure increased student achievement. There are many other factors that affect student learning. The data indicate that the amount of school district expenditures is not the only factor that is related to student achievement. In other words, the keys to excellence in student achievement may lie outside of conventional measures of increasing the overall monetary investment in instructional expenditures. Money must be targeted toward specific programs that are designed to meet the specific needs of individual students. The data also strongly indicated that other factors not included in this study had a stronger impact on a student's achievement than money. (Clark, 2002, pp. 130–133)

Two things are noteworthy from Clark's recommendations for further research. First, he has aligned his recommendations with his research questions. Second, he has adhered to the maxim: "Stay close to the data." His recommendations are based on his data.

CONCLUSIONS

Sometimes the "Conclusions" section is omitted. At other times, conclusions are incorporated into the discussion section. The conclusions section of the final chapter is very important, because it is the summative statement of the researcher's study. Its function is similar to the summaries provided at the end of each chapter, except that the conclusions section is the conclusion of the whole study. It provides closure to the entire project. Every dissertation and master's thesis should end with conclusions.

Conclusions are assertions based on the findings. By reading your conclusions, readers discover to what extent research questions posed have been answered or to what extent hypotheses are sustained or not sustained. Thus, conclusions address issues that support or fail to support your theoretical framework. For example, if a hypothesis has been supported by the data, then the researcher can conclude that the data support the validity of the theory, which was being tested in the study. Qualitative researchers may use trends or themes, which emerged in their findings as a basis for potential theory building. In this case, the conclusions section provides the researcher's sense of how findings of the study contribute to the knowledge base.

A common error made by students is drawing more conclusions than the data warrant. Conclusions must not be generalized beyond what the data can support. Again, we call your attention to the maxim: "Stay close to the data." Another common error found in the conclusions section is that what are supposedly conclusions are actually summaries. Conclusions like the following can be found in numerous dissertations and master's theses: "Mean scores for males and females were not significantly different." The statement merely recalls a finding derived from analyzing the data. This finding needs to be interpreted in a way that will lead to a conclusion about what it means in terms of your research questions or hypotheses. Finally, you may include supplemental findings in the conclusion section not addressed in your research questions or hypotheses, providing you have included the analyses in the Results Chapter. These analyses will appear under the heading "Additional Analyses" in Chapter Four. It is inappropriate to introduce new data anywhere in the Discussion Chapter.

Sally Craycraft (1999) presented a conclusions section in her study of brain dominance and leadership styles of school superintendents and business chief executive officers. (See Example 10.6.)

Example 10.6

Conclusions

The findings of this study expanded the work of previous researchers in the area of leadership style and brain dominance characteristics. This investigation revealed that persons in the top executive level educational administration position (school superintendents) are characterized by a brain dominance style, which prefers the logical, analytic, organized, and controlled processes of the left hemisphere. A further assessment of the brain dominance results found in this study showed school superintendents generally lacking intuitive, conceptualizing right-brained skills required of leaders administering in a setting characterized by the need for risk-taking and acceptance of change. Business chief executive officers, on the other hand, are more right brained, preferring more intuitive, conceptual, interpersonal, and holistic processes. Significant differences were also found between the brain dominance mean scores for male and female leaders, with each group showing a stronger preference for left and right hemispheres, respectively.

The management/leadership literature indicates that most American organizations are experiencing dramatic change processes due to changes in technology, financial resources, and retrenchment of organizational structures and the people who work in them. The literature suggests a need for executive leadership that is able to visualize images of the future and articulate that vision to the followers in ways that empower them to change. (Craycraft, 1999, p. 108)

Note that Craycraft provided a brief but comprehensive discussion of conclusions from her study. Note also that she has "stayed close to the data"; that is, her conclusions are based on her findings.

SUMMARY

The final chapter of your dissertation may have any one of the following titles or a combination thereof: "Summary," "Discussion," "Implications," "Recommendations," and/or "Conclusions." The final chapter of your dissertation or master's thesis needs to include all of these elements. In this chapter, we provided advice on the contents of each of these elements. This advice was supported with examples from completed dissertations. We also suggested that qualitative dissertations and theses may not necessarily follow this pattern. In qualitative dissertations and theses, researchers frequently integrate results and the discussion of those results in one or more chapters. In the next chapter, we provide advice on how to prepare for and defend your proposal and final document.

PART IV

The Defense and Afterward

11

The Proposal and Final Oral Defense

Most universities require that you meet formally with a faculty committee twice, during which you defend your research project. The first meeting is the proposal meeting. The second meeting is the final oral defense. The proposal meeting is held before you begin to collect your data. The final oral defense is held after you have collected and analyzed your data and have written your entire dissertation or master's thesis. Our university decided that proposals should consist of Chapters One, Two, and Three of the dissertation. This practice is becoming commonplace at many other institutions. However, universities use a variety of formats for preparing the dissertation proposal. These formats can range from a 10- to 20-page description of your proposed study to the completion of the first three chapters of the dissertation. Thesis proposals are typically less formal.

It is your responsibility to schedule the proposal meeting. You should schedule your proposal meeting at least three weeks in advance of the proposal defense. Submit a quality, hard-copy document to your committee at the time you set the defense date, with a reminder memorandum indicating the date, time, and location of the defense.

You can take a number of steps to help ensure a successful proposal meeting: (a) prepare a well-written document, (b) know the format of the defense, (c) prepare your presentation, (d) practice your presentation, and (e) anticipate questions.

PREPARE A WELL-WRITTEN DOCUMENT

You can increase the chances that your proposal meeting will go well if you prepare a well-written document. Do not pressure your chair or committee to meet with you if your written document requires additional work. Make sure your chair has read and approves the final draft of your proposal. In this way, you will have your chair's support. Once your final draft is approved by your chair, you can submit the document to committee members. If the manuscript you submit to your committee is well written and carefully prepared (i.e., no spelling errors or poor grammar, no missing references, tables and figures match text, clear printed copies), you will begin your proposal meeting with a favorable impression. On the other hand, a poorly prepared document is likely to be perceived by your committee as the mark of an imprecise researcher.

KNOW THE FORMAT

The committee chair usually begins the proposal meeting by introducing the committee and explaining the procedures to be followed. Then you are asked to introduce yourself, make a brief statement about your professional background, and present a 25- to 35-minute summary of your proposal. This summary should cover all the major aspects of your research plan—the problem, purpose, theoretical framework, research questions or hypotheses, and methodology. The presentation should be clear and concise.

Questions from the committee follow your presentation. These questions and your responses occupy most of the meeting, which normally takes between one and two hours. Usually, questioning is conducted in one of two basic ways: Each member asks an uninterrupted segment of questions, with the committee chair acting as moderator; or questions are posed from any committee member on any aspect of the document. The round-robin format tends to break down in most cases after the first hour or so, with an increase in cross-fire questions from any member of the committee on any aspect of the document.

After the committee has completed its questioning, the committee chair will call for further questions. It there are no further questions, you will be asked to leave the room. The committee will then deliberate, concerning both your performance during the proposal defense and the adequacy of your research plan. Finally, the committee will vote on the acceptability of your research proposal.

Committees typically use four options in deciding the result of a proposal defense: (a) approval as submitted (this option is rare); (b) conditional approval, pending minor changes; (c) conditional approval, pending major changes; and (d) denied approval (this option is also rare, but it does happen occasionally). In the latter case, a waiting period is usually required before the proposal defense can be repeated. Typically, only one reassessment is permitted.

When the committee has reached a decision, you will be called back into the room. The chair of the committee will announce the decision. Changes required in the document are summarized orally by the committee chair. An official approval form is circulated for committee members' signatures before the meeting is adjourned. Subsequently, the committee chair attaches a memorandum to the approval form, containing a list of the revisions agreed upon in the meeting. The chair will then meet with you and go over the changes agreed to in the proposal defense.

PREPARE YOUR PRESENTATION

If you are in a field where PowerPoint is used for presentations (e.g., education and business), consider doing a PowerPoint presentation. PowerPoint will provide your presentation visually, so the committee will focus on the screen, not on you, and you can refer to the monitor as you speak. Provide committee members copies of your PowerPoint slides. In order to remain within the time allotted for your presentation (25 to 35 minutes), do not exceed 40 slides. Make a backup of transparencies from your PowerPoint slides in case the equipment fails on the day of your presentation. Nevertheless, we suggest you bring your own laptop computer and present your PowerPoint presentation from your own equipment.

The presentation you give will set the tone for the rest of the meeting. After you are introduced by your committee chair, begin your presentation by thanking your committee by name (Dr. Jones, Dr. Smith . . .) for all the help they have given you. Smile and make eye contact with your committee members. Take the opportunity to stand. This puts you in a dominant position, while all others in the room are seated. Tell the committee members how you became interested in your study. Keep it brief and professional. You might say something like this: "For some time now, I have been interested in variables that might have an effect on student achievement. In reviewing the literature, I have come across three variables that may be related to student achievement, namely: academic emphasis, collective efficacy, and faculty trust. I have decided to pursue this line of inquiry in my research."

Then, use this introduction to begin briefly reviewing the literature in this area. Concentrate on the literature directly related to your own study. Briefly summarize previous studies. Emphasize major findings. Then, lay the groundwork for your theoretical framework. Briefly present your theoretical framework. This brief discussion of your theoretical framework will lead to your research questions or hypotheses. State each research question or hypothesis (1, 2, 3, and so on).

Then move into your methodology. Describe your participants. Tell how you will acquire them. Describe your independent and dependent variables. Discuss the instrument(s) you will use. Mention reliability and validity of these measures. Describe your data collection procedures (e.g., questionnaires, in-depth interviews, observation, and document analysis). Be specific here. Discuss how you will analyze your data for each research question (hypothesis), theme, or variable.

Conclude by thanking your committee members for their interest in your research and for the time they devoted to reading many drafts of your proposal document.

The following outline may help you to prepare your proposal and final oral defense (see Table 11.1). It follows the five-chapter dissertation model we have presented in this book.

Table 11.1   Sample Presentation Outline

I. Introduction
Greeting
Background of the study
Statement of the problem
Purpose of the study
Significance of the study
Operational definitions (list only)
Theoretical framework
Research questions (or hypotheses)

II. Literature Review
The literature review can be integrated with the elements above, as suggested in the aforementioned example.

III. Method
Participants
Instrumentation
Validity
Reliability
Data Collection
Data Analysis
Limitations
Delimitations
Assumptions
These three integrated sections typically constitute the proposal defense.

IV. Results

V. Discussion, Implications, and Conclusions
All five sections constitute the final oral defense with emphasis on the results and discussion of those results.

PRACTICE YOUR PRESENTATION

As mentioned previously, you will be asked to give a 25- to 35-minute presentation of your research plan. It is a good idea to practice this presentation alone, as well as in front of an audience. Time your presentation. Students frequently underestimate the time it takes to make a presentation. As a result, they end up rushing through the most important part of their research plan: the methodology, especially during the proposal defense. In addition to practicing and timing your presentation, practice responding to questions about your research that may be asked by your committee. You can do this with other students or alone. Law students routinely engage in numerous "mock trials," as part of their training, before trying a case in front of a jury.

Find out where your proposal meeting will be held. Go and look at the room. Check to see if the equipment you will need is available, such as a blackboard, an overhead projector, a screen, or PowerPoint equipment. If any items you will need are absent, make arrangements for them well in advance of your proposal meeting. If possible, practice your presentation in the same room your proposal meeting will be held.

ANTICIPATE QUESTIONS

Questions from the committee follow your presentation. It is difficult to predict the questions committee members will ask in a proposal defense. However, the committee will almost certainly engage you in detailed questioning about your methodology during the proposal defense. This is because the Methodology Chapter provides the specific steps you plan to take to carry out your study. When committee members sign the approval form at the end of your proposal meeting, they are in essence supporting your methodology. That is, they are affirming that your methodology will provide an adequate test of the research questions or hypotheses you proposed (Heppner & Heppner, 2004).

Therefore, you can expect that the committee will focus on detailed aspects of your methodology. Most research involves sampling issues. They may inquire about the manner in which you selected your participants. They may ask about the extent to which your study can be generalized to other populations. They may inquire about the instruments you plan to use and the validity and reliability of these measures. If you plan to create you own instrument, they are certain to ask about your plans to validate the instrument and details about your pilot study. They may ask you about any potential internal and external threats to validity and steps you will take to minimize these. You may be asked questions about ethical issues, or about strategies to ensure anonymity and confidentiality of your participants.

You should expect to be asked questions about your plans for data collection. The committee may ask how you plan to analyze your data. We have found that detailed questioning about statistical analysis is usually not a major focus in proposal meetings. This is because most universities, like our own, have what is called "a resident statistician." He or she teaches the statistics course(s) and usually serves as a committee member on all quantitative studies. If not, the resident statistician consults with the students on their statistical analyses. Typically, many of the finer points of statistical analysis are intensified after the proposal has been approved, but prior to data collection, although a rough schema is usually required at the time of the proposal meeting. If your study is qualitative, the committee will certainly question you on your data collection procedures (e.g., in-depth interviews, focus groups, document analysis) and the analytic processes you will employ.

You must be able to answer detailed questions about your methodology. These are questions you can anticipate, and that you can prepare to answer prior to the proposal meeting. The detail with which committee members will question you on these issues will depend on the thoroughness with which you have prepared your written document.

In sum, after your proposal has been approved and you obtain clearance from your institution's Human Subjects' Committee, you can begin collecting and analyzing your data. Having collected and analyzed your data, you will then write the remaining chapters. Once you have finished writing the remaining chapters and have received approval from your committee chair, you will schedule the final oral defense.

FINAL ORAL DEFENSE

The final oral defense is similar to the proposal meeting. Therefore, much of the advice provided thus far regarding scheduling and presenting the proposal applies here. That is, similar to the proposal meeting, you will be asked to present, in this case, a 30- to 40-minute summary of your study. In this meeting, you will describe all the major aspects of your study—the problem, purpose, brief literature review, theoretical framework, research questions or hypotheses, method, results, and interpretation. However, in the final oral defense, you will focus less on the literature, rationale, and method of the study and more on the results and interpretation of those results. Thus, in your final oral defense, committee members will ask you to describe what you did, what you found, and what it means.

When responding to questions, you should observe two basic principles: (a) listen carefully and (b) respond both respectfully and scientifically. This means that you listen to and acknowledge every question posed by a committee member, and you respond to each question professionally, using a well thought out rationale. We recommend that you prepare and practice the 30- to 40-minute summary, as well as ways of responding to questions from the committee. A few examples follow.

It is important to listen carefully to every question. This will ensure that you answer the question asked. Answer questions completely yet succinctly. Do not give a lecture.

If you do not understand a question, ask the committee member to rephrase the question. Or you might paraphrase the question yourself to make sure you heard it correctly.

Perhaps a committee member will say: "Are you familiar with the recent article by X and Y on . . . What did you think of their findings in relation to yours?" Do not panic if you have not read the article. Say, "No, I am not familiar with their work. Could you please give me the reference, and I will read it." X and Y's study may be only remotely related to yours, so do not agree to any more than reading it. Missing a question or two will not result in a failed oral defense.

Suppose a committee member offers a suggestion for strengthening your study that implies another study. You might respond by saying, "That is a very interesting point, but I believe it is beyond the scope of this study." Such a response is fine, but an even better response would be: "That is a very interesting point. I agree with you. I will add it to my section on recommendations for further research." In the latter response, you have recognized the merit of the committee member's idea and have agreed to include it in your document. This is what Stephen Covey (1991) would call a "win-win" situation. You have acknowledged the committee member's idea, and the change to your document is minimal.

Does this mean that you have to agree with all committee members' suggestions? Of course, not. For example, suppose a committee member offers another procedural option that she feels will strengthen your study. The suggestion seems to be gaining momentum among other committee members during the meeting. You have listened openly to the faculty member's suggestion, but you do not agree. Describe the rationale you used in making the decision. Say: "Here was my rationale for selecting that particular procedure . . . " Give a relatively detailed explanation of your decision, supported by data and author references. You have acknowledged the faculty member's suggestion, and you have provided a scientific response. Usually the strategy works. The issue is settled. Again, you have created another win-win situation.

Say another committee member questions one of your summary data tables, claiming that it does not contain the proper heading for the statistical procedure used. This will be an easy change to make. Agree with the professor. Say: "I agree with you. It certainly clarifies the table." Your chair will have the final decision in matters like these, and in this case, the statistician's opinion will be sought. The point is, you have responded respectfully during the meeting. This constitutes another win-win situation.

Another committee member begins asking a long series of questions based on an earlier draft of your document. It is obvious to all that he has not read the final version of the document. Maintain your composure. Very skillfully and systematically respond to each question one-by-one, in each case referring to the page number in the revised document. For example, say: "I have added to that explanation on page 38; I have revised that table on page 144," and so on. Resist the temptation to express your true feelings of frustration and disappointment at the faculty member's lack of attention to details. Remember, he or she may be on numerous dissertation committees. Always respond respectfully and professionally to all questions.

Expect a certain amount of posturing. This behavior takes the form of mini-lectures or long convoluted, rambling comments, which are not really questions at all. This behavior by a faculty member is intended to impress other committee members with the speaker's knowledge about your topic. Let the faculty member have his or her say. Do not interrupt. When he or she concludes, say: "That is an important point." Say nothing else, and get ready for the next question. Once again, you have created another win-win situation. You respectfully acknowledged the faculty member's ideas, which has resulted in no change to your document.

TIPS FOR AVOIDING COMMON MISTAKES

Preparation is the key to a successful dissertation proposal and final oral defense. The proposal usually consists of the first three chapters of the thesis or dissertation: introduction, review of the literature, and methodology. The final oral defense consists of an examination of the entire document, including the Results and Discussion Chapters. These two important meetings are the culmination of a long preparation process. Throughout the process, you have been guided by a dissertation or thesis chair. By the time of your final oral defense of your dissertation or thesis, you have thoroughly reviewed the literature, designed the methodology, and conducted the study under the guidance of your chair and committee. The dissertation or thesis was written with the advice and consultation of the entire committee. Every member of the committee has seen the document and has critiqued it prior to the final oral defense meeting. With all this preparation and scrutiny, the final defense should proceed smoothly.

Nevertheless, it is not uncommon to encounter some problems at this stage of the process. Why does this happen? We provide a half-dozen tips on how to avoid such problems (Castetter & Heisler, 1984; Mauch & Park, 2003; Newman, Benz, Weis, & McNeil, 1997; Sternberg, 1981).

1. *You lack mastery of the substance of your dissertation.* Your chair has been misled about how much of the document—the literature review, the research design, the data collection, and the data analysis—was really completed or understood by you. Because of this, serious weaknesses surface at the final oral defense, which are then pursued by the committee. Make certain that you have total mastery of the dissertation or master's

thesis and how each section of the document relates to the knowledge base. Although you pay someone to do your data analysis, you will be held accountable for understanding the results.

2. *You convince your chair that you are ready for the final defense.* Your chair, feeling pressured, allows you to come to the final defense before your document is thoroughly and carefully completed, and before it represents a work of excellence. Get your chair's approval of the entire document before setting the defense date, and do not pressure your chair into agreeing to a defense date until your document is ready.

3. *You have failed to gain approval of successive stages and chapters of the dissertation from committee members.* In some programs, the dissertation process is still so vague that the student can proceed with the bulk of the dissertation or thesis without being scrutinized by faculty. Set up weekly or monthly meetings with your chair and crucial committee members. Such a schedule will keep you and your examiners on the same page throughout the process.

4. *Your dissertation is not well packaged for the final defense.* An often neglected aspect of packaging is the two- or three-page *abstract* that University Microfilms International requires at the beginning of all dissertations. The first substance item that catches the wary reader's eye is the abstract. Make it a terse yet complete overview of the dissertation, including the purpose embedded in the knowledge base of the discipline, a conveyance of its contribution, the research questions or hypotheses developed from the problem examined, the methodologies employed in collecting and analyzing the data, the major findings, discussion of the results, and implications for practice. Your abstract should project the central themes from each chapter of the dissertation or thesis, condensed into one or two paragraphs each.

5. *The appearance of the final draft copy of your dissertation is neglected.* This is another important aspect of packaging your dissertation for the final defense. Use a high-quality laser printer for the final draft of the dissertation that the committee receives. From our experience, the Helvetica font seems to produce darker, more distinct copies than other fonts. Helvetica is also easier to read than many other fonts. Take care in preparing your tables symmetrically on each page and avoid white space at the bottom of the pages of your dissertation. This will require careful planning of all of your tables before you begin to write the chapter. According to the American Psychological Association, you may reduce the tables to 10 point and single space some items when space is needed.

6. *You lack "informed consent" about the defense. Informed consent* is a term used in medicine when surgeons inform patients about the procedures or risks of a particular operation to be performed. In the context of an oral defense, *uninformed consent* means that you have neither a clear picture of

what will likely transpire during the defense nor what can go wrong. In such a state, you may experience predefense fear, during-defense paralysis, and postdefense depression. The best way to have informed consent about how dissertation defenses are conducted in your department is to attend one or more defenses. The final oral defense is typically open to the public, and doctoral students are encouraged to attend. If you cannot attend a defense at your institution, talk to someone who has recently successfully defended a dissertation in your department. We provided a detailed description of what is likely to transpire at a dissertation defense in this chapter, under the heading "Know the Format." Most of the suggestions in that section are applicable to both the proposal defense and the final oral defense of the dissertation.

SUMMARY

The essence of the discussion in this chapter is that the best preparation for a dissertation or thesis defense is through meticulous preparation of the written document and the meeting itself. Thus, know what you did, why you did it, what you found, and what it means. The mark of an excellent researcher is one who becomes her or his own harshest critic.

In the next chapter, we provide advice on how to prepare your dissertation or master's thesis for wider dissemination, including professional presentations and print media.

12

Presenting and Publishing Your Dissertation

Y ou have defended your dissertation, made any necessary corrections, and submitted the required copies to your university library. Your dissertation may be consulted by students who are interested in your topic; it may be requested by other universities through the interlibrary loan system; and it may be referenced in other dissertations, books, or journal articles. However, your research will not reach a wide audience in this way.

Publishing your dissertation is the way you can get it into the mainstream of academic ideas, rather than having it sit on a shelf and collect dust in your university library. You can disseminate your research to a wider audience in a number of ways, including: (a) presentations, (b) job interviews, (c) academic journals, (d) books, (e) chapters in books, (f) the popular press, (g) Internet publishing, and (h) desktop publishing.

PRESENTATIONS

Formats for presentations include department colloquia; presentations at state, regional, national, and international professional conferences; and presentations at job interviews. In many departments, graduate students, faculty, or invited guests have opportunities to present their research in colloquia (also called "brown bags") to anyone interested in attending. You can reach a larger audience, however, if you present your research at state, regional, national, and international meetings. Presenting at department colloquia and state and regional meetings will give you practice for presenting at the more prestigious national and international conferences.

If your career aspirations lean toward academia, presentations at national and international meetings will count more heavily on your curriculum vitae than state and regional meetings. National and international conferences provide a number of different presentation formats. They include paper presentations, poster sessions, organized symposia, workshops, round table discussions, panel discussions, fireside chats, and invited addresses. Research based on dissertations and master's theses are most appropriate for the first two formats: paper presentations and poster sessions. Therefore, we will concentrate our discussion on these two formats.

Paper Presentation

Abstracts and proposals must be submitted well in advance of a national or international conference. For example, the American Educational Research Association (AERA), which meets in April annually, requires that submissions be received by early August. The University Council for Educational Administration (UCEA), which meets in November each year, requires that submissions be received by early May. Thus, presenting your study at national meetings such as these requires advanced planning. You may wish to check specific organizations' Web sites to determine deadlines for presentation submissions.

If you plan to present your research at one of the aforementioned national conferences, you will need to submit electronically a 50-word abstract and a three-page proposal of your study. Other organizations may require a different submission format. Much of the groundwork will have been done, providing you have prepared a stellar abstract for *Dissertation Abstracts International*. The three-page proposal should contain the following items: problem, theoretical (or conceptual) framework, method, results, and implications. About two-thirds of the proposal should describe the method and results. Reviewers will want to know the most important details of the study. The abstract is a brief summary of the proposal.

Following are examples of an abstract (see Example 12.1) and a proposal (see Example 12.2). Although a variety of session formats are available to presenters, these examples represent submissions that were accepted for paper presentations at the annual meeting of the American Educational Research Association (AERA) in April 2007. These submissions to AERA were based on Allen Garner's (2005) doctoral dissertation. They are typical submissions and may serve as models for your own submissions.

Example 12.1

Managerial Tasks of Superintendents in Large, Medium, and Small School Districts

Abstract

Superintendents' managerial tasks performed in large, medium, and small school districts was the focus of this study. Three research questions guided the investigation concerning level of involvement, differences of involvement, and priority of tasks performed. Glass's (2004) *Superintendent Management Grid* was administered to a national sample of 2,000 school superintendents randomly selected by computer through the Market Data Retrieval Company. After three requests, 1,042 superintendents returned usable instruments (52%). Inferential statistics revealed 87 significant differences between large, medium, and small school districts with respect to Glass's five management domains: financial management, facility management, personnel management, student personnel and special services, and support services. The study provides implications for the preparation of school superintendents.

Example 12.2

Managerial Tasks of Superintendents in Large, Medium, and Small School Districts

1. Objectives

The managerial of tasks of school superintendents "differs greatly among districts of varying size, wealth, and program configuration" (Glass, 2004, p. 17). The purpose of this study was to examine the managerial tasks of school superintendents in large, medium, and small school districts. Specifically, this superintendent study was intended to: (1) examine the *level of involvement* of school superintendents in large, medium, and small school districts with respect to Glass's (2004) five areas of school management: financial management, facility management, personnel management, student personnel and special services, and support services; (2) examine the *differences of involvement* of school superintendents in large, medium, and small school districts with respect to Glass's five areas of school management; and (3) examine the *priority of tasks performed* by school superintendents with respect to Glass's five areas of school management.

2. Perspective(s)

The following managerial tasks are common to every school district regardless of size and wealth: financial management, facility management, personnel management, student personnel and special services, and support services. Financial management includes the following functions: fiscal planning, budgeting/forecasting/demographics, accounting/cash management, purchasing/contracts, inventory management, materials distribution, risk management, salary/wage management, and worker's compensation. Facility management includes replacement, maintenance, retrofit, technology, and equipment. Personnel management includes the following functions: needs assessment, recruitment, evaluation, induction, staff development, record keeping, payroll, fringe benefits, safety/environment, negotiations/contract management, and grievance management. Student personnel and special services include program organization and management, supervision of services, assessment/compliance, adjudication of problems, student health, and school attorney. Support services include student transportation, food services, and contracting. They are prescribed actions both in highly centralized or decentralized systems. Most of these management functions are closely monitored by state departments and other regulatory agencies. They constitute a nonnegotiable managerial imperative for superintendents to supervise, coordinate, perform, and be held accountable by the school board and community.

The level of superintendent participation in the preceding management areas is primarily determined by district size, not training, experience, or personal inclination. Larger school districts have larger central office staffs than smaller districts allowing the superintendent to assign and delegate many management responsibilities to others. In most of the 14,500 American school districts, however, superintendents perform the tasks themselves or share them with one or two other administrators. We adopted the four levels of management devised by Glass (2004) in an earlier study (Level 1—Supervise: The superintendent has little if any direct involvement; Level 2—Coordinate: The superintendent has coordinator role and is directly involved; Level 3—Co-Worker: The superintendent is actually performing some of the work; Level 4—Do It: The superintendent performs the task) devised by Glass (2004). Also we adopted school district sizes (large, medium, small), which were used in each of the American Association of School Administrator (AASA) ten-year superintendent studies.

3. Methods

Participants:

A national sample of 1,042 superintendents participated in the study. The responding school superintendents' responses were placed in one of the following three categories: (a) large for those with an enrollment of 10,000 and over, totaling 86 school districts; (b) medium for those with an enrollment of 1,600 to 9,999 students, totaling 282 school districts; and (c) small for those with an enrollment of 1 to 1,599 students totaling, 674 school districts.

Instrumentation:

A useful instrument for examining the managerial tasks of school superintendents is Glass's superintendent management grid (2004). The instrument contains 36 management tasks divided into five categories: (a) financial management, (b) facility management, (c) personnel management, (d) student personnel and special services, and (e) support services.

The instrument was modified slightly for this study: First, numbers were added to help clarify and organize constructs. Next, percentages were added to the four levels of superintendent involvement to help provide clarification for respondents which included the following: (a) level 1 supervise at 25%, (b) level 2 coordinate at 50%, (c) level 3 co-worker at 75%, and (d) level 4 do it all at 100%. Finally, section two of the survey instrument was added to include demographic information. Reliability and validity of the superintendent management grid is reported elsewhere (Glass, 2004). A Cronbach alpha was conducted with the present sample to measure reliability and internal consistency of the instrument. The Cronbach alpha was .96 ($n = 1,042$).

4. Data Sources

The superintendent management grid, together with a cover letter and self-addressed envelope, was mailed to a national sample of 2,000 superintendents randomly selected by computer through the Market Data Retrieval Company. All surveys were coded to a master list of the sample for identification in order to calculate return percentages. After two additional requests, 1,042 superintendents returned usable instruments (52% return rate). The Statistical Package for Social Sciences (SPSS) software was used to analyze and describe the data. Data were coded and inputted into the computer on all responses from surveys returned. Size of school district (large, medium, and small) was used as the dependent variable. Combinations of descriptive and inferential statistics were utilized to analyze the data. Descriptive analysis was used to characterize superintendent respondents with the following demographic information: (a) gender, (b) ethnicity, (c) age, (d) highest degree earned, (e) total years in education, (f) total years as superintendent, (g) number of superintendent positions held, and (h) school district size. Descriptive analysis was also used to identify the level of involvement (Level 1–4) superintendents have in the work tasks of large, medium, and small school districts in the following areas of school management: (a) financial management, (b) facility management, (c) personnel management, (d) student personnel and special services, and (e) support services. Additionally, analysis variance (ANOVA) was used to compare differences of responses of superintendent management tasks with school district enrollment. Due to the fact that significant mean differences were evident between different sized school districts, a Turkey post hoc analysis was performed to determine precisely where the significant mean differences were found. Effect size was also calculated on all inferential statistics. Finally, descriptive analysis was used to rank order superintendent managerial tasks by school district size.

5. Results

Analysis of variance (ANOVA) revealed 87 significant differences of superintendent involvement according to school district size. First, superintendent involvement in financial management revealed 24 significant differences among superintendents of large, medium, and small school districts. Subsequently, there were 11 significant differences among superintendent respondents in facility management. In addition, the study of superintendent involvement in personnel management revealed 27 significant differences. Furthermore, there were 18 significant differences among superintendent respondents in student personnel and special services. Finally, superintendent involvement in support services revealed seven significant differences in responses.

Descriptive methods revealed that financial management was the most important area of school management for superintendents, followed by personnel management, student personnel and special services, facility management, and support services. The demographics of the current superintendent study were quite similar to the Glass, Björk, and Brunner (2000) national AASA study.

6. *Educational Importance of the Study*

Not only are current superintendent preparation programs offered by universities not uniform, but also certification programs vary from state to state. In the past, certification requirements have driven the content of superintendent preparation. Certification or licensing codes generally require university coursework and passing a state exam. In approximately 30 states, the certification or licensing code is closely or loosely based on seven standards developed by the Educational Leadership Constituent Council (2002) for a K–12 principal position. The application of generic principal standards may be due to the traditional structure of many university superintendent programs being mere extensions of principal preparation (Kowalski & Glass, 2002).

This paper does not debate the appropriateness of existing superintendent preparation but has implications for developing a superintendent executive management program consisting of five domains of management: financial management, personnel management, student personnel and special services, facility management, and support services. Each domain can be developed into an instructional and performance module and should be a collaborative effort between the university, professional associations, and the state agency.

The abstract and three-page proposal was sent electronically, single-spaced, and in 12-point type to AERA. The documents included as Examples 12.1 and 12.2 are reproduced here exactly as they were submitted. The proposal was accepted as a paper presentation at the annual meeting of AERA in April 2007. These are the typical submissions required by national organizations such as AERA and UCEA, and many others. Note how Garner's submission, which is based on his dissertation, conforms to our earlier recommendations concerning contents of proposals submitted to national meetings.

Preparing a Paper Presentation

In Chapter 11, we provided you with many suggestions for preparing a presentation for your proposal and final oral defense. Much of that information applies here. Following are a few additional suggestions for presenting a paper at a national or international conference.

1. Submit a copy of your paper to your session discussant at least two weeks prior to your presentation date.

2. Observe time limits set for presenters. Usually four presenters per session are allowed 10 to 15 minutes each, followed by questions from the audience.

3. Practice reading your paper to determine how much time you will need. Adjust the length accordingly. If you will be using PowerPoint, adjust the number of slides appropriate for the time allotted. We recommend that you bring your own equipment (e.g., laptop computer). Make transparencies of your slides as a backup in case your PowerPoint does not work.

4. Familiarize yourself with the layout of the room prior to your presentation, and set up your PowerPoint prior to your presentation.

5. When presenting your paper, maintain eye contact with your audience periodically, enunciate, and show enthusiasm by varying the pitch and modulation of your voice.

6. Stay within your time limit. Look at your watch when you begin talking, or set a timer on the podium.

7. During the questioning portion of the presentation, answer questions completely and succinctly.

8. Make a sufficient number of copies of your paper available for your audience.

If you follow these suggestions, it is likely that you will make a successful presentation.

Poster Session

The poster session is a relatively new innovation. Researchers are assigned positions in a room where each one displays key elements of her or his research and discusses it with whomever attends. For a poster session, you prepare a visual layout of your research that parallels the content of a paper presentation. The various sections of your paper, namely problem (or purpose), theoretical framework (or perspectives), method, results, and implications, are typed and attached to a 3-foot by 5-foot poster. The type should be readable at a distance of about two or three feet. As to organization of your paper, allocate one page for purpose, theoretical framework, and implications, two pages each for method and results, and display no more than three tables or figures. You can start by using the three-page proposal to develop your poster. Both formats (paper presentation and poster session) require a 50-word abstract and a 3-page single-spaced proposal. The poster display allows other researchers to stop by your poster, read its contents, and discuss it with you if they wish. Prepare a handout of the contents of your poster, which can be distributed to interested persons.

JOB INTERVIEW

Another means of disseminating your research to a wider audience is a job interview. Of course, in this case, your primary motive is to use your dissertation or master's thesis to secure a position. Suppose, for example, that you are one of three finalists for a faculty position at a college or university. You have been invited to campus for two days to meet with faculty, administrators, and students. As part of the interview, you are required to make a one-hour presentation (including questions) on your research interests. How do you prepare for this event?

First, consider your audience. Your audience is likely to be composed of faculty, students, and administrators. Faculty will be interested in your potential as a teacher, scholar, and colleague. Students will be interested in your potential as their teacher and what they can learn from you. Administrators will be interested in all of the above. At this point, all three finalists are probably about even based on their paper credentials, or they would not have been invited to make a presentation. Therefore, it is important that you make a solid presentation. The presentation you make will set the tone for the rest of the interview.

Second, as mentioned in Chapter 11, practice your presentation alone and in front of a group. Perhaps you have already presented an abbreviated version of your dissertation or master's thesis at a local, state, or national conference. This has given you some practice. But such presentations were only 10 to 15 minutes in length at those conferences. You could read your paper, if done skillfully, without losing your audience. A 45-minute presentation followed by 15 minutes of questions is different and more demanding. If you read your paper for 45 minutes, you will surely lose your audience. What you need to do is learn your content so well that you do not have to read your paper. However, if you cannot memorize the content, then practice reading the paper with as much enthusiasm—variation in pitch, tone, and modulation of your voice, as well as periodic eye contact with your audience—as possible. "The trick to reading a paper . . . is to appear not to be reading it" (Madsen, 1992, p. 134). An even better approach is to do a PowerPoint presentation. This way you can refer to your paper off your laptop monitor. The audience will focus on the screen, and not on you. Provide slides of your PowerPoint, so your audience can follow you using either the screen or your slides. We recommend that you work off your own laptop computer. Make transparencies of your PowerPoint slides as a backup and use an overhead projector should your PowerPoint equipment fail.

Third, what should be included in your presentation? Follow the guidelines for the preparation of a conference paper or poster session: problem, theoretical framework (or perspectives), method, results, and implications. Provide a brief overview of the research problem. Do not spend much time reviewing the literature, but discuss theories that undergird your study. Simply state your research questions or hypotheses. Spend most of your time describing the methodology (e.g., in-depth interviews, focus groups, document analysis, instruments, or experiments) and the results. Conclude by discussing implications of the results (i.e., what is the significance of your study). Thank everyone for attending, and wait for questions. Much of the advice we provided in Chapter 11 regarding questioning during the proposal and final oral defense applies here. Recall the advice we provided in Chapter 11 for responding to questions: you should observe two basic principles when responding to questions: (a) listen carefully and (b) respond both respectfully and scientifically.

ACADEMIC JOURNALS

If you intend to pursue a career in higher education, you need to consider very carefully the requirements for tenure. If you want to achieve tenure, you will need to amass an appropriate number of important articles in high-quality, peer-reviewed journals. At the time of the tenure decision, most universities want to see a long list of quality published articles. The requirement for a research university is about three articles per year. Smaller colleges and universities, oriented toward teaching and undergraduate students, might require only one article per year.

Having completed the doctorate recently, your first step is to determine how many articles can be published from your dissertation. We believe that any dissertation of seminal importance can produce multiple journal articles. For example, your literature review may be so comprehensive and of such high quality that it would be suitable for publication in a review journal. In addition, you may have developed a piece of computer software during the course of your study that could be described in a specialized journal that focuses on computers. Perhaps you have developed a new statistical procedure or variant of an existing procedure while conducting your study that could be described in a short statistics handbook. Or, you might have discovered a different set of factors based on a factor analysis of the instrument(s) you used in your study, a description of which might be appropriate for publication in a journal that specializes in measurement issues.

The scheme outlined above—a review article, a computer software article, a statistical procedure article, and a measurement article—derived from your dissertation could constitute the beginning of a publication plan for tenure.

Note that we are speaking here about submitting multiple papers derived from your dissertation that describes independent parts of the total document. We are not speaking about creating several publications based on the results from a single database. This practice constitutes duplicate publication (Cone & Foster, 2007). Consult the *American Psychological Association Publication Manual* (5th ed., 2001) for further discussion of this issue.

Select a Suitable Journal

Determining where to send your manuscript involves three important factors: (a) selecting a journal that matches your topic, (b) selecting a journal that matches you career goals, and (c) selecting a journal that is appropriate for your study (Heppner & Heppner, 2004).

First, find a journal that publishes the types of articles that match your dissertation topic. A particular discipline may have a dozen or more journals. Typically, each one will focus on a particular type of article it publishes, such as empirical articles, theoretical articles, or practitioner articles. For example, within educational administration, *Educational Administration Quarterly* publishes primarily empirical research. *The Journal of Educational Administration* publishes primarily conceptual and empirical studies. *Educational Leadership* and *Phi Delta Kappan* publish primarily applied articles on educational leadership and education in general, respectively, as well as some empirical articles with definitive implications for practice. Thus, select a suitable journal that matches your dissertation topic. Read the journal's mission statement and its guidelines for manuscript submission. In addition, peruse the contents of the primary journals in your discipline to get a feel for the type of articles published in them. And, of course, consult with your dissertation chair.

Second, your career goals will determine the most suitable journal for your manuscript. For example, if you are interested in working as a consultant or as an administrator in a public school, then you should choose to publish in a journal that focuses on practitioner articles. However, if you intend to build a career in a research university, you should submit your work to a prestigious empirical journal. Academic departments in research universities will only favorably consider articles published in top-tier journals.

Following are a dozen Tier 1 journals in educational administration for those professors interested in building a career teaching educational administration at a prestigious research university. (See Table 12.1.)

Table 12.1   Tier 1 Journals in Educational Administration

Educational Administration Quarterly	*Review of Research in Education*
Journal of Educational Administration	*Educational Evaluation & Policy Analysis*
Journal of School Leadership	*Harvard Educational Review*
Educational Researcher	*Teachers College Record*
American Educational Research Journal	*Educational Management & Administration*
Review of Educational Research	*Journal of Educational Research*

Third, determine the most prestigious journal that is suitable for your manuscript. Many journals are available in any given discipline, but not all journals are of the same quality or scientific rigor. Academics classify journals into a rough hierarchy as to quality as follows: excellent (Tier 1), above average to average (Tier 2), and below average to marginal (Tier 3). This rough classification system is based primarily on three factors: refereeing systems, acceptance rates, and citation scores. For example, some journals may not be refereed (i.e., they do not peer review manuscripts) and may have very high acceptance rates. Other journals have a refereeing system and may have a very low acceptance rate. Some journals have high citation scores, while other journals are cited less often. Generally, the higher the rejection rate, the higher the quality of the journal. However, there are exceptions to this general pattern. In many social and behavioral science disciplines, some prestigious journals do not operate on the basis of a refereeing system. In addition, some universities place importance on *citation scores.* This is a calculation of how often other researchers cite an article from a specific journal. The more often a specific journal is cited, the higher the quality the journal is judge to be. Citation scores for most journals can be found in the *Social Science Citation Index* and the *Humanities Citation Index.*

One good source of information on the characteristics of journals is *Cabell's Directory of Publishing Opportunities* (2006). It lists more than 4,000 specialized and professional journals by discipline. For each journal it supplies (a) submission addresses; (b) publication guidelines, including manuscript length, copies required, computer submission requirements, format, and manuscript style; (c) review information, including number of external reviewers, acceptance rate, time required to review, reviewer's comments, and invited articles; (d) circulation data, including primary audience, frequency of issue, copies per issue, publisher; (e) manuscript topics; and (f) manuscript guidelines.

Now that you have determined the level of quality of various journals, you should evaluate the level of scientific rigor of your manuscript. If your dissertation is a two-variable study using correlation, it is not likely to be published in a Tier 1, empirical journal. It may be more suitable for a Tier 2 or Tier 3 journal. However, if your study was a test of a new theory, used an underrepresented population not traditionally used in the past, or employed an advance-level statistical procedure, like structural equation modeling, it might be accepted in a Tier 1, empirical journal. Moreover, if your study was qualitative, and your analyses were solid, it too might be accepted in a Tier 1 journal.

Prepare the Manuscript

After selecting a suitable journal, the next step is to prepare the manuscript for publication. Most APA-style journal articles include the following sections: abstract, introduction, method, results, and discussion. These sections parallel the sections (or chapters) of a dissertation or master's thesis. Pare down your dissertation so that these sections of your document are shorter and more focused, or build up the conference proposal you submitted to AERA or UCEA, or other national or international annual meeting "call for papers." Read the guidelines for manuscript submission found in the journal you have selected, and follow them exactly.

Observe the following maxim when preparing your manuscript: "Write, print, edit, revise, polish, get feedback, and revise again." Repeat this cycle as many times as it takes to get a publication-ready manuscript. Write a first draft concentrating on getting your thoughts in written form. Do not worry about how your ideas are organized at first. Print your writings and edit them on the hard copy. Avoid on-screen editing, which is usually confined to simple corrections. At the revision stage, focus on organizing your ideas into a clear argument sequence and linking closely related points. Then polish the text using topic sentences, transitions, and closure sentences, as discussed in Chapter 7. Get feedback on your polished text from well-respected and published colleagues. Based on the feedback you receive, revise again. Repeat this cycle until you are completely satisfied that your manuscript is ready for submission to the journal of your choice.

Submit the Manuscript

Submit the required number of copies to the address provided in the most recent issue of the journal you selected. Send the manuscript *Return Receipt Requested*. This postal method requires a signature from a receiver where the journal is housed. When you receive the receipt in the mail, you will know your manuscript arrived safely. Most editors will acknowledge receipt of your manuscript by letter. They will usually indicate who is handling your manuscript, typically an associate editor. If you have not received such an acknowledgment letter within four weeks of submission, contact the editor (by e-mail, telephone, or letter) to inquire about the status of your manuscript.

You will receive a decision on your manuscript. Journal editors typically use four categories of response: (a) acceptance with no changes;

(b) conditional acceptance pending changes; (c) rejection, accompanied by two or more anonymous reviews; and (d) revise and resubmit. In the latter case, the editor encourages the author to revise the manuscript and resubmit it for additional consideration. The "conditional acceptance pending changes" and the "revise-resubmit" decisions are very common nowadays. In the former case, you have an acceptance. It doesn't get much better than that, for "acceptance with no changes" is very rare. Thus, revise the manuscript as soon as possible, following the suggestions provided by the reviewers. You do not have to make all suggestions recommended if you do not agree with them, but you must respond to each suggestion. The "revise-resubmit" decision is, in essence, no decision. You may decide to revise and resubmit, or submit the manuscript to another journal, using the suggestions from reviewers to improve the manuscript.

BOOKS

Books can be divided into two main types—trade books and academic books. Trade books are intended for the general public and can be found in commercial bookstores, public libraries, and publisher's catalogs. Academic books, including textbooks and monographs, are intended for academic audiences, such as students and faculty in colleges and universities, and practitioners in the field. Most social and behavioral science research is best suited for publication in academic books. However, some may appeal to the general public and qualify for publication in trade books.

Most dissertations or master's theses are best suited for publication as research monographs. A monograph is a detailed study of one particular topic (e.g., organizational climate and pupil control ideology, as mentioned in Chapter 7). It is at the opposite end of a continuum from a best-selling textbook. Sales for monographs total in the low hundreds as compared textbooks, which may sell in the thousands.

Why is it worth publishing a monograph? There are at least three reasons: (a) to disseminate your research to a larger audience, (b) to add accomplishments to your curriculum vitae, and (c) to improve your citation score (i.e., how many times your work is cited in the professional literature) (Dunleavy, 2003). The citation score is often used by research universities as one criterion in making tenure decisions. The more often your work is cited by other scholars the better, and the more prestigious the journal the better yet.

Possible publishers to approach with a book proposal include: (a) major university presses, such as Teachers College Press, Columbia University; (b) major commercial publishers with monograph lists; (c) less well-known university presses; (d) smaller or lesser-known commercial publishers with monograph lists; or (e) vanity presses. The first four choices are legitimate publications, the first one being the best choice. Do not even consider vanity presses. A book published by a vanity press may impress your friends, but it cannot be used to build your curriculum vitae in your bid for tenure in most colleges and universities.

After considering possible publishers, your next task is to prepare a book proposal. Most book publishers want to know (a) about your project, (b) about the contents, and (c) about the market. Following are book proposal guidelines issued by Corwin Press. (See Example 12.3.)

Example 12.3

Part 1: About the Project

Rationale: Why are you writing the book? What will it accomplish? Why do people need help on the topic at this time? Is the topic of increasing importance rather than passing or declining importance? How does the book meet the need you have identified?

Knowledge Base: What is the research or experience base for the information in the book? Briefly describe any special studies or previous work relevant to the content.

Nature of Content: Do you provide a "broad brush" approach or a detailed, comprehensive treatment of the topic? How will the book be applicable to practice?

Alternative Title Possibilities: Along with your current working title, please suggest several alternative titles. We strive for titles that clearly communicate to all audiences the topic, purpose, and usefulness of our publications.

Competing or Related Works: Please list the author, title, and publisher of the main competing or related books, and tell us how your book would differ or be superior.

Special Materials: Describe any elements in the book that will help illustrate the textual discussions (for example, cases, flowcharts, forms, summaries, annotated bibliography, glossary, and so on.) How many tables, figures, and exhibits do you anticipate using?

Length and Schedule: How many double-spaced, typewritten pages do you anticipate the manuscript will have? Include special materials, tables, figures, and the reference section in the page count. When do you expect to have your manuscript ready? (Please be realistic in planning your schedule.)

Other Publishers: Which other publishers are considering your project?

Author: What experience, background, or other qualifications do you have that make you uniquely qualified to undertake this project? Please attach your curriculum vitae or resume.

Part 2: About the Contents

Outline of Contents and Chapter Descriptions: Please provide an outline with all part and chapter titles indicated. Also, include a few sentences about the purpose and contents of each chapter along with specific details and examples.

Sample Chapters: Do not wait until the manuscript is completed to submit the prospectus. Instead, send it with one or two sample chapters. When we learn of projects in the early stages, we can point out potential problems and offer editorial suggestions. Of course, if the manuscript is complete, or nearly so, then send copies of all that is available.

Part 3: About the Market

Primary Audience: What is the primary market for the book? Professionals in what specific field/subfield? What associations or specific divisions of professional organizations or professional journals would provide highly targeted mailing lists for promoting your book?

Secondary Audience: Are there other audiences that might be interested in the book, but to a lesser degree? Please be as realistic and as specific as possible in describing who will buy the book.

Uses: What would the book help the audience do, understand, improve, carry out, etc.? Distinguish between the use for the practitioner audiences and the uses for training workshops or whatever other distinction is most meaningful.

Potential Course Adoptions: In addition to sales to individual practitioners and academics, Corwin Press books are often used as supplements in college university courses, staff development workshops, and other training settings. If your book has the potential for such use, please provide as much specific information as possible as to the types of courses and approximate enrollments.

(Corwin Press Book Prospectus Guidelines, 2000)

Send your book proposal, together with your curriculum vitae to two or three publishers on your first attempt. Precede your submission with a brief telephone conversation with the acquisitions editor for your discipline. Most publishers have a Web site on which publication guidelines can be found. Read the guidelines carefully.

A dissertation or master's thesis is rarely ready for publication as a book. Dissertations and master's theses are published as a book only after considerable editing and revision. Here are some general suggestions for making your dissertation suitable for publication as a book: (a) delete excessively repetitive text found in most dissertations; (b) decrease substantially the number of tables and figures, references, excessive lists, and academic jargon; and (c) eliminate most of the literature review (unless your book will be a historical treatise).

CHAPTERS IN BOOKS

Abbreviated versions of your dissertation or master's thesis may be published in an edited book. First, the editor of the volume selects the authors who will be asked to submit chapters for the edited book. Such was the case with *The Changing World of School Administration*—25 chapters (Perreault & Lunenburg, 2002) and *Shaping the Future*—28 chapters (Lunenburg & Carr, 2003). Second, papers presented at a conference can comprise an edited book's contents.

POPULAR PRESS

The popular press includes magazines, newspapers, and newsletters. Compared with journal articles, books, and chapters in books, they are brief, free of jargon, and often suggest applications of the research results for lay people. An advantage of the popular press as compared to the more academic venues is that they may reach more readers. The disadvantage is that these are not refereed publications and, therefore, do not carry much weight in the academic community. Appearances on radio and television can also be included in the category of the popular press.

INTERNET PUBLISHING

Recently we have witnessed the World Wide Web as a publishing venue. The Web consists of millions of information servers and millions of users at more than a million sites. The growth of the Internet and World Wide Web has created a new outlet for reports of research. At the present time, researchers can distribute their research reports via the Internet and World Wide Web in two main ways. Both involve electronic transmission to a specific site. For example, in the first case, an author can transmit a document to a user at their network address. One such site appropriate for the receipt of research reports is Connexions, a project of Rice University. The research report, after acceptance and any necessary editing by the author, is placed on the Connexions network by category of topic. The second alternative is for an author of a research report to transmit the manuscript via the Internet to the editor of a journal that issues its product on the Internet.

One example is the online journal *Advancing Women in Leadership* (see http://www.advancingwomen.com).

DESKTOP PUBLISHING

Equipped with a word processing program, an author can create a book that can appear like a professionally typeset document. With the use of a copy machine, the same author can print copies of the manuscript. Many authors have typesetting equipment, but few have bindery equipment. Therefore, binding a book or journal pages would need to be contracted out to a professional bindery at the author's expense. Of course, desktop publishing, as well as the popular press, are not considered legitimate publications in the academic community, and, therefore, would carry little weight regarding tenure decisions.

PLANNING THE WRITING PROCESS

One of the major problems beginning assistant professors face in getting ready for tenure is the shortage of time. Amassing a suitable number of important articles in top-tier, refereed journals is difficult for some, especially with the competing demands of teaching, service, and family. Once you begin teaching, it will seem as though you cannot find the time to write. The keys to your writing success and publishing success are planning and discipline. Following are tips for organizing the writing process (Dunleavy, 2003; Heppner & Heppner, 2004; Luey, 2004). (See Example 12.4.)

Example 12.4

Tip No. 1. Establish regular, predetermined writing times. For example, some authors find it helpful to set aside two or three half-days or one full day (8–9 hours) each week for writing. Others write for two hours every day. Still others may prefer to reserve writing blocks of 6–8 hours one or two times a week. It doesn't matter when, where, or what you write, at least in the beginning. Make certain that you establish regular, predetermined writing times, and make them inviolable. Writing regularly greatly increases the level of writing productivity, as well as the quality of the writing.

Tip No. 2. Just write. If you find it difficult to write during your regular, predetermined writing times, do not stop writing, but instead, just write a first draft. Do not worry about how your first draft is organized. Concentrate instead on expressing your ideas. Then, later you can rearrange your ideas into a single, clear sequence of arguments. For example, you may decide that eight typed pages is a good level of productivity for a full eight-hour day of writing. Then set a minimum goal of writing six typed pages in a full day of writing. Reward yourself in some way for reaching your writing goal.

Tip No. 3. The order of the writing task need not be linear. We have suggested that an APA-style journal article contains the following sections: abstract, introduction, method, results, and discussion. You do not have to write the manuscript from beginning to end, (i.e., write the abstract page and continue linearly through the manuscript). Start with the easiest task and progress to the more difficult tasks. Perhaps the method section is the easiest for you to write. Then begin there. When this task is accomplished, you will feel that you are making progress and will be ready to focus on the next task. Also, some sections may take longer to write than others. Thus, you might plan the writing tasks in relation to the amount of time you have available to write. For example, if you have a large block of time to write on a given day, it may be sufficient to write the first draft of the introduction, which usually takes the longest time to write. However, if you have a small block of time, you may wish to tackle a smaller task.

Tip No. 4. Write, print, edit, revise, polish, get feedback, and revise again. A good draft of the manuscript is not ready to submit for publication. Follow the suggested cycle above. Write your ideas. Next print out your writings and edit them on your hard copy print out. Avoid on-screen editing, which tends to be confined to simple corrections rather than textual improvements. Once you have edited the text, extend and clarify the manuscript if needed. After you have made revisions and further polished the manuscript, ask several well-published colleagues to read it and provide critical, editorial feedback. Ask them specifically to provide critical feedback. Then revise again based on the feedback you receive.

Tip No. 5. The best writing does not happen under pressure. Successful professional writing takes time: time to reflect, time to read, time to write, time to get feedback, time to evaluate the writing, and time to repeatedly revise the manuscript. "A manuscript should be written and revised at least five times, and more for inexperienced writers." This is a tip that doctoral students should follow before submitting their work to their committee chair. One of the authors of this book had a conversation a few years ago with a doctoral student who was attending a major research university. She told him that she was going to submit her dissertation chapters to her dissertation chair the following day "to get his reaction." The author of this book said to the student: "Are you completely satisfied that your dissertation chapters are the very best work you can do. If not, consider revising them until you are absolutely certain your chapters cannot be improved any further by yourself. Then, and only then, should you submit them to your chair." This is sound advice to any writer. We find that many of our doctoral students submit their first draft to us "to get our reaction." Ninety-nine times out of a hundred, we send it back for further revision.

Tip No. 6. Writing does not just happen. Writing should be planned. Authors can exercise control over the process. The production of a quality product requires sustained effort over time. If you follow the aforementioned tips, your chances of delivering a quality product will improve.

SUMMARY

In this chapter, we discussed many important issues regarding disseminating your research to the professional community and lay public. This needs to be done as soon after your final oral defense as possible. Dissertations and master's theses can and should be published in one venue or another depending on your career goals. We concluded the chapter with some tips on planning the writing process. The mark of an excellent writer is one who becomes his or her own harshest critic.

APPENDIX A

Initial Letter Soliciting Participation

UNIVERSITY LETTERHEAD

College of Education
Address

Date

Principal's Name
and Address

Dear _____:

Two hundred principals have been selected to participate in a basic research project in educational administration being conducted at XYZ University. Enclosed is a questionnaire-type instrument, which is employed to secure:

1. Your opinions concerning certain aspects of principal-teacher relationships
2. Your opinions on a number of important social and personal questions

The forms do not take long to complete; the time required by most individuals varies from ten to fifteen minutes. Since we are collecting opinions, there are no correct or incorrect answers. All that is necessary is that you give your frank opinion. Your responses will be strictly confidential; all replies are anonymous, and no individual or school will be named in any report of the research.

Please read the directions carefully and then proceed to answer all the questions. Some of the questions may be difficult to answer with the information given, but please respond to each statement as well as you are able, following the directions.

Your prompt attention and cooperation will be greatly appreciated, as it is a prerequisite to the success of this research. Thank you.

Sincerely,

John Smith   Tom Jones, Ph.D.
Doctoral Student   Professor

P.S.: You will receive a report of the research, probably early next year, but perhaps sooner.

APPENDIX B

First Follow-Up Letter

UNIVERSITY LETTERHEAD

College of Education
Address

Date

Principal's Name
and Address

Dear _____:

About two weeks ago, you were one of the 200 school principals who received a questionnaire-type instrument in connection with a basic research project in educational administration being conducted at XYZ University. These forms do not take long to complete; the time required by most individuals varies from ten to fifteen minutes.

Your prompt attention and cooperation will be greatly appreciated, as it is a prerequisite to the success of this research. Thank you.

Sincerely,

John Smith   Tom Jones, Ph.D.
Doctoral Student   Professor

P.S.: If you have misplaced the questionnaire, please drop the enclosed coded post card in the mail and you will receive another copy of the instrument by return mail.

APPENDIX C

Second Follow-Up Letter

UNIVERSITY LETTERHEAD

College of Education
Address

Date

Principal's Name
and Address

Dear _____:

About three weeks ago you were one of 200 principals who received a questionnaire-type instrument in connection with a basic research project in educational administration being conducted at XYZ University. These forms do not take long to complete; the time required by most individuals varies from ten to fifteen minutes.

Enclosed is another copy of the questionnaire, in case you have misplaced the original. Your responses will be strictly confidential; all replies are anonymous, and no individual or school will be named in any report of the research.

Your prompt attention and cooperation will be greatly appreciated, as it is a prerequisite to the success of this research. Thank you.

Sincerely,

John Smith   Tom Jones, Ph.D.
Doctoral Student   Professor

P.S.: If the individual to whom this letter is addressed is no longer in the position, the new principal should respond to the questionnaire. You will receive a report of the research, probably early next year, but perhaps sooner.

APPENDIX D

Dissertation Proposal Outline (Correlational)

PREDICTING GRADUATION RATES: AN ANALYSIS OF STUDENT
AND INSTITUTIONAL FACTORS AT UNIVERSITY COUNCIL FOR
EDUCATIONAL ADMINISTRATION (UCEA) PUBLIC UNIVERSITIES

Problem:

1. To examine the relationship between graduation rates at University Council for Educational Administration public universities and student SAT scores and students graduating in the top 10% of their high school class.

2. To examine the relationship between the graduation rates at University Council for Educational Administration public universities and students paying out-of-state tuition and students from underrepresented populations (i.e. African American, Hispanic, Asian, and Native American).

3. To examine the relationship between the graduation rates at University Council for Educational Administration public universities and the percent of full-time faculty and the average salary of full-time faculty.

4. To examine the relationship between the graduation rates at University Council for Educational Administration public universities and class size (i.e., percent of classes with fewer than 20 students; percent of classes with 50 or more students).

5. To examine the relationship between the graduation rates at University Council for Educational Administration public universities and total student educational expenditures (i.e., tuition and fees, cost of instruction, research, student services).

Literature:

Graduation Rates:

American College Test (1999); Braxton & Mundy (2001); Caison (2004); Chronicle of Higher Education (1999); Engle, Reilly, & Levine (2003); Goenner & Snaith (2003); Horn & Carroll (1998); Mangold, Bean, Adams, Schwab, & Lynch (2002); Pascarella & Terenzini (1991); Schuh (1999); Tinto (1993).

Student Factors:

Braustein & McGrath (1997); Credle & Dean (1991); Engle, Reilly, & Levine (2003); Gardner, Keller, & Protrowski (1996); Goenner & Snaith (2003); Gold (1995); Good, Halpin, & Halpin (1992); House (1992); Payne, Pullen, & Padgett (1996); Porter (2003); Rowser (1997); Schuh (1999); Schwartz & Washington (2002); Tinto (1987).

Institutional Factors:

Astin (1983); Chronicle of Higher Education (2005); Goenner & Snaith (2003); Jacoby & Garland (2004); Landrum (2001); U.S. News & World Report (2006).

Research Questions:

1. What is the relationship between graduation rates at University Council for Educational Administration public universities and student SAT scores?

2. What is the relationship between graduation rates at University Council for Educational Administration public universities and students graduating in the top 10% of their high school class?

3. What is the relationship between graduation rates at University Council for Educational Administration public universities and the percent of students paying out-of-state tuition?

4. What is the relationship between graduation rates at University Council for Educational Administration public universities and the percent of students of underrepresented populations (i.e. African American, Hispanic, Asian, and Native American)?

5. What is the relationship between graduation rates at University Council for Educational Administration public universities and the percent of full-time faculty?

6. What is the relationship between graduation rates at University Council for Educational Administration public universities and the average salary of full-time faculty?

7. What is the relationship between graduation rates at University Council for Educational Administration public universities and class size (i.e., percent of classes with fewer than 20 students; percent of classes with 50 or more students)?

8. What is the relationship between graduation rates at University Council for Educational Administration public universities and total student educational expenditures (i.e., tuition and fees, cost of instruction, research, and student services)?

Design:

1. Sample:

Sixty-three public universities in the University Council for Educational Administration (UCEA)

2. Data Collection:

All data for the sample are available in: (1) The Chronicle of Higher Education Almanac Issue 2005–2006, (2) U.S. News and World Report 2006 Edition of America's Best Colleges, (3) The U. S. Department of Education Graduation Survey retrieved at The Education Trust: College Results Online, and (4) Integrated Postsecondary Education Data System (iPEDS) Spring 2001–2004 Data File.

3. Data Analysis:

Research Question 1. A Pearson Correlation will be used to determine if there is a statistically significant relationship between graduation rates at University Council for Educational Administration public universities and student SAT scores.

Research Question 2. A Pearson Correlation will be used to determine if there is a statistically significant relationship between graduation rates at University Council for Educational Administration public universities and students graduating in the top 10% of their high school class.

Research Question 3. A Pearson Correlation will be used to determine if there is a statistically significant relationship between graduation rates at University Council for Educational Administration public universities and the percent of students paying out-of state tuition.

Research Question 4. A Pearson Correlation will be used to determine if there is a statistically significant relationship between graduation rates at University Council for Educational Administration public universities and the percent of students from underrepresented populations (i.e. African American, Hispanic, Asian, and Native American).

Research Question 5. A Pearson Correlation will be used to determine if there is statistically significant relationship between graduation rates at University Council for Educational Administration public universities and the percent of full-time faculty.

Research Question 6. A Pearson Correlation will be used to determine if there is a statistically significant relationship between graduation rates at University Council for Educational Administration public universities and the average salary of full-time faculty.

Research Question 7. A Pearson Correlation will be used to determine if there is a statistically significant relationship between graduation rates at University Council for Educational Administration public universities and class size (i.e., percent of classes with fewer than 20 students; percent of classes with 50 or more students).

Research Question 8. A Pearson Correlation will be used to determine if there is a statistically significant relationship between graduation rates at University Council for Educational Administration public universities and total student education expenditures (i.e., tuition and fees, cost of instruction, research, and student services)?

The Pearson Correlation describes and measures the linear relationship between two variables. However, correlation tells us nothing about the predictive power of variables. Multiple regression analysis will be utilized to predict values of the dependent variable (graduation rates) from the independent variables found to be significantly correlated (student and institutional factors). For example, if the Pearson Correlation reveals a strong and significant relationship between SAT scores and graduation rates, a regression analysis will help identify a model that allows us to predict graduation rates based on students' SAT scores. Thus, highly ranked colleges and universities can use the regression model to predict that a student entering college with an SAT score of 1400 should have a 97% chance of graduation.

Contribution:

1. To determine the relationship between graduation rates at University Council for Educational Administration public universities and student SAT scores and students graduating in the top 10% of their high school class

2. To determine the relationship between graduation rates at University Council for Educational Administration public universities and students paying out-of-state tuition and students from underrepresented populations (i.e. African American, Hispanic, Asian, and Native American)

3. To determine the relationship between graduation rates at University Council for Educational Administration public universities and the percent of full-time faculty and student-faculty ratio

4. To determine the relationship between graduation rates at University Council for Educational Administration public universities and student tuition and fees

APPENDIX E

Dissertation Proposal Outline (Analysis of Variance and Regression)

THE RELATIONSHIP OF SUPERINTENDENT LEADERSHIP STYLES TO STUDENT ACHIEVEMENT AND SCHOOL DISTRICT FINANCIAL AND DEMOGRAPHIC FACTORS

Problem:

1. To determine differences in superintendents' leadership styles and student achievement as measured by Academic Excellence Indicator System (AEIS) school district ratings of *exemplary, recognized, academically acceptable,* and *low performing.*

2. To examine the relationship between superintendents' leadership styles and student achievement as measured by TAAS scores in reading, writing, and mathematics.

3. To examine the relationship between superintendents' leadership styles and 11 selected school district financial and demographic factors, such as (a) percent of economically disadvantaged students, (b) percent of limited English proficient students, (c) percent of minority populations, (d) percent of special education students, (e) percent of gifted and talented students, (f) percent of career and technology students, (g) per pupil cost for instruction, (h) percent of operating expenses spent on instruction, (i) percent of operating expenses spent on extracurricular activities, (j) amount of local tax value per pupil, and (k) pupil-teacher ratio.

4. To examine the relationship between student achievement as measured by school district TAAS scores in reading, writing, and mathematics and 11 school district financial and demographic factors, such as (a) percent of economically disadvantaged students, (b) percent of limited English proficient students, (c) percent of minority populations, (d) percent of special education students, (e) percent of gifted and talented students, (f) percent of career and technology students, (g) per pupil cost for instruction, (h) percent of operating expenses spent on instruction, (i) percent of operating expenses spent on extracurricular activities, (j) amount of local tax value per pupil, and (k) pupil-teacher ratio.

Literature:

Transformational Leadership:

Bass (1981, 1985); Bass & Avolio (1990, 1993, 1994, 1995); Bass, Avolio, & Goodheim (1987); Bennis & Nanus (1985); Bright (1987); Buck (1989); Burns (1978, 1984); Byrd (1987); Downton (1973); Hampton, Summer, & Webber (1987); Hoover (1987); House (1977); King (1989); Koh (1990); Orr (1990); Roberts (1985); Rouche (1989); Sergiovanni (1990, 1992); Smith (1982); Stogdill (1963); Tichy & Devonna (1986); Tichy & Ulrich (1984); Zaleznik (1989).

Student Achievement:

Educational Economic Policy Center (1994); Firestone (1991); Goals 2000: Educate America Act (1994); Heck, Larsen, & Marcoulldes (1990); Heller (1994); Johnson, Lein, & Ragland (1997); Mace-Matluck (1987); McCord (1996); National Commission on Excellence in Education (1983); Newmann, King, & Rigdon (1997); Shavelson (1991); Texas Education Agency (1997); Vornberg (2000); Zigarelli (1996).

Accountability and the Superintendent:

Alpin & Daresh (1984); Buck (1989); Cawelti (1981); Clark, Clark, & Campbell (1993); Collier (1987); Collier, Sclafani, & Estes (1987); Cuban (1988); Duigan (1980); Ford (1999); Fullan (1993, 1998); Geery (1997); Lunenburg & Ornstein (2000); Marks (1981); Mintzberg (1973); Palmaffy (1998); Pankratz & Petrosko (2000); Sergiovanni (1992); Schlechty (1990, 2000); Siccone (1997); Wallace (1985).

Financial and Demographic Factors:

Brookover & Lezotte (1979); Coleman (1966); Crisfield (1999); Educational Economic Policy Center (1994); Golden (1999); Tomlinson (1980); Turner (1999).

Research Questions:

1. What differences exist in superintendent leadership styles and student achievement as measured by Academic Excellence Indicator System (AEIS) school district ratings of *exemplary, recognized, academically acceptable,* and *low performing*?

2. What is the relationship between superintendents' leadership styles and student achievement as measured by school district TAAS scores in reading, writing, and mathematics?

3. What is the relationship between superintendents' leadership styles and 11 selected school district financial and demographic factors,

such as (a) percent of economically disadvantaged students, (b) percent of limited English proficient students, (c) percent of minority populations, (d) percent of special education students, (e) percent of gifted and talented students, (f) percent of career and technology students, (g) per pupil cost for instruction, (h) percent of operating expenses spent on instruction, (i) percent of operating expenses spent on extracurricular activities, (j) amount of local tax value per pupil, and (k) pupil-teacher ratio?

4. What is the relationship between student achievement as measured by school district TAAS scores in reading, writing, and mathematics and 11 selected financial and demographic factors, such as (a) percent of economically disadvantaged students, (b) percent of limited English proficient students, (c) percent of minority populations, (d) percent of special education students, (e) percent of gifted and talented students, (f) percent of career and technology students, (g) per pupil cost for instruction, (h) percent of operating expenses spent on instruction, (i) percent of operating expenses spent on extracurricular activities, (j) amount of local tax value per pupil, and (k) pupil-teacher ratio?

Design:

1. Sample:

207 school districts in Texas

207 superintendents and 3 principals from each school district (one representing each school level: elementary, middle, high school)

420,000 students (approximately)

2. Instrumentation:

Multifactor Leadership Questionnaire (Bass & Avolio, 1985)

TAAS tests in reading, writing, and mathematics (TEA Web site)

Financial and demographic factors (PEIMS-TEA Web site)

3. Data Collection:

a. MLQ (self-report version) administered to the superintendent and the MLQ (principal version) administered to three principals in the 207 school districts

b. TAAS scores in reading, writing, and mathematics retrieved from the TEA Web site

c. Eleven financial and demographic factors retrieved from the TEA Web site

4. Data Analysis:

Research Question # 1: 12 ANOVAs computed for each of the 12 subscales of the MSQ to determine differences in superintendents' leadership styles among the four school district ratings.

Research Question # 2: Three stepwise multiple regression analyses computed to determine MSQ predictors of school district TAAS scores in reading, writing, and mathematics.

Research Question # 3: 12 forward stepwise multiple regression analyses computed to determine financial and demographic factor predictors of the 12 subscales of the MLQ. For those scales significantly related to financial and demographic factors, backward stepwise multiple regression analyses computed to determine financial and demographic factor predictors of the MSQ subscales.

Research Question # 4: Three forward stepwise multiple regression analyses computed to determine financial and demographic factor predictors of school district TAAS scores in reading, writing, and mathematics.

Contribution:

1. To determine the influence of superintendent leadership on school district ratings

2. To determine the influence of superintendent leadership on student achievement as measured by TAAS scores in reading, writing, and mathematics

3. To determine relationships between 12 MSQ subscales and 11 school district financial and demographic factors

4. To determine relationships between 11 school district financial and demographic factors and TAAS scores in reading, writing, and mathematics

APPENDIX F

Dissertation Proposal Outline
(Multivariate Analysis of Variance)

THE RELATIONSHIP BETWEEN BRAIN DOMINANCE AND LEADERSHIP STYLE OF SCHOOL SUPERINTENDENTS AND BUSINESS CHIEF EXECUTIVE OFFICERS

Problem:

1. To explore the prevailing brain hemisphere characteristics and self-perceived leadership styles of school superintendents and business chief executive officers.

2. To investigate the effects of intervening variables such as affiliation (business or education), gender, experience level, and age on brain hemisphere characteristics and leadership style.

Literature:

Brain Research:

Agor (1983, 1984, 1985); Andrews (1980); Begley & Carey (1981); Blakeslee (1980); Bogen (1977); Bogen & Gogen (1969); Bunderson (1988); Bunderson, Olsen, & Herrmann (1984); Carnine (1990); Cassell (1978); Chall & Mirsky (1978); Cicchette (1991); Cohen (1979); Cone (1981, 1982); Coulson & Strickland (1983a, 1983b, 1996); DeBono (1971, 1985); Eccles (1973); Edwards (1979, 1982); Epstein (1974, 1978, 1984); Fagan (1979); Finn (1983); Ford (1987); Freeman (1995); Garrett (1976); Gaylean (1981); Gaylin (1976); Garmon (1985); Gazzaniga (1967, 1983, 1985a, 1985b); Geschwind (1979); Goldstein (1985); Goleman (1977); Gorovitz (1982); Gowan (1981); Grefe (1982); Hardyck & Haapanen (1979); Hart (1975, 1978, 1981, 1983); Hatcher (1983); Herrmann (1981a, 1981b, 1981c, 1982a, 1982b, 1988, 1989, 1996); Hutson (1984); lronson (1984); Jaynes (1976); Kane & Kane (1979); Kanter (1983); Katz (1978); Kerensky (1983); Kimura (1973, 1978, 1985); Kinsbourne (1975, 1982); Leaffer (1980); Levitt (1963); Levy (1972, 1978, 1980, 1983); Levy & Trevarthen (1976); Lynch (1986); Maguire (1990); McCallum & Glynn (1979); McKenney & Keen (1974); McLean (1978); McQueen (1984); Mintzberg (1976); Nebes (1974); Norris (1984, 1985a, 1985b, 1985c, 1986, 1988); Oates (1979); Ornstein (1972, 1978); Ornstein & Brandwein (1977); Ornstein & Thompson (1984); Owens (1986); Perelle & Ehrman (1983); Piatt (1983); Reitz (1986); Restak (1979); Reynolds & Torrance (1980); Riggs (1991); Ross (1990); Samples (1980); Satz (1979); Schkade & Potvin (1981); Scott-Soler (1991); Segalowitz (1983); Sperry (1964, 1973, 1975); Springer & Deutsch (1990); Spruill (1986); Suojanen

(1976); Torrance (1981); Trevarthen (1980); Trotter (1976); Wallace (1992); Wenger (1982); Wessman (1987, 1988); Witelson (1977); Wittrock (1977); Youngblook (1981); Zelinski & March (1976); Zemke (1984).

Leadership:

Anasse (1984); Argyris (1962); Artise (1984); Barnard (1938); Barnard (1968, 1976); Barrett & Yoder (1980); Blake & Mouton (1964); Burke (1980); Cleveland (1985); Coulson & Strickland (1983); Cuban (1988); Culbertson (1976); Davidson (1987); DeBono (1971, 1985); Drucker (1982); Dunigan (1980); Dwyer (1984); ERS (1986); Farkes (1979); Fielder (1969); Freeman (1995); Graham (1980); Greenleaf (1977); Griffiths (1966); Guglielmino (1979); Henderson & Nutt (1980); Hersey (1986); Hersey & Blanchard (1977, 1979, 1982); Hersey & Stinson (1980); Heyberg (1966); Huckaby (1980); Jung (1923); Katz (1974); Kouzes & Posner (1990); Levitt (1963); Lynch (1986); Macoby (1981, 1982); McGregor (1960); Mesenburg (1983); Mintzberg (1976); Paulsen (1982); Peters & Waterman (1982); Pitner & Ogawa (1981); Pondez (1978); Reitz (1986); Riggs (1991); Roethlisberger (1941); Ross (1990); Rowan (1986); Scott-Soler (1991); Selznick (1957); Sergiovanni (1979); Snyder & Anderson (1987); Spruill (1986); Stodgill (1948, 1970); Stodgill & Coons (1957); Sweeney (1982); Tannenbaum & Schmidt (1958); Taggert, Daniel, Roby & Kroeck (1985); Taggert & Roby (1981); Turner (1979); Vecchio (1981); Walter, Caldwell, & Marshall (1980); Weisenberg & Grunfield (1966); Wessman (1987); Wonder & Donovan (1984); Zaleznick (1964, 1977).

Research Questions/Hypotheses:

Research Questions:

1. What are the brain dominance preferences of superintendents and chief executive officers?

2. Which brain dominance patterns are most prevalent among superintendents and chief executive officers?

3. What differences exist between brain dominance profiles in terms of (a) affiliation (business or education), (b) gender, (c) years of experience, and (d) age?

Hypotheses:

1. There is no significant difference in brain dominance preferences exhibited between superintendents of schools and business chief executive officers.

2. There is no significant difference in brain quadrant scores between superintendents and chief executive officers.

3. There is no significant difference in brain quadrant scores between males and females.

4. There is no significant difference in brain quadrant scores due to experience level.

5. Age is not a significant influence in determining brain quadrant scores.

Design:

1. Sample:

707 subjects from a database compiled by Herrmann International (1988–1998)
408 (599) Chief Executive Officers and 299 (366) Superintendents
610 males and 97 females

2. Instrumentation:

Herrmann Brain Dominance Instrument (HBDI)—Thinking Styles Assessment

3. Procedure:

Analysis of data elements obtained from the administration of the HBDI

a. Profile Codes—numeric representation of preference for the use of each of the four quadrants

b. Right/Left and Cerebral/Limbic Dominance Raw Scores—used to determine differences among the groups

c. Four Quadrant Scaled Scores—used to determine differences among the groups

d. Key Descriptors, Work Elements, Twenty Questions—provided descriptive information about the work characteristics and leadership style of the groups (represent their behavioral preferences for decision making and interaction with others)

4. Statistical Analysis:

a. Multivariate Analyses
   – MANOVA (multivariate analysis of variance)
   – MANCOVA (multivariate analysis of covariance)

b. Analysis of Covariance (ANCOVA)

Contribution:

1. Influence the content and design of future educational administration training programs.

2. Have implications for the recruitment, selection, and training of educational administrators.

3. Guide individuals into the most appropriate course of study within the administration field.

4. Provide specific areas of focus for personal choices for professional development of practicing administrators.

5. Assist in selecting advanced-degree candidates for educational administration programs.

6. Provide initial information on the cognitive styles of educational administrators that may reflect on barriers to educational change and innovation.

APPENDIX G

Dissertation Proposal Outline (Qualitative)

THE MOTIVATIONAL IMPACT OF ONLINE ELECTIVE
COURSES: AN ANALYSIS OF THE MOTIVATIONAL
ORIENTATION OF AT-RISK NINTH-GRADERS ENROLLED IN
TRADITIONAL AND ONLINE ELECTIVE COURSES

Problem:

1. To examine the differences in the intrinsic goal orientation of at-risk ninth-grade students enrolled in online elective courses, as compared to at-risk ninth-grade students enrolled in traditional elective courses.

2. To examine the differences in the extrinsic goal orientation of at-risk ninth-grade students enrolled in online elective courses, as compared to at-risk ninth-grade students enrolled in traditional elective courses.

3. To examine the differences in the task value of at-risk ninth-grade students enrolled in online elective courses, as compared to at-risk ninth-grade students enrolled in traditional elective courses.

4. To examine the differences in the learning control beliefs of at-risk ninth-grade students enrolled in online elective courses, as compared to at-risk ninth-grade students enrolled in traditional elective courses.

5. To examine the differences in the self-efficacy for learning and performance of at-risk ninth-grade students enrolled in online elective courses, as compared to at-risk ninth-grade students enrolled in traditional elective courses.

6. To examine the differences in the test anxiety level of at-risk ninth-grade students enrolled in online elective courses, as compared with students enrolled in traditional elective courses.

7. To examine student perception of online instruction and traditional instruction as a means of developing motivational strategies.

Literature:

At-Risk Students:

Bransford et al. (1999); Brophy (1998); Conley (1992); Diem & Katims (1998); Egan & Gibb (1997); Ferguson (2000); Gaustad (1991); George & McEwin (1999); Jones (1988); Jones & Watson (1990); Jukes (2000); Levine

& Ornstein (1993); Malone et al. (1997); Marshall (1999); McCombs (2000); National Assessment of Educational Progress (1990); SCANS (1991); Renchler (1993); Ruff (1993); Shank & Jona (1999); Texas Education Agency (1996, 2000); Thornburg (1999); Vacha & McLaughlin (1992); Wehlage, Rutter, & Turnbaugh (1987); Yellen (1998).

Attribution Theory:

Anderman & Midgley (1998); Raffini (1993); Stage, Muller, Kinzie, & Simmons (1998); Stipek (1988); Weiner (1985).

Goal Theory:

Condry & Chambers (1978); Herzberg (1959); Keller (1987); Lepper (1988); Maehr & Midgley (1991); Maslow (1954); McInerney (1997); Middleton & Midgley (1997); Ryan, Hicks, & Midgley (1997); Small (1997); Wlodkowski (1981).

Self-Determination Theory:

Deci & Ryan (1985); Deci, Vallerand, Pelletier, & Ryan (1991); Midgley & Feldlaufer (1987); Salisbury-Glennon, Gorrell, Sanders, Boyd, & Kamen (1999).

Technology and Online Courses:

Andrews & Marshall (2000); Burnham, Miller, & Ray (2000); Bornas (1997); Carroll (2000); Gershon & Bergstrom (1991); Guan, Wang, Young, Owen, & Andrew (1999); Jones, Valdez, Nowakowski, & Rasmussen (1994); Means (1997); Richardson (1973); Ruppert & Smith (1996); Southwest Educational Development Laboratory (2000); Taylor, McKay, Culp, Baumann, & Elinich (1997); Sherman (1998);Wendt-Keswick (1999); Young (1996).

Research Questions:

1. What is the difference in the intrinsic goal orientation of at-risk ninth-grade students enrolled in online elective courses, as compared to at-risk ninth-grade students enrolled in traditional elective courses?

2. What is the difference in the extrinsic goal orientation of at-risk ninth-grade students enrolled in online elective courses, as compared to at-risk ninth-grade students enrolled in traditional elective courses?

3. What is the difference in the task value of at-risk ninth-grade students enrolled in online elective courses, as compared to at-risk ninth-grade students enrolled in traditional elective courses?

4. What is the difference in the learning control beliefs of at-risk ninth-grade students enrolled in online elective courses, as compared to at-risk ninth-grade students enrolled in traditional elective courses?

5. What is the difference in the self-efficacy of at-risk ninth-grade students enrolled in online elective courses, as compared to at-risk ninth-grade students enrolled in traditional elective courses?

6. What is the difference in the test anxiety levels of at-risk ninth-grade students enrolled in online elective courses, as compared to at-risk ninth-grade students enrolled in traditional elective courses?

7. What are the perceptions of students enrolled in online elective courses compared to students enrolled in traditional elective courses, regarding the elective course's role as a means of developing motivational strategies?

Design:

1. Sample:

a. 169 at-risk ninth-grade students enrolled in online elective courses

b. 169 at-risk ninth-grade students enrolled in traditional elective courses

c. All participants are enrolled in one large suburban district north of Houston, Texas

2. Instrumentation:

a. The Motivated Strategies for Learning Questionnaire (MSLQ) (Pintrich, Smith, Garcia, & McKeachie, 1991)

b. Three student focus groups

c. Sixty open-ended student questionnaires

3. Data Collection:

a. MSLQ administered to the 169 at-risk ninth-grade students enrolled in online elective courses and to 169 at-risk ninth-grade students enrolled in traditional elective courses.

b. Student responses collected in three separate focus groups of at-risk ninth-grade students enrolled in online elective courses and ninth-grade students enrolled in traditional elective courses.

c. Student responses derived from open-ended interview questions administered to 30 at-risk ninth-grade students enrolled in online elective classes and to 30 at-risk ninth-grade students enrolled in traditional elective classes.

4. Data Analysis:

Research Question # 1:

t test for independent samples to determine differences in the level of intrinsic goal orientation between at-risk ninth-grade students enrolled in online elective courses and at-risk ninth-grade students enrolled in traditional elective courses.

Research Question #2:

t test for independent samples to determine differences in the level of extrinsic goal orientation between at-risk ninth-grade students enrolled in online elective courses and at-risk ninth-grade students enrolled in traditional elective courses.

Research Question #3:

t test for independent samples to determine differences in task value between at-risk ninth-grade students enrolled in online elective courses and at-risk ninth-grade students enrolled in traditional elective courses.

Research Question #4:

t test for independent samples to determine differences in learning control beliefs between at-risk ninth-grade students enrolled in online elective courses and at-risk ninth-grade students enrolled in traditional elective courses.

Research Question #5:

t test for independent samples to determine differences in self-efficacy between at-risk ninth-grade students enrolled in online elective courses and at-risk ninth-grade students enrolled in traditional elective courses.

Research Question #6:

t test for independent samples to determine the level of test anxiety between at-risk ninth-grade students enrolled in online elective courses and at-risk ninth-grade students enrolled in traditional elective courses.

Research Question #7:

a. Three student focus groups designed to elicit more information on the relationship between enrollment in online elective courses and the development of motivational strategies, which include: (a) intrinsic goal orientation, (b) extrinsic goal orientation, (c) task value, (d) learning control beliefs, (e) self-efficacy, and (f) test anxiety. Focused interviews will last from 45 to 60 minutes, and they will be recorded and transcribed in order to permit identification of emergent themes and triangulation.

b. Open-ended interviews will be conducted with 30 at-risk ninth-grade students enrolled in online elective courses and with 30 at-risk ninth-grade students enrolled in traditional elective courses. Open-ended interviews will last from 30 to 45 minutes, and they will be recorded and transcribed in order to permit identification of emergent themes and triangulation.

Contribution:

1. To determine the relationship between the enrollment of at-risk ninth-grade students in online elective courses and the development of motivational strategies, which include: (a) intrinsic goal orientation, (b) extrinsic goal orientation, (c) task value, (d) learning control beliefs, (e) self-efficacy, and (f) test anxiety, as measured by student responses on six separate MSLQ subscales

2. To determine the perceptions of at-risk ninth-grade students regarding the relationship between enrollment in online elective courses and the development of motivational strategies, which include: (a) intrinsic goal orientation, (b) extrinsic goal orientation, (c) task value, (d) learning control beliefs, (e) self-efficacy, and (f) test anxiety, as measured by student responses provided in focus groups and open-ended interviews

3. To refocus school reform efforts so that the impact of online technology on motivational strategies is considered

4. To provide a model of instruction that would help to motivate at-risk ninth-grade students through the use of online instruction

APPENDIX H

Qualitative Research Critique

1. Bibliographic Information (APA Style): State the title of your attached study in APA format.

2. Problem: What is the problem or need? (State it.) Is it stated clearly? (Explain.) Is it logical? (Explain.) Is the problem convincing? (Explain.)

3. Purpose: What is the purpose? (State it.) Does it focus the research? (Explain.) Does the purpose follow the problem statement logically? (Explain.) Has the researcher convinced you that this study is worthwhile? (Explain.)

4. Theoretical Framework: On what is the theoretical framework based? (Explain it.) If none is stated, please indicate that and try to surmise what it might be from the literature presented.

5. Prior Research or Literature Review: What previous work has been done leading up to this study? (You will need to do a search in dissertations and journals to determine if any major research piece is missing: for example, a name of a researcher that keeps appearing.) Is there any major body of research missing?

6. Method Research Question(s): What is/are the research question(s)? (List them.) Are the research questions specific and clear? Why or why not? Are the research question(s) related to the purpose? (Explain.)

7. Method—Data Collection and Analysis: Are participants (How many?), sampling techniques (How were they selected and was this technique appropriate and accurate—answer both: appropriate for the study and accurate?), and context for the study explicit and appropriate? (Explain.) Is the research design clear? Explain the design and whether it is appropriate for the study; was something else more appropriate? Are the collection and analysis based on solid referenced methods? (Explain.) Are the methods the best choice in the study? (Explain.) What improvements would you suggest?

8. Definition(s): Which terms are defined? Are the definitions operational? Are the definitions included within the introduction or within the methods section of the report? If there are no terms, then did the researcher include those in the written text? What terms are appropriate for this study?

9. Credibility and Reliability Issues in Design: What does the author say regarding issues of credibility and/or generalizing ability internal and/or external validity? Respond to *each* of the internal/external validity issues as referenced in qualitative research.

10. Method Instrumentation: Describe the instrument(s) for interviews, focus groups, and so forth. Were they preexisting, or specially created? How were they related? How was reliability established?

11. Ethics: Does the author discuss ethical issues? Do you see any ethical issues in the study? Are the ethical issues properly taken care of?

12. Limitations and Delimitations: What limitations/delimitations are identified? How do these limit generalizability, and does it matter? To what extent do the limitations/delimitations (stated or unstated) affect the value of the research?

13. Results and Discussion: Are the research questions answered? How and sufficiently? Is existing literature brought into the discussion? Are supportive representative statements used from the data when appropriate?

14. Implications and Recommendations: What are the implications from the research for practice and what recommendations for theory, further research, and/or practice are presented?

SOURCE: © Beverly J. Irby. Used with permission.

APPENDIX I

Agreement: Guidelines for Chairing a Dissertation

The following are guidelines that I want all doctoral students to consider as they determine whether to ask me to serve as chair of their dissertation.

Role of the Dissertation Chair

1. The dissertation chair's job in completing the dissertation is to assist in facilitating the process, giving direction, and providing quality control.

2. The dissertation chair and the student work together to determine the committee members. The student must clear all committee members with the dissertation chair.

3. All work on the dissertation must be approved by the dissertation chair before the student will be permitted to forward chapters of the dissertation to other committee members. That is, as chapters of the dissertation are approved by the dissertation chair, but not before, the chair will direct the student to forward completed chapters to the committee members.

4. The dissertation chair and the student will complete a realistic timeline for the completion of the dissertation; however, it is not the responsibility of the dissertation chair to keep the student on the timeline.

Function of the Proposal

1. The dissertation proposal must be thoroughly understood by the student, from the statement of the problem through the review of the literature to the methodology, before defending the proposal.

2. The dissertation proposal must be delivered to all committee members two weeks prior to the proposal defense.

3. Once the proposal has been approved, be aware that it is not a contract; rather, it is a guide. The actual dissertation may be altered slightly as the dissertation chair and committee members work through the process of completing the dissertation with the student.

4. The student will PROOFREAD thoroughly the dissertation proposal and assure that the proposal is free of typographical and grammatical errors, and obvious omissions.

Preparation of the Dissertation

1. Each student must become familiar with the dissertation format by reviewing my publication, *Writing a Successful Thesis or Dissertation: Tips and Strategies for Students in the Social and Behavioral Sciences,* and other dissertations on the student's topic.

2. Each student must become familiar and must be sufficiently knowledgeable of the research design, including the specific statistical tests or the qualitative method or combination of the two, and table headings and format. The student must do this by reading research and statistics books and by reviewing dissertations or research studies using the particular method. The student must find those dissertations, theses, research studies, or books on his or her own.

3. The student should expect to write as many drafts of the dissertation proposal and the dissertation as is necessary to render it in acceptable form for wider distribution. However, the first draft of each chapter the student submits to the dissertation chair should be in as perfect form as is humanly possible. The dissertation chair will ask for explanations of the statistical tests, why the student chose the particular test, or, in the case of qualitative method, why the specific method(s) were selected.

4. The student should expect to hire an external editor and/or a statistician.

5. Before submission to the chair and subsequent distribution to committee members, the student will PROOFREAD thoroughly each chapter for typographical and grammatical errors, and obvious omissions. Use, but do not rely exclusively on, spell check to detect errors. Proofreading means reading the dissertation word for word from the front matter through to the vita.

Dissertation Defense

1. The chair will not authorize the student to schedule the dissertation defense date until the chair has received and corrected *all* chapters of the dissertation.

2. After approval by the chair, all chapters of the dissertation must be delivered to all committee members at least two weeks prior to the dissertation defense.

3. The student must have the *entire* dissertation completed by the dissertation defense date. This includes all front pages (title page, signature page, dedication, abstract, acknowledgements, table of contents, list of tables, list of figures) and back pages (references, appendixes, and vita).

4. The student will PROOFREAD thoroughly again the entire dissertation, take personal responsibility for its contents, and assure that the entire dissertation is free of typographical and grammatical errors, and obvious omissions. It is expected that the dissertation will be in *publishable* form at the time of the dissertation defense.

Graduation

1. The student may project a target date for graduation (December, May, or August); however, if the student is not ready according to standards set forth by the dissertation chair or other committee members, then the student will not graduate at that particular date.

2. The completion of the graduation process involves the routing of the completed dissertation as follows: Dissertation Committee, Director of the Doctoral Program, Graduate School, Library, Department Chair, Education Dean, and Registrar. Therefore, deadlines for the dissertation defense must be enforced.

3. For December graduations, defense of the dissertation must occur at or prior to October 1.

4. For May graduations, defense of the dissertation must occur at or prior to March 1.

5. For August graduations, defense of the dissertation must occur at or prior to June 1.

Required Copies of the Dissertation

Required copies of the completed dissertation for doctoral students in education are as follows:

1. Library	2 (acid free, 20% cotton bond)
2. Dean, College of Education	1
3. Chair, Dissertation Committee	1
4. Committee Members	4 (one for each member)
5. Center for Doctoral Research	2
6. Bell & Howell/UMI	1
Total	11

Headings

Boldface type is not permitted in headings. Most dissertations will use three levels of headings. For three levels of headings, use the following format:

CENTERED UPPERCASE HEADING (All chapter headings)

Centered Uppercase and Lowercase Heading (Level 1)

Flush Left, Italics, Uppercase and Lowercase Side Heading (Level 2)

Indent, italics, lowercase paragraph heading ending with a period. (Level 3)

For use of more than three levels of headings, consult the most recent edition of the *Publication Manual of the American Psychological Association*.

An example follows:

CHAPTER III

METHODOLOGY

Instrumentation (Level 1)

The Multifactor Leadership Questionnaire (Level 2)

Reliability. (Level 3)

Validity. (Level 3)

_____   _____
Dissertation Chair   Student's Signature, Date

_____

APPENDIX J

Checklist for Dissertation Quality

Following is a list of questions to consider when evaluating the quality and content of each chapter and section within each chapter of your dissertation. Not all questions are appropriate for all studies, and not all institutions, departments, and committees will be expecting the same content in each chapter. However, we have structured this checklist in accordance with the recommended content of a five-chapter dissertation.

CHAPTER I: INTRODUCTION

Background of the Study

Have you described how your study fits into the larger context of theory and practice? _____

Is adequate background presented for all the variables or concepts in the study? _____

Is the background of the problem presented clearly (e.g., educational trends related to the problem, unresolved issues, social concerns)? _____

Have the majority of the references cited been published within the past five years? _____

Statement of the Problem

Is adequate information presented for an understanding of the problem? _____

Is the problem clearly stated? _____

Is there a description of what has already been done related to the problem? _____

Is the relationship of the problem to previous research made clear? _____

Is there a logical transition that leads directly to the purpose of the study? _____

Have the majority of the references cited been published within the past five years? _____

Purpose of the Study

Is the purpose of the study related to the statement of the problem? _____

Is the purpose of the study stated clearly and succinctly? _____

Have the majority of the references cited been published within the past five years? _____

Significance of the Study

Is it clear how this study will add to the body of knowledge (theory or practice)? _____

Does the study have the potential of being presented at a national conference? _____

Does the study have the potential of being published in an academic journal?   _____

Have the majority of the references cited been published within the past five years?   _____

Definition of Terms

Are the terms used in the study adequately defined so that their usage is clearly understood?   _____

Theoretical Framework

Have you provided a brief description of the relevant theory(ies) to be utilized in approaching the problem?   _____

Have you reviewed the major variables or concepts and their interrelationships derived from the existing theoretical work?   _____

Have you described a connection between these theoretical constructions and your research questions or hypotheses?   _____

Have you utilized theory as a heuristic device to examine and interpret qualitative data?   _____

Research Questions

Are the research questions related to the problem and the purpose?   _____

Are the research questions well stated; e.g., (a) all variables clarified, (b) avoidance of "how" or "why" questions, (c) theoretical constructs clarified (achievement, success, intelligence)?   _____

Is the kind of measurement obvious (e.g., description, relationship, differences)?   _____

Is each research question testable?   _____

Limitations

Are limitations well defined (methodology, data, analysis)?   _____

Delimitations

Are the delimitations well defined (e.g., timeframe, location, sample, criterion)?   _____

Assumptions

Are your assumptions clearly stated?   _____

Organization of the Study

Is there a transition to Chapter Two and the chapters following? (Typically Chapter One ends with an overview of the entire dissertation.)   _____

CHAPTER II: REVIEW OF THE LITERATURE

Introduction

Does Chapter Two begin with an introduction using an *advance organizer*
to prepare the reader for the content of the chapter?   _____

Body

Is the review of the literature comprehensive?   _____
Does the review of the literature cover all variables or concepts in
the study?   _____
Does the review of the literature contain at least 50 references?   _____
Are all references cited relevant to the problem?   _____
Have the majority of the references cited been published within the
past five years?   _____
Are references cited completely and accurately?   _____
Are authors who make the same point combined in a single citation?   _____
Is there an overabundance of direct quotations?   _____
Is each major section of the review of the literature summarized
without a summary heading (e.g., in sum, in summary, in short)?   _____
Have you searched all available sources in your review of literature?   _____

Summary

Does the Review of the Literature Chapter conclude with a summary
of the literature review and a transition introducing the next chapter? _____

CHAPTER III: METHODOLOGY

Introduction

Does the chapter begin with an introduction, using an *advance organizer*
to prepare the reader for the content of the chapter?   _____

Selection of Participants

Are the size and major characteristics of the population studied described? _____
Are the procedures and criteria for selecting the sample clearly described? _____
Is the sample size large enough for the method of research used?   _____
Are the size and major characteristics of the sample described?   _____

Instrumentation

Is a rationale given for the selection of the instruments used?   _____
Are the purpose and content of each instrument described?   _____
Is the validity of each instrument described?   _____
Is the reliability of each instrument described?   _____

Are the instruments appropriate for measuring the variables
studied?   _____

If an instrument was developed specifically for the study, are the
procedures involved in its development and validation described?   _____

If an instrument was developed specifically for the study, are
administration, scoring, and interpretation procedures fully described? _____

If an instrument was developed, was a pilot test conducted with a
different sample than was used in the study?   _____

If interviews were used, were procedures described for determining
interviewer bias?   _____

When necessary, were interobserver or interrater reliability assessed? _____

Data Collection

Are the procedures for collecting data described in sufficient detail
to permit replication by another researcher?   _____

If a pilot study was conducted, are its execution, results, and effect on
the current study described?   _____

If the study was qualitative, were internal validity strategies described
(e.g., triangulation, member checks, peer examination)?   _____

Data Analysis

Were the statistics used appropriate for the study?   _____
Are the appropriate statistics reported for each test?   _____
For statistical tests, are sufficient statistics presented (e.g., mean,
standard deviation)   _____
In a qualitative study, are the themes and patterns appropriately labeled? _____

Summary

Does the chapter conclude with a summary and a transition to
Chapter Four?   _____

CHAPTER IV: PRESENTATION
AND ANALYSIS OF DATA

Introduction

Does the chapter begin with an introduction, using an *advance organizer* to
prepare the reader for the contents of the chapter?   _____

Demographic Descriptive Statistics

Are demographic descriptive statistics of the sample presented in
table form?   _____

Are appropriate headings used to help the flow and organization of the
chapter (e.g. research questions (hypotheses), themes, or variables?)   _____
Research Question (or Hypothesis) One

Research Question (or Hypothesis) Two

Etc.

Are the tables and figures (if any) well organized and easy to understand?   _____
Are the data in each table and figure described in the text?   _____
Are tests of significance properly cited using appropriate degrees of
freedom; e.g., $[F(2,71) = 14.87, p < .001$ or $F(2,71) = 0.14, p > .05]$?   _____
Were post hoc tests calculated when appropriate?   _____
Were effect sizes reported when appropriate?   _____
Is this chapter free of interpretation? (In qualitative studies, factual
and interpretive information is sometimes intermingled to sustain
reader interest.)   _____
In a qualitative study, is there a balance of direct quotations and
description to enhance the meaning of themes and patterns?   _____
Is there a summary of key findings in table form when appropriate?   _____

Summary

Does the chapter end with a summary of the entire chapter and a
transition to Chapter Five?   _____

CHAPTER V: SUMMARY, DISCUSSION, AND CONCLUSIONS

Introduction

Does the chapter begin with an introduction, using an *advance organizer*
to prepare the reader for the contents of the chapter?   _____

Summary of the Study

Is there a brief summary of the entire study?   _____

Discussion of the Findings

Are the findings discussed within the framework of previous studies,
the theoretical rationale, and the review of the literature?   _____

Implications for Practice

Are the implications derived from the findings?   _____
Are implications made for theory and practice?   _____

Recommendations for Further Research

Are recommendations for further research clearly implied from the study?   _____

Conclusions

Do the conclusions highlight the important aspects of the study?   _____
Are the conclusions derived from the findings?   _____

References

Adler, P. S., & Borys, B. (1996). Two types of bureaucracy: Enabling and coercive. *Administrative Science Quarterly, 41*, 61–89.

Agboo, S. A. (2001). Enhancing success in American Indian students: Participatory research at Akawanese as part of the development of a culturally relevant curriculum. *Journal of American Indian Education, 40*(1), 31–55.

Ajzen, I. (1985). From intentions to actions: A theory of planned behavior. In J. Kuhl & J. Beckmann (Eds.), *Action control: From cognition to behavior* (pp. 11–39). New York: Springer Verlag.

Aldrich, H. E. (1979). *Organizations and environments*. Englewood Cliffs, NJ: Prentice Hall.

American Psychological Association. (2001). *Publication manual of the American psychological association* (5th ed.). Washington, DC: Author.

Anastas, J. W. (1999). *Research design for social work and the human services*. New York: Columbia University Press.

Anderson, D. P. (1964). *Organizational climate of elementary schools* (Research Monograph No. 1). Minneapolis: University of Minnesota, Educational Research and Development Council.

Andrews, J. H. M. (1965). School organizational climate: Some validity studies. *Canadian Education and Research Digest, 5*, 317–334.

Appleberry, J. B. (1969). The relationship between organizational climate and pupil control ideology. *Dissertation Abstracts International, 31*(8), 3797A. (UMI No. 7021337)

Arnold, S. K. (2006). Teacher preparation and formal mentoring at a regional university in south Texas. *Dissertation Abstracts International, 66*(11), A.

Ashton, P. T., & Webb, R. B. (1986). *Making a difference: Teachers' sense of efficacy and student achievement*. New York: Longman.

Astin, A. W. (1991). *Assessment for excellence*. New York: Macmillan.

Astin, A. W. (1993). *What matters in college?* San Francisco: Jossey-Bass.

Astin, A. W. (1997). How good is your institution's retention rate? *Research in Higher Education, 34*(6), 647–658.

Astin, A. W. (2005). Making sense out of degree completion rates. *Journal of College Student Retention: Research, Theory, and Practice, 7*(1), 5–17.

Azodi, D. S. (2006). *Principal leadership, trust, and teacher efficacy*. Unpublished doctoral dissertation, Sam Houston State University, Huntsville, Texas.

Baier, A. (1986). Trust and antitrust. *Ethics, 96*(2), 231–260.

Bamberg, W. (2004). An application of the synergistic leadership theory to the leadership experience of five female superintendents leading successful school districts. *Dissertation Abstracts International, 65*(8), 2842A. (UMI No. 3143574)

Bandura, A. (1977). Self-efficacy: Toward a unifying theory of behavioral change. *Psychological Review, 84*, 191–215.

Bandura, A. (1997). *Self-efficacy: The experience of control*. New York: Freeman.

Barber, B. (1984). Creating bytes of language. *Language Arts, 59*, 472–475.

Barrett, D. S. (1999). Information systems: An exploration of the factors impacting effective utilization. *Journal of Research on Computing in Education, 33,* 1–2.

Barrett, D. S. (2000). Factors and their effect in the principals' utilization of a management information system. *Dissertation Abstracts International, 61*(8), 3002A. (UMI No. 9982139)

Barry, J., & Hederman, R. (2000). *Report card on American education: A state-by-state analysis 1976–1999.* Washington, DC: American Legislative Exchange Council.

Basham, V. P. (1988). A study of the status of strategic planning in Kentucky school districts. *Dissertation Abstracts International, 50*(4), 834A. (UMI No. 8914132)

Basham, V., & Lunenburg, F. C. (1989). Strategic planning, student achievement, and school district financial and demographic factors. *Planning and Changing, 20*(3), 158–171.

Bass, B. M., & Avolio, B. J. (1994). *Improving organizational effectiveness through transformational leadership: An inquiry into transformational leadership.* Thousand Oaks, CA: SAGE.

Bean, H. C. (1983). Computerized word processing as an aid to revision. *College Composition and Communication, 34,* 146–148.

Bean, M. (2007). Physical activity in elementary school girls: Implementation and theory-based evaluation of girls on the run. *Dissertation Abstracts International, 67*(04), B.

Below, P. J., Morrissey, G. L., & Acomb, B. L. (1987). *The executive guide to strategic planning.* San Francisco: Jossey-Bass.

Bennett, W. J. (1988). *American education: Making it work.* Washington, DC: U.S. Government Printing Office, Superintendent of Documents.

Benz, C. R., Bradley, L., Alderman, M. K., & Flowers, M. A. (1992). Personal teaching efficacy: Developmental relationships in education. *Journal of Educational Research, 85*(5), 274–286.

Berger, J. B. (2001). Understanding the organizational nature of student persistence: Empirically-based recommendations for practice. *Journal of College Student Retention: Research, Theory, and Practice, 3,* 3–21.

Best, J. W. (1981). *Research in education* (4th ed.). Englewood Cliffs, NJ: Prentice Hall.

Black, L. T. (2003). The development and validation of the principal efficacy scale. *Dissertation Abstracts International, 64*(11), 3912A. (UMI No. 3112222)

Blair, D. (2001). Principals' leadership styles, school ratings, and principals' time spent on instructional leadership and management tasks. *Dissertation Abstracts International, 63*(7), 2419A. (UMI No. 3059689)

Bogdan, R., & Biklen, S. (2007). *Qualitative research for education: An introduction to theory and methods.* Boston: Allyn & Bacon.

Bollen, K. A., & Curran, P. J. (2006). *Latent curve models: A structural equation perspective.* Hoboken, NJ: Wiley.

Boone, R. A. (1985). *The revision processes of elementary school students who write using a word processing computer program.* Eugene, OR: University of Oregon Press.

Bradley, V. (1982). Improving students' writing with microcomputers. *Language Arts, 59,* 732–743.

Brause, R. S. (2004). *Writing your doctoral dissertation.* London: Routledge Falmer.

Bridgewater, S. R. (2006). Preschool school psychology training: Assessing the perceived level of training and competence of preservice school psychologists to provide social-emotional assessment and mental health services in early childhood settings. *Dissertation Abstracts International, 67*(5), DAI-A. (UMI No. 3217411).

Brown, A. F. (1967). Reactions to leadership. *Educational Administration Quarterly, 3,* 62–73.

Brown, G., & Irby, B. J. (1994). Needed: A theory including women executives in the rural culture. In D. Montgomery (Ed.), *Conference proceedings of rural partnerships: Working together* (pp. 19–24). Austin, TX: The American Council on Rural Education (ACRES).

Brown, R. J. (1965). *Organizational climate of elementary schools* (Research Monograph No. 2). Minneapolis: University of Minnesota, Educational Research and Development Center.

Brownell, M. T., & Pajares, F. M. (1996). The influence of teachers' efficacy beliefs on perceived success in mainstreaming students with learning and behavior problems: A path analysis. *Research Bulletin, 27*(3, 4), 11–24.

Brunner, C. C. (2000). Unsettled moments in settled discourse: Women superintendents' experiences of inequality. *Educational Administration Quarterly, 36*(1), 76–116.

Bryce, H. J. (1987). *Financial and strategic management for nonprofit organizations.* Englewood Cliffs, NJ: Prentice Hall.

Burns, J. M. (1978). *Leadership.* New York: Harper & Row.

Byrne, B. M. (2006). *Structural equation modeling with EQS: Basic concepts, applications, and programming.* Mahwah, NJ: Erlbaum.

Cabell, D. W. E. (Ed.). (2006). *Cabell's directory of publishing opportunities.* Beaumont, TX: Cabell.

Cadavid, V. (1986). Locus of control and pupil control ideology as related to dimensions of burnout. *Dissertation Abstracts International, 47*(9), 3393A. (UMI No. 8622964)

Caison, A. (2004). Determinants of systemic retention: Implications for improving retention practice in higher education. *Journal of College Student Retention: Research, Theory, and Practice, 6*(1), 3–22.

Camilus, J. C. (1986). *Strategic planning and management control: Systems for survival and success.* Lexington, MA: Lexington Books.

Campbell, D. T., & Stanley, J. C. (1963). *Experimental and quasi-experimental designs for research.* Chicago: Rand McNally.

Carey, K. (2004). *A matter of degrees: Improving four-year colleges and universities.* Washington, DC: Education Trust.

Castetter, W. B., & Heisler, R. S. (1984). *Developing and defending a dissertation proposal* (4th ed.). Philadelphia: University of Pennsylvania.

Cattell, R. B. (1966). The scree test for the number of factors. *Multivariate Behavioral Research, 1*, 245–276.

Cervone, D. (2000). Thinking about self-efficacy. *Behavior Modification, 24*(1), 30–56.

Charters, W. W. (1964). *Teacher perceptions of administrator behavior* (Cooperative Research Project No. 929). St. Louis: Washington University, U.S. Department of Health, Education, and Welfare, Office of Education.

Choi, J. W. (2005). Acculturation and physical activity in Korean immigrant women *Dissertation Abstracts International, 66*(4), 1977B. (UMI No. 3173715).

Choi, N., Fuqua, D. R., & Griffin, B. W. (2001). Exploratory analysis of the structure of scores from multidimensional scales of perceived self-efficacy [Electronic version]. *Educational and Psychological Measurement, 61*(3), 475–489.

Christensen, G. S. (2004). *What matters for immigrant achievement cross-nationally? A comparative approach examining immigrant and non-immigrant student achievement.* Unpublished doctoral dissertation, Stanford University, Stanford, CA.

Christensen, J. M. (2003). Technology integration correlates in high-performing elementary schools. *Dissertation Abstracts International. 63*(07), 2514A. (UMI No. 3059690)

Christopher, F. P. (2006). Accommodating English language learners in mainstream secondary classes: A comparative study of professional development delivery methods. *Dissertation Abstracts International, 67*(02), A.

Chung, W. (2006). The effects of presentation pace and modality on learning a multimedia science lesson. *Dissertation Abstracts International, 67*(06), A.

Clark, K. D. (2002). Student achievement, demographics, and property wealth as related to the allocation of educational resources in public school districts. *Dissertation Abstracts International, 63*(11), 3798A. (UMI No. 3072046)

Clark, S. L. (2005). The effect of specific versus generalized supervisory feedback on counseling self-efficacy of counselors-in-training. *Dissertation Abstracts International, 66*(11), DAI-B. (UMI No. 3197603).

Coate, D., & VanderHoff, J. (1999). Public school spending and student achievement: The case of New Jersey. *CATO Journal, 19*(1), 85–100.

Cohen, J. (1988). *Statistical power analysis for the behavioral sciences* (2d ed.). Hillsdale, NJ: Erlbaum.

Cohen, J. (1992). A power primer. *Psychological Bulletin, 112*, 155–159.

Coladarci, T. (1992). Teachers' sense of efficacy and commitment to teaching. *Journal of Experimental Education, 60*(4), 323–337.

Coleman, J. C. (2003). The congruence between superintendents' and school boards' expectations of the superintendent and student achievement. *Dissertation Abstracts International, 64*(11), 3913A. (UMI No. 3112224)

Coleman, J. S., et al. (1966). *Equality of educational opportunity.* Washington, DC: U.S. Government Printing Office.

Collier, R. M. (1983). The word processor and revision strategies. *College Composition and Communication, 34,* 149–155.

Cone, J. D., & Foster, S. L. (2007). *Dissertations and theses from start to finish.* Washington, DC: American Psychological Association.

Connelly, F. M., & Clandinin, D. J. (1990). Stories of experience and narrative inquiry. *Educational Researcher, 19*(5), 2–14.

Cook, C. L. (2006). The questions we ask: A study of tutor questions and their effect on writing center tutorials. *Dissertation Abstracts International, 67*(2), 577A. (UMI No. 3206641).

Cook, T. D., & Campbell, D. T. (1979). *Quasi-experimentation: Design and analysis issues for field settings.* Boston: Houghton Mifflin.

Coon-Carty, H. M. (1998). The influence of subject-specific academic self-concepts on academic achievement from a Vygotskian developmental perspective: A longitudinal investigation. *Dissertation Abstracts International, 59*(06), 3091B.

Corbett, D., Wilson, B., & Williams, B. (2005). No choice but success: *Learning from urban schools. Educational Leadership, 62*(6), 8–12.

Corbin, J. M., & Strauss, A. L. (1990). Grounded theory research: Procedures, canons, and evaluative criteria. *Qualitative Sociology, 13*(1), 3–21.

Corwin Press Book Prospectus Guidelines. (2000). Retrieved August 26, 2007, from http://www.corwinpress.com/publish.nav

Corwin, R. G., & Wagenaar, T. C. (1976). Boundary interaction between service organizations and their publics: A study of teacher-parent relationships. *Social Forces, 55,* 471–492.

Council of Graduate Schools. (2002). *The role and nature of the doctoral dissertation: A policy statement.* Washington DC: Author.

Covey, S. R. (1991). *The seven habits of highly effective people.* New York: Simon & Schuster.

Craig, T. (1995). Achieving innovation through bureaucracy. *California Management Review, 33*(10), 8–36.

Craycraft, S. J. (1999). *The relationship between brain dominance and leadership style of school superintendents and business chief executive officers.* Unpublished doctoral dissertation. Sam Houston State University, Huntsville, Texas.

Creighton, L. M. (2006). *Predicting graduation rates: An analysis of student and institutional factors at University Council for Educational Administration public universities.* Unpublished doctoral dissertation. Sam Houston State University, Huntsville, Texas.

Creswell, J. W. (2007). *Qualitative inquiry and research design: Choosing among five traditions.* Thousand Oaks, CA: SAGE.

Cronbach, L. J. (1951). Coefficient alpha and the internal structure of tests. *Psychometrika, 16,* 297–334.

Crown, W. H. (1998). *Statistical models for the social and behavioral sciences: Multiple regression and limited-dependent variable models.* Westport, CT: Praeger. Retrieved January 6, 2007, from Questia database.

Culver, S. M., Wolfe, L. M., & Cross, L. H. (1990). Testing a model of teacher satisfaction for blacks and whites. *American Educational Research Journal, 20*(1), 1–25.

Cuttance, P. (2001). The impact of teaching on student learning. In K. Kennedy (Ed.), *Beyond the rhetoric: Building a teaching profession to support quality teaching* (pp. 35–55). Canberra, Australia: Australian College of Education.

Cyert, R. M., & March, J. G. (1963). *A behavioral theory of the firm.* Englewood Cliffs, NJ: Prentice Hall.

Daiute, C. (1986). Physical and cognitive factors in revising: Insights from studies with computers. *Research in the Teaching of English, 20,* 141–159.

Dalton, D., & Hannafin, M. J. (1987). The effects of word processing on written composition. *Journal of Educational Research, 80,* 338–342.

Damanpour, F. (1991). Organizational innovation. *Academy of Management Journal, 34,* 555–591.

Daresh, J., & Playko, M. (1995). *Supervision as a proactive process: Concepts and cases.* Prospect Heights, IL: Waveland Press.

Davis, F. D. (1989). Perceived usefulness, perceived ease of use, and user acceptance of information technology. *MIS Quarterly, 13*(3), 319–340.

Davis, S. H. (1998). Superintendents' perspectives on the involuntary departure of public school principals: The most frequent reasons why principals lose their jobs. *Educational Administration Quarterly, 34*(1), 59–90.

Deal, T. E., & Peterson, K. D. (1994). *The leadership paradox: Balancing logic and artistry in schools.* San Francisco: Jossey-Bass.

Delaney, D. D. (2005). An exploratory study of the leadership behaviors of principals in state-funded prekindergarten programs. *Dissertation Abstracts International, 67*(1), 43A. (UMI No. 3202835)

Dembo, M. H., & Gibson, S. (1985). Teachers' sense of efficacy: An important factor in school improvement. *Elementary School Journal, 86*(2), 173–184.

Denzin, N. K. (1978). *Sociological methods.* New York: McGraw-Hill.

Denzin, N. K., & Lincoln, Y. S. (1994). *Handbook of qualitative research.* London: SAGE.

Denzin, N. K., & Lincoln, Y. S. (Eds.). (2005). *The SAGE handbook of qualitative research* (3d ed.). Thousand Oaks, CA: SAGE.

Dishaw, M. T., & Strong, D. M. (1999). Extending the technology acceptance model with task-technology fit constructs. *Information Management, 36*(1), 9–21.

Dorin, H., Demmin, P. E., & Gabel, D. (1990). *Chemistry: The study of matter.* (3d ed.). Englewood Cliffs, NJ: Prentice Hall.

Drees, W. F. (2006). *The prediction of academic and credentialing success in an allied health program.* Unpublished doctoral dissertation, Sam Houston State University, Huntsville, Texas.

Drew, C. F. (1980). *Introduction to designing and conducting research* (2d ed.). St. Louis, MO: C. V. Mosby.

Dunleavy, P. (2003). *Authoring a PhD: How to plan, draft, write and finish a doctoral dissertation.* New York: Palgrave Macmillan.

Edmonds, R. (1979). Some schools work and more can. *Social Policy, 9,* 28–32.

Eisenhardt, K. M. (1989). Building theories from case study research. *Academy of Management Review, 14,* 532–550.

Epstein, J. L., & McPartland, J. M. (1978). *Quality of school life administration and technical manual.* Boston: Houghton Mifflin.

Ericksen, J. B. (2006). Developing a theory about how early elementary special education teachers approach literacy learning with student with significant disabilities. *Dissertation Abstracts International, 67*(03), 896A.

Erickson, D. A. (1965). Essay review: Some misgivings concerning a study of leadership. *Educational Administration Quarterly, 1,* 52–59.

Erickson, D. A. (1967). The school administrator. *Review of Educational Research, 37,* 417–420.

Evans, S. A. (2006). A validation study of a measurement of technology integration skills for pre-service teachers. *Dissertation Abstracts International, 67*(02), A.

Feldvebel, A. M. (1964). The relationship between socioeconomic status of the school's patrons, organizational climate in the school and pupil achievement level. *Dissertation Abstracts.* (UMI No. 10599)

Ferguson, K. E. (1984). *The feminist case against bureaucracy.* Philadelphia: Temple University Press.

Field, A. (2000). *Discovering statistics using SPSS for Windows: Advanced techniques for the beginner.* Thousand Oaks, CA: SAGE.

Fishbein, M., & Ajzen, I. (1975). *Belief, attitude, intention, and behavior: An introduction to theory and research.* Reading, MA: Addison-Wesley.

Fitzgerald, J. (1987). Research on revision in writing. *Review of Educational Research, 57*(4), 481–506.

Fitzgibbon, C., & Morris, L. (1987). *How to analyze data.* Newbury Park, CA: SAGE.

Flagg, J. T. (1965). The organizational climate of schools: Its relationship to pupil achievement, size of school, and teacher turnover. *Dissertation Abstracts, 26,* 818–819A.

Flowers, L. A. (2004). Retaining African American students in higher education: An integrative review. *Journal of College Student Retention: Research, Theory, and Practice, 6*(1), 23–38.

Gall, M., Borg, W., & Gall, J. (1996). *Educational research: An introduction.* White Plains, NY: Longman.

Gall, M. D., Gall, J. P., & Borg, W. R. (2007). *Educational research: An introduction* (8th ed.). Boston: Allyn & Bacon.

Gardner, J. R., Rachlin, R., & Sweeney, H. W. (1986). *Handbook of strategic planning.* New York: Wiley.

Garner, D. A. (2005). Management tasks and functions of school district superintendents. *Dissertation Abstracts International, 66*(4), 1225A.

Gay, L. R, & Airasian, P. (2000). *Educational research: Competencies for analysis and applications* (6th ed.). Upper Saddle River, NJ: Merrill/Prentice Hall.

Gay, L. R., Mills, G. E., & Airasian, P. (2006). *Educational research: Competencies for analysis and applications* (8th ed.). Upper Saddle River, NJ: Merrill/Prentice Hall.

Gibson, S., & Dembo, M. H. (1984). Teacher efficacy: A construct validation. *Journal of Educational Psychology, 76*(4), 569–582.

Gitonga, S. K. (2006). A phenomenological inquiry of beginning counselors' experience of their first counseling position. *Dissertation Abstracts International, 67*(03), A.

Glaser, B. G. (1978). *Theoretical sensitivity: Advances in the methodology of grounded theory.* Mill Valley, CA: Sociology Press.

Glaser, B. G., & Strauss, A. L. (1967). *The discovery of grounded theory: Strategies for qualitative research.* Chicago: Aldine.

Glass, T. E., Björk, L. G., & Brunner, C. C. (2000). *The study of the American superintendency 2000.* Arlington, VA: American Association of School Administrators.

Goldring, E. B. (1995). School administrators as boundary spanners. In S. B. Bacharach & B. Mundell (Eds.), *Images of schools* (pp. 283–314). Thousand Oaks, CA: Corwin Press.

Gorton, R. A., & Snowden, P. (1993). *School leadership and administration: Important concepts, case studies, and simulations.* Madison, WI: Brown & Benchmark.

Greenfield, W. D. (1995). Toward a theory of school administration: The centrality of leadership. *Educational Administration Quarterly, 31,* 61–85.

Grejda, G. F., & Hannafin, M. J. (1991). The influence of word processing on the revisions of fifth graders. *Computers in the Schools, 8*(4), 89–102.

Grejda, G. F. & Hannafin, M. J. (1992). Effects of word processing on sixth graders' holistic writing revisions. *Journal of Educational Research, 85,* 144–149.

Gross, N., & Herriott, R. E. (1965). *Staff leadership in public schools: A sociological inquiry.* New York: Wiley.

Guskey, T. R., & Passaro, P. D. (1994). Teacher efficacy: A study of construct dimensions. *American Educational Research Journal, 31*(3), 627–643.

Gustafson, T. J. (1985). *Microcomputers and educational administration.* Englewood Cliffs, NJ: Prentice Hall.

Guy, R. M. (1970). The relationship between organizational climate, leadership, and progress. *Dissertation Abstracts International, 30,* 3679A.

Hale, J. (1965). A study of the relationship between selected factors of organizational climate and pupil achievement in reading, arithmetic, and language. *Dissertation Abstracts International, 26,* 5817A.

Hall, R. H. (1991). *Organizations: Structure, process, and outcomes.* Englewood Cliffs, NJ: Prentice Hall.

Hallinger, P., & Heck, R. (1997). Exploring the principal's contribution to school effectiveness. *School Effectiveness and School Improvement, 8*(4), 1–35.

Halpin, A. W. (1956). *The leadership behavior of school superintendents.* Chicago: Midwest Administration Center, University of Chicago.

Halpin, A. W., & Croft, D. B. (1963). *The organizational climate of schools.* Chicago: Midwest Administration Center, University of Chicago.

Hartley, M., & Hoy, W. K. (1972). Openness of school climate and alienation of high school students. *California Journal of Educational Research, 23,* 17–24.

Hawisher, G. (1987). The effects of word processing on the revision strategies of college freshmen. *Research in the Teaching of English, 21,* 145–159.

Henson, R. K. (2001). *Teacher self-efficacy: Substantive implications and measurement dilemmas.* Keynote address given at the annual meeting of the educational Research Exchange, Texas A&M University, College Station, Texas. Retrieved February 7, 2006, from http://www.emory.edu/EDUCATION/mfp/effpage.html

Heppner, P. P., & Heppner, M. J. (2004). *Writing and publishing your thesis, dissertation, and research.* Belmont, CA: Thomson/Brooks Cole.

Heppner, P. P., Kivlighan, D. M., & Wampold, B. E. (1999). *Research design in counseling* (2nd ed.). Belmont, CA: Wadsworth.

Herbert, E., Lee, A., & Williamson, L. (1998). Teachers' and teacher education students' sense of efficacy: Quantitative and qualitative comparisons. *Journal of Research and Development in Education, 31(4),* 214–225.

Hernandez, J. C. (2000). Understanding the retention of Latino college students. *Journal of Student Development, 41,* 575–588.

Hernandez, R. M. (2004). An analysis of superintendent and school board perceptions of the factors of the synergistic leadership theory. *Dissertation Abstracts International, 65*(8), 2848A. (UMI No. 3143582)

Hersey, P. (1976). Situational leadership: Some aspects of its influence on organizational development. *Dissertation Abstracts International, 37*(1), 438A. (UMI No. 7614691)

Hersey, P., & Blanchard, K. H. (2007). *Management of organizational behavior* (8th ed.). Mahwah, NJ: Prentice Hall.

Hinojosa, M. A. (2005). A comparison of academic achievement of economically disadvantaged elementary students served in Title I Part A programs: Targeted assistance versus schoolwide models. *Dissertation Abstracts International, 66*(07), 2452A.

Hirschhorn, L. (1997). *Reworking authority: Leading and following in a postmodern organization.* Cambridge, MA: MIT Press.

Hodge, B., & Anthony, W. (1991). *Organizational theory: A strategic approach.* Boston: Allyn & Bacon.

Hoke, M. C. (2006). A case study of the effects of a total compensation strategy on the culture of a nonprofit organization. *Dissertation Abstracts International, 66*(11), B.

Holtkamp, L. W. (2001). The validation of the organizational and leadership effectiveness inventory. *Dissertation Abstracts International, 62*(7), 2300A. (UMI No. 3020890)

Hoy, W. K. (1998). Self-efficacy: The exercise of control. *Educational Administration Quarterly, 34*(1), 153–158.

Hoy, W. K., & Clover, S. J. (1986). Elementary school climate: A revision of the OCDQ. *Educational Administration Quarterly, 22,* 93–110.

Hoy, W. K., & Miskel, C. G. (1982). *Educational administration: Theory, research, and practice* (2nd ed.). New York: Random House.

Hoy, W. K., & Miskel, C. G. (2001). *Educational administration: Theory, research, and practice* (6th ed.). New York: McGraw-Hill.

Hoy, W. K., & Sweetland, S. R. (2000). School bureaucracies that work: Enabling, not coercive. *Journal of School Leadership, 10*(6), 525–541.

Hoy, W. K. & Tarter, C. J. (1997). *The road to open and healthy schools: A handbook for change, elementary and middle school edition.* Thousand Oaks, CA: Corwin Press.

Hoy, W. K., Tarter, C. J., & Hoy, A. W. (2006). Academic optimism of schools: A force for student achievement. *American Educational Research Journal, 43*(3), 425–446.

Hoy, W. K., & Woolfolk, A. E. (1993). Teachers' sense of efficacy and the organizational health of schools. *Elementary School Journal, 94*(4), 355–372.

Huntsman, W. G. (1986). Long-range educational planning practices in the twelve unified school districts in Maricopa County, Arizona. *Dissertation Abstracts International, 47*(12), 4254A. (UMI No. 8705746)

Hurtado, S. (2000). The campus racial climate. In C. Turner, M. Garcia, A. Nora, & L. I. Rendon (Eds.), *Racial and ethnic diversity in higher education* (pp. 485–506). Needham Heights, MA: Simon & Schuster.

Irby, B. J., Brown, G., Duffy, J., & Trautman, D. (2002). The synergistic leadership theory. *Journal of Educational Administration, 40*(4), 304–322.

Irby, B. J., Brown, G., & Trautman, D. (1999, August). *Analysis of thirteen leadership theories for an androcentric bias.* Paper presented at the National Council of Professors of Educational Administration, Jackson Hole, Wyoming.

Igbaria, M., Zinatelli, N., Cragg, P., & Cavaye, A. (1997). Personal computing acceptance factors in small firms: A structural equation model. *MIS Quarterly, 21*(3), 279–305.

Ivancevich, J. M., Donnelly, J. H., & Gibson, J. L. (1980). *Managing for performance.* Dallas, TX: Business Publications.

Jackson, S., & Schuler, R. S. (1985). A meta-analysis and conceptual critique of research on role ambiguity and role conflict in work settings. *Organizational Behavior and Human Decision Processes, 36*, 17–78.

Jacobs, D. (1974). Dependency and vulnerability: An exchange approach to the control of organizations. *Administrative Science Quarterly, 19*, 45–59.

Jencks, C. (1972). *Inequality: A reassessment of the effect of family and schooling in America.* New York: Basic Books.

Jodry, E. O. (2001). Hispanic academic advancement theory: An ethnographic study of students participating in an urban Texas high school advanced diploma program. *Dissertation Abstracts International, 63*(07), 2436A.

Johnson, B. L., & Fauske, J. R. (2000). Principals and the political economy of environmental enactment. *Educational Administration Quarterly, 34*(1), 59–90.

Johnson, R. B., & Onwuegbuzie, A. J. (2004). Mixed methods research: A research paradigm whose time has come. *Educational researcher, 33*(7), 14–26.

Kanner, L. T. (1974). Machiavellianism and the secondary schools: Teacher-principal relations. *Dissertation Abstracts International, 35*(6), 3344A. (UMI No. 7427329)

Katz, D., & Kahn, R. L. (1978). *The social psychology of organizations* (2nd ed.). New York: Wiley.

Kerlinger, F. N. (1986). *Foundations of behavioral research* (3rd ed.). San Diego, CA: Harcourt Brace.

Kerr, C. (2001). *The uses of the university.* Cambridge, MA: Harvard University Press.

Kim, J., & Mueller, J. (1978). *Factor analysis: Statistical methods and practical issues.* Thousand Oaks, CA: SAGE.

Kortz, W. J. (2002). Measuring the effects of the accelerated reader program on third grade English language learners' reading achievement in dual language programs. *Dissertation Abstracts International, 63*(11), 3860A. (UMI No. 3072050)

Kottkamp, R. B., Mulhern, J. A., & Hoy, W. K. (1987). Secondary school climate: A revision of the OCDQ. *Educational Administration Quarterly, 23*, 31–48.

Krathwohl, D. R. & Smith, N. L. (2005). *How to prepare a dissertation proposal.* Syracuse, NY: Syracuse University Press.

Krejcie, R. V., & Morgan, D. W. (1970). Determining sample size for research activities. *Educational and Psychological Measurement, 30*, 608.

Kreuger, R.A. (1988). *Focus groups: A practical guide for applied research.* London: SAGE

Kuh, G. D. (2005). Student engagement in the first year of college. In M. L. Upcraft, J. N. Garner, & B. O. Barefoot (Eds.), *Challenging and supporting the first-year student: A handbook for improving the first year of college* (pp. 86–107). San Francisco: Jossey-Bass.

Kuhn, T. (1962). *The structure of scientific revolutions.* Chicago: University of Chicago Press.

Kvale, S. (1996). *Interviews: An introduction to qualitative research interviewing.* Thousand Oaks, CA: SAGE.

Lather, P. (1991). *Getting smart: Feminist research and pedagogy within the postmodern.* New York: Routledge.

Lawrence, P. R., & Lorsch, J. W. (1967). *Organization and environment: Managing differentiation and integration.* Boston: Harvard University Graduate School of Business Administration Press.

Lesure-Lester, G. E., & King, N. (2004). Racial and ethnic differences in social anxiety among college students. *Journal of College Student Retention: Research, Theory, and Practice, 6*(3), 359–367.

Lewis, J. (1983). *Long-range and short-range planning for educational administration.* Boston: Allyn & Bacon.

Lewis, J. A. (2006). Do juvenile drunk driving laws really work? An interrupted time-series analysis of Pennsylvania's zero-tolerance juvenile alcohol law. *Dissertation Abstracts International, 67*(02), A.

Likert, R. (1961). *New patterns of management.* New York: McGraw-Hill.

Lincoln, Y. S., & Guba, E. G. (1985). *Naturalistic inquiry.* Newbury Park, CA: SAGE.

Loeffler, C. A. (2005). The relationship of adult learning styles and perceived factors involved in online graduate education leadership programs. *Dissertation Abstracts International, 66*(4), 1244A. (UMI No. 3171978)

Loehlin, J. C. (2004). *Latent variable models: An introduction to factor, path, and structural equation analysis.* Mahwah, NJ: Erlbaum.

Long, T. J., Convey, J. J., & Chwalek, A. R. (1985). *Completing dissertations in the behavioral sciences and education.* San Francisco: Jossey-Bass.

Luey, B. (2004). *Revising your dissertation.* Berkeley: University of California Press.

Lunenburg, F. C. (1969). *A validation of the OCDQ in elementary schools.* Unpublished master's thesis. Seton Hall University, South Orange, New Jersey.

Lunenburg, F. C. (1972). *Organizational climate, dogmatism, and pupil control ideology.* Unpublished doctoral dissertation. University of Ottawa, Ottawa, Ontario, Canada.

Lunenburg, F. C. (1982). A model of organizational effectiveness. *The School Administrator, 39*(9), 37–39.

Lunenburg, F. C. (1984). *Pupil-control orientation: Individual and organizational correlates.* Lexington, MA: Ginn.

Lunenburg, F. C. (1991a). Educators' pupil control ideology as a predictor of educators' reactions to pupil disruptive behavior. *High School Journal, 74*(2), 81–87.

Lunenburg, F. C. (1991b). Pupil control ideology and behavior as predictors of environmental robustness: Public and private schools compared. *Journal of Research and Development in Education, 24*(3), 15–19.

Lunenburg, F. C. (2000). *Revision of the instructional leadership/management tasks profile (Tech. Rep. No. 1).* Huntsville, TX: Sam Houston State University, Center for Research and Doctoral Studies in Educational Leadership.

Lunenburg, F. C. (2002). Improving student achievement: Some structural incompatibilities. In G. Perreault & F. C. Lunenburg (Eds.), *The changing world of school administration* (pp. 5–27). Lanham, MD: Rowman & Littlefield.

Lunenburg, F. C. (2003). The post-behavioral science era: Excellence, democracy, and justice. In F. C. Lunenburg & C. S. Carr (Eds.), *Shaping the future* (pp. 36–55). Lanham, MD: Rowman & Littlefield.

Lunenburg, F. C. (2006). Heuristics in decision making. In F. English (Ed.), *Encyclopedia of educational leadership and administration* (pp. 455–457). Thousand Oaks, CA: Sage.

Lunenburg, F. C., & Cadavid, V. (1992). Locus of control, pupil control ideology, and dimensions of teacher burnout. *Journal of Instructional Psychology, 19*(1), 13–22.

Lunenburg, F. C., & Carr, C., (Eds.). (2003). *Shaping the future.* Lanham, MD: Rowman & Littlefield.

Lunenburg, F. C., & Columba, L. (1992). The 16PF as a predictor of principal performance: An integration of quantitative and qualitative research methods. *Education, 113*(1), 68–73.

Lunenburg, F. C., & Irby, B. J. (2000). *High expectations: An action plan for implementing goals 2000.* Thousand Oaks, CA: Corwin Press.

Lunenburg, F. C., & Mankowsky, S. A. (2000, April). *School bureaucratization, pupil control ideology, and pupil control behavior.* Paper presented at the annual meeting of the American Educational Research Association, New Orleans, Louisiana.

Lunenburg, F. C., & O'Reilly, R. R. (1974). Personal and organizational influence on pupil control ideology. *Journal of Experimental Education, 42*(3), 31–35.

Lunenburg, F. C., & Ornstein, A. O. (2000). *Educational administration: Concepts and practices* (3rd ed.). Belmont, CA: Wadsworth.

Lunenburg, F. C., & Ornstein, A. O. (2004). *Educational administration: Concepts and practices* (4th ed.). Belmont, CA: Thomson/Wadsworth.

Lunenburg, F. C., & Ornstein, A. O. (2008). *Educational administration: Concepts and practices* (5th ed.). Belmont, CA: Thomson/Wadsworth.

Lunenburg, F. C., & Schmidt, L. J. (1987). Pupil disruptive behavior: Development and factor structure of an operational measure. *Educational and Psychological Measurement, 47*(4), 1081–1085.

Lunenburg, F. C., & Schmidt, L. J. (1989). Pupil control ideology, pupil control behavior, and the quality of school life. *Journal of Research and Development in Education, 22*(4), 36–44.

Lutz, D. (2006). *The relationship between a bilingual federal grant program and student academic achievement in public schools.* Unpublished doctoral dissertation. Sam Houston State University, Huntsville, Texas.

Mackinnon, D. P., Nohre, L., Cheong, J., Stacey, A. W., & Pentz, M. A. (2001). Longitudinal relationship between the alcohol warning label and alcohol consumption. *Journal of Studies on Alcohol, 62*(2), 221. Retrieved December 31, 2006, from http://www.questia.com/PM.qst?a=o&d=5001008334

Madsen D. (1992). *Successful dissertations and theses.* San Francisco: Jossey-Bass.

Malhota, Y. (1998). Role of social influence, self-determination, and quality of use in information technology acceptance and utilization: A theoretical framework and empirical field study. *Dissertation Abstracts International, 59–07A, 2606.

Mangold, W. D., Bean, L. G., Adams, D. J., Scwab, W. A., & Lynch, S. M. (2002). Who goes, who stays? An assessment of the effect of a freshman mentoring and unit registration program on college persistence. *Journal of College Student Retention: Research, Theory, and Practice, 4*(2), 95–122.

Martin, R. (1980). *Writing and defending a thesis or dissertation in psychology and education.* Springfield, IL: Charles C. Thomas.

Martin, J., & Knopoff, K. (1999). The gendered implications of apparently gender-neutral theory: Rereading Weber. In E. Freeman & A. Larson (Eds.), *Ruffin lecture series, vol. 3: Business ethics and women's studies.* Oxford, UK: Oxford University Press.

Martin-Lucchesi, J. (1990). *Superintendents and unsuccessful principals: A study in Washington state.* Unpublished doctoral dissertation, Washington State University, Spokane, Washington.

Maslach, C., & Jackson, S. E. (1981). *Burnout inventory research edition manual.* Palo Alto, CA: Consulting Psychologists Press.

Mauch, J. E., & Park, N. (2003). *Guide to successful thesis and dissertation* (5th ed.). New York: Marcel Dekker.

Maxwell, R. E. (1967). Leader behavior of principals: A study of ten inner-city elementary schools of Flint, Michigan. *Dissertation Abstracts, 28,* 2950A.

McCoy, V. A. (2005). Humor, hope, and gratitude scores as predictors of attitudes toward persons with disabilities. *Dissertation Abstracts International, 67*(03), 126B.

McFadden, D. M. (2006). An investigation of the lived experience of spirituality and religion in the lives of those diagnosed with severe or chronic mental illness. *Dissertation Abstracts International, 67*(04), B.

Menconi, J. P. (2006). A case study: Principal perspectives of the strengths and weaknesses of looping and multiage education. *Dissertation Abstracts International, 67*(04), A.

Merriam, S. B. (1998). *Qualitative research and case study applications in education.* San Francisco: Jossey-Bass.

Merriam-Webster Inc. (1986). *Merriam-Webster's ninth new collegiate dictionary.* Springfield, MA: Author.

Meyer, D. J. (2000). Evaluating urban elementary bilingual classrooms through the four-dimensional bilingual pedagogical theory. *Dissertation Abstracts International, 61*(8), 3031A. (UMI No. 9982143)

Meyer, J. W., & Scott, W. R. (1992). *Organizational environments: Ritual and rationality.* Newbury Park, CA: SAGE.

Meyertons, J. E. (2006). An examination of faculty experiences with hybrid formats. *Dissertation Abstracts International, 67*(05), A.

Michaels, R. E., Cron, W. L., Dubinsky, A. J., & Joachimsthaler, E. A. (1988). Influence of formalization on the organizational commitment and work alienation of salespeople and industrial buyers. *Journal of Marketing Research, 25,* 376–383.

Miles, R. (1980). *Macro organizational behavior.* Santa Monica, CA: Goodyear.

Miles, M. B., & Huberman, A. M. (1994). *Qualitative data analysis: A sourcebook for new methods* (2nd ed.). Thousand Oaks, CA: SAGE.

Miller, H. E. (1969). An investigation of organizational climate as a variable in pupil achievement among 29 elementary schools in an urban school district. *Dissertation Abstracts, 29,* 9987A.

Miller, W. D. (2003). An inquiry related to students', recent graduates', and program directors' experiences and perceptions as participants in doctoral cohorts in educational leadership programs. *Dissertation Abstracts International, 64*(7), 2332A. (UMI No. 3098502)

Mishler, E. (1986). The analysis of interview-narratives. In T. Sarbin (Ed.). *Narrative psychology: The storied nature of human conduct* (pp. 233–255). New York: Praeger.

Miskel, C. G., & Ogawa, R. (1988). Work motivation, job satisfaction, and climate. In N. J. Boyan (Ed.), *Handbook of research on educational administration* (pp. 279–304). New York: Longman.

Morgen, S. (1994). Personalizing personnel decisions in feminist organizational theory. *Human Relations, 47*(6), 665–684.

Morris, M. G. (1996). A longitudinal examination of information technology acceptance: The influence of system experience on user perceptions and behavior. *Dissertation Abstracts International, 57*(7), 3125A. (UMI No. 9640131)

Morrissey, G. L., Below, P. J., & Acomb, B. L. (1988). *The executive guide to operational planning.* San Francisco: Jossey-Bass.

Murphy, J. (1990). The educational reform movement of the 1980s: A comprehensive analysis. In J. Murphy (Ed.), *The educational reform movement of the 1980s: Perspectives and cases* (pp. 3–55). Berkeley, CA: McCutchan.

Neuman, W. L. (1997). *Social science methods: Qualitative and quantitative approaches.* Boston: Allyn & Bacon.

Newman, I., Benz, C. R., Weis, D., & McNeil, K. (1997). *Theses and dissertations: A guide to writing in the social and physical sciences.* Lanham, MD: University Press of America.

Nicholas, L. N., Virgo, H. E., & Wattenberg, W. W. (1965). *Effects of socioeconomic setting and organizational climate on problems brought to elementary school offices.* Unpublished report. Detroit, MI: Wayne State University.

Nightingale, D., & Cromby, J. (Eds.) (1999). *Social constructionist psychology.* Buckingham, UK: Open University Press. Retrieved May 1, 2007, from http://www.psy.dmu.ac.uk/michael/qual_reflexivity.htm

Nora, A. (2001). *How minority students finance their higher education.* New York: ERIC Clearinghouse on Urban Education. (ERIC Document Reproduction Service No. ED460243).

Null, E. J. (1967). *Organizational climate of elementary schools* (Research monograph No. 3). Minneapolis: University of Minnesota, Educational Research and Development Council.

Nwankwo, J. J. (1979). The school climate as a factor in students' conflict in Nigeria. *Educational Studies, 10,* 267–279.

Nygren, B. (1992). Two-party tune up. *American School Board Journal, 179*(7), 35.

Ogawa, R. T. (1996). Bridging and buffering relations between parents and schools. *University Council for Educational Administration Review, 3,* 37.

Olejnik, S. E. (1984). Planning educational research: Determining the necessary sample size. *Journal of Experimental Education, 53,* 40–48.

Ozawa, Y. (2006). Authentic communication for Japanese language learning: A single case study of Midwestern university students. *Dissertation Abstracts International, 67*(02) A.

Pajares, F. (1996). Self-efficacy beliefs in academic settings. *Review of Educational Research, 66*(4), 543–578.

Parkay, F. W., Currie, G. D., & Rhodes, J. W. (1992). Professional socialization: A longitudinal study of first-time high school principals. *Educational Administration Quarterly, 28,* 43–75.

Parkay, F. W., Greenwood, G., Olejnik, S., & Proller, N. (1988). A study of the relationships among teacher efficacy, locus of control, and stress. *Journal of Research and Development in Education, 21*(4), 13–22.

Pascarella, E. T., & Terenzini, P. T. (2005). *How college affects students, vol. 2: A third decade of research.* San Francisco: Jossey-Bass.

Pascarella, S. V. (1985). A field test of Hersey and Blanchard's situation leadership theory. *Dissertation Abstract International, 46*(5), 1149A. (UMI No. 8515695)

Pascarella, S. V., & Lunenburg, F. C. (1988). A field test of Hersey and Blanchard's situational leadership theory. *College Student Journal, 22*(1), 4–7.

Patton, M. Q. (1990). *Qualitative evaluation and research methods* (2nd ed.). Newbury Park: CA, SAGE.

Patton, M. Q. (2002). *Qualitative evaluation and research methods* (4th ed.). Newbury Park, CA: SAGE.

Perl, S. (1979). The composing process of unskilled college writers. *Research in the Teaching of English, 13,* 317–336.

Perreault, G., & Lunenburg, F. C., (Eds.). (2002). *The changing world of school administration.* Lanham, MD: Rowman & Littlefield.

Petrie, T. A., Hartranft, F., & Lutz, K. (1995). The relationship between teacher efficacy and administrative perceptions of effectiveness. *High School Journal, 78*(2), 73–77.

Pfeffer, J., & Salancik, G. R. (1978). *The external control of organizations.* New York: Harper & Row.

Pfeiffer, J. W. (1986). *Strategic planning: Selected readings.* San Diego: University Associates.

Plaxton, R. (1965). Principal personality and school organizational climate. *CSA Bulletin, 4*(5), 34–39.

Potter, J. (1996). Discourse analysis and constructionist approaches: Theoretical background. In J. Richardson (Ed.), *Handbook of qualitative research methods for psychology and the social sciences* (pp. 124–140). Leicester: BPS Books.

Punch, K. F. (1967). *Bureaucratic structure in schools and its relationship to leader behavior: An empirical study.* Unpublished doctoral dissertation, University of Toronto, Toronto, Ontario, Canada.

Quon, G. (2006). Gendered patterns of participation in classroom talk interaction. *Masters Abstracts International, 44*(06).

Randles, H. E. (1964). The effects of organizational climate on beginning elementary teachers. *Dissertation Abstracts International, 25*(12), 7049A. (UMI No. 6505673)

Reed, J. G., & Baxter, P. M. (2003). *Library use: A handbook for psychology* (3rd ed.). Washington, DC: American Psychological Association.

Rice, R. K. (1968). The relationship between organizational climate and student achievement. *Dissertation Abstracts, 29*, 1731A.

Robbins, S. (1990). *Organizational theory: Structure, design, and applications.* Englewood Cliffs, NJ: Prentice Hall.

Rodriguez, P. A. (2005). A study of advanced placement calculus programs in selected high schools in the county of San Bernardino, California. *Dissertation Abstracts International, 66*(08), 2862A.

Rotter, J. B. (1966). Generalized expectancies for internal versus external control of reinforcement. *Psychological Monographs, 80*(1, Whole No. 609).

Rowan, B., Raudenbush, S. W., & Cheong, Y. K. (1993). Teaching as a non-routine task: Implications for the management of schools. *Educational Administration Quarterly, 29*, 479–500.

Rudestam, K. E., & Newton, R. R. (2007). *Surviving your dissertation* (3rd. ed.). Thousand Oaks, CA: SAGE.

Rutgers University, Camden. (2003, August). *Table/graph format in interpretation.* Retrieved September 15, 2003, from http://sociology.camden.rutgers.edu/curriculum/format.htm

Salvato, J. L. (2006). The parental regulations used to monitor television viewing among elementary school students. *Masters Abstracts International, 44*(05).

Sargeant, J. C. (1967). *Organizational climate of high schools* (Research monograph No. 4). Minneapolis: University of Minnesota, Educational Research and Development Council.

Schlosberg, T. V. (2004). An international case study: The transportability of the synergistic leadership theory to selected educational leaders in Mexico. *Dissertation Abstracts International, 64*(07), 2337A. (UMI No. 3098504)

Schmidt, L. J. (1987). Relationships between pupil control ideology, pupil control behavior, and the quality of school life. *Dissertation Abstracts International, 48*(2), 276A. (UMI No. 8704860)

Schnell, C. A., & Doetkott, C. D. (2002). First year seminars produce long-term impact. *Journal of College Student Retention: Research, Theory, and Practice, 4*(4), 377–391.

Scott, W. R. (1998). *Organizations: Rational, natural, and open systems* (4th ed.). Englewood Cliffs, NJ: Prentice Hall.

Selznick, P. (1957). *Leadership in administration.* New York: Harper & Row.

Senatra, P. T. (1980). Role conflict, role ambiguity, and organizational climate in a public accounting firm. *Accounting Review, 55*, 594–603.

Senge, P. (1990). *The fifth discipline: The art and practice of the learning organization.* New York: Doubleday.

Sergiovanni, T. J. (1995). *The principalship: A reflective practice perspective.* Needham Heights, MA: Allyn & Bacon.

Shakeshaft, C. (1989). *Women in educational administration.* Newbury Park, CA: SAGE.

Siemers, E. E. (2006). Children's aggression at recess: Examining the relationship between the playground environment, aggressive behavior, and reports of worry. *Dissertation Abstracts International, 67*(03), A.

Slater, J. N. (2001). Application of motivation theory: An analysis of the motivation of at-risk ninth-grade students enrolled in online courses. *Dissertation Abstracts International, 62*(7), 2334A. (UMI No. 3020895)

Slavin, R. E. (1992). *Research methods in education: A practical guide.* Englewood Cliffs, NJ: Prentice Hall.

Smylie, M. A., Conley, S., & Marks, H. M. (2002). Exploring new approaches to teacher leadership for school improvement. *LSS Review, 1*(2), 18–19.

Solomon, R. C., & Flores, F. (2001). *Building trust in business, politics, and life.* New York: Oxford University Press.

Sowell, E. J., & Casey, R. J. (1982). *Research methods in education.* Belmont, CA: Wadsworth.

Spillane, J. P., & Louis, K. S. (2002). School improvement processes and practices: Professional learning for building instructional capacity. *LSS Review, 1*(2), 12–13.

Sprinthall, R. C. (2000). *Basic statistical analysis* (6th ed.). Needham Heights, MA: Allyn & Bacon.

Stanfield, V. S. (2000). The usefulness of the college student inventory as a needs assessment tool in community colleges. *Dissertation Abstracts International, 62*(7), 2324A. (UMI No. 3020897)

Stanford, J., Oates, B., & Flores, D. (1995). Women's leadership styles: A heuristic analysis. *Women in Management Review, 10*(2), 6–16.

Steinhoff, C. R. (1965). *Organizational climate in a public school system.* Washington, DC: U.S. Office of Education, Cooperative Program Contract No. OE-4–225, Project No. S-083, Syracuse University.

Stern, G. G. (1970). *People in context: Measuring person-environment in education and industry.* New York: Wiley.

Sternberg, D. (1981). *How to complete and survive a doctoral dissertation.* New York: St. Martin's Griffin.

Stogdill, R. M., & Coons, A. E. (1957). *Leader behavior: Its description and measurement.* Columbus: Ohio State University, Bureau of Business Research.

Stoner, J., Freeman, A., & Gilbert, D. (1995). *Management.* Englewood Cliffs, NJ: Prentice Hall.

Stubbs, M. (1983). *Discourse analysis: The sociolinguistic analysis of natural language.* Chicago: University of Chicago Press.

Swetnam, D. (2004). *Writing your dissertation: How to plan, prepare, and present successful work* (3rd ed.). Oxford, UK: How To Books.

Tagiuri, R. (1968). The concept of organizational climate. In R. Tagiuri & G. H. Litwin (Eds.), *Organizational climate: Explorations of concepts.* Boston: Harvard University Graduate School of Business Administration, Division of Research.

Tallerico, M. (1999). Women and the superintendency: What do we really know? In C. C. Brunner (Ed.), *Sacred dreams: Women and the superintendency* (pp. 29–48). Albany: State University of New York Press.

Taylor, S., & Todd, P. A. (1995). Understanding information technology usage: A test of competing models. *Information Systems Research, 6*(2), 144–176.

Telem, M. (1995). The potential impact of information technology on the high school principal: A preliminary exploration. *Journal of Research on Computing in Education, 27*(3), 281–296.

Texas Education Agency. (2000). *Snapshot 2000: 1999–2000 school district profiles.* Austin, TX: Author.

Thanasui, P. L. (2005). The influence of past abuse on heterosexual cohabiting couples' relationship types. *Dissertation Abstracts International, 66*(06), 2118A.

Thielemann, H. (2004). The effectiveness of enrollment management programs in universities and community colleges. *Dissertation Abstracts International, 65*(8), 2922A. (UMI No. 3143585)

Thompson, B. (1984). *Canonical correlation analysis: Uses and interpretation.* Thousand Oaks, CA: SAGE.

Thompson, B. (2000). *A suggested revision to the forthcoming 5th edition of the APA publication manual.* Retrieved October 4, 2006, from http://www.coe.tamu.edu/~bthompson/apaeffec.htm.

Thompson, B. (2004). *Exploratory and confirmatory factor analysis.* Washington, DC: American Psychological Association.

Thompson, L. C. (2003). An investigation of the relationships between exposure to on-the-job challenges and self-reported changes in leadership behavior and characteristics. *Dissertation Abstracts International, 64*(03), 988A.

Thompson, P. B. (2006). Performance creativity: The role of self, meaning, and cultural significance in a Montessori environment. *Dissertation Abstracts International. 67*(05), A.

Tinto, V. (1999). Taking retention seriously: Rethinking the first year of college. *NACADA Journal, 19*(2), 5–9.

Togneri, W. (2003). *Beyond islands of excellence: What districts can do to improve instruction and achievement in all schools—A leadership brief.* Washington, DC: Learning First Alliance.

Tong, F. (2006). *Oral English development and its impact on emergent reading achievement: A comparative study of transitional bilingual and structured English immersion models.* Unpublished doctoral dissertation, Texas A&M University, College Station, Texas.

Tong, R. (1989). *Feminist thought.* San Francisco: Westview.

Trautman, D. (2000). A validation of the synergistic leadership theory: A gender inclusive leadership theory. *Dissertation Abstracts International, 62*(7), 2598A. (UMI No. 3020899)

Truslow, K. O. (2004). An analysis of gender differences of public school superintendents' conflict management modes in relation to the synergistic leadership theory. *Dissertation Abstracts International, 65*(8), 2859A. (UMI No. 3143586)

Tsai, Y.-C. (2006). *Schooling effectiveness: Multilevel analysis of PIRLS reading achievement for English-language majority and minority students in the United States and Singapore.* Unpublished doctoral dissertation, Sam Houston State University, Huntsville, Texas.

Tschannen-Moran, M., & Hoy, A. W. (2001). *The teachers' sense of efficacy scale.* Columbus: Ohio State University.

Tschannen-Moran, M., & Hoy, W. K. (2000). A multidisciplinary analysis of the nature, meaning, and measurement of trust. *Review of Educational Research, 70*(4), 547–593.

Tschannen-Moran, M., & Hoy, W. K. (2001). Teacher efficacy: Capturing an elusive construct. *Teaching and Teacher Education, 17,* 783–805.

Tschannen-Moran, M, & Hoy, W. K. (2002, April). *The influence of resources and support of teachers' efficacy beliefs.* Paper presented at the annual meeting of the American Educational Research Association, New Orleans, Louisiana.

Tschannen-Moran, M., Hoy, A. W., & Hoy, W. K. (1998). Teacher efficacy: Its meaning and measure. *Review of Educational Research, 68*(2), 202–248.

van Eden-Moorefield, B. M. (2005). Links between the statuses of gay men in relationships and couple identity: A theoretical extension and examination. *Dissertation Abstracts International, 66*(08), 3109A.

Visscher, A. J., & Spuck, D. W. (1991). Computer assisted school administration and management: The state of the art in seven nations. *Journal of Research on Computing in Education, 21*(1), 146–168.

Wallace, R. C. (1985). *The superintendent of education: Data based instructional leadership* (Report No. LROC-1985–87). Pittsburgh University, Learning Research and Development Center. (ERIC Document Reproduction Service No. ED 256060)

Watkins, J. F. (1968). The OCDQ: An application and some implications. *Educational Administration Quarterly, 4*(2), 46–60.

Weber, M. (1947). *The theory of social and economic organizations* (T. Parsons, Ed.; A. M. Henderson & T. Parsons, Trans.) New York: Free Press.

Weick, K. E. (1978). The spines of leadership. In M. W. McCall & M. M. Lombardo (Eds.), *Leadership: Where else can we go?* (pp. 37–61). Durham, NC: Duke University Press.

Weick, K. E. (1995). *Sensemaking in organizations.* Thousand Oaks, CA: SAGE.

Wheeler, F. (1985). Can word processing help the writing process? *Learning, 3,* 54–62.

Wiggins, T. W. (1972). A comparative investigation of principal behavior and school climate. *Journal of Educational Research, 66,* 103–105.

Wilbur, C. E. (2005). Using organizational development strategies to facilitate major technological change. *Dissertation Abstracts International, 66*(06), 2134A.

Willig, C. (2001). *Introducing qualitative research in psychology: Adventures in theory and method.* Buckingham, UK: Open University Press.

Willower, D. J., Eidell, T. L., & Hoy, W. K. (1967). *The school and pupil control ideology.* University Park: Pennsylvania State University.

Willower, D. J., Eidell, T. L., & Hoy, W. K. (1973). *The school and pupil control ideology* (rev. ed.). University Park: Pennsylvania State University.

Wooderson-Perzan, M. K. (2000). The relationship of superintendent leadership styles to student achievement and school district financial and demographic factors. *Dissertation Abstracts International, 61*(8), 3020A. (UMI No. 9982149)

Woodruff, E., Bereiter, C., & Scardamalia, M. (1982). On the road to computer-assisted composition. *Journal of Educational Technology Systems, 10,* 133–148.

Woolfolk, A. E., & Hoy, W. K. (1990). Prospective teachers' sense of efficacy and beliefs about control. *Journal of Educational Psychology, 82,* 81–91.

Yates, S, J., Taylor, S., & Wetherall, M. (2001). *Discourse as data: A guide for analysis.* London: SAGE.

Yin, R. K. (1994). *Case study research design and methods* (2nd ed.). Thousand Oaks, CA: SAGE.

Zaharias, J. (1983). Microcomputers in the language arts classroom: Promises and pitfalls. *Language Arts, 60,* 990–995.

Index

CORWIN
PRESS

The Corwin Press logo—a raven striding across an open book—represents the union of courage and learning. Corwin Press is committed to improving education for all learners by publishing books and other professional development resources for those serving the field of PreK–12 education. By providing practical, hands-on materials, Corwin Press continues to carry out the promise of its motto: **"Helping Educators Do Their Work Better."**